Curtain Calls

Curtain Calls

British and American Women and the Theater,

——————1660–1820 ——————

Edited by Mary Anne Schofield and Cecilia Macheski

OHIO UNIVERSITY PRESS 𝄞 ATHENS

© copyright 1991 by Ohio University Press
Printed in the United States of America
All rights reserved
Ohio University Press books are printed on acid-free paper ∞
Library of Congress Cataloging-in-Publication Data

Curtain calls : British and American women and the theater, 1660–1820
    / edited by Mary Anne Schofield and Cecilia Macheski.
        p.   cm.
    Includes bibliographical references and index.
    ISBN 0-8214-0957-3
    1. Women in the theater—Great Britian—History.   2. Women in the
theater—United States—History.   3. English drama—Women authors—
History and criticism.   4. American drama—Women authors—History
and criticism.   5. Feminism and theater—Great Britian—History.
6. Feminism and theater—United States—History.   7. Women in
literature.   I. Schofield, Mary Anne.   II. Macheski, Cecilia.
PN2582.W65C87   1991
792'.092'241—dc20   90-44396
                                                                        CIP

to our teachers and our students

Contents

3
The Dresser

4
Set Change: The Colonial Scene

5
Critical Reviews

THE ACTRESS' PRAYER!!

Hear me Dramatic Sifters, gay THALIA, and fublime MELPOMONE, be *Guardians* to your fupplicant, and aid her in her profeffion.—Well ye know the hair-breadth fcrapes I have encountered fince my *Elopement* and *Trip to Scotland*, evading the vigilance of my *Duenna*, braving *The School for Scandal*, and venturing *Neck or Nothing*, for TOMMY TRAP, the Tragedian. Oh! he was a jewel of an *Actor*, the grand prop of a Country Company, the *fide-wing* as it were of Theatrical Genius, and though a *Poor Gentleman*, and frequently in the *Road to Ruin*, he was the *Pizarro* of my heart, and I was to him the very *Oba* of perfection!

But TOMMY is no more!!—The *O. P.* and *P. S.* that marked his *exits* and his *entrances* mourn him, and if he had failings, they are loft behind the *Curtain* of oblivion!

Protect, I befeech ye, our little community, and may our *fhares* be trebled; divide the *candle-ends* in equal proportions, and give additional *honefty* to our *door-keeper*, who, I am apprehenfive, requires a large increafe of that neceffary article! *Prompt*, I befeech ye, the Town's-people to aid my forth-coming *benefit*, and open the proud hearts of the family of the THROG-MORTONS', fo that they may *all* appear at the Theatre at an early hour, even down to Mrs. DICKENS, the methodift houfe-keeper! And laftly, I pray ye, fhould I ever reach the *boards* of a London Theatre, may my terms be as enormous as my abilities are confpicuous, and finally my labours be crowned with the *coronet* of honor, and that I may become a convert to domeftic happinefs.

SPRAGG, PRINTER, 17, BOW-STREET, COVENT-GARDEN.

"The Actress' Prayer."

Acknowledgments

L ifting "the Curtain of Oblivion" and answering "the actress' prayer," we present *Curtain Calls*, the first collection of critical essays to examine British and American women and their roles in the eighteenth-century theater. Traditional studies have attempted to drop the curtain and exclude a large number of these women from the playbill of literary history. *Curtain Calls*, in response to a renewed interest in women's studies, raises the curtain for long overdue reviews and qualified ovation.

If the applause, in some cases, is qualified, our thanks to the following people is not. We offer a standing ovation to: our colleagues and staff of the English Departments of LaGuardia Community College, C.U.N.Y., and St. Bonaventure University; Mary Leahy, Rare Book Curator of the Bryn Mawr College Library; Judith Moore; Mrs. Frank Sussler, Curator of Prints, The Lewis Walpole Library; Anne M. Schofield; Georgiana Ziegler, Rare Book Collection, Van Pelt Library; and Holly Panich, our editor, and Helen Gawthrop without whose patience and guidance this book would have remained only a prompter's copy.

And, if like Frances Burney's heroine, we have "now acted [our] part, and acted it to [our] own satisfaction," we can say, "the curtain dropt when . . . nature resumed her rights and the . . . [female] heart was no longer disguised or repressed" (Frances Burney, *Cecilia*. 1782; rpt. London: Virago Press, 198).

List of Illustrations

"Mrs. Cibber as Cordelia"
Horace Howard Furness Memorial Library,
Special Collections Van Pelt Library,
University of Pennsylvania

Prologue

> I here and there o'heard a Coxcomb cry,
> Ah, Rot it—'tis a Woman's Comedy.

Thus Aphra Behn brings us into a new era for women in the British theater, and greets her opposition in the epilogue to *Sir Patient Fancy* (1678). She continues to defend her brazen endeavor of turning playwright as the epilogue goes on:

> Why in this age has Heaven allow'd you more,
> And Women less of Wit than heretofore? We
> Once were fam'd in story, and could write
> Equal to Men; cou'd govern, nay, cou'd fight.

Over a century later, the issue of female authorship still required tactful handling; in the prologue to *I'll Tell You What* (1785), which George Colman wrote for author Elizabeth Inchbald, he appeals to the audience:

> Our Author, is a Woman—that's a Charm
> Of Power to guard herself and Play from Harm.
> The Muses, Ladies Regent of the Pen,
> Grant Women skill, and Force, to write like men.
> Yet they, like the Aeolian Maid of Old,
> Their Sex's Character will ever hold:
> Not with bold Quill too roughly strike the Lyre,
> But with the *Feather* raise a soft Desire.

In the lines of these addresses to the audience, we find a convenient measure of the changing status of women in the theater from the Restoration to the French and American revolutions. While the interval was marked by some advances in the status of women authors, whatever gains were made were celebrated cautiously, as the later prologue suggests. Nonetheless, in the later decades we find at least one significant gain by which to chart progress from the earlier years if we look at the most telling factor: money. However uncertain the evidence concerning Aphra Behn's life, most recent studies agree that she died in illness and poverty, even though she wrote at a feverish pace in her last years. Elizabeth Inchbald, and especially Sarah Siddons, in contrast, both died wealthy women, and never were coy about the fact that financial security for themselves and their families was a strong motive in their success.

For each woman who chose a career in the theater world of the eighteenth century, there is a unique tale of good or bad fortune, disaster, bankruptcy, or riches "beyond the dreams of avarice," or, for some, fame. Whether acting, writing, reviewing, or stage-managing, women played a major, if frequently unacknowledged, role in the history of the theater from the late seventeenth through the early nineteenth centuries. From Aphra Behn's earliest plays through the glorious celebrity of Sarah Siddons, women molded the taste of the age and carved out in the theater one of the few available opportunities for independence and renown. Like the novelists discussed in *Fetter'd or Free?* these women endured insults, seductions, and rapes, but unlike their scribbling sisters whose celebrity and survival depended upon a printed text, the women of the theater faced the demands and frequently the humiliation of public scrutiny not only of their words but also of their bodies.

Not all the women who tried the theater succeeded, of course, and even the best faced opposition as they challenged the male stronghold of playwriting and theater managing. *Curtain Calls* maps the new territory as these pioneering women staked it for their own and chronicles their lives, their triumphs, and their losses. We begin with Aphra Behn, whose first play was staged in 1670, and conclude in the early decades of the nineteenth century with Inchbald and Siddons. The 150 years encompassed between their lives contain the careers of dozens of lesser-known women, a network, as Dr. Johnson would have it, reticulated and decussated with talent and tribulation.

Curtain Calls is divided into six sections. The first, "Dramatis Personae," focuses on the lives of the women who labored in the theater, not as glamorous stars but as the unsung heroines, "the hardworking journey-women without whose efforts the theaters could not have operated" (Langhans). As the first of the four essays in "Dramatis Personae," Edward Langhan's "Tough Actresses to Follow" begins our reconstruction of the eighteenth-century stage by focusing on "a more balanced picture of performers' training, tribulations, contract arrangements, incomes, chances of advancement, power in company affairs, behavior on- and off-stage, and talent." He recovers the lives of such figures as "Susanna Verbruggen, who must have been just as good a comedienne as Kitty Clive but lacked Clive's connections; that splendid tragic actress Mary Porter, whose life was too exemplary to attract biographers; Priscilla Wilford, who went from rags to riches; promising Miss Robins, who didn't make it; unpromising Mary Ann Yates, who did; difficult Henrietta Smith; ill-fated Susan Warwick; and diligent Elizabeth Willis," among others, providing the modern scholar critic with a more equitable view of how "[w]omen in Restoration and eighteenth-century theaters had to struggle for acceptance in a world dominated by men," and "not only survived but endured."

We chose to focus on such women in this book because we believe that a more accurate picture of the eighteenth-century stage can be gleaned than through the often distorted or popularized versions of lives of theater celebrities like Kitty Clive, Nell Gwynn, or Fanny Kemble. The career of Margaret Cavendish dramatizes this distortion of theater history by illustrating what happens when sensationalism replaces scholarly investigation. In the second essay in this section, Linda R. Payne recasts the tabloid "history" of the Duchess of Newcastle, often labeled "Mad Madge" because of her "iconoclastic heroines who are clearly autobiographical and provide us with fascinating insights into the feelings, values and dreams" of the author. Payne argues that "Cavendish's heroines play out the dramas of identity and self-determination that women faced then—and now. Just as the two heroine types suggest Margaret as she was and Margaret as she dreamed herself, so the major heroic plots about powerful, influential women project her seemingly unrealizable dreams against the subplots featuring appropriately dutiful and modest women sorting through the domestic trials of the real world." Payne concludes that Cavendish's "dream world is populated by women who dare to live their lives without restraint and women who warn them that to do so means failure or death." Unlike Cavendish, Elizabeth Inchbald was notorious for her virtue, but even she, as Cecilia Macheski argues in the third essay, felt compelled to write her own life through portraits and diaries, thus attempting to forestall the malevolent tongues and pens of the same theater historians who had ridiculed "mad Madge." Ironically, so successful was her campaign against scandal that she suppressed her own fame, and dislodged herself from the very place in the record she hoped to secure. Like Langhans's Mary Porter, "too exemplary to attract biographers," Inchbald suffered what is perhaps a worse fate—a bad biographer. To correct the damage done by James Boaden's memoirs of her life, Macheski turns to Inchbald's portraits as an alternative form of biography, suggesting that as we seek to reconstruct the history of women, we may need to reconsider our very methodology. Pat Rogers, in the final essay in "Dramatis Personae," presents the career of one woman who was "not less than a goddess, or more than a prophetess inspired by the gods," as Hazlitt claimed. Sarah Siddons, unlike her predecessors and most of her contemporaries on the stage, "towered above her sex" and secured both fame and fortune to a degree unprecedented. Rogers asserts that "linguistic usage, one which departs from older gender-related vocabulary, and allows to a prominent woman a wider range of qualities than those traditionally associated with 'feminine' strengths and virtues," is responsible for Siddons's near mythic identity both in her time and in subsequent records of the theater. He charts the development of the Siddons mythos from "eyewitness accounts, recollections such as those of Hazlitt, the biographies of Boaden and Campbell, and the portrayal of her by Sir Joshua Reynolds and other artists" to show that her "combination of high histrionic talent with a blameless private life" results in her enshrinement as a superstar in the dramatis personae of theater history.

By injecting into eighteenth-century theater history these revisionist perspectives, we correct earlier misconceptions that inclined toward simplistic dismissal or such mythic enshrinement of women. Hoping neither to enshrine Mary Porter nor dethrone Mrs. Siddons, we prefer to establish a more informed dramatis personae for the eighteenth-century theater.

The shift from public response to Cavendish as a figure of ridicule to Siddons's success at the end of the century was only possible, the next section of *Curtain Calls* argues, because of the struggles women endured in order to establish themselves in a theater system that was dominated by men and patronage. In "Stage Business," we anatomize David Garrick who, among others, dictated even more emphatically than did the Lord Chamberlain what a theater audience experienced. Maureen E. Mulvihill's "A Feminist Link in the Old Boys' Network: The Dramatic Career of Katherine Philips," examines Katherine's spectacular success in the theater as an accessible case-study in the politics of authorship during the Restoration. While acknowledging Philip's status as "the most celebrated English woman writer of the seventeenth-century," Mulvihill also warns that "Reassessing a legend is dangerous business." But in the case of Katherine Philips's, whose achievement has been overstated since the late seventeenth-century, to the detriment of more skilled women writers, some contextualizing of Philips's life, work, and career is long overdue. The obvious weakness in Philips's studies to date is an unwillingness to accept the 'Orinda' myth for what it really was: a remarkable literary campaign conceived and promoted by Philips's herself and some of the literary bosses of the Restoration old boys' newwork." Mulvihill "takes into account the full play of [Philips's] support base" in Stuart London, Dublin, and Wales, and locates "a career distinguished by astute networking and (heretofore unacknowledged) artistic individualism."

By the revolution of 1688, however, the playwright-patronage relationship shifted, and Deborah Payne notes the dynamism of the relationship between spectator and peer in the next essay, observing the "tension between patronage as compelling cultural symbol and enfeebled material." Behn managed to get a start in the theater without the intervention of a patron, and throughout her career, her relationship to the patronage system remained problematic with Behn very susceptible to the vagaries of audience taste. Payne concludes that her "Liminal status within the Restoration theater . . . permits her to stand aside in these dedications and flout the conventions of the *ancien regime*." In the final analysis, though, Behn does not fit this "royalist/patronal/male dynamic."

Such patriarchal control is well-documented in the case of David Garrick's relationship with Elizabeth Griffith, Hannah Cowley, and

Hannah More. But, as Betty Rizzo argues, women like Griffith learned to use the ubiquitous patronage system to their own ends: "An author, it was generally believed, must appease both Garrick's vanity (by flattery) and his cupidity (by allowing him to edit one's manuscript for a fee) before his play could be accepted. Griffith flattered Garrick shamelessly, acknowledged his collaboration in her plays more than once, in writing, and also both played defenseless and, when she could, heaped guilt upon him for having failed in chivalry. It became more dangerous to him to fail or criticize her than to aid her. This final twist . . . was her own invention." Griffith's best triumph, Rizzo concludes, "and her best revenge, was her knowledge that she herself had never yielded the initiative, never ceased plotting and ploying in the best Restoration comedy tradition, in order to attain her first objective—the successful establishment of her children."

Ellen Donkin continues this thread by examining the violent controversy that erupted between Hannah More and Hannah Cowley upon the death of their "stage father" Garrick in 1779. So strong was Garrick's influence that after his death both women found themselves "bereft of essential sponsorship; they floundered in the maelstrom of the theatrical marketplace." "It was Garrick's mixed legacy," Donkin concludes, "to late eighteenth-century theater that he created opportunities for women playwrights, but was unable to influence the institution of theater sufficiently to insure them a sense of belonging after he was gone." It would take the later efforts of women like Inchbald and Siddons to alter that theater institution sufficiently and shift public awareness around women in the theater.

The death of Garrick brings us to the end of "Stage Business" and to the end of the patronage system so familiar to Philips and Behn. "Garrick's praiseworthy guidance and help to women playwrights during his career as manager," as Donkin tell us, "had created in them a correspondingly strong need to distance themselves and their work from the power of his authority and authorship, in order to continue working after his death."

The old boys' network that channeled women's stage careers through male taste and funding sources forced women as early as Aphra Behn to don male attire in order to circumvent the restrictions patrons like Garrick mandated. However much women learned to

manipulate the patronage system by Griffith's time, they were nonetheless so confined by this system that it was only when they adopted
male attire that they could freely express themselves.

"The Dresser," our third section, defines a "new language to talk
about old sex," according to Kendall's opening essay, which pre-
pares us for the subsequent essays, all of which contribute to a definition of cross-dressing as not mere costuming but as a vehicle for the
exploration of new sexual identities and roles. While Garrick's
patronage coerced women into deceptive parts, Queen Anne's assistance, in contrast, "contributed to a temporary fashion for the public
expression of eroticism between women," Kendall argues. Further,
she queries the viability of applying twentieth-century "new language" like "lesbian" or "bisexuality" to "old" sexual behavior mirrored in dramatic texts. In the second essay in the section, Frances M.
Kavenik "explores Behn's shift from portrayal of the most lively and
hedonistic" female characters to "characters less openly libertine"
and more committed to moral reform after the popish plot, and identifies "the doubleness of her claims and the doubleness of her vision"
in Behn's creation of "a new sexual space from which to speak."
When Jessica Munns claims that Behn "does not flirt, she asserts,"
we continue the definition of "The Dresser," a section that underscores the prevalence of disguise as subliminal text. She continues
the examination of Behn and "literary androgyny" by claiming
that Behn "defended her right to write like a man," citing Behn's
preface to *The Lucky Chance*. Nancy Cotton refines the definition of the sexual space that Behn inhabits when she responds to
Kavenik and Munns by suggesting that "Behn wrote from her own
gender perspective rather than aping the attitudes or genres of her
nearest male counterparts." By scrutinizing Behn's *The Rover*,
Etherege's *Man of Mode* and Wycherley's *The Plain Dealer*, Cotton
constructs a viable definition of "pattern hero," concluding that the
"portrayal of the hero" is determined not by genre "but authorial attitude." The fourth and final essay in this section turns from Behn to
her contemporary, Mary Pix, whose plays share Behn's device of
"breeches parts." Edna L. Steeves demonstrates that the popular
appeal of cross-dressing made for Pix's successful career.

Successful careers were not confined by geographical boundaries.
A burgeoning colonial theater borrowed structures and sometimes

shared actors with Britain, but more importantly derived its own voice from the political revolution in America. The fourth section of this book, "Set Change: The Colonial Scene," takes us across the Atlantic, where two female playwrights were using the drama for political propaganda, both feminist and republican. Doreen Alvarez Saar notes that Susannah Rowson "takes conventions of the sentimental novel and uses them as underpinnings of the three major themes in the play *Slaves in Algiers*: slavery, feminism, and democracy." Jean B. Kern, in studying Mercy Otis Warren, concludes that Warren used conventional English forms to tackle the problems of the new confederacy. Kern's final estimate is that "the very act of writing [plays] made her a participant in a war from which her gender excluded her." In the third piece in this section, Mary Anne Schofield provides a survey of little-known but popular women playwrights in post-revolutionary America—Margaret Faugeres, Madam Gardie, Mrs. Marriott, and Judith Sargent Murray. The oddity of form illustrated by Murray's *The Gleaner* points to the cultural differences separating the emerging colony from the homeland. In America critics like Murray struggle to find a voice; such was not the case in Britain where, as "Critical Reviews" demonstrates, criticism by women was already a well-developed craft.

Both Katharine M. Rogers and Constance Clark focus on the work of a single reviewer to convince us that from at least as early as 1719, and continuing for a full century, women worked as critics. Rogers argues that by 1819, Inchbald was practicing as an established and recognized professional critic and journalist while Clark's reading of Corinna's *Critical Remarks* shows us the imperfect but important first stages of dramatic criticism by an untrained writer.

The next section, "Playbill," contains two studies designed not only to provide new insights but also to suggest directions for further critical research. William J. Burling, in "Their Empire Disjoyn'd: Serious Plays by Women on the London Stage, 1660–1737," surveys "some current critical approaches to serious drama" as well as defining the category, and offers generalizations about the themes and plots that proved most appealing to women dramatists. Judith Philips Stanton offers statistical data examining "the rate at which women started writing plays compared to other genres," and the success of their venture.

By the latter part of the century, novels exhibited more dramatic qualities, while plays assumed a more novelistic quality of being read rather than performed. Mrs. Inchbald, for example, was invited by her publishers to compile *The British Theatre*, a twenty-five volume edition of plays for which she wrote critical prefaces so that readers could take the drama to their closets; at the same time, *A Simple Story*, her first novel, relies heavily on the dramatic techniques of dialogue and setting.

In our final section, then, "Closet Drama: From the Play to the Novel," two essays examine the Janus-like relationship between novel and drama. Douglas Butler, in his discussion of Susannah Centlivre's plots and Whig politics, reminds us of the cross-fertilization that exists between these literary forms. Rose Zimbardo further investigates the interplay between drama and the novel by examining the hybrid nature of Behn's productions for theater and closet audience, concluding that Behn's "works, chronologically considered, reflect the drastic changes in dramatic imitation of nature that occurred during her period."

The novel, though, is another domain. *Curtain Calls* is about the stage, and the women who, behind the scenes or on the boards, made a living in the theater. The essays collected here revive lost reputations, reconstruct theater history, and, we hope, kindle interest in these women whose careers, whose plays, and whose work, deserve a critical encore.

1

Dramatis Personae

"Mrs. Siddons, old Kemble, and Henderson Rehearsing in
the Green Room." Courtesy of the Print Collection,
The Lewis Walpole Library, Yale University.

Tough Actresses to Follow

EDWARD A. LANGHANS

My title has multiple meanings. I propose to seek out not the great actresses of the British Restoration and eighteenth-century theater, about whom much has already been written, but the players whose activities are harder to trace. I want also to look for those actresses who were hardened troupers—survivors in a world of fierce competition. The stars are important, of course, but also significant are those women who were exceptionally talented but have been neglected by historians and overshadowed by the stars, and whose careers are sometimes difficult to follow. They are unsung heroines who seldom acted leading roles but were hard-working journeywomen without whose efforts the theaters could not have operated. Information about some of those who have been forgotten provides a more balanced picture of performers' training, tribulations, contract arrangements, incomes, chances of advancement, power in company affairs, behavior on- and off-stage, and talent. My subjects include Susanna Verbruggen, who must have been just as good a comedienne as Kitty Clive but lacked Clive's connections; that splendid tragic actress Mary Porter, whose life was too exemplary to attract biographers; Priscilla Wilford, who went from rags to riches; promising Miss Robins, who didn't make it; unpromising Mary Ann Yates, who did; difficult Henrietta Smith; ill-fated Susan Warwick; and diligent Elizabeth Willis.

Those actresses who rose to the top of their profession could command top salaries that were often on a par with those earned by leading actors. During 1799–1800, for example, Dorothy Jordan received £31 10s weekly, the same as John Philip Kemble. Kemble's sister,

Sarah Siddons, if *The London Stage* listing is correct, was paid £31 10s per *night* (Hogan 1968, 3:2204–5)! At first glance that might suggest that there was no discrimination, but Kemble was the manager of Drury Lane Theatre and probably had hidden perquisites that gave him more than Mrs. Jordan but perhaps not as much as his celebrated sister. Indeed, it is extremely difficult to compare the financial status of different performers, because articles of agreement varied considerably. Some players were engaged by the season, some by the night; some were under long-term contracts; some had choice benefit nights guaranteed; some received benefits free of house charges; some were paid whether they acted or not (that was one of Mrs. Jordan's perks); some had wardrobes provided by the management; and so on. Most extant salary lists indicate that the men generally fared better than the women, but not always. A Covent Garden Theatre paylist for 1767–68, published in *The London Stage*, shows that the highest paid men received £2 15s daily; the highest paid women, £1 3s 4d daily—a great discrepancy. On the other hand, the lowest salary for women was 3s 4d daily (about £32 annually) and the lowest for men 2s 6d (Stone 3:1269–70). For purposes of comparison, in 1767 a clerk earned c50 annually; a plain, coarse suit of clothes cost him £4 10s (George 1926, 167, 369n). But Covent Garden's paylist in September 1760, in *The London Stage*, shows the highest-paid actress, Miss Macklin, at c300 for the season and the highest-paid actor, Sparks, at £250 (Stone 1962, 2:815–16). The conclusion must be that without more paylists and much fuller information on contracts it is dangerous to draw conclusions about performers' incomes.

As the above figures indicate, however, we can say that there was a vast disparity in salaries between the top and bottom; players in the highest rank—some paylists show four ranks—did very well indeed and usually had their benefits early in the spring, when profits to them would be greater. Those poor players at the bottom must have had trouble just surviving. A hard-working journeywoman performer may serve as an example. Elizabeth Willis (c.1669–1739) was an actress, singer, and dancer who began her stage career in the 1690s and performed for almost fifty years, mostly at Drury Lane. She augmented her income by acting at the late summer fairs in London and at the theater in Richmond, Surrey. Rarely did she play roles of importance; she was a utility actress, absolutely essential to a troupe; someone must play those minor characters. In addition to her own chores, she coached her two daughters and brought them on the stage in 1704, probably to add to the family income. A manuscript salary list at the Public Record Office (LC 7/3) titled the "Establishmt of ye Company" and dating about 1703 shows Mrs. Willis at an annual salary of £35 to £40, next to the lowest scale for actresses. She may never have risen much above that, but she had the satisfaction of knowing that some men named for the same rank were on the same pay scale. And she was perhaps better off than a common seaman, who earned half what she was paid but was provided food and a place to sleep (George 1953, 150–51).

Mrs. Willis was a fine player. Thomas Davies in his *Dramatic Miscellanies* wrote of her acting of the Old Lady in *Henry VIII*: "Mrs. Willis, a most excellent actress in low humour, played this small, and I believe, generally thought, insignificant part, many years. She threw into this old lady, as well as into every thing she acted, so much truth and nature, that the audience never dismissed her without marks of approbation. . . . She lived to a great age with its worst companion, poverty" (Davies 1784, 1:422–23).

Some actresses, for financial gain, became company managers or co-managers: Anne Bracegirdle and Elizabeth Barry shared with Thomas Betterton the management of the Lincoln's Inn Fields Theatre in the early 1700s; Sarah Baker was the head of provincial players from Sadler's Wells Theatre in the 1770s; Teresa Cornelys (though a singer, not an actress) became a purveyor of fashionable entertainments in London in the 1770s; Mary Ann Yates joined James and Frances Brooke in the management of the King's Theatre (opera house) from 1773 to 1778; the eccentric Charlotte Charke was in and out of management in the 1730s and 1740s; Madame Violante led a troupe of entertainers in the 1720s; Anne Oldfield shared briefly in the management of the Queen's Theatre in 1709; Hannah Lee operated booth theaters at the late summer fairs in the first half of the eighteenth century. There is no way of knowing how much influence over company affairs the leading actresses may have had if they were not actually sharing in the management. The women were outnumbered by the men (because playwrights all the way back to the ancient Greeks rarely wrote plays with more female than male characters), but the salaries of some of the actresses suggest that the best of them held their own in a male-dominated profession.

Performers usually learned their trade by training under an experienced player, often an actor-manager. But that did not necessarily assure them success. David Garrick was probably the best teacher of acting during the eighteenth century, and one of his discoveries and greatest disappointments was a Miss Robins. In the 22–24 November 1774 issue of the *Middlesex Journal, and Evening Advertiser* appeared a puff (that got the girl's name wrong, calling her Roberts): "This lively lass, of eighteen, having been under the tuition of the great *theatrical school-master*, who has been indefatigable in his endeavours to introduce a pupil on the stage, who shall be an honor to himself, and an acquisition to the dramatic world" was soon to appear in *The Country Girl* (Garrick's alteration of Wycherley's *The Country Wife*). The production opened at Drury Lane on 1 December, and the same correspondent had high praise for the young actress:

> From her admirable conception of the character, and easy stile of performing it, we are convinced she has derived no small improvement from the ablest theatrical instructor. Her voice is pleasing and comprehensive, as was evident from her song in the last act; yet we think she was a little unfortunate in pitching it rather too low in the dialogue, though done in order the more strongly to mark the simplicity of the character. Her figure is of middle size, but elegantly turned: and her features so stamped as to admit of a variety of characteristic impressions.

Garrick's prompter, William Hopkins, noted in his manuscript "diary" (now at the Folger Shakespeare Library):

> Miss Robins made her first appearance upon the Stage in the part of the Country Girl   an agreeable figure as a Woman & also in Breeches—she has a particular Cuddenish [foolish] way with her wch is not amiss in this Character, but I am afraid it will be a disadvantage to her in any other.   Mr G. took great pains with her, & a long time in Training her before he brought her out   he wrote & introduc'd a Song in the part and a *New Prologue* to introduce her & alter'd the *Epilogue*.   all which & the Lady were very well receiv'd. (Stone 1962, 3:1852)

Then something went wrong. *The Country Girl* was performed only four times, through 16 December. When Miss Robins played Leonora in *The Padlock* on 22 December she sang out of tune, Hopkins noted, and received some hisses (Stone 1962, 3:1858). After one more performance, *The Padlock* was shelved, and when it was revived in May 1775, Miss Robins was not in the cast. Indeed, she was not named in any playbills that season after Christmas 1774. The following season Garrick relegated her to a Country Lass in *May Day*; by 9 December 1775 she was dropped from the cast and evidently left the stage. The Highfill-Burnim-Langhans *Biographical Dictionary* shows hundreds of similar cases of young hopefuls who did not make it.

Just the opposite of Miss Robins was Mary Ann Yates, whose first attempts were abysmal. As Mary Ann Graham she tried Anna Bullen in *Henry VIII* in January 1753 in Dublin for the actor-manager Thomas Sheridan but, according to the *European Magazine*, she was too fat and had no vocal power. Sheridan tried to convince her that she would not get anywhere as an actress, but that did not stop her. She lost some weight and the following year was in London. *Theatrical Biography* in 1792 recounted her trials:

> [A]fter a few rehearsals it was found her person only spoke in her favour, and merely on this account she was taken in under the double character of *dresser* and *mute*, at the inconsiderable salary of *twenty shillings per week*.
>
> Naturally possessing the seeds of theatric genius, her inclinations strongly supported them, and she neglected no opportunity to observe [the] best performers, and turn that observation to advantage: it was a long time, however, before she was permitted to speak; at last an opportunity presented itself; the sudden illness of one of the actresses, where a good figure was necessary, obliged the prompter to look round the theatre for an immediate supply; Mrs. Yates being the only person remarkably happy in this respect, was asked whether she would *attempt* it; her heart bounded at the question, she sat down to it with avidity, and, after awhile, made herself so perfect in it, that her performance, like a talismanic power, broke the spells of her *quondam* silence, and she was immediately called up to fill characters of more consequence, whilst her salary was proportionably increased.

The London Stage shows her first advertised appearance at Drury Lane as Marcia in *Virginia* on 25 February 1754. The prompter,

Richard Cross, noted that she was deservedly applauded (Stone 1962, 1:411). Garrick had been her tutor, and after him the veteran actor Richard Yates instructed her, wooed her, and married her. But Garrick dropped her from the Drury Lane roster at the end of her first season, after which the playwright Arthur Murphy helped to train her. Garrick rehired Mrs. Yates in 1756–57. Davies in his *Life of David Garrick* told of her first real success:

> Mrs. Yates was then a young actress of merit, who had occasionally given some proofs of genius, but was so unacquainted with the stage, that it was thought hazardous by the manager to trust so great a part as Mandane [in Murphy's *The Orphan of China*] to her performance. However, Mr. Murphy having privately consulted the lady, she promised to undertake it, if he would take the pains to instruct her. (Davies 1780, 1:220–22)

Instruct her he did, and Garrick let her play the role with the effect that "Mrs. Yates, from her excellent acting of Mandane, became immediately a favourite with the public" (Davies 1780, 1:222). She developed into one of Garrick's finest actresses—difficult, imperious, but immensely talented. In 1774–75 she received from Drury Lane c800 for the season (c26 10s weekly), twice as much as her nearest female competitor, Elizabeth Younge, and almost twice as much as the highest-paid actor, William Smith (Stone 1962, 3:1898). Not bad for an actress who had such a shaky start.

Mrs. Yates became a star, one of the lucky and talented few. Susan Warwick was another lowly house servant who also served as a supernumerary actress, but her story is a sad one. We know virtually nothing about her except her accident on 1 October 1736 at Covent Garden Theatre, reported in the *Daily Post and General Advertiser* the following day:

> Last night in the Entertainment of Dr Faustus [*The Necromancer*, a spectacular pantomime] . . . when the Machine wherein were Harlequin, the Miller's Wife, the Miller and his Man, was got up to the full Extent of its flying, one of the Wires which held up the hind part of the Car broke first, and then the other broke, and the Machine, and all the People in it fell down upon the Stage; by which unhappy Accident the young Woman who personated the Miller's Wife had her thigh broke, and her

"Mary Ann Yates as the Tragic Muse"
Engraving by Valentine Green after Romney, 1772
By permission of the Trustees of the British Museum

Kneepan shatter'd, and was otherways very much bruised, the Harlequin had his Head bruised, and his Wrist strained; the Miller broke his Arm; and the Miller's Man had his Scull so fractured that his Life is despaired of. (Scouten 1961, 2:603)

Two days later the *Daily Advertiser* said that James Todd, who had acted the Miller's Man, had died. "Susan Warwick, who represented the Miller's Wife, lies at the point of Death at the infirmary at Hyde-Park Corner" (Scouten 1961, 2:604). In the show she had been standing in for the dancer-actress Mrs. Anthony Moreau; stars did not have to risk the hazards of the trade. We do not know if Susan Warwick survived.

Though all performers hoped they would eventually appear on the London stage, especially at one of the major houses, Drury Lane or Covent Garden, there were far more of them active in the provinces, where they could be big fish in little ponds. For example, Henrietta Smith acted only two roles in London, in the summer of 1786 at the Haymarket Theatre, the major "minor" playhouse in London. Her career was otherwise Irish and provincial: Dublin, Cork, Belfast, Hull, Edinburgh, Sheffield, Doncaster, York, Leeds, Norwich (?), Brighton (?)—too many Smiths for positive identification—Bath, Bristol, and who knows where else? She spent several seasons in the 1780s with Tate Wilkinson's company on the York circuit, playing leading roles (some of her Shakespearean parts were Juliet, Lady Anne, Portia, and Rosalind). She was a valuable actress to Wilkinson, but she was also a pain in his neck. In his *Wandering Patentee* he recorded several examples of Mrs. Smith's difficult behavior, the last one leading to a break:

"Fontainbleau, or our Way in France," was got up that season [1784–85], and I gave its first representation (after being at the expence of Music, Scenery, &c.) for Mrs. Smith's benefit, on Saturday, Feb. 26, 1785: I cast Lady Bull to Mrs. Smith; Miss Bull to Mrs. Jordan. Mrs. Smith, though proper for the character, yet disliked so much the playing it, that notwithstanding her having the compliment of it the first representation for her own benefit, yet we quarrelled because I refused a particular requisite when she represented that character; and she was so foolish as to put in practice what she said she would, that was, spoil the character every time she played it; and no compliment to her wisdom or her folly; for she really kept her word most rigidly, and when she was losing her own reputation, gloried in thinking she vexed the manager: We quarrelled so much at Leeds on the subject, that we agreed to part at the expiration of articles, the end of May 1786, and never were friends again in Yorkshire. (Wilkinson 1795, 2:182–83)

Fortunately, Mrs. Smith was an exception. Most performers, female and male, were hard-working and uncomplaining.

It was not easy for a performer to make it to the top. Talent was necessary, but good connections often helped almost as much. Consider the case of Priscilla Wilford. She was a barmaid at Bret's Coffee House, according to the actress George Anne Bellamy in her *Apology*—not always a reliable source (1785, 1:198). Calling herself Mrs. Stevens, Priscilla came on stage in 1730 as Jenny in *The Generous Free-Mason* at the Oates-Fielding booth theater at Bartholomew Fair—a very humble beginning. John Rich, the manager of Lincoln's Inn Fields, hired her for the 1730–31 season and gave her a solo benefit in March 1731—an indication of Rich's interest in her person rather than her talent, probably, for during her acting career she seldom played leading roles (Emilia in *Othello*, Celia in *Volpone*, and Lady Macduff in *Macbeth* are typical of her line). By 1740–41 she had worked her way up to 6s 8d daily; a leading actress like Kitty Clive was earning seven times that. But Priscilla had made herself a useful actress and, according to Mrs. Bellamy, John Rich's housekeeper (Bellamy 1785, 1:198). In October 1744 Priscilla left the stage and married Rich. Mrs. Bellamy said, "That lady's regards were only shewn to those who bask in sunshine; and not to poor beings enveloped in a cloud of distress" (1785, 4:121). Mrs. Rich was a Methodist convert and "thought of nothing but praying and accumulating wealth for herself and her spouse" (Bellamy 1785, 1:197). Smollett in *Roderick Random* (1748)—another source to be approached with caution—said of Rich ("Mr. Vandal"): "the poor man's head, which was not naturally very clear, had been disordered with superstition, and he laboured under the tyranny of a wife and the terror of hell-fire at the same time" (Smollett 1979, 394).

Mrs. Rich, though no longer acting, seems to have remained active at the playhouse (Covent Garden, where the company moved in 1732), but in what capacity is not clear. The accounts show payments to her from time to time. When John Rich died in 1761, Mrs. Rich joined with the singer John Beard in the management of the theater, though she seems to have been a silent partner. Rich had left her rich. With her four daughters she shared the profits of the Covent Garden patent, which was sold in 1767 for £60,000. When Priscilla Rich died in 1783 she left a lengthy will (Public Record Office, probate 12 March 1783) that shows her to have had a very considerable estate. It also shows her to have been a remarkably generous woman and not the miser Mrs. Bellamy described. She left bequests to a great number of people who were related to her only by marriage, and she gave sizable amounts of money to dozens of others. Priscilla Wilford Rich had played her cards very well.

A splendid, hard-working actress who has not received the attention she deserves is the tragedienne Mary Porter. By all accounts she was one of the finest actresses of the eighteenth century, easily the equal of Mrs. Cibber though lacking her singing ability (and temperament) and evidently as talented as Anne Oldfield. But Mary Porter did not lead a scandalous private life, and biographers have not shown much interest in such players (witness the several biographies of notorious Nell Gwyn).

In the 1706–7 season at the Queen's Theatre, Mary was paid only 40s weekly, and a letter from her to the Lord Chamberlain complained that she deserved more. Her petition of 22 October 1707 said:

When several of the Gentlewomen who played Principal Parts, either neglected or were sick, she [Mrs. Porter] at a night's notice study'd and play'd them perfect the next night and to satisfaction, for which she hop'd for encouragement or at least to have had such Parts given her by which she might have gain'd reputation when there was more time to study. But instead thereof generally those Parts were given to such as were below her.

That she was postponed in her Benefit Play to all the younger actors, and not admitted to have it till the 2d of May last when the Town was almost empty and may Fayre was begann. (Public Record Office LC 7/3)

Mary had to fight for recognition and fair treatment by theater managers, but by 1720, after more than twenty years on stage, she had succeeded to leading roles in both comedy and tragedy. Her tragic characters were her best—Alicia in *Jane Shore*, Desdemona in *Othello*, Monimia in *The Orphan*, Lady Macbeth, Belvidera in *Venice Preserv'd*, and Zara in *The Mourning Bride* made her the successor of her mentor, Elizabeth Barry. Though Mary Porter was not blessed with beauty and a good voice, she overcame those shortcomings with an intensity and dignity that was remarked by a number of critics. Thomas Davies (himself an actor) in his *Dramatic Miscellanies* expressed the typical reaction to her work: "Where the passions predominated, she exerted her powers to a supreme degree; she seemed then to be another person, and to be informed with that noble and enthusiastic ardour which was capable of rousing the coldest auditor to an equal animation. Her deportment was dignified with graceful ease, and her action the result of the passion she felt" (Davies 1784, 3:467). Mrs. Porter "concealed the art of her profession so skilfully, that she seemed to realise the passions, and to be inspired with the various situations of her characters" (Davies 1784, 3:207). She was similarly commended by Dr. Johnson, Horace Walpole, Benjamin Victor, James Thomson, Aaron Hill, Mrs. Delany, and Charles Macklin—all good authorities. And she won an adoring public: Mrs. Delany noted that Drury Lane was packed whenever Mrs. Porter acted.

Another remarkable yet neglected actress was Susanna Percival Mountfort Verbruggen, whose life was filled with tragedy but who filled theaters with laughter. She was born about 1667, the daughter of Thomas Percival, a minor London performer. By 1681 she had begun her acting career, and in 1686 she married the promising player William Mountfort. The parish registers of St. Giles in the Fields and St. Clement Danes show that Susanna and William had at least four children: Susanna, born on 27 April 1690 (she became an actress and died insane in 1720); Edward, born on 1 April, died on 3 May 1691; Elizabeth, born on 22 March 1692, died a week later; Mary, christened at St. Clement's on 27 April 1693, was being carried by Susanna when William Mountfort was murdered on the night of 9–10 December 1692. The murderer, Lord Mohun, was found not guilty by the House of Lords, and Mrs. Mountfort had to drop an appeal in order to save her father, who had been sentenced to death for clipping.

Despite the tragedies in her personal life, she continued her stage career; indeed, she probably had to survive, for William Mountfort's will, dictated as he was dying, gave no indication of a large estate. From the beginning Susanna's specialty was comedy; she acted in a number of plays now forgotten, but two of her early parts—Harriet in *The Man of Mode* by Etherege and Belinda in Congreve's *The Old Bachelor*—suggest her forte: witty characters in high comedy. She was also popular in her younger years in breeches parts: Thomas Southerne wrote the title role in *Sir Anthony Love* for her. In January 1694 Susanna married the actor John Verbruggen, and it was as Mrs. Verbruggen that she played her finest roles and established herself as London's best comedienne. Articles of agreement at the Public Record Office (LC 7/3) drawn up on 10 April 1695 show her to have been a sharer in the Drury Lane company with a guarantee of c105 per season; that put her close to her new husband's salary (c3 weekly for her, c4 for him; he was ranked with George Powell as a leading actor in the troupe).

Can Colley Cibber's comments on Susanna Verbruggen in his *Apology* (1740) and Anthony Aston's *Brief Supplement* (1748) to the *Apology* be trusted? Both Cibber and Aston were themselves actors, and Aston, especially, called a spade a spade. His physical description of Mrs. Verbruggen in her later years (she died in 1703) was not very flattering ("thick legs and thighs, corpulent and large posteriours"), but he thought highly of her craftsmanship as an actress. "She was all Art," he said, "and her Acting all acquir'd, but dress'd so nice, it look'd like Nature. There was not a Look, a Motion, but what were all design'd; and these at the same Word, Period, Occasion, Incident, were every Night, in the same Character, alike; and yet all sat charmingly easy on her. . . . Whatever she did was not to be call'd Acting; no, no, it was what she represented: She was neither more nor less, and was the most easy Actress in the World" (Cibber 1889, 2:313).

Cibber acted with Mrs. Verbruggen at Drury Lane in the late 1690s and early 1700s and in his *Apology* gave her a much fuller treatment than most of the performers he described, and if only half of his praise was deserved, Susanna must have been quite an actress. He was writing of her in retrospect, but he was very circumstantial:

In a Play of D'urfey's now forgotten, call'd *The Western Lass*, which Part she acted, she transform'd her whole Being, Body,

Shape, Voice, Language, Look and Features, into almost
another Animal, with a strong *Devonshire* Dialect, a broad
laughing Voice, a poking Head, round Shoulders, an uncon-
ceiving Eye, and the most bediz'ning dowdy Dress that ever
cover'd the untrain'd Limbs of a Joan Trot. To have seen her
here you would have thought it impossible the same Creature
could ever have been recover'd to what was as easy to her, the
Gay, the Lively, and the Desirable. Nor was her Humour limited
to her Sex; for, while her Shape permitted, she was a more adroit
pretty Fellow than is usually seen upon the Stage: Her easy Air,
Action, Mien, and Gesture quite chang'd from the Quoif to the
cock'd Hat and Cavalier in fashion. People were so fond of seeing her a Man, that when the Part of *Bays* in the *Rehearsal* had
for some time lain dormant, she was desired to take it up, which
I have seen her act with all the true coxcombly Spirit and
Humour that the Sufficiency of the Character required.

But what found most Employment for her whole various Excellence at once, was the Part of *Melantha* in [Dryden's]
Marriage-Alamode. Melantha is as finish'd an Impertinent as
ever flutter'd in a Drawing-Room, and seems to contain the
most compleat System of Female Foppery that could possibly be
crowded into the tortured Form of a Fine Lady. Her Language,
Dress, Motion, Manners, Soul, and Body, are in a continual
Hurry to be something more than is necessary or commenda-
ble. . . . The first ridiculous Airs that break from her are upon
a Gallant never seen before, who delivers her a Letter from her
Father recommending him to her good Graces as an honourable
Lover. Here now, one would think, she might naturally shew a
little of the Sexe's decent Reserve, tho' never so slightly cover'd!
No, Sir; not a Tittle of it; Modesty is the Virtue of a poor-soul'd
Country Gentlewoman; she is too much a Court Lady to be
under so vulgar a Confusion; she reads the Letter, therefore,
with a careless, dropping Lip and erected Brow, humming it
hastily over as if she were impatient to outgo her Father's Com-
mands by making a compleat Conquest of him [the young man]
at once; and that the Letter might not embarass her Attack,
crack! she crumbles it at once into her Palm and pours upon
him her whole Artillery of Airs, Eyes, and Motion; down goes
her dainty, diving Body to the Ground, as if she were sinking

under the conscious Load of her own Attractions; then launches into a Flood of fine Language and Compliment, still playing her Chest forward in fifty Falls and Risings, like a Swan upon waving Water; and, to complete her Impertinence, she is so rapidly fond of her own Wit that she will not give her Lover Leave to praise it; Silent assenting Bows and vain Endeavours to speak are all the share of the Conversation he is admitted to, which at last he is relieved from by her Engagement to half a Score Visits, which she *swims* from him to make, with a Promise to return in a Twinkling. (Cibber 1889, 1:166–69)

Just as Mary Porter entered fully into her characters, so, too, with thorough professionalism, did Mrs. Verbruggen. In 1745 *An Essay on the Theatres* in *The Harleian Miscellany* praised Kitty Clive's comic talent and called her the true successor to Susanna Verbruggen; that was high praise for both.

Women in Restoration and eighteenth-century British theaters had to struggle for acceptance in a world dominated by men, and it is remarkable how many not only survived but endured. Records of their activity are sparse (except for the stellar or notorious ladies), but what evidence we have shows that many were tough actresses to follow.

Works Cited

Aston, Anthony. *See* Cibber, Colley.

Bellamy, George Anne. 1785. *An Apology for the Life of George Anne Bellamy, Late of Covent-Garden Theatre.* 6 vols. London.

Beveridge, Lord, et al. 1965. *Prices and Wages in England.* London: Cass.

Cibber, Colley. 1889. *An Apology for the Life of Mr. Colley Cibber* (with Anthony Aston's *Brief Supplement*). Ed. Robert W. Lowe. 2 vols. London.

Davies, Thomas. 1780. *Memoirs of the Life of David Garrick, Esq.* 2 vols. London.

―――. 1784. *Dramatic Miscellanies.* 3 vols. London.

European Magazine, January 1753.

George, M. Dorothy. 1926. *London Life in the XVIIIth Century.* New York: Knopf.

―――. 1953. *England in Transition.* 1967 reprint. Baltimore: Penguin.

The Harleian Miscellany. 1745. Vol. 5. London.

Highfill, Philip H., Jr., Kalman A. Burnim, and Edward A. Langhans. 1973–. *A Biographical Dictionary of Actors, Actresses, Musicians, Dancers, Managers, and Other Stage Personnel in London, 1660–1800.* 12 vols. Carbondale: Southern Illinois Univ. Press.

Hogan, Charles Beecher, ed. 1968. *The London Stage* 1660–1800, part 5, 1776–1800. 3 vols. Carbondale: Southern Illinois Univ. Press.

Middlesex Journal, and Evening Advertiser, 22–24 November 1774.

Public Record Office, London: MS. Lord Chamberlain's accounts, LC 7/3.

St. Clement Danes MS parish registers at the Guildhall Library, London.

St. Giles in the Fields MS parish registers at the church, London.

Scouten, Arthur H., ed. 1960. *The London Stage* 1660–1800, part 3, 1729–47. 2 vols. Carbondale: Southern Illinois Univ. Press.

Smollett, Tobias. 1979. *The Adventures of Roderick Random*. Ed. Paul-Gabriel Bouce. Oxford: Oxford Univ. Press.

Stone, George Winchester, Jr., ed. 1962. *The London Stage* 1660–1800, part 4, 1747–76. 3 vols. Carbondale: Southern Illinois Univ. Press.

Theatrical Biography, 1792.

Wilkinson, Tate. 1795. *The Wandering Patentee; or, A History of the Yorkshire Theatres From* 1770 *to the Present Time* 4 vols. York.

Dramatic Dreamscape: Women's Dreams and Utopian Vision in the Works of Margaret Cavendish, Duchess of Newcastle

LINDA R. PAYNE

Margaret Lucas Cavendish, Duchess of Newcastle, was jeered by her Restoration contemporaries both high and low, male and female. Often known as "Mad Madge," she was described by Pepys as "a mad, conceited, ridiculous woman" whose husband was "an ass to suffer her to write what she writes to him and of him" (Pepys 1926, 514). Dorothy Osborne declared that "there are many soberer people in Bedlam" and that her friends were "much to blame to let her go abroad" (Fraser 1984, 122). Other charges, also leveled against almost every woman who dared to write, included sexual immorality and plagiarism from male authors.

Even today, more attention is focused on her outlandish dress and unpredictable behavior than on her work. Gilbert and Gubar, using her as a type for their "madwoman" figure, agree that she probably *was* mad (Gilbert and Gubar 1979, 62–63), while Angeline Goreau implies as much in suggesting that the progressive worsening of her "eccentricities" might have been caused either by "natural evolution" or "the effects of the conflict of her ambitions and her sex" (Goreau 19).

Yet this "fantasticall" figure was the first English woman to publish extensively, and she tried her hand at every available genre: poetry, fiction, biography, scientific and philosophical treatises, but most prolifically in drama. Cavendish has gained recognition in recent years as one of the first important biographers, and her scientific and philosophical works are regarded with some amused interest for their marked originality and oddness in a speculative era. Her drama and fiction, however, are generally regarded as failures and given very little attention. Although she published nineteen dramatic works in two collections, *Plays* (1662) and *Plays Never Before Printed* (1668), none of them was produced, and their publication was undoubtedly due to the fortune and influence of her husband, William. Her fiction is almost never read.

The wits, Cavendish complained, condemned her plays because they were not made up according to the "Rules of Art." Critics through the years have been less kind. Virginia Woolf called them "intolerable" and found Cavendish's writings "a vision of loneliness and riot . . . as if some giant cucumber had spread itself over all the roses and carnations in the garden and choked them to death" (Woolf 1929, 59–60). Marjorie Nicolson declared that criticizing Cavendish was beyond her scope, that just to read her one needed to bring order out of chaos (Nicolson 1948, 224). Even sympathetic biographer Douglas Grant describes the plays as "confused," a "delta of tedium," "utterly undramatic," and "a collection of disconnected scenes" (Grant 1957, 162–63).

Cavendish herself saw the problems in her plays, calling them "tedious" and "somewhat long" (Cavendish 1662, A3^c), "like dull dead statues" (Cavendish 1662, A3^b), "dull and flat by reason they have not the high seasoning of Poeticall Salt" (Cavendish 1662, A5^a–5^b), and, generally, "not so well done but that there will be many faults found" (Cavendish 1662, A5^d).

In fact, in the first collection, through nine prefaces "To the Readers," an epistle dedicatory to "My Lord," and "A General Prologue to all my Playes," she alternately apologized for their flaws and justified them as deliberate breaks from convention. It is while comparing her plays to those of her husband that she described them as "dull dead statues," for which reason, she said,

> I send them forth to be printed, rather than keep them concealed in hopes to have them first Acted; and this advantage I have, that is, I am out of fear of having them hissed off from the Stage, for they are not like to come thereon; but were they such as might deserve applause, yet if Envy did make a faction against them, they would have had a public Condemnation; and though I am not such a Coward, as to be afraid of the hissing Serpents, or stinged Tongues of Envy, yet it would have made me a little Melancholy to have my harmless and innocent Playes go weep-

ing from the Stage, and whipt by malicious hard-hearted jurors.
(Cavendish 1662, A3[a-b])

She excused the seeming tedium her plays would present on the stage
as a product of their length, since "having much variety in them, I
could not possibly make them shorter, and being long, it might tire
the Spectators, who are forced, or bound by the rules of civility to sit
out a Play, if they be not sick" (Cavendish 1662, A3[d]).

However, the length is probably not really so much the problem as
their apparent lack of form or structure. Cavendish's apologies for
such flaws typically reveal both insecurity and a defiant carelessness:
"for besides that I want also the skill of scholarship and true writing,
I did many times not peruse the copies that were transcribed, lest they
should disturb my following conceptions; by which neglect . . .
many errors are slipped into my works" (Cavendish 1667, xxxvii).

She explains the lack of coherence by declaring herself a poet
rather than a tailor:

> I have heard that such Poets that write Playes, seldom or never
> join or sew the several scenes together; they are two several Pro-
> fessions, at least unusual for rare Poets to take that pains
> . . . but I like as a poor Taylor was forced to do all my self, as to
> cut out, shape, join, and sew each several scene together, with-
> out any help or direction . . . but howsoever, I did my best
> indeavour, and took great pains in the ordering and joining
> thereof, for which I hope my Learned Readers will pardon the
> errors therein and excuse me the worker thereof. (Cavendish
> 1662, A5[d])

Her unconventional structures extend even to the technical side of
her writing: grammar, syntax, and, alas, spelling. However, as she
saw it,

> I do perceive no strong reason to contradict but that everyone
> may be his own grammarian if by his natural grammar he can
> make his hearers understand his sense. . . . But language
> should be like garments, for though every particular garment
> hath a general cut, yet their trimmings may be different, and not
> go out of the fashion. (Cavendish, *World's Olio* 1655, 93–94)

In fact, she seemed to consider the kind of ordered logic and "rules" which much of her audience expected from literature to be a masculine trait. She even went so far as to declare it "against nature for a woman to spell right" (Cavendish, *World's Olio* 1655, 93–94). Women are strong on fancy, while reason is a man's domain. Women's brains "work usually in a Fantasticall motion . . . not so much by Rules and Methods as by choice" (Cavendish 1653, A⁴). In her first collection of poetry, *Poems and Fancies* (1653), she declared her disdain for the rules of art:

> Give me the free and noble style,
> Which seems uncurbed, though it be wild
> . . . Give me a style that Nature frames, not art,
> For art doth seem to take the pedant's part;
> And that seems noble, which is easy, free,
> Not to be bound with o'er-nice pedantry.
> (Cavendish 1653, 158)

Cavendish wrote "Fancy," as she called her creative writing, "to recreate the Mind, and withdraw it from its more serious Contemplations" (Cavendish 1653, A³–A⁴), her more serious inquiries into "truth" or "reason." Her gender bias not only evidences itself in her artistic method, or at least in justification of it, but also in her portrayal of female characters. Mastery over language itself is often shown as inaccessible to women, primarily because of its corruption by men. Women achieve various degrees of success in traditionally masculine endeavors according to their access to traditional masculine tools. Paradoxically, other equally heroic women deliberately choose the domestic sphere in rejection of society's decadent—and primarily masculine—structures.

Perhaps it is also within the scheme of Cavendish's canon as "fancy" or a woman's dream world that we can appreciate her "disconnected scenes." Such dreamscapes seem appropriate to works so obviously filled with the dreams of both heroines and playwright. In *The Presence* (1668), the princess and her ladies spend their days dreaming, finding in dream lovers fulfillment not to be found at court. In a fantasy never explained by rational process, the princess awakens one day to find her dream made flesh—and, no less, a prince in disguise.

The Duchess, not finding her dreams flesh, could at least give them substance on paper, explaining that she created the fantasy domain of *The Description of a New World, Called the Blazing-World* (1668) because,

> though I cannot be Henry V or Charles I, yet I will endeavour to be Margaret the First, and though I have neither Power, Time, nor Occasion to be a giant Conqueror like Alexander or Caesar, yet rather than not be Mistress of a world, since Fortune and the Fates would give me none, I have made one of my own.
> (Cavendish, *Blazing World* 1668, A2)

Admitting that she wrote for recognition and identity outside the domestic sphere, in the preface to *Nature's Pictures Drawn by Fancies Pencil* (1651) she declared, "That my ambition of extraordinary Fame, is restless, and not ordinary, I cannot deny: and since all Heroic Actions, Publick Employments, as well Civil as Military, and Eloquent Pleadings, are deni'd my Sex in this Age, I may be excused for writing so much" (Cavendish 1656, C4).

So her works present one vision after another of women achieving such goals. Queens, counselors, belles, scholars—all are projections of Cavendish's visions of power. There are also intriguing glimpses of strong, platonic relationships between women, and perhaps a bit of flirtation with lesbianism. These amazon heroines may be actual warriors, like Lady Victoria in *Bell in Campo* (1662), who recruits and leads a victorious female army of "Heroickesses," convinced that with equal education women will prove "as good Souldiers and Privy Counsellors, Rulers and Commanders, Navigators and Architectors . . . as men are" (2.9). In addition to her noble actions, her eloquent speeches gain approval for a sort of Bill of Rights for Women, and represent Cavendish's finest dramatic writing.

Or the heroines might be scholars, like Lady Sanspareille of *Youths Glory, and Deaths Banquet* (1662), who gains fame and regard as a philosopher and orator both from the great men of her time and a very compelling queen. Or take the case of Lady Orphant of *Loves Adventures* (1662)—she's something of both. In order to be near the man she loves she takes on male identity and disguise. As the page "Affectionata," she astounds the army with both her genius for strategy and her valor in battle, quickly moving up to a command post. Her reputation nets her a summons to Rome, and during her visit to the Vatican she debates with the College of Cardinals and is offered a cardinal's hat by the pope himself. She also "gets her man," of course, although he first adopts her as his son!

One aspect of the unusual vision of author and heroines is rejection of the traditional marriages of the time. *The Matrimonial Trouble* (1662) chronicles nine bad marriages, while the masque performed by the women of the *Convent of Pleasure* (1662) is also designed as antimarriage propaganda. Ten scenes depict women beaten by drunken husbands, dying in childbirth, or suffering as their own children die. In the words of the epilogue, "Marriage is a curse we find, / Especially to Women kind, / From the Cobler's wife we see, / to Ladies, they unhappy be." The heroine, Lady Happy, asserts that marriage to the "best of men, if any best there be . . . [brings] more crosses and sorrows than pleasure, freedom, or happiness" and has thus separated herself from men, "who made the female sex their slaves" (1.2).

The negative matrimonial examples in the plays include both the common commercial alliances of the time and also relationships based on passion. Although Lady Wagtail, one of the fashionable gossips of *Love's Adventures*, insists that "there's none of the effeminate Sex but takes it for a disgrace to lie an old maid, and rather than dye one, they will marry any man that will have them" (part 2, 1.5), a number of Cavendish heroines prove her wrong. Doltche, for instance, in *The Comedy Named the Several Wits*, rejects the notion of arranged marriage: "If my Father desires me to dye, I shall satisfie his desire, for it is in my power to take away my own life, when I will; but it is not in my power to love those my Father would have me; for love is not to be commanded, nor directed, nor governed, nor prescribed, for love is free, and not to be controuled" (1.4).

Some of the heroines speak convincingly against marriage as a trap for women but eventually accept exceptional men with potential for truly equal relationships. This seems to have been the case with the duchess herself, who obviously loved her husband deeply and dramatically proved her devotion to him through many years of poverty, yet was proud to say that she had never known what it was to be "in love." Lady Bashful of *Loves Adventures* reluctantly agrees to marry the man she has come to love truly, but insists on a private ceremony rather than making a pageant that would hypocritically dramatize triumph in taking on an institution of enslavement. Lady

Happy will marry the prince who has infiltrated her *Convent of Pleasure* only after he has gradually won her esteem and love while masquerading as a woman.

Other heroines maintain their resolve and their celibacy. Grand Esprit and Ease of *The Wits Cabal* (1662), Single in *The Matrimonial Trouble*, and, most notably, Sanspareille in *Youths Glory* insist on their right to remain single. Sanspareille perhaps makes her case most convincingly, in a multi-page oration which she delivers while dressed in white Satin "like as a Bride," to her father and an entire audience "which are all Lovers." She cunningly begins by treating the responsibility and drudgery of marriage for men, but then moves on to her strongest point:

> but to treat or discourse of married women, is to discourse of a most unhappy life, for all the time of their lives is insnared with troubles . . . I do as faithfully believe it, as if I were experienced therein: On which faith, I made a vow never to marry, since I hear men are so hard to please and apt to change; wherefore if I were marryed, instead of discoursing of several arguments, I should be groaning and sighing, and weeping, with several pain and vexations. . . . (Part 2, 2.5)

Not only can Cavendish's heroines envision life without marriage, but they can also envision life without men. Two of her plays include utopian schemes, communities of women. Each of the works takes its name from its utopian society.

In *The Female Academy*, the academy is established for the "well-born (or antient descent)" and rich. Men are excluded, except for observing from a grate, as are less elite women, who have yet a separate grate. The word goes out, "If you would have your Daughter virtuously and wisely educated, you must put her into the Female Academy." Viewing Cavendish's ideals for education, we see the ladies learning by making orations (just as the author seemed to prefer her own speculations to any kind of research or systematic observation). Each morning and afternoon the members of the academy assemble to listen to one after another of the young women discoursing on such issues as "whether or not women may equal men in wit or wisdom" (yes to wit, no to wisdom), "the behavior of our sex," friendship, honesty, "vanity, vice, and wickedness," "boldness and bashfulnesse," "virtuous courtships and wooing Suiters," poetry, and theater. One favorite topic is to discourse on discourses. The men of the neighborhood, lustful, jealous, and threatened, determine to break the strength of the Academy by marching in protest and blowing trumpets around the compound.

Revealing quite a different vision, the convent in *The Convent of Pleasure* is a retreat not for asceticism but rather for sensual delights. The Lady Happy has established it because she believes that

> men are the only troublers of Women; for they only cross and oppose their sweet delights, and peaceable life; they cause their pains, but not their pleasure . . . those Women where Fortune, Nature, and the gods are joined to make them happy, were mad to live with Men, who make the Female sex their Slaves. . . .

She vows,

> But I will not be so inslaved, but will live retired from their Company. Wherefore, in order thereto, I will take so many Noble Persons of my own Sex . . . whose Births are greater than their Fortunes, and are resolv'd to live a single life, and vow Virginity; with these I mean to live incloister'd with all the delights and pleasures that are allowable and lawful; My Cloister shall not be a Cloister of restraint, but a place for freedom, not to vex the Senses but to please them. (1.2)

The cloister, it is reported, has "conveniencey for much Provision, and hath Women for every Office and Employment: for though she hath not above twenty Ladies with her, yet she hath a numerous Company of female servants, so as there is no occasion for Men" (2.2). The staff includes "Women-Physicians, Surgeons and Apothecaries" (2.1). Cavendish describes at great length the lavish decor and "conveniencies" of the convent, the dress provided the ladies, the choicest meats of each season, as well as the lush grounds and gardens. In a song, Lady Happy promises,

> We'll please our Sight with Pictures rare.
> Our Nostrils with perfumed Air.
> Our Ears with sweet melodious Sound,

Whose Substance can be no where found
. . . Variety each Sense shall feed,
And Change in them new Appetites breed.
(2.2)

The recreations of the cloistered ladies not only delight their senses and aesthetics, but also provide for fulfilling their dreams. Through their pageants and skits the dramatic medium itself becomes central in multiple layers of plays within plays. A sequence in which fantasies come to life gives the work a dreamlike—and eerily modern—quality. A pastoral scene appears and a princess (dressed as a shepherd) woos Lady Happy (dressed as a shepherdess), discussing "innocent love" and the platonic desire to "mingle souls together" in a kiss. The pasture vanishes and the scene (without changing) opens into a rocky shore with the princess as Neptune and Lady Happy as a sea goddess. They make verses about their beautiful lives in the sea, until the scene again vanishes.

Cavendish exposed her view of dreams and creativity in her self-reflexive fiction, *Description of the Blazing World* (1668). Immaterial spirits instruct the Empress's friend, the Duchess of Newcastle, that

> every human Creature can create an Immaterial World fully in-habited by Immaterial Creatures, and populous of Immaterial subjects, such as we are, and all this within the compass of the head or scull . . . also he may alter that World as often as he pleases, or change it from a Natural World, to an Artificial . . . a World of Ideas, a World of Atoms, a World of Lights, or whatsoever his Fancy leads him to . . . and enjoy as much pleasure and delight as a World can afford you. (96–97)

The world created by the fictional Duchess of Newcastle is, of course, the Blazing World created by the historical Duchess of Newcastle.

Although many of Cavendish's plot lines and characters seem to represent an author creating new structures to undermine the patriarchal order, others paradoxically undercut this purpose. While Cavendish has envisioned and portrayed a fascinating and encouraging complexity of women's roles in a man's world, she also reveals a striking ambivalence about a woman's choice of those roles. Both the utopian communities of *The Female Academy* and *The Convent of*

Pleasure promise rich and unusual fulfillment for women, frightening those outside by their potential for upheaving the social order, yet ultimately each turns out to be fruitless.

Much is made of education for the Female Academy, holding up lofty, though abstract, goals and ideals for women. However, after a number of gestures in a feminist direction, the status quo is restored. In the final scene, the matron reveals to the insecure men that the ladies have committed themselves to the academy in order to become better wives, and "have learn'd so much Duty and Obedience, as to obey to what they shall think fit" (5.29).

In the other ostensibly feminist stronghold, the Convent of Pleasure, Lady Happy finds herself more and more attached and attracted to a beautiful princess who has joined her ranks, and questions, "Why may I not love a woman with the same affection I could a Man?" (4.1). Alas, we never learn the answer to that question because the princess turns out to be a prince in disguise. The ambivalence is particularly interesting in this most unusual instance of sexual cross-identity: the audience is not in on the masquerade, and the "princess" in turn further cross-dresses (as a man dressed as a woman-dressed-as-a-man), assuming masculine dress and roles for the playacting with which the women frequently amuse and instruct themselves. As Lady Happy assumes her new position as princess, the Convent is, of course, forgotten.

Cavendish undermines much of the potential feminine power of the other works to comparable effect. In addition to the amazon or heroic heroines, there is also another major character type generally found either as a foil to the main heroine or as a focus of an important subplot. This woman is generally more conventional: quiet, seeking to please, devoted to her traditional duties and the man she loves. In most cases Cavendish emphasizes that the character is shy to the point of painfulness—just as the author described herself in her single days as a lady of Queen Henrietta's court.

Jacqueline Pearson, in "Women may discourse . . . as well as men," classifies the two types of heroines as speaking women and silent women. Both have exemplary qualities, but play two different types of roles in the world, distinguished by their access to language—which is itself molded and manipulated by men—the golden key to success, or even survival, in a man's world. In at least six of Cavendish's plays the "heroic" heroines make public orations, pointedly demonstrating their mastery over language. The silent women, however, recognizing that they lack meaningful language, deliberately reject the corrupt language typically available to women and which characterizes other females as gossips, liars, and cheats.

Two plays feature sub-heroines, both known as Lady Bashful, who suffer great malice and gossip from the court and fashionable society because they lack the expected social graces. In *The Presence*, the Ladies Wagtail and Self-Conceit and Quick-Wit mock the Lady Bashful for her unsociable behavior and try to embroil her in scandal when she omits conventional social forms. When asked if she came to court to be thought a fool, she responds,

> No, I came to learn Wisdom, and to improve my Understanding, and if I can meet no Vertue, Worth, nor Honour to take Exampels from, yet I may observe the Follies, so as to shun them where or whensoever I meet them; and though ignorance is thought a defect, either in Nature, or Breeding, yet it is not accounted a crime, nor a deadly sin; and as long as they cannot think by my Carriage I am base, wanton, or wicked, I do not care how they think of my Wit or Bashfulness. (Cavendish, *Plays Never Before Printed* 1668, Scenes "designed to be put into the Presence" but "print[ed] . . . by themselves," 4)

Lord Loyalty sees Lady Bashful's sterling qualities through her quiet demeanor and weds her, much as the dashing Duke of Newcastle had wed the blushing maid of honor who held such similar sentiments.

The Lady Bashful of *Love's Adventures* similarly asserts that her bashfulness is based on fear of dishonoring herself and not on any shame in her person or actions. When visited by the Ladies Wagtail and Amorous and the Sirs Bolde and Exception of fashionable society she trembles and shakes, either stammering, or being struck entirely mute with terror. Yet she, too, attracts wooers, although desiring none. She finds least troublesome the attentions of Sir Serious Dumb, who courts her by notes, thereby disturbing her privacy the least. When he is attacked by another suitor, Bashful realizes her love for him, disarms the challenger, and threatens him with his own sword. "Fear gave me confidence . . . love gave me courage" (part 2, 1.8), she tells Dumb. He, it turns out, is not really mute, but has foresworn language to merit her esteem through action rather than corrupt words. Through him Cavendish most pointedly dramatizes the issue that serves as such a strong undercurrent in her work.

Lady Innocent of *Youths Glory, and Deaths Banquet* is a victimized heroine more akin to those of the era's romances. Yet it is corrupt language that persecutes her—in this case the lies of her rival Lady Incontinent. Finding herself accused of immorality and lies, Innocent trusts in the virtue and judgment of her guardian and fiancé Lord de l'Amour to be able to discern the truth: "To what purpose should I speak? . . . silence, and patience, shall be my two companions" (part 2, 2.9). But when framed for stealing from Incontinent, despairing of finding language to answer the charges, she decides that only her death can demonstrate her to innocence her fiancé. So suicide becomes a triumphant action, prompting her stricken lover also to take his own life in her tomb.

These heroines show that within the domestic realm (the real world, perhaps), women must trust to modest and virtuous lives to speak for them and achieve a respect above their normal station—respect that they cannot gain by competing on the same basis with the men who manipulate that world and its language. They can claim a kind of power over their own lives and sometimes those around them, but it is a power in stark and somewhat perplexing contrast to that wielded by the heroines of the main plots.

Perhaps *Youths Glory* provides the most disturbing manifestation of Cavendish's ambivalence. Silent Lady Innocent, who must commit suicide in order to communicate her innocence, is set opposite that most articulate of scholars and individualists, Lady Sanspareille. Sanspareille succeeds in earning the world's respect, but then inexplicably sickens and dies. Was it just too inconceivable that this remarkable woman could continue to bloom in a public role, particularly when further estranged from her sex by her vow of celibacy?

Cavendish's ambivalence toward her heroines seems to mirror the insecurity that shines through all the apologies and prefaces about her own efforts to master the written word: she alternately portrays her vocation as a heroic assay into the male competitive sphere and a harmless diversion for days insufficiently filled with domestic duties in a wealthy and childless household. She apologizes for one of her first ventures into publication, *The Philosophical and Physical Opinions*, confessing to His Excellence the Lord Marquis of Newcastle, "I have somewhat erred from good housewifery, to write Nature's Philosophy, where, had I been prudent, I should have translated natural philosophy into good housewifery" (*Philosophical Opinions* 1655, a²).

Like her statements concerning her own vocation, within the plays Cavendish's contrasting visions of female power are juxtaposed jarringly against each other. Perhaps her complex and contorted structures may also be part of her struggle to project the full complexities of her ambivalences. Part of what makes her plays seem disconnected is the rapid alternation of short scenes from each plot or subplot with those of the others, or sometimes simply with a few lines by anonymous passersby commenting chorus-like on the action or filling in a strand of exposition. Certainly one aim of this technique must be to maintain a high level of suspense—after all, this is the typical structure of pot-boilers and the modern soap opera—but the ponderous number of scenes that results (as many as thirty to fifty in one part of a two-part play) and the choppiness of the transitions are not comfortable even for reading, and would certainly be unstageable. (I would suggest, however, that although the works are at heart plays of ideas rather than of dramatic action, with extensive editing and rearranging of scenes, three—*Love's Adventures, Bell in Campo*, and *The Convent of Pleasure*—may contain the dramatic elements and liveliness necessary to succeed on stage.)

Furthermore, while most of Cavendish's plays were untheatrical, written during the interregnum while the theaters were closed and without any sense of the visual dimensions of that medium, they may have a greater appeal to the modern imagination than they did for her own time. Surrealistic scenes—sometimes little more than a fleeting series of tableaux or images—and fantasy sequences seem now as if they could have been written for film. Perhaps the most striking example of this is *The Convent of Pleasure*, in which the medium itself becomes central in multiple layers of plays within plays. In addition to the masque on the hardships of women are the scenes in which the ladies of the Convent, particularly Lady Happy and the princess/prince, appear in shifting scenes representing their fantasies.

But beyond the problems of structural coherence, the lack of a unified vision or direction would have prevented Cavendish from gaining a popular audience. The tensions inherent in her ambivalence could not be exploited because they are never resolved, probably not even for the playwright. The rigid expectations of her society concerning the way in which theater as a public ritual builds and climaxes are not conducive to portraying uncertainty. On the other hand, the presence of unresolved conflicts can be a powerful force on the page rather than the stage. There is a private dimension to reading which allows the suggestion of multiple meanings for both writer and reader. Our finest literature is usually rich in the unresolved conflicts and ambivalences of real life.

Regardless of what degree of self-awareness she possessed or expressed, Cavendish's heroines play out the dramas of identity and self-determination that women faced then—and now. Just as the two heroine types suggest Margaret as she was and Margaret as she dreamed herself, so the major heroic plots about powerful, influential women project her seemingly unrealizable dreams against the subplots featuring appropriately dutiful and modest women sorting through the domestic trials of the real world. That Cavendish could not live within the bounds of her own world is evident in her unconventional behavior—and the ridicule it drew, including the world's refusal to take her writing seriously. She may have deprecated her abilities and her writing, but she never stopped writing. Wielding her pen was her own form of heroic action by which she could stay within the proscribed confines of domesticity and yet break out to test ideas and dreams women had never dared claim before.

Her dream world is populated by women who seek to live their lives without restraint and others who warn them that to do so means failure or death. The inventive alternatives Cavendish devised reveal not only exceptional creativity but also courage. Her ultimate ambivalence—a woman equal to any earthly man who finally runs up against some insidious inexplicable force that will not let her live (whether it be a patriarchal god or her own "unnaturalness")—is more a collapse of faith than a failure of fancy.

Works Cited

Bowerbank, Sylvia. 1984. "The Spider's Delight: Margaret Cavendish and the 'Female' Imagination." *ELR* 14: 392–408.

Cavendish, Margaret Lucas. 1668. *The Description of a New World, called the Blazing-World. Written by the thrice Noble, Illustrious, and Excellent Princesse, the Duchess of Newcastle.* London: A. Maxwell.

————. 1667. *The Life of the thrice Noble, High and Puissant Prince William Cavendish, Duke, Marquess, and Earl of Newcastle; Earl of Ogle; Viscount Mansfield; and Baron of Bolsover, of Ogle, Bothal and Hepple . . . Written by the thrice Noble, Illustrious, and Excellent Princess, Margaret, Duchess of Newcastle, his wife.* London: A. Maxwell.

————. [1953]. *Memoirs of William Cavendish, Duke of Newcastle, and Margaret his Wife: The Life of William Cavendish, Duke of Newcastle, to Which is Added the True Relation of My Birth Breeding and Life* Ed. C. H. Firth. London: George Routledge & Sons.

————. 1656. *Natures Pictures drawn by Fancies Pencil to the Life. Written by the thrice Noble, Illustrious, and Excellent Princess, the Lady Marchioness of Newcastle. In this volume there are several feigned Stories of Natural Descriptions, as comical, Tragical, and Tragi-Comical, Poetical, Romancical, Philosophical, and Historical, both in Prose and Verse, some all Verse, some all Prose, some mixt, partly Prose, and partly Verse. Also there are some Morals, and some Dialogues; but they are as the Advantage Loaves of Bread to a Bakers dozen; and a true Story at the latter end, wherein there is no Feignings.* London: J. Martin and J. Allestrye.

————. 1666. *Observations upon Experimental Philosophy. To which is added, The Description of a new Blazing World. Written by the thrice Noble, Illustrious, and Excellent Princesse, the Duchess of Newcastle.* London: A. Maxwell.

————. 1664. *CCXI. Sociable Letters, Written by the thrice Noble, Illustrious, and Excellent Princess, the Lady Marchioness of Newcastle.* London: William Wilson.

————. 1662. *Orations of Divers Sorts, Accomodated to Divers Places. Written by the thrice Noble, Illustrious and Excellent Princess, the Lady Marchioness of Newcastle* London.

————. 1655. *The Philosophical and Physical Opinions, Written by her Excellency, The Lady Marchionesse of Newcastle.* London: J. Martin & J. Allestrye.

————. 1662. *Playes written by the thrice Noble, Illustrious and Excellent Princess, the Lady Marchioness of Newcastle.* London: John Martyn, et al.

————. 1668. *Plays, never before Printed. Written by the thrice Noble, Illustrious, and Excellent Princesse, the Duchess of Newcastle.* London: A. Maxwell.

————. 1653. *Poems, and Fancies: Written by the Right Honourable, the Lady Margaret Countesse of Newcastle.* London: J. Martin, and J. Allestrye.

————. 1655. *The Worlds Olio. Written by the Most Excellent Lady the Lady M. of Newcastle.* London: J. Martin and J. Allestrye.

Evelyn, John. 1905. *Diary of John Evelyn, to which are added a Selection of Familiar Letters.* Vols. 2 and 3. London: Bickers and Sons.

Fraser, Antonia. 1984. *The Weaker Vessel.* New York: Knopf.

Gilbert, Sandra M. and Susan Gubar. 1979. *The Madwoman in the Attic.* New Haven: Yale Univ. Press.

Goreau, Angeline. 1983. "Aphra Behn: A Scandal to Modesty." In *Feminist Theorists.* Ed. Dale Spender. New York: Pantheon Books, 8–27.

———. 1985. *The Whole Duty of a Woman.* New York: Dial.

Grant, Douglas. 1957. *Margaret the First.* Toronto: Univ. of Toronto Press.

Jones, Kathleen. 1988. *A Glorious Fame: The Life of Margaret Cavendish, Duchess of Newcastle, 1623–1673.* London: Bloomsbury.

Mintz, Samuel I. 1952. "The Duchess of Newcastle's Visit to the Royal Society." *JEGP* 51: 168–76.

Nicolson, Marjorie. 1948. *Voyages to the Moon.* New York.

Paloma, Dolores. 1980, "Margaret Cavendish: Defining the female self." *Women's Studies* 7:55–66.

Pearson, Jacqueline. 1985. "Women may discourse . . . as well as men': Speaking and Silent Women in the Plays of Margaret Cavendish, Duchess of Newcastle." *TSWL* 4:33–45.

Pepys, Samuel. 1926. *Everybody's Pepys: The Diary of Samuel Pepys 1660–1669.* Abr. and ed. O. F. Morshead. New York: Harcourt, Brace.

Woolf, Virginia. 1929. *A Room of One's Own.* London: Bloomsbury.

Herself as Heroine: Portraits as Autobiography for Elizabeth Inchbald

CECILIA MACHESKI

Are portraits a form of autobiography, or biography? Or are they a peculiar middle ground where the subject can interfere and partially control the image, yet where the portrait artist has the final say? In another essay in this section, Pat Rogers notes the importance both Sarah Siddons and Sir Joshua Reynolds placed on the creation of gesture, and the desire each expressed to be recognized as the originator of the pose that became so renowned in "The Tragic Muse." Such concern with what modern celebrities and their agents know as "image" was shared by Siddons's friend and fellow actress, Elizabeth Inchbald (1753–1821). While her celebrity on the stage was minor compared to that of the great Siddons, Inchbald became familiar to the same audiences through her achievements as a playwright, novelist, and critic. In looking for answers to the questions posed here about the nature of portraits and their relationship particularly to autobiography, I suggest that, especially for women, the written record of a life is often inadequate and disappointing, and that the biographer must turn to alternate media to create a complete picture of a female subject whose career encompassed so transitory and ephemeral a field as the stage.

In turning to portraits of Mrs. Inchbald to fill out the life record available in print, I suggest that we must revise our notions of autobiography, and of biographical method, when we are treating subjects for whom the traditional methods and opportunities for recording and analyzing life history were unavailable. As the eighteenth-century response to the published lives of Colley Cibber and his notorious daughter Charlotte Charke reveal, public accep-

"Mrs. Inchbald." After Cook, engraved by Walker.
Collection of Cecilia Macheski.

tance of autobiography was not easy to acquire. The reading public was inclined to view the task of making public an intimate life record as a gesture of scandalous egoism. Thus for a woman concerned with reputation, and accustomed to being in the public eye, the notion of creating an autobiography was at once attractive yet cause for careful planning to avoid the scandal attached to Charke and her kind. Inchbald's solution—to create an autobiographical record through portraits—is better appreciated if we glance first at the outline of her career and next at some recent theories on the nature of autobiography.

To the eighteenth-century British reading public, the published works of Elizabeth Inchbald were judged far superior to those of many of her contemporaries. The applause of audiences and the respect of critics supported her through a long, successful career as a writer for the stage. A beautiful woman, judged vain by some and frugal by others, she made a lifelong campaign of surviving by her pen when the death of her actor husband left her in poverty and her insistent stutter kept her stage success at a modest level. She had been raised a Roman Catholic, and while her religious fervor seems to have waned through most of her life, she returned to a strong interest in evangelical Christianity in her retirement years (Macheski 1984).

Crucial to her success was an almost uncanny ability to measure and mirror the temper of her times, reflected in her sympathy with Jacobin causes and her insistence on female virtue. (Thus, while she could espouse the political causes of Godwin and Holcroft, she would later refuse to acknowledge Mary Wollstonecraft when she and Godwin cohabited.) Inchbald's adaptability is further evident in her experiments with genre as she shifted from farce to drama to novel, molding each to meet audience taste and at the same time to incorporate her own sensibility in her texts.

The complex and fascinating question of just what, exactly, shapes an autobiographical record has recently become the concern of psychologists like Jerome Bruner and anthropologists such as Vincent Crapanzano.[1] While space limitations here must confine us to only a sketch of the relevant theories, we can glean enough to illuminate the nature of Inchbald's somewhat eccentric autobiographical method. In essence, these theories of personal history suggest that each individual who constructs an autobiography is constrained by rules of genre and style; that is, the shape of the life as it is printed is as much a function of genre as of what actually happened in the life. Bruner notes that there are three categories of life history, using terms borrowed from Hayden White: the *annal*, which records merely facts or happenings; the *chronique*, or plot, which creates a "clot of meaning"; and the *histoire*, in which a moral construct is generated for the events in the life. He suggests that the very act of telling separates self from the subject about which one is writing, even though that subject is oneself. The self-report is interpretive, and used for self-location, both placing the subject within a cultural context, and at the same time individualizing him or her as well. Bruner is using his discoveries to help understand the way in which memory works to schematize, select, or organize experience. Crapanzano's work, especially as reported in *Tuhami*, is related; he argues, based on field work done in Morocco, that Western anthropologists and psychologists often misunderstand subjects from other cultures because they fail to take into account the importance of their own presence as an influence on the way those subjects report their experiences. *Tuhami* is an experiment in acknowledging and recording the observer's relationship to his subject as well as the results of the study.

What Bruner and Crapanzano can help us do in the field of literary study is to reconsider the angle from which we view subjects like Inchbald, whose careers and whose extant life records do not fit the norm we have come to expect from such great self-historians (and mythologizers) as, say, Henry James or Samuel Richardson. Yet rather than dismissing Inchbald because she did not hand down an established canon about her life in carefully preserved letters and journals, what Bruner's method directs us toward is an appreciation of the extant, if eccentric, material if it provides us with the *histoire* that helps make sense of the mere facts.

In Inchbald's case, her biographer, James Boaden, can, in this new light, be dismissed as a mere recorder of the equivalent of the *annal*. His compilation of the mere facts of her life lacks sympathy, insight, or any attempt at constructing an analysis. Similarly, Inchbald's own diary/account books, a handful of which survive in the Folger Shakespeare Library, disappoint the avid biographer because they too are little more than *annal*. In these tiny pocket memorandum books she recorded expenses and visitors, but had little space to comment on how these daily commodities affected her. The volumes of the later years, when Inchbald was more established in her career, move slightly toward *chronique* as she records in a few lines her loneliness, or her criticism of a play.

To find the *histoire* then, we cannot look in these sources. We must look, instead, for the record in which Mrs. Inchbald interprets herself, placing herself, as Bruner suggests, both in a cultural context and yet individualizing her image. And for this record we must turn to the portraits.

That a woman of Inchbald's beauty and wide popularity should sit for many portraits is hardly surprising, but these pictures are more than a mere publicity stunt. They are her attempt to find her own voice or genre for her autobiographical report. In the transformation of dress, posture, and general style the portraits mirror the author's remarkable responsiveness to the tastes of the times, and her ability to make fashions suit her own interests. Like her personal papers, moreover, the portraits suggest how deeply patterned with introspection was her nature, how frequent and intelligent her self-evaluations. Evidence of the changing nature of her image provided by the portraits offers a striking contrast to the flatness of life that Boaden, a priggish biographer, described. While this prudish compiler tends to conceal much of the conflict and change in Inchbald's life, the visual record can be used to countermand Boaden's conclusions. It is in fact her pictures, even more than her diary, that offer us the most representative image of the dynamic, observant, woman.

Inchbald's intense introspection may be in part the result of her Roman Catholic heritage with its doctrine of confession and its tradition of writers like St. Augustine. But perhaps a man, however great his sins, could more easily confess than a woman, even by the eighteenth century. Thus, though the practice of self-analytical meditation was available, Inchbald no doubt felt the need to redefine the form it would take to suit her temper and her times. Public self-examination became more easily possible through the genre of the portrait than the confessional text. But such introspection also suits the consciousness of a writer, and it is thus not so surprising that Inchbald kept a diary regularly for fifty years. The discipline implied by such a practice carried over into her published work, and argues for the sincerity of the values expressed in her novels and plays, since many incorporated autobiographical material. Thus, the autobiographical impulse was strong for Elizabeth Inchbald, but her gender

M^{RS}. INCHBALD.

"Mrs. Inchbald." Attributed to Thomas Lawrence.
Collection of Cecilia Macheski.

and by extension her limited education required that she shape the
product of that impulse to suit her own voice, and to conform with
the prejudices of her day. Though she could attempt to translate
Rousseau's *Confessions*, in other words, she could not so readily
transcribe her own. Her solution was to turn to portraits. Ironically,
then, the portraits, designed for public view and obviously manufac-
tured and manipulated by the painter, can still be read as far more
private autobiographical statements than her own written account
book diaries. Readers of the tiny day books come away disappointed
with the merely factual record they contain (what Bruner calls the
annal), but those who turn to the portraits find in them something
closer to his *chronique*, and, perhaps, even a bit of the *histoire*.

Louis Joughin's study of Mrs. Inchbald includes an index of all known portraits (1932, 529–35). From these, I have selected five, chiefly because of their availability as prints and bookplates—making them among the more public statements—and because they cover the active years of the writer's stage and literary career. Five portraits cover the years from 1787, when she had just begun to see her plays become regular items in the London theater repertory, and 1814, when she was fifty-five years old and living in retirement.

The earliest (Fig. 1), engraved by Walker from a drawing by Cook, is dated September 1787. It celebrates Inchbald's success as a writer of comic drama, surrounding the oval portrait with iconography suggesting her life in the theater. Drapery fills the upper left and right corners and forms a dark ground against which glows a quill pen on a bed of roses and a second device, probably a mirror. In the lower left is a lyre; on the right rest the emblems of comedy, including the traditional mask and a small figure of a jester. This formal neoclassical iconography identifies Inchbald's roots in the Augustan world and her apprenticeship on the stage made popular by Garrick and Sheridan. Within this formal and symbolic frame, the actress and playwright sits, glancing to her left with a look of accomplishment. The face is serene, marked by a rather long and slender nose, distinct, slightly rakish eyebrows, forthright eyes, and a shapely mouth. The features in this early image are sharpened slightly to suggest classical sculpture, an effect enhanced by the pompous hair and a formal wig, piled high and hanging in long curls on both shoulders. The impression is almost masculine, especially as she is shrouded in a generous piece of drapery that conceals the outline of her figure. The overall effect is distinctly neoclassical.

Of the three middle pictures two are undated, while the third, from 1806, is closest to the George Dance drawing dated c. 1808–14, which, unfortunately, cannot be reproduced here. The two remaining pictures, like the others, present the subject in half-length in costumes varying radically from that of the 1787 bust. In each, Inchbald sports long, romantic hair, a more strikingly youthful and feminine appearance, and a more shapely outline. Thus while each picture shows the changes in artistic taste and style that marked the transitional period of the 1790s and early 1800s, each portrait likewise shows Inchbald's adaptation to her time, and her continuing interest in revising her visual autobiography.

Figure 2 presents the subject in a romantic pose, face resting gently on her left hand as she stares away from the audience as if in a reverie. The hair is again piled high, as she emphasizes her stage "trademark" of playing without the conventional wig. The artist suggests the natural color of her curls, free from powder and cascading onto her bosom. Her countenance is softer, her eyes made particularly striking by hints of shadow. The mouth is familiar from the 1787 picture and the nose, softened, is still long and slender. This artist, possibly Thomas Lawrence (Joughin 1932), gives prominence to her chin and cheek bones, and overall creates the most flattering of the images. Her dress here is cut low in the bodice and is the most ornate of any we see. A lacy handkerchief frames the neckline and is tied in a knot in the center, while soft white cuffs highlight the wrist that supports her cheek. The suggestion is of preromantic influences, of a free-spirited woman confident of her talent and aware of the newer tastes in fashion that combine eighteenth-century love of ornament with softer lines and contours. If this is indeed the 1795 portrait to which Joughin refers we find in this image of a liberal mind the author of the successful *A Simple Story* on the eve of the publication of her second novel.

The next picture (Fig. 3) shows a pronounced simplification of dress as the subject now wears a light-colored Empire-style dress suggesting the Grecian lines favored during the Regency. She looks remarkably like a heroine from a novel by Jane Austen, or, indeed, by herself. To the clean line of the dress is contrasted an exuberant plumed hat or turban, possibly suggesting an earlier date. Soft curls tumble down her back. The expression is similar to, though plainer than the one in the previous portrait. The artist captures a more austere visage, although the brow, nose, and lips confirm the authenticity of the subject. It is the portrait of a sensible woman, as if the face were to contrast with the extravagant headdress. The eyes look almost directly ahead, unlike the earlier sidewards glances. Behind the figure the artist suggests clouds, as if Inchbald had been painted out of doors rather than in a studio.

The portrait dated 1806 (Fig. 4) is, according to Joughin, by an unknown artist. It was used as the frontispiece for *The British Theatre*. Here the writer, now in her early fifties, retains the youthful appearance of a girl, although her dress suggests that of an older woman. The hair looks shorter, falling in soft curls only to her col-

"Mrs. Inchbald." From *La Belle Assembleé*.
Collection of Cecilia Macheski

"Mrs. Inchbald." Frontispiece to **The British Theatre.**
Collection of Cecilia Macheski.

lar. She is seated rather stiffly in a small chair and her arms rest on a
table as she stares directly at the viewer. The eyes are drawn with
thicker lids, softening her frontal glance. The small pointed mouth
and long slender nose seem unchanged in the decades since the
theater portrait of 1787. There is a look of resignation about her, and
an almost inquisitive stare aimed at the viewer. A white handkerchief
frames her neck and tucks into the modestly cut bodice of the stiff-
looking fabric of a dress of plain design. As the reputable Mrs.
Inchbald of 1806, she wears a dark-colored garment lacking ornament, and only in this do we find a clue to her age and increasingly
conservative tastes as she turned in her later years to serious concern
with evangelical religion.

The final drawing (Fig. 5) presents a profile of the author when she was at least fifty-five, and possibly as old as sixty-one. Finally we see age registered by the artist, probably because of the less formal nature of the sitting. A matronly cap conceals most of her hair, and the plain dress, similar to the one in the 1806 portrait, suggests a severity in her appearance. The face is still intelligent, but quieter, caught in repose, suggesting introspection but neither pride nor vanity. The simplicity and "ordinary" tone reinforce the impression of her character found in the later diaries.

"Elizabeth Inchbald" by George Dance,
reproduced by permission of the National Portrait Gallery, London.

These portraits, then, form a life history, a personal history, recording the fluctuations and self-assessments that form the true *histoire*. The life is not merely recorded as a series of factual events, but is interpreted both by the writer and by her relationship with the portrait painter who helped her construct a definition for her self.

The visual record is of course ambiguous, open to the interpretation of the viewer and the accusation of mere vanity as a motive rather than the moral construction necessary for the genuine *histoire*. The fact, however, that unlike so many of the women who are the subjects of *Curtain Calls,* Elizabeth Inchbald made a conscious effort toward autobiography through her diaries and her many portraits, and that she had the time and, eventually, the money to indulge this interest, seems evidence enough to encourage us to read the portraits as a form of serious personal history.

What conclusions, then, can we draw from the visual record? In having her portrait painted and sketched so often, Elizabeth Inchbald is aligning herself with a new tradition of Fame. As Jessica Munns notes elsewhere in this collection, Aphra Behn confronted a notion of Fame as a masculine domain from which she was rigorously excluded. What Inchbald's portrait history tells us is that by the 1790s women had learned to make Fame a territory in which they could not only dwell, but also even rule.

Inchbald's portraits are, finally, part of a female tradition of iconography that emerged in the visual arts in the later eighteenth century, validated most emphatically by its transference from the high art of a woman like Angelica Kauffmann to the embroideries of dozens upon dozens of schoolgirls and women. I am thinking specifically of a print by Kauffmann of Fame at the tomb of Shakespeare (Fig. 6). The illustration shows a female, Fame, dressed in Grecian-style attire, mourning at a tomb engraved with the Bard's name, upon which she is tossing flower petals. So popular did this image become that female academies both in Britain and in the United States (especially the one run by novelist Susannah Rowson) from the 1790s until the 1830s recorded variations on the theme in memorial embroideries. While particulars changed, the genre remained recognizable and decidedly the exclusive domain of women.[2]

While the portraits of Elizabeth Inchbald do not directly allude to this tradition—we do not find the authoress garbed as Fame, for

"Fame at Shakespeare's Tomb." After Angelica Kauffmann.
Collection of Cecilia Macheski.

instance, as Siddons posed as The Tragic Muse—I suggest that there is, nonetheless, an echo of the Fame tradition in Inchbald's images. The familiarity and power of Kauffmann's picture is undeniable, but I argue that it is also subversive and feminist. For in this portrait of Fame, the great male poet is represented by a stone tomb marker, while Fame, the woman, is the central image. Who, then, is more important? Does the woman empower the poet, or is she a mere figurehead? I like to think that Kauffmann chose her image to assert her own power as an artist and the power of women in general to endure. Perhaps such a reading is too whimsical, but there is no question that we have come a long distance from the disgruntled attacks of Behn against the male cabal that opposed her. Kauffmann, perhaps, asserts a new power for women, not to be the mere counterparts of men, but to control their own celebrity. It is Fame who raises Shakespeare to his stature as famous, even if her flowers will fade long before his tomb crumbles, and we can infer that it is she who could cast him into the nether regions of, say, a few disdainful lines in *The Dunciad*. Can we, in fact, read Kauffmann's image as a form of self-portrait? Has she, in this single portrait, made herself both Fame and famous?

However speculative such queries must remain, there is no question that women in the eighteenth century, and especially those who chose a life on the stage, sought to have Fame's flowers, however transitory, strewn upon their own paths. In an era when the writing of autobiography was still an occupation restricted to marginal members of society like Charlotte Charke, women were obliged to find other media in which to record their histories. In the case of Mrs. Inchbald, the portrait proved an ideal form. As for each sitting she chose a new style or posed in a different way, she interacted with the artist for whom she sat in the same way that she played to her audience when she wrote for the stage. Neither relationship jeopardized her individuality, for she remained able to define her own notion of self even as she explored ways to transform that self from woman to heroine. Thus the portraits become her version of *histoire*, a unique genre in which she tried to analyze her growth from Augustan actress to autobiographical novelist to critic and celebrity.

If modern feminists are inclined to find Elizabeth Inchbald's exploitation of her acknowledged beauty distasteful, her celebration of her self misguided, perhaps they are too hasty in their estimate. For in the self she created by means of her portraits, this woman achieved something that only a century earlier had seemed unattainable: financial independence, literary productivity, and Fame.

Notes

1. For my understanding of these theories I am indebted to a Mellon proseminar sponsored by The City University of New York in 1987, which was directed by Vincent Crapanzano and at which Jerome Bruner was a guest. The theories Dr. Bruner proposed are from a work in progress on personal history.

2. While no exhaustive studies have yet been done connecting these schoolgirl embroideries to a literary and historical context, the most comprehensive cataloguing of mourning pictures is available in Betty Ring, *American Needlework Treasures: Samplers and Silk Embroideries from the Collection of Betty Ring* (New York: E.P. Dutton and Museum of American Folk Art, 1987).

Works Cited

Joughin, G. Louis. 1932. "The Life of Elizabeth Inchbald." Unpublished dissertation, Harvard University.

Macheski, Cecilia. 1984. "A Feeling Mind: The Early Literary Career of Elizabeth Inchbald (1753–1821)." Unpublished dissertation, The City University of New York.

"Towering Beyond Her Sex": Stature and Sublimity in the Achievement of Sarah Siddons

PAT ROGERS

The homage she has received is greater than that which is paid to Queens. The enthusiasm she excited had something idolatrous about it; she was regarded less with admiration than with wonder, as if a being of a superior order had dropped from another sphere to awe the world with the majesty of her appearance. She raised Tragedy to the skies, or brought it down from thence, It was something above nature. We can conceive of nothing grander. She embodied to our imagination the fables of mythology, of the heroic and deified mortals of elder time. She was not less than a goddess, or than a prophetess inspired by the gods. Power was seated on her brow, passion emanated from her breast as from a shrine. She was Tragedy personified. She was the stateliest ornament of the public mind.—William Hazlitt, "Mrs. Siddons" (*Examiner*, 15 June 1816)

In 1804 the miscellaneous writer Mary Pilkington brought out one of the first, if not the very first, among volumes of collected biographies of notable women. The full title was *Memoirs of Celebrated Female Characters, who have Distinguished themselves by their Talents and Virtues in Every Age and Nation; containing the most Extensive Collection of Illustrious Examples of Feminine Excellence ever Published; in which the Virtuous and the Vicious are Painted in their True Colours.* Well over 300 women are covered inside 350 duodecimo pages; the entries run from Agrippina to Zoe (wife of the emperor Romanus), from Joan of Arc to Catherine the Great, from Charlotte Corday to Ninon L'Enclos. Lucretia of legendary memory is present, but not Lucrezia Borgia. Comparatively few living persons are included, amongst them Mrs. Inchbald, Angelica Kauffmann, the ladies of Llangollen, Mrs. Piozzi, Hannah

More, and the sculptress Anne Damer; there is also one infiltrator in the shape of the Chevalier D'Eon, who had been living as a woman for a quarter of a century and was believed to be one. Some mythical personages appear, such as "Egee, Queen of the American Amazons," together with individuals who have almost moved from history into myth, such as Lady Godiva. A high proportion of the women present are queens, empresses, consorts, aristocrats, or courtesans. High independent achievement and autonomous celebrity are not conspicuous until the most recent entries, where for the first time women were attaining the possibility of living their own lives and speaking in their own voices. But even here a modern reader will raise her or his eyebrows on noticing the omission of Mary Wollstonecraft and Fanny Burney.

Some of the highest commendations are bestowed, not surprisingly, on Sarah Siddons, whose entry is garnished with an engraving of the well-known portrait by Sir Thomas Lawrence. Women, too, were acquiring a face of their own, and as we shall see Mrs. Siddons was a celebrity much depicted in contemporary portraiture. The entry begins in a characteristic manner: "This favourite child of Melpomene has long been the ornament of the English stage, and amidst the various allurements of which are naturally attached to such a situation, she has preserved the purity of an unsullied name" (Pilkington 321).[1] A common thread in almost all eulogies of Siddons is her combination of high histrionic talent with a blameless private life.[2] Mrs. Pilkington had the courage to mention some disagreeable stories which had been attached to Siddons, notably alleged "parsimony of disposition and callosity of heart," only to dismiss these as slander. She also alludes to a criticism that had been made of Siddons as an actress: "The countenance of this celebrated actress is peculiarly adapted to express the different passions of the mind, but with regard to her voice there are two opinions; one is, that she modulates it completely, and the other, that it wants variety and change." However, she quotes a previous biographer who claimed for Siddons not just "a majestic person" but also a well-modulated voice; he concludes, "the flexibility of her features, the expression of her eyes, and the grace of her deportment, have seldom been equalled" (Pilkington 321–22). All in this is a handsome tribute to Sarah, though not as fulsome a commendation as she had received from her greatest admirers. In this essay I shall look at a number of early assessments of her acting and behavior off-stage. The evidence is drawn from eyewitness accounts, recollections like those of Hazlitt, the biographies by Boaden and Campbell, and the portrayal of her by Joshua Reynolds and other artists. The aim will be to discover the terms in which she was habitually praised and to see how this marks a new phase in linguistic usage—one which departs from older gender-related vocabulary, and allows to a prominent woman a wider range of qualities than those traditionally associated with "feminine" strengths and virtues.

I

"The person of Mrs. Siddons," writes James Boaden, "rather courted the regal attire, and her beauty became more vivid from the decoration of her rank [as Euphrasia, in Arthur Murphy's *Grecian Daughter*]. The commanding height and powerful action of her figure, though always feminine, seemed to tower beyond her sex" (Boaden 1831, 1:312). Boaden's life first appeared in 1827; a new edition appeared in 1831, the year in which Siddons died. The same writer produced biographies of John Kemble (brother of Siddons), Mrs. Jordan, and others. His work was shortly followed by a rival compilation by the poet Thomas Campbell (1834). Together these lives provide a full picture of the kind of regard in which Siddons was held, and they will be central sources for this study. The emphasis which Boaden lays on Siddons's commanding physical stature is crucial to understanding her innovative cultural role. Betraying as the concessive "though still feminine" may appear, it is in fact the clue to a real liberation in vocabulary and outlook. One could say that Siddons extended the range of the feminine, that is, she made permissible the attribution to women of a less restricted and timid set of human qualities. Through her stage presence she made the idea of women in command a less frightening notion, and ultimately she must have affected the way in which women were able to conduct themselves in ordinary life.[3]

There is universal agreement that Siddons, in tragic roles at least, inspired unprecedented awe in those who witnessed her performances. Boaden quotes a contemporary description, possibly written by himself, when Siddons first appeared in her great part as Isabella in Southerne's *The Fatal Marriage*, at Drury Lane in October 1782:

> There never, perhaps, was a better stage figure than that of Mrs.
> Siddons. Her height was above the middle size, but not all
> inclined to the embonpoint. There is, notwithstanding, nothing
> sharp or angular in the frame; there is sufficient muscle to
> bestow a roundness upon the limbs, and her attitudes are, there-
> fore, distinguished equally by energy and grace. The symmetry
> of her person is exact and captivating. Her face is peculiarly
> happy, and features being finely formed, though strong, and
> never for an instant seeming overcharged, like the Italian faces,
> nor coarse and unfeminine under whatever impulse. On the
> contrary, it is so thoroughly harmonised when quiescent, and so
> expressive when impassioned that most people think her more
> beautiful than she is. So great, too, is the flexibility of her coun-
> tenance, that the rapid transitions of passion are given with a
> variety and effect that never tire upon the eye. Her voice is natu-
> rally plaintive, and a tender melancholy in her level of speaking
> denotes a being devoted to tragedy; yet this seemingly settled
> quality of voice becomes at will sonorous or piercing, over-
> whelms with rage, or, in its wild shriek, absolutely harrows up
> the soul. Her sorrow, too, is never childish; her lamentation has
> a dignity which belongs, I think, to no other woman; it claims
> your respect along with your tears. Her eye is brilliant and vary-
> ing like the diamond; it is singularly well placed; 'it pries,' in
> Shakespeare's language, 'through the portal of the head,' and
> has every aid from brows flexible beyond all female parallel,
> contracting to disdain, or dilating with the emotions of sym-
> pathy or pity or anguish. Her memory is tenacious and exact,
> her articulation clear and distinct, her pronunciation systematic
> and refined.

The writer goes on to observe that Siddons avoids all studied tricks,
making for a stage action that is "always proper, picturesque, graceful, and dignified." His final tribute might almost fit the performers
in Vincent Crummles's company, if not those of Mrs. Jarley's wax-
works: "So natural are her graduations and transitions, so classical
and correct her speech and deportment, and so intensely interesting
her voice, form, and features, that there is no conveying an idea of the

pleasure she communicates by words. She must be seen to be known. . . . She is an original; she copies no one, living or dead, but acts from Nature and herself" (Boaden 1831, 1:287–89).

It should be noted that several observers commented on the power of Mrs. Siddons's "eye" or gaze. Boaden himself, in connection with her performance of Juliet in middle age, remarks that "her art had more impressed her features than her age," and adds, "The eye . . . perfectly answered the mind; and what is or can be so essential to an actress as this visual eloquence?" The same power had been regularly noticed in the case of Garrick, whose natural successor Siddons was often taken to be. Even in later life when at her readings in public it was necessary that "she assisted her distant sight by glasses," she managed to make an expressive prop from her spectacles, by "waving them from time to time before her." It was well known that Garrick had not been very encouraging toward her in the days of her unsuccessful early appearance in London, and this was imputed by many to jealousy—the reason Tom Davies gave, for instance, to James Beattie. For his part Beattie stated in 1784 that "Garrick never affected me half as much as Mrs. Siddons had done." He noted a resemblance between her countenance and her great predecessor's, which had apparently also been noted by Reynolds (Boaden 1831, 2:387).[4]

More important, however, than sheer physical looks were the qualities of dignity and majesty which derived from some inner force. Words like "noble" are commonly employed in evoking this attribute, and a representative passage is this from Boaden:

> There was a male dignity in the understanding of Mrs. Siddons, that raised her above the helpless timidity of other women; and it was certainly without surprise and evidently with profound admiration, that [the audience] heard this NOBLE BEING assert her innocence and demand protection. (2:116)[5]

Leaving aside the equivocal nature of the epithet in "male dignity," this is indicative of the unparalleled respect which the actress inspired. "Helpless timidity" was emphatically not the sort of quality she brought to the women she portrayed on the stage, and in private life after her retirement she struck those who met her with a comparable dignity. An American witness, George Ticknor, said after seeing her at Byron's house in 1815 that she "had one of the most

dignified and commanding figures" he had ever beheld. "Her conversation," he continues, "corresponded well with her person. It is
rather stately, but not, I think, affected and though accompanied by
considerable gesture, not really over-acted. . . . She formed a singular figure by Lady Byron, who sat by her side, all grace and delicacy,
and thus showed Mrs. Siddons's masculine powers in the stronger
light of contrast." The traditional "feminine" virtues of grace and
delicacy, we are invited to feel, were eclipsed by the force of presence
Siddons (Paston 1902, 287–88).[6]

As for those who saw her in the theater, there is widespread agreement. Benjamin Robert Haydon spoke of the awe her Juno-like
demeanor and "majestic presence" called out. He also thought,
when Siddons gave a private reading of *Macbeth* in 1821, that she
acted the central role better than either Kemble or Kean. James
Northcote told Hazlitt that "if you had not seen Mrs. Siddons, you
could have no idea of her. . . . She was like a preternatural being
descended to earth. I cannot say Sir Joshua had done her justice."[7] We
shall return to Reynolds's picture of *The Tragic Muse*; it is enough
for the moment to recall that Hazlitt was to write his own still more
impassioned praise: "She was not less than a goddess or a prophetess
inspired by the gods. Power was seated on her brow, passion emanated from her breast like a shrine." Her countenance remained fixed
in his imagination through his long years of solitude and despair.
She was able to "quench the blaze of surrounding beauty in silent
tears." The affective value of her acting is regularly imaged as a mode
of power.[8]

Hazlitt and Northcote were by no means alone in sensing something preternatural about Siddons. De Quincey ended his literary
reminiscences with these words: "I shall always regard my recollections of Mrs. Siddons as those in which I chiefly have an advantage
over the coming generation; nay, perhaps over all generations; for
many centuries may revolve without producing such another transcendent creature." This is from a man who had intimately known
Wordsworth, Coleridge, Southey, and many others (Masson 1898,
2:454). Similarly we read in a biography of Frances Sheridan, by her
granddaughter Alicia LeFanu, of "the full blaze of transcendent
merit in Mrs. Siddons," which triumphs over the jealousy of rivals
(383).

One can well understand that poor undistinguished William Siddons came to feel that his wife was "too grand a thing for me." The full extent of "Siddonian idolatry" is expressed perhaps by Anna Seward (the phrase is her own).

> She far outstrips that ideal perfection which, through life, I have vainly searched for in the theatre. Her energy, her pathos, her majestic scorn, is inspired by the same sensibility and nobleness of soul, which produces all the varied expressions of these passions in Giovanni's singing, and casts the Yates, the Crawfords, and the Youngs at the same immeasurable distance, at which he throws every other singer in the world. . . . Mrs. Siddons in the theatre, and Giovanni in the orchestra, have made all amusements, dramatic, and musical, so insipid where they are not [that] . . . to a play I will not be dragged when the sun of excellence withdraws her beams. . . . (Pearson 68–69)

We may note here two matters: the quasi-operatic nature of the actress, and the unfavorable light thrown on other leading actresses, even the celebrated Mary Ann Yates. It is central to the aggrandisement of Sarah Siddons that other performers, recent or contemporary, are seen to be thrown into the shade, such is the novelty of her achievement.[9] The gravamen of such tributes is summarized in one short sentence by Mrs. Piozzi, when she writes to her friend Sophia Pennington in 1801 of "the greatest and only unrivalled female this century last expired has pretended to produce" (Knapp 224). Piozzi's high regard for Siddons seems to have been reciprocated: Campbell quotes her pleasure on receiving "a note or a visit from Reynolds, Mrs. Piozzi, [Lord Chancellor] Erskine, Burke, Sheridan, or Malone (1834, 2:129–30). James L. Clifford adds: "In this list it is interesting that Mrs. Piozzi was the only woman whom Mrs. Siddons mentioned on a par with Reynolds, Burke or Malone. On her side Mrs. Piozzi elevated the actress to the pedestal left vacant by [Arthur] Collier and Johnson. Her temperament always needed someone to adore, someone to look up to and serve proudly. . . . Mrs. Siddons now became this most intimate companion, and the correspondence between the two gives proof of the lasting quality of the relationship" (336). It is odd that it has taken two centuries for us to see some qualities in Piozzi herself comparable to those of her friend, whose talent blazed forth so unmistakably in her own lifetime.

Years earlier, Mrs. Thrale—as she then was—had received an

account from Samuel Johnson of a visit from Siddons. The passage can be found in Boswell's *Life*, under October 1783, and is followed by a description of the meeting which was given to the biographer by John Philip Kemble. Johnson mentions the "great modesty and propriety" with which his visitor behaved, and seemed almost prepared to send the actress back to some kind of theatrical kitchen; but he attempts a mild gallantry by promising to "hobble out to the theatre myself" if Siddons should again perform Queen Katherine in Shakespeare's *Henry VIII*. It would not be easy to show that Johnson shared in the general enthusiasm for the trail-breaking attributes of Siddon's acting style, but his very avoidance of modish fan-jargon helps us to perceive the nature of the impact which Siddons had made on more impressionable theater-goers.[10]

II

One area of critical vocabulary is especially applicable to Siddons, and this is the most remarkable testimony to her revolutionary qualities. On a number of occasions her idolaters are driven to employ the word "sublime" or its derivatives. This is in some sense a reversal of semantic alliances, because the cult of sublimity has tended to link grandeur with rough, raw, wild, savage, untamable aspects of nature, and with associated psychological attributes. Meanwhile, the beautiful went with regularity and harmony. Burke's own analysis of *The Sublime and the Beautiful* (1757) consistently interprets the data in this way, and consequently identifies the sublime with masculine values as against the beautiful, or prettily feminine. Equally, Reynolds opposes a massive and dramatic sublime with a finicky beautiful in his fourth *Discourse* (1771): "The Sublime impresses the mind at once with one great idea; it is a single blow: the Elegant indeed may be produced by repetition; by an accumulation of many minute circumstances." Similarly in the last *Discourse* (1790) Reynolds argues that sublimity has such an overpowering effect that "the little elegancies of art in the presence of these great ideas thus greatly expressed, lose all their value" (Wack, 65, a76).[11] It was precisely the sublime in these terms which spectators recognized in the great stage performances of Siddons, contrary to all order and decorum in the rules of gender identity.

Anna Seward is again representative, when she writes to Thomas

Whalley of a tour Siddons made in 1795: "Your matchless friend has been performing most of her celebrated characters at Birmingham. The dejecting nature of my bodily sensations counteracted the longings of my spirit after those sublime representations of high-strung feelings and conflicting passions, till I saw Mrs. Siddons announced for Hermione, and Catherine the Shrew" (Pearson 1936, 168). Another example is provided by Campbell, when he quotes William Godwin on Siddons as Zara in *The Mourning Bridge*. According to Godwin, "in spite of Garrick's superior versatility, Mrs. Siddons showed at times conceptions of her characters" which Godwin thought "more sublime than anything even in Garrick's action." Further, "the disdain and indignation of Siddons, in *Zara*, engrossed all attention, and swept away the possibility of interest in anything else. Her magnificence in the part was inexpressible" (Campbell 1834, 1:190). Again we find Siddons's acting imaged as an irresistible force of nature. Two small riders may be added. First, we know that Godwin's wife Mary Wollstonecraft was also an admirer of the actress—"even Mrs. Siddons would not have tempted me out today," she once wrote to Godwin (Wardle 367).[12] Second, the French or Italian habit of referring to a performer as *"the* Siddons" seems to have few precedents in English usage. Again Siddons had broken the former mold of linguistic habit.

Campbell also cites his friend James Ballantyne on the "extraordinary sublimity of her feelings and expressions." As Queen Katherine, "her form seems to expand, and her eye to burn with a fire beyond human." Even more explicit is Hazlitt's eulogy: "Grandeur was the cradle in which her genius was rocked; for her to be, was sublime!" In a famous passage Hazlitt wrote, "We can conceive of nothing grander. It was something above nature. It seemed almost as if a being of a superior order had dropped from a higher sphere to awe the world with the majesty of her appearance (Campbell 1834, 2:143–45; Manvell 301). Like other observers, Hazlitt unconsciously strays into a rhetoric not just of deification but also of secular heroicization. Siddons, one could say, made the great heroines fully heroic for the first time; instead of tremulous victims, they become figures of dignity and strength.[13] Thus Anna Seward contrasts Siddons with actresses like Susannah Cibber and Hannah Pritchard, in the way she augments "pathos" and "justness" with variety, vocal dexterity, and majesty of form (Reason 177–78). Again Garrick is the only possible rival; in fact, Siddons had entered an exclusive enclosure previously reserved for the greatest male tragedians. In doing so, she challenged the accepted modes of perceiving concepts like the sublime; by all earlier definitions, Siddons had committed a category error in presenting female identities on the stage and achieving an effect grander than pathos or virtue in distress. It is well known that she did reduce Charles James Fox, Burke, and others to tears (Sichel 1909, 134).[14] Horace Walpole may have been more resistant: "Were I five and twenty, I suppose I should weep myself blind" (Lewis, 1937–83, 29:282), but few hearts were stony enough to hold out when she played Calista or Isabella.

Nevertheless, the lachrymose as such was not the main thing, as it had been for earlier specialists in sentimental drama. Her relative lack of success in comedy, which is so widely attested, may be partly attributable to the merely lifesize dimension of the charaters she was required to play there. (Boaden also complains about the malapropisms she was forced to utter in Garrick's farce Lethe. [183, 2:274–75].) The overriding fact in all this can be stated simply: Siddons was an actress on the heroic scale, and her surpassing talents only shone out when she was playing a role in keeping with her majestic stage bearing. Pertinently, Seward remarked of her as Rosalind, "the playful scintilliations of colloquial wit . . . suit not the dignity of the Siddonian form and countenance (Pearson 91). In others words, sublimity curdles in the proximity of comedy. As Horace Walpole observed, even "Mrs. Siddons's warmest devotees do not hold her above a demi-goddess in comedy (Lewis 1937–38, 34:3).[15] It was universally agreed that destiny had marked her out for tragedy, the grandest and most dignified of dramatic kinds.

III

In order to understand how Siddons came to attain this eminence, the most useful line of approach is through an important essay by Edgar Wind, entitled "Hume and the Heroic Portrait." Wind argues, apropos of Reynolds's depiction of Garrick, that "when the reputation of an actress depends on her being cast as the Muse of art, in a dumbshow, then we can gauge the extent to which the stage, from being a place where the actor played a part, had become a place where the actor himself was given heroic stature by the part he played" (41).

At this juncture Wind is not directly concerned with Siddons; he has just referred to Garrick's Shakespearean event called *The Jubilee* (1769), where a leading actress (actually, George Anne Bellamy) took part in a processional mime. But the relevance of this insight is equally clear for Siddons. A few pages later Wind turns directly to the famous picture of Mrs. Siddons as the Tragic Muse. His comments are especially pertinent to our concerns here:

> Significantly, at the time of the painting, Mrs. Siddons had never yet played the Tragic Muse. Mrs. Yates was then the queen of tragedy, with exclusive claims to this symbolic role. Romney glorified her in this part. His picture was painted a few years after the first production and idealizes both the pose and the costume. In his portrait of Mrs. Siddons, however, Reynolds was anticipating theatrical developments and therefore not bound by any actual performances. . . . the actress is portrayed as if, as an actress, she is being inspired, whereas she should, as a Muse, herself inspired. (45–46)

Wind goes on to discuss the issue of whether Siddons herself invented the pose adopted in the painting (as she claimed), or Reynolds devised it himself; Wind believes the latter to be more probable, and adds, "The fact that an actress vied with a painter in claiming credit for a gesture in one of his pictures shows how much importance was attached to their invention." We are told that Mrs. Siddons actually went on to impersonate the Tragic Muse a year after the painting had been exhibited: "She thrust out her rival Mrs. Yates with such panache the reverberations of the contest can still be sensed in the contemporary pictoral record." Finally we move to Gainsborough's equally famous portrait: "He took pains to remove every sign of the heroic style from her expression and bearing. It embodies nothing but the ideal of natural social composure—the elegant woman at her ease." A contemporary critic remarked that "all the graces of private station" could not make the picture popular, "so prevalent is the striking form of action and of character over the mild and unimpassioned deportment of private life."[17]

There are several paradoxical features here. For one thing, Mrs. Siddons was specifically the woman who had shown that life upon the wicked stage need not bring with it any blameworthy personal associations; she, above all, exhibited "mild and unimpassioned deportment" in her family life. A long list could be compiled of commentators who stress this fact: De Quincey may speak for many: "Nothing could exceed the amiable, kind, and unassuming deportment of Mrs. Siddons." Even the king himself was "a professed admirer of her manners in private life (Masson 2:453; Boaden, 1831, 2:260). At the same time it was Siddons who had brought the heroic style to a new pitch of histrionic virtuosity. She had indeed brought to the stage some of the attitudes associated with portraiture; her statuesque poses had possessed the same clean, simple, and powerful lines which critics and theorists demanded of the figures in a setpiece of historical (i.e. heroic) painting.[17]

Siddons had reached this point because she understood the art so thoroughly. Campbell remarks that "Mrs. Siddons had the right to be painted as the Tragic Muse, for her very manner in society was marked by an abstractedness and reserve that were the result of her studiousness." More especially her own sense of what was involved in theatrical peformance ran in this direction: "The quality of abstraction" as she put it, "has always appeared to me to be so necessary in the art of acting" (Campbell 1834, 1:140; 2:214). John Loftis has related this quality to one play in which she enjoyed great success, Sheridan's *Pizzaro:* "Personalities and moral and political issues have a kind of schematic simplicity, removed from complicated ambiguities. . . . Neither Elvira nor any other character in the play can be regarded as much more than an 'abstraction' (Loftis 1976, 138–39). Siddons was able to remove her own personality from the role, and yet convey a sense that the heroism of the character infused her own being. This is another version of Diderot's *paradoxe sur le comédien.*

A third oddity lies in the fact that Reynolds, who immortalized Siddons as the transcendent actress, may not have admired her without qualification. He got on well with her socially, regularly dining in her company. He attended her private performances, and we know that he enjoyed sitting in the orchestra stalls at Drury Lane, trumpet to his ear, in the company of Burke, Sheridan, Windham, and Fox.[18] But we have also an entry in the diary of Joseph Farington which concerns Reynolds's own niece: "Talking of Mrs. Siddons Lady Inchiquin said that Sir Joshua Reynolds often declared that she was an actress who never *made him feel*," and there are other signs that he was ready to make fun of her excessive dignity (Greig, 1:273;

Hudson 182). All this indicates is that the painting is not a mere reflection of histrionic power, but an abstracted, schematized version of tragic acting at large. *Pace* Wind, it depicts the Muse, but the Muse under the Siddonian aspect.

It is encouraging, if a little surprising, to find that Boaden faced the central issues raised by the Reynolds portrait as long ago as 1827. He writes:

> Sir Joshua had a difficulty; he had to combine portrait with mythology, the *woman* with the MUSE. Had he intended the latter merely, the substance of the dress would have been more solid, and contained fewer small parts; as he blended the characters the materials are of modern usage, and the *forms* alone exceed the dignity of the actress's toilet. . . . The kind of expression given to the face, which is very beautiful, seems an *abstraction* of TRAGEDY; contemplating its essence rather than its forms, its effects rather than its properties. (Boaden 1831, 2:89)

The sentiments here are admirably in accord with Reynolds's own artistic theory, as outlined in the *Discourses*. However, there was a problem of perception in that Siddons had grown too large in her own dramatic personality for such an abstraction to be easily achieved by the viewing public. When Reynolds painted Mrs. Billington as St. Cecilia in 1789, there was no danger that the audience would confuse even this gifted singer with the patron saint of music. (He had already depicted Elizabeth Sheridan in a similar role a decade earlier.) For centuries women had posed as figures of mythology, safe in the knowledge that their own human potential was limited by social convention and that there could be no risk of their own identity blurring the abstract scheme. Hence, as Marina Warner has argued, the profusion of female allegories in statuary; women could more easily represent Justice, because they had no share in the mundane practical world of administering justice.

It was quite otherwise with Siddons. She had assumed a stature within the high cultural life of the nation which gave her an authentically heroic, if not almost mythical, identity. Just how clearly this "favourite child of Melpomene" had come to possess a recognizable public image is indicated by a criticism made by the well-known satirical observer of the art world, "Anthony Pasquin," when

Thomas Lawrence exhibited his portrait of Siddons in 1796. Pasquin's comments on the "Portrait of a Lady" are these:

> It is no more like her than Hebe is similar to Bellona. We have here youth, flexibility of features, and an attempt at the formation of beauty, to denote a lady who is proverbially so stern in her countenance that it approaches to savageness,—so determined in the outline of her visage, that it requires the delusion of the scene to render it soft and agreeable, and who is so far from being young, that her climacteric will be no more. (Goldrina 1951, 111)

The last ungracious remark is quite false (Sarah was only just past forty; the "climacteric" was always set at sixty-three—it has nothing to do with the menopause). But Pasquin describes what was certainly a general sense of stern-faced, "unfeminine" persona which had come to be hers. "Savageness" again connoted the sublime; Bellona is an unusual referent, but not altogether an unflattering one. The lowering gaze of Siddons on stage expressed an extension of the permissible female vocabulary of emotions.

One further instance of the popular view of Siddons must be mentioned. In 1784, following the immense success of *The Tragic Muse*, James Gillray produced a parodic version of the Reynolds picture entitled *Melpomene*. It shows Siddons as avaricious and hard-hearted (common charges), and in the words of a recent commentator, "While Reynolds contrived through expression and viewing angle to idealize Mrs. Siddons's face, Gillray's profile confirms Walpole's verdict of "neither nose nor chin according to the Greek standard, beyond which both advance a good deal" (Penny 1986, 384–85). In this print Siddons is very positively a human being masquerading as Melpomene, rather than the muse made actual within a human frame. Her bodily configurations are crucial to Gillray's aim of reduction and caricature. This is to reverse the process by which Reynolds had helped to blur the distinction between the woman and the muse, the individual and the general, the local and the mythical. In effect, Gillray is seeking to reinstate Siddons as a mere woman, and an infallible one at that.

Not long before Siddons died, Sir Thomas Lawrence gave a presidential address to the Royal Academy, in the heritage of the Reynolds

Discourses. One of his contentions was that "the Picture by Sir Joshua Reynolds of Mrs. Siddons as the Tragic Muse, is the finest female portrait in the world." (This was a view, incidentally, in which James Barry and John Opie would have concurred [Goldring 1951, 303].)[19] The address was circulated and reached Mrs. Siddons herself. She wrote to Lawrence in 1824 of the "various and thronging ideas" that filled her, "situated as I am, with respect to the glorious Picture so finely eulogised, and with its illustrious Panegyrist." She ended, "could we change persons, I would not exchange the gratification you have experienced this *sublime* tribute of praise, for all the fame it must accumulate on the memory of the Tragic Muse" (Goldring 1951, 303). Probably she was recalling the remark by Reynolds, passed on to us in her own memoirs, that he wished to go down to posterity on the hem of her garment. It was *The Tragic Muse* which ratified a judgment already widely expressed by those who witnessed Siddons on stage: she embodied the sublime, rather than simply impersonating it. She had achieved a mode of greatness that could only be expressed in art through epic vocabulary.

IV

Finally, back to *Celebrated Female Characters,* from which we began. It is a worthy and much needed compilation, in spite of its resolutely improving tone. And in an age when female achievement was systematically and, as it were, formally depressed (rather than casually and culpably, as today), it is good to have such a volume, with entries for underrated women who are still receiving only grudging recognition in many quarters. But none of the other worthies—Mary Astell or Lucy, Countess of Bedford, or George Anne Bellamy (to go no further through the alphabet)—could be advanced to real heroic status. The moral character, real or supposed, of Aphra Behn disqualified her. Often very little information could be gleaned about important figures of the past: Mary Pilkington could find only a few lines to write about "Anne Broadstreet" [Bradstreet], and this was no fault of the compiler. Only one woman in recent history had raised herself to a commanding place in the English culture, and stood at the head of a profession in a way which even the most bigoted apologist for masculinist values could not deny. This was Sarah Siddons, who had attained this eminence without compromise either of her own instincts or of the public mores of her time.

Her career was one of the first examples of a *Heldenleben*, and her success in the most august branch of drama ensured that female heroics need no longer be confined to tender and sentimental attitudinizing.[20] Her amazing achievement is still imperfectly recognized. It is greatly to her credit that she inspired the admiration of so many women, and distinguished ones at that—Piozzi, Montagu, Hannah More, Anna Seward, and others. De Quincey bizarrely thought that the presence of Siddons was "positively painful and humiliating" through "the degradation which it inflicted upon other women." He describes her leaving the table at a dinner party, when "by the mere necessity of her regal deportment, she dwarfed the whole party, and made them look ridiculous; though Mrs. H. More, and other ladies present, were otherwise really women of very pleasing appearance" (Masson, 2:453–54). Siddons certainly dwarfed other women in the grandeur of her being, on and off the stage; but though she inspired awe, she also made heroism a more conceivable goal for her sex. Fanny Burney described an early meeting with Siddons, and pays tribute to her modest and unaffected demeanor. Yet there was also the stately side of her bearing: "She has, however, a steadiness in her manner and deportment by no means engaging. Mrs. Thrale . . . said,—'Why, this is a leaden goddess we are all worshiping! However, we shall soon gild it' " (Burney 1842: 200–02). There was no need, in truth, to gild the goddess, as Mrs. Thrale realized in the course of time. If she was reverenced more than she was loved, then that was the condition of her achievement, if women were to escape from the small back-room of history: for epic heroes had never put the highest priority on being loved, and female heroes would wisely learn the same lesson. Sarah Siddons had earned full-hearted respect, against the grain of a sexist culture and she deserves as much today.

Notes

I wish to thank Barbara Looney for her help in the preparation of this essay, especially in locating and transcribing some of the material used.

1. For Pilkington, principally a children's author, see *A Dictionary of British and American Women Writers 1660–1800*, ed. Janet Todd (London: 1984), 252.

2. Contrasts are usually drawn with the less respectable lives of such former stage

favorites as Peg Woffington, Anne Oldfield, or George Anne Bellany ("This unfortunate, frail female," as the entry in Pilkington begins, 48). Similarly, Fanny Burney writes of Siddons, "She is a woman of excellent character, and therefore I am very glad she is thus patronized, since Mrs. Abington, and so many frail fair ones, have been thus noticed to be great." See *Diary and Letters of Madame D'Arblay*, ed. Charlotte Barrett (London: Colburn, 1842), 2: 202. Notice the emphasis on the word "frail," precisely the antonym of words applied to Siddons. John Byng, who made a special detour to see her perform in Birmingham on 2 July 1792, went backstage and found her a woman of "retired notions." *The Torrington Diaries*, ed. C. B. Andrews, rev. Fanny Andrews (London: Eyre and Spottiswoode, 1954), 451.

3. Boaden begins by observing that "Biography but seldom selects its ornaments from the gentler sex. Women are devoted as much by nature as custom to its domestic duties" (Boaden 1831, 1:1–2)—orthodox masculine self-protection. But progress has made it possible for women to become prominent on the stage, so that "the author of the sublime and beautiful [Edmund Burke] has found no difficulty in commemorating Mrs. Siddons even with Garrick himself" (1:3). As the book evolves, Boaden might have been led to question how minutely accurate his term "the gentler sex" is, in the light of Siddons's achievement.

4. Sir William Forbes, *An Account of the Life and Writings of James Beattie* (New York, Brisban and Brannan 1907), 371–72. John Byng enjoyed "the highly wrought exhibition of Mrs. Siddon's performance as Catherine in Henry 8th" although he thought in the new Drury Lane Theatre the performance was "lost and sent to wast. . . ." Garrick retired "of the proper time" for "even his fine eye" and would not register in this "vast void." Entry for 14 May 1796, in *Torrington Diaries*, 479.

5. A rare dissenting voice was that of a French lady who thought that Siddons lacked the "dignity and grace" of her own countrywomen. See *Reminiscences of Michael Kelly*, ed. Theodore Hook (New York: Blom, 1969), 207.

6. On the other hand, in her domestic life Siddons is cast in a traditional nurturing role: see Sophie de la Roche on the tender matter of a sick child, quoted by Rosamond Bayne-Powell, *Travellers in Eighteenth-century England* (London: Murray, 1951), 80.

7. Douglas Goldring, *Regency Portrait Painter: The Life of Sir Thomas Lawrence, P.R.A.* (London: MacDonald, 1951), 290; Margaret Greaves, *Regency Patron: Sir George Beaumont* (London: Bentley, 1984), 244. See also Northcote (33) on young ladies of quality peeping at Mrs. Siddons "with all the same timidity and curiosity as if it were some preternatural being—he was sure more than if it had been the Queen."

8. Quoted by Roger Manvell, *Sarah Siddons: Portrait of an Actress (New York: Putnam,* 1971), 301; Stella Margetson, *Leisure and Pleasure in the Eighteenth Century* (London: Cassell, 1970), 177. Boaden has a curiously hesitant and unenthusiastic passage speculating on what Siddons might have been like, in comparison with her brother's performances of the role (1831, 1:281–82). It was said to be one of her most applauded characters; Thomas Campbell, *The Life of Mrs. Siddons* (London: Effingham, 1834), 1:79. On another private occasion Mrs. Sid-

dons locked herself in a room with Mrs. Thrale and acted out the part of Sir Anthony Absolute "quite inimitably": Walter Sichel, *Sheridan* (London: Constable, 1909), 1:497. This last is the judgment of Mrs. Thrale herself, who was hard to please.

9. Campbell (1834, 1:93–149) has a section on British actresses up to the time of Siddons. Mrs. Yates is termed "the most commanding personage . . . before Mrs. Siddons" (1:145). For an example of what Sheridan considered "a presumptuous innovation" as Lady Macbeth, see Campbell, 2:38.

10. James Boswell, *The Life of Samuel Johnson*, ed. G. B. Hill and L. F. Powell (Oxford: Clarendon, 1934–50), 4:242–43. Boaden has a significant passage in the peroration to his biography: "Her place in society was assigned her by the general feeling of her merits; and she was approached with a reverence such as Dr. Johnson used to excite in those he knew his talents and virtues" (2:409). It would surprise most of those who still honor Johnson with such respect to know that Siddons once claimed a comparable rank.

11. See part 2, section 1 of Burke's *Essay* for the power of the sublime to fill the mind "so that it cannot entertain any other" project, precisely the faculty attributed to Siddons (see, e.g., Campbell, 1:190).

12. Mrs. Montagu once admitted that though she could easily resist the common run of invitations, a chance to meet Mrs. Siddons at the table of Reynolds had proved irresistible: "I run the hazard of catching cold when a great character in the Drama of human life, or poetick fiction is exhibited;" see *Mrs. Montagu: 'Queen of the Blues,'* ed. Reginald Blunt (London: Constable, 1923), 2:203. Richard Cumberland shows matters in a different light when he depicts Siddons as giving sensible replies to silly questions at the gathering of Bluestockings assembled by Mrs. Montagu; see John Doran, *A Lady of the Last Century* (London: Bentley, 1973), 299–300.

13. Siddons's own reviews of the role of Constance in Shakespeare's *King John* are set out at length in Campbell, 2:211–21. She sees the character as "noble in mind, and commanding in person and demeanor" (2:212), and calls her affliction "of so sublime and intense a character, that the personation of its grandeur . . . almost overwhelms the mind that meditates its realization" (2, 225).

14. William Roberts, *Memoirs of the Life and Correspondence of Mrs. Hannah More* (London: Seely, 1834), 2:54. For Burke's own admission of the tears Siddons called out, see *Reflections on the Revolution in France*, ed. Conor Cruise O'Brien. (Harmondsworth: Penguin, 1969), 175–76.

15. John Byng thought that her comic powers were "very great . . . had she not been curbed"; entry for 8 June 1790: *Torrington Diaries*, 237.

16. For an account of Siddons as portrayed by various artists, concluding that, "the essence of her stage personality was her innate majesty," see Mrs. Clement Parsons, *The Incomparable Siddons* (New York: Blum, 1969), 59–62. Parsons states that Siddons "identified her personality with sublime parts" (245).

17. It is interesting to recall that Anne Damer not only sculpted Siddons in the role of The Tragic Muse, but actually gave her lessons in art. See P. S. Noble, *Anne Seymour Damer* (London: Kegan Paul, 1908), 84, 164–65,

18. Boaden, 2:146; W. T. Whitley, *Artists and their Friends in England 1700–1799*

(New York: Blum, 1968), 2:34; Derek Hudson, *Sir Joshua Reynolds* (London: Bles, 1958), 208–9. For her part, Siddons admitted in her *Reminiscences* that as "an ambitious candidate for fame," she frequented Reynolds's gatherings in the hope of meeting "all the good, the wise, the talented, the rank and fashion of the age." See Albert Boime, *Art in an Age of Revolution 1750–1800* (Chicago, Univ. of Chicago Press, 1987), 200.

19. See Farington, vol. 1:308; Forbes, *Beattie*, 371; Penny, *Reynolds*, 325.

20. See the comments of Siddons's fellow actors on the "fearful resemblance of reality" she was able to achieve, the "terrible" fidelity of her performances, and "her heroic loveliness" as assembled by Campbell, 1:169–71. See also Bartley's description of the way in which he was "stunned by the commanding entrances" Siddons made in *Edward IV*: "the giantess burst upon view" (Campbell 1834, 1:266–87).

Works Cited

Andrews, C. B., ed. 1954. *The Torrington Diaries.* London: Eyre and Spottiswoode.

Boaden, James. 1831. *Memoirs of Mrs. Siddons.* 2d ed. London: Colburn and Bentley.

Burney, Fanny. 1842. *Diary and Letters of Madame D'Arblay* Ed. Charlotte Barrett. London: Colburn.

Campbell, Thomas. 1834. *The Life of Mrs. Siddons.* London: Effingham.

Goldring, Douglas. 1951. *Regency Portrait Painter: The Life of Sir Thomas Lawrence, P.R.A.* London: Macdonald.

Lewis, W. S., ed. 1937–38. *The Correspondence of Horace Walpole.* New Haven: Yale Univ. Press.

Loftis, John. 1976. *Sheridan and the Drama of Georgian England.* Oxford: Blackwell.

Masson, David, ed. 1896. *The Collected Writings of Thomas De Quincey.* London: Black.

"Paston, George." [Emily Morse Symonds.] 1902. *Side-Lights on the Georgian Period.* London: Methuen.

Penny, Nicholas, ed. 1986. *Reynolds.* London: Royal Academy and Weidenfeld and Nicolson.

Pearson, Hesketh, ed. 1936. *The Swan of Litchfield.* London: Hamilton.

Pilkington, Mary. 1804. *Memoirs of Celebrated Female Characters.* London: J. Harris et al.

Sichel, Walter. 1890. *Sheridan.* London: Constable.

Wark, Robert, ed. 1975. *Sir Joshua Reynolds' Discourses on Art.* New Haven: Yale Univ. Press.

Wind, Edgar. 1986. *Hume and the Heroic Portrait: Studies in Eighteenth-Century Imagery.* Oxford: Clarendon.

Additional References:

Clifford, James L., 1968. *Hester Lynch Piozzi (Mrs. Thrale)* (Oxford: Clarendon, 2nd ed.).

Grieg, James (ed.), 1922–28. *The Farington Diary* (London: Hutchinson).

Hudson, Derek, 1958. *Sir Joshua Reynolds* (London: Bles).

Knapp, O. G. (ed.), 1914. *The Intimate Letters of Hester Piozzi and Penelope Pennington* (London: Lane).

Manvell, Robert, 1971. *Sarah Siddons: Portrait of an Actress* (New York: Putnam).

LeFanu, Alicia, 1824. *Memoirs of Mrs. Frances Sheridan* (London).

Wardle, Ralph M. (ed.) 1929. *Collected Letters of Mary Wollstonecraft* (Ithaca: Cornell University Press).

2

Stage Business

"Mrs. Siddons as Constance in King John.*"*
Detail from "Mrs. Billington and Mrs. Siddons." Courtesy of the
Print Collection, The Lewis Walpole Library, Yale University.

A Feminist Link in the Old Boys' Network: The Cosseting of Katherine Philips

MAUREEN E. MULVIHILL

The Restoration is significant in the history of English feminism because it witnessed the advance of women playwrights in the professional theater. The first decade of the Restoration was graced by four newcomers: Katherine Philips (*Pompey*, 1663; *Horace*, 1668), Frances Boothby (*Marcelia*, 1670), Aphra Behn (*The Forc'd Marriage*, 1670), and Elizabeth Polwhele (*The Faithful Virgins*, [1670/71][1]). Behn was the most prolific and commercially successful in this first wave of dramatic ingénues, Boothby and Polwhele the most obscure. Katherine Philip's place in this cluster of female dramatists is preeminent, as it was Philips who first broke ground for women in the English and Irish theater. For a brief moment in theater history, Philips was a *cause célèbre*, and her dazzling career provided the important precedential model for aspiring literary women. Philips was the first "Sappho" of the English-speaking world, and the first woman to have her work produced on the Dublin and London stage. Her success, in fact, may well have pointed the way for Behn; for when Behn made her début with *The Forc'd Marriage*, mounted by the Duke's Company in the summer of 1670, she was succeeding Philips, whose dramatic translations from Pierre Corneille had been enthusiastically received several years before.

Katherine Philips's contemporary fame rested on two translations from the French classical tragedy of Corneille: his *La Mort de Pompée* (1642), translated by Philips in 1663 and brilliantly staged the same season in Dublin's new Theatre Royal in Smock Alley; and

Corneille's *Horace* (1640), partially translated by Philips shortly before her sudden death in 1664, and produced in 1668 at Dublin's Theatre Royal and also before the court of Charles II. Philips's *Pompey* and *Horace* were published soon after their premières, and each saw sell-out editions in Dublin and London. (The first issue of the Dublin *Pompey*, 500 copies, was sold within weeks.) Philips's reputation as "the Matchless Orinda," rapturous poet of "female Friendship," came slightly later and now is seeing a revival.[2] But Philips initially made her mark in the Anglo-Irish theatre, not the poetic coteries of the Restoration court.

Notices on Philips after her death do not scant her dramatic talent. Estimates in David Erskine Baker's *Biographica Dramatica* (1764), for example, celebrate her success in playwrighting (2:157, 288). And contradicting Sir Edmund Gosse's assessment that Katherine Philips "sank into utter darkness" in the early eighteenth century is William Roberts's work, which traces something of Philips's popularity up through the late 1800s.[3] Philips's rapid ascent to celebrity was astonishing, given harsh male prejudice against women writers at that time. Her chaste, comely verse and unimpeachable reputation set the standard for female excellence. In fact, so dominant was the cult of "Orinda" during the later-Stuart period that women writers, especially poets, found themselves hard-pressed to compete with Philips, and so began working alternative literary markets—drama, essay-periodical, and particularly the novel. But no matter how overdrawn the portrait, Katherine Philips showed that a public career in literature was possible for a woman in the seventeenth century, even if she were a commoner. While Philips's *oeuvre* is lean—a single published folio of 116 original poems and five verse-translations from the French, two dramatic translations from Corneille, and an incomplete collection of letters—"Orinda" was the undisputed darling of her era and the most celebrated woman in seventeenth-century Anglo-Irish letters.

Reassessing a legend is dangerous business. But in the case of Katherine Philips, whose achievement has been overstated since the late seventeenth century (to the detriment of more skilled women writers), some *contextualizing* of Philips's life, work, and career is long overdue. The obvious weakness in almost all Philips studies to date is an inability to appreciate the "Orinda" myth for what it really was: a remarkable literary campaign conceived and promoted by Philips herself, her relatives, and some of the literary bosses of the Restoration old boys' network.

Philips's grand if brief career was a collaborative product created by Philips and several powerful male allies. Her principal literary productions—the Corneille translations—were orchestrated by influential men of the late seventeenth-century literary world. Philips found effective comrades in Stuart London, Dublin, and southwest Wales, the triple base, as we shall see, of her elaborate operations. Without in any way wishing to discredit Katherine Philips (indeed her support by preeminent men of letters further attests to her talent), I am eager to explore this underplayed aspect of her career as a case-study in supportive relations between men and women of letters at this time. Moreover, based on Philips's published correspondence, it appears that her camaraderie with male confidants and literary advisors resulted in a progressive unfolding of a surprisingly assertive authorial ego.

With the single exception of Lucy Brashear's essay on Philips in *The Anglo-Welsh Review* in 1979, this dimension of Philips's artistic temperament and career has been overlooked in Philips studies thus far.[4] Brashear suggests that Philips always was on the climb, dating from her early days in Wales in the 1650s, when she strategically began creating the "Orinda" persona by broadly circulating her poems, and, moreover, by addressing them to notables of only slight acquaintance, such as Henry Vaughan, one of Philips's many new Welsh relatives after her marriage in 1648.[5] Brashear even (ingeniously) suggests that Philips may well have "engineered" the pirated edition of her own poems in 1664.

My reconstruction of Philips, slightly more tempered and comprehensive, takes into account the full play of "Orinda" 's support-base and its strong influence throughout the three phases of her career, a career distinguished by its astute management, networking, and heretofore unacknowledged artistic individualism. But before I can begin to properly make my case, the stage must first be set for Philips's entrance with some introductory remarks on the sensitive literary climate of the Restoration and its representation in today's feminist criticism.

*Prologue: Feminist Angst vs. the
Politics of Female Authorship*

My genealogical researches into the powerful Phillipps clan, seated at Picton Castle, Pembrokeshire, Wales, the line into which Katherine Philips *née* Fowler married in 1648, have led me to a fresh perspective on the phenomenon of the professional English woman writer who first emerged during the later-Stuart period. As we know, many women writers began to go public during the Restoration. Some asserted their new literary identity by publishing their initials on the title pages of their work. Others, such as Sarah Egerton, Jane Barker, Anne Lady Winchilsea, and Mary Lady Chudleigh, boldly published their surnames. Observing the broad literary and political connections of the Phillipps group in Wales and its key role in launching Katherine Philips, I have begun to examine the professional beginnings and sponsorship of other women writers of their period (particularly the poet-playwright "Ephelia," apparently of the interrelated Proud-Phillips-Milton line) with an eye to the largely unacknowledged role of their male allies and the networks they sometimes made available to the young female entrants.

This new line of inquiry is frankly deconstructive of the new feminist reconstructive criticism. So we begin by looking at things squarely. The new recovery work on women writers of the Restoration and eighteenth century has produced both admirable results and questionable tendencies. On the positive side, it has performed superlatively: by resurrecting a new canon of obscured writings; by identifying female coteries and patronesses; by producing at a brisk rate a body of new reference tools, biographies, and criticism; and by reprinting many essential feminist texts heretofore out of print for generations.[6] This flurry of aggressive feminist activity in the American, British, and Canadian academies bodes well for a deep reconstruction of the canon, with women writers more equitably represented.

Yet, despite its appreciated gains, a fair amount of the recent criticism promotes a point of view (by now almost a premise) which is disturbing and historically unsupportable. I refer to the perception that insists on an adversarial relationship between men and women of letters. Promoters of such a vantage point romanticize female professionals, especially the writers, as a disenfranchised, beleaguered minority whose work was carried out in some sort of vague literary and psychological isolation. The more strident adherents speak of male "victimization" of women. Exclusivity, otherness, and, above all, *feminist angst* are assigned these "pioneers" as inevitable conditions of their gender and "unique" historical position. One commentator on Restoration literature writes: "[Aphra Behn] was a writer who not only insisted on being heard, but [who] successfully forced the men who dominated the jealous literary world of Restoration England to receive her as an equal. . . . I began a life of Aphra and saw in her a heroine . . . a feminist heroine" (Goreau 1980, 3, 5). A historian characterizes early English women writers as a distinct social and intellectual subgroup, hellbent on feminist reform: "They were mavericks, operating in a largely hostile environment, who employed bits and pieces of the social and intellectual criticism they found about themselves to understand and to change women's lives" (Smith 1982, 66). A third example comes to hand from a feminist literary critic who claims that women writers suffered ordeals of identity, as cultural definitions of female propriety condemned individualism and certainly the pursuit of a career: "The struggle each of these women waged to create a professional identity was in large measure defined by the social and psychological forces of this ideal of proper—or innate—femininity" (Poovey 1984, x). Feminist anthologists are now joining the fray with descriptions of women writers as *"guerrilleras"* storming the bastions of the patriarchal establishment (Greer 1988,1). Broad historical judgments and psychologizing of this nature have begun to appear with increasing frequency in feminist studies. These tendencies, I suggest, are misleading because they do not stand up against available historical evidence on how women of the pre-Modern era broke into literary professions and began shaping careers.

Now, unarguably, the young women writers of the early-modern era were mercilessly ridiculed by *some* male writers. Robert Gould, an undervalued Restoration poet-playwright, attacks Behn and "Ephelia" in his blistering antifeminist *Satyrical Epistle* as "hackney Writers" whose verse was "as vicious as their Tails" (1691). Anne Countess of Winchilsea was roundly jeered by Pope's circle in *Three Hours After Marriage*, a successful farce of 1717. Artemisia, the female speaker in Rochester's most polished social satire, *A Letter from Artemisia . . . to Chloe* (1679), begins her verse-epistle with a thirty-one-line summary of contemporary male bias against women writers. "Whore is scarce a more reproachful Name / Than Poetess," she writes her friend (Vieth 1968, 105:25–26). Moreover, women were systematically barred from such early old boys' networks as the universities at Oxford and Cambridge, the Royal Society, and that prototype of the English club, the ubiquitous coffee house. Yet, the record also shows that women's writings *did get into print*.[7] This hard fact of history suggests that overt patriarchal oppression of women did not carry over into the literary establishment; if it had, their work would not have been published and sponsored at all. The flourishing London book trade (the commercial arm of the literary old boys' network) appreciated the market potential of the new books by women. And, as the women went on to show, theirs was not ephemera but work of lasting value. Publishers cultivated this new breed of writer through complimentary prefaces which, in turn, stimulated interest in the buying public. Benjamin Crayle promoted Jane Barker in his edition of her *Poetic Recreations* (1688). Richard Bassett remarked on the uniqueness of a book he published in 1700, *The Nine Muses,* a collection of elegies on the death of Dryden written exclusively by women.[8] Bernard Lintot, publisher of Pope's *Homer,* ensured a receptive audience for Katherine Philips's *Letters,* which he published in 1705, by soliciting commendatory verses for the book. Other London bookmen, such as James Courtney, John Taylor, and James Nott, publishers respectively of *Female Poems . . . By Ephelia* (1679), Sarah Egerton's *Female Advocate* (1687), and Egerton's *Poems* (1703), gave visibility to their new authors and, moreover, heightened their commercial profile, by seeing their work through subsequent editions.

Then, as now, an integral dynamic in the politics of authorship was finding a place on the circuit. This meant establishing bonds and useful contacts with contemporaries who had already "arrived." Comandeering the authorship circuit, of course, was that well-oiled machine of the literary brotherhood, the old boys' network, a privately-held club of literary brokers who materially determined the success or failure of many careers. We know, for example, that senior male writers sometimes made themselves available to sponsor and advise their talented male juniors. Dryden gave a healthy boost to the early career of William Walsh by gracing Walsh's *Dialogue Concerning Woman* (1691) with a substantial preface. Or consider the

Mrs. Catherine Philips, attributed to Sir Peter Lely.
Courtesy Lord Sackville, Knole, England. The back of the portrait bears the manuscript inscription "Rochester's Orinda."

early career of John Gay. In a letter dated 23 August 1714, Pope advised the young Gay on his *Fan,* a courtship-and-marriage allegory. Sir Richard Steele also assisted Gay when he recommended *The Fan* in *The Englishman* (10 December 1717), one of Steele's several successful essay-periodicals. Consider, too, the team of classical translators who assisted Dryden in his *Juvenal* of 1692. And Pope proceeded similarly, with a battery of "Auxiliaries," in launching his Homer during the period 1712 to 1726. There was also the Scriblerus Club, that literary fraternity of Pope, Swift, Gay, Parnell, Harley, and Arbuthnot, which produced satire on bad writers and "false Taste." Examples of such professional camaraderie, fraternal links, and career-boosting are legion in the careers of professional men of letters. To a large extent, this is the very stuff of literary history.

But not a few of the literary "good ole boys" also gave a generous hand-up to so-called petticoat-authors, especially at the outset of their careers. Rochester and Dryden, though members of rival coteries, found a mutual friend in Aphra Behn, and they collaborated with her to a far greater extent than Behn scholars have yet to acknowledge (O'Donnell 1986, 159, 214, 283). Dryden is especially interesting on this score. As his foremost bibliographer observed, Dryden was "something of a favorite with the [literary] ladies" (Macdonald 1939, 305). This is an important dimension of the laureate's literary life which James Winn broaches in his impressive *John Dryden and His World* (1987) and which he presently is examining in a study of gender in Dryden's aesthetics. Dryden counselled the young poet Elizabeth Thomas (his "Corinna"); he expressed to Walsh and Jacob Tonson respectful interest in the verse of Mary Lady Chudleigh;[9] and he was so well regarded by his female contemporaries that upon his death in 1700 he was honored by the collection of their elegies, mentioned above. Further evidence exists in supportive relationships between John Dunton and Elizabeth Singer Rowe, Swift and Delariviére Manley, Joseph Johnson and Mary Wollstonecraft, and George Hickes and Elizabeth Elstob.[10]

Female authorship was a sensitive literary and social issue throughout the Restoration and most of the eighteenth century. No one close to the material denies that. But the facts also show that the victimization school of feminist studies lacks historical grounding. As the literary register tells us, the old boys' network was not without some female rewards.

Katherine Philips: A Life and A Career
(in Three Acts)

The brief but successful dramatic career of Katherine Philips is a fine case-study in supportive partnership between literary men and women. Indeed, Philips's entire literary life, from her *Pompey* (1663) to her *Poems* (1667), and *Letters* (1705), was carefully managed by influential male confidants, relatives, and literary associates. Moreover, as her correspondence reveals, Philips's guided initiation in the politics of authorship was evidently so gratifying an experience that she began to develop a confident sense of herself as an important, independent presence of her day. Because her personal background is essential to my case, let me illustrate the privileged career development and marketing of Katherine Philips within the main lines of her biography.

1. London. The first phase of Philips's life centered in London, site of her early beginnings. Katherine Phillips *née* Fowler was born in London in 1631 into an upper-middle-class English family. Her father, John Fowler, was a prosperous tradesman, a "clothmaker" (Barnes 1867, 63; Souers 1931, 7). Her mother Katherine Oxenbridge had married down in her match with Fowler, as she descended from a prestigious English pedigree of the fourteenth century, one which included Dr. Daniel Oxenbridge of the Royal College of Physicians and Lady Elizabeth Tyrwhitt *née* Oxenbridge, a lady-in-waiting to Queen Katherine Parr and governess to Princess Elizabeth Tudor.[11] Lady Tyrwhitt, one of two writing women in Katherine Philips's maternal line, produced *Morning and Evening Prayer* (1574, 16mo), dedicated to Elizabeth and preserved in the British Library. A second literary model for young Katherine Philips would have been her maternal grandmother Katherine Oxenbridge *née* Harby, an amateur poet and an acquaintance of the poet Francis Quarles.[12] To date, Philips scholars have failed to suggest that Katherine Philips was quite plausibly inspired by these two precedential models of female authorship in her own family. This often is the case among early women writers, I have found, whose models are traceable through their matrilineal line.

Literate around the age of four, according to contemporary accounts, young Katherine received training in the rudiments at home, from her cousin the governess Mrs. Blackett. At the age of eight, she began formal training at Mrs. Salmon's fashionable boarding-school for girls at Hackney, where the precocious Philips displayed signs of literary aptitude. It was here that she made her first principal career contact in the person of Mary Aubrey, of the distinguished Welsh royalist Aubreys, who became the dear "Rosania" of Philips's poems. Mary Aubrey helped to ensure Philips's fame by relating essential facts of her life and career to her cousin John Aubrey, whose biographical sketch of Philips continues to be the foundation of all Philips studies, from Philip Sourers's monograph (1931) down to the Rev. Patrick Thomas's useful Ph.D. dissertation (1982, University of Wales). This schoolgirl relationship between Philips and Mary Aubrey blossomed into enduring friendship. Most important of all, it was the first of several profitable connections between Katherine Philips and the Welsh peerage.

2. *Wales*. The second phase of Katherine Philips's life and nascent literary development centered in Wales, that lesser London to the west which gave us such literary personalities as John Aubrey, the Vaughans, Nell Gwyn, and the blind poet Anna Williams of Samuel Johnson's circle. The 1640s were turbulent years for young Katherine and her mother. John Fowler, Katherine's father, died in 1642, after which Katherine's mother married one George Henley of London at St. Andrew's Church on 4 May 1643 (*Mormon International Genealogical Index*, 2d ed., 1988:67, 928; Limbert 1989, 2–3). But this second marriage was also short-lived, and again we find Katherine Philips's mother a widow. But again she remarried, so that by 1646 Katherine's mother was the second wife of a prominent landowner in the Welsh peerage. At the age of fifteen, young Katherine left London with her mother to relocate to Pembrokeshire in southwest Wales. This would soon become the scene of her literary apprenticeship.

Katherine's second stepfather was Sir Richard Phillipps, second Baronet, of the Picton Castle Phillipps line, a prestigious family in the Welsh peerage and wealthy landowners with broad social and political ties throughout Wales, England, and Ireland (NLW MS 12359D; Philipps 1906, 23–26). This Welsh clan was also a strong literary and philanthropic power in southwest Wales, as active benefactors of unfortunate writers.[13] A widower when he married Katherine's mother, Sir Richard was related by law to the Dryden line, as his first wife was Elizabeth Dryden, an aunt of John Dryden's. The poet-laureate of the Restoration, then, was a cousin of Katherine Philips's. Dryden acknowledged their kinship and acquaintance in a letter to the young poet Elizabeth Thomas, published by Charles Ward (1942, 98; Kunitz and Haycraft 1952, 409–10). It was Philips's relative Dryden who promoted her as "Matchless," a seldom-mentioned but significant fact in Philips studies; and, as Cowley would do in an elegiac ode to "Orinda" prefixed to the first authorized edition of her work in 1667, Dryden praised Philips as the female laureate of the Restoration in his elegiac ode to the poet-painter Anne Killigrew (1685).

When Katherine Philips's second stepfather died in 1648, Dame Phillipps soon took a fourth husband, Major Philip Skippon, also a Welsh notable. Skippon died in 1660. Four times widowed, Katherine Philips's mother had become one of the wealthiest women in Wales. By the time of her death in 1678, she would live to see her daughter a wife, mother, poet, dramatic translator, and literary toast of the English-speaking world.

Marriage, motherhood, and the poetic celebration of platonic friendship between women were the principal concerns of Katherine Philips's late teens and early womanhood. Her mother and their new Welsh relations had selected a husband for young Katherine, one James Philips of Cardigan. A widower and Oxford men, Philips was a Parliamentarian and a political power in southwest Wales and in London. He also was related by blood and marriage to the Picton Castle Phillipps line.[14] At the time of their marriage in August 1648, Katherine was seventeen years old, James Philips fifty-four (Chester 1887, 2:281). For an arranged marriage, theirs was a reportedly happy union, which produced two children, a son Hector, who died in infancy (see "On Little Hector Philips," Katherine's most affecting lyric), and a daughter Katherine, who married into the prominent Wogan family of Boulston, Pembrokeshire, also a cadet branch of the ancient Phillipps line (Phillips 1858, 202–3).

Before her public life in literature, Katherine Philips composed intimate lyrics for a small circle of Welsh friends and relatives. Fame never was a goal early on, or so she adamantly claimed in her letters. Philips confined herself to Cardigan during the late 1640s and throughout the 1650s, attending to new domestic duties, but also producing a substantial body of verse devoted largely to her signature theme, female friendship.[15] The center of Philips's emotional life, one gathers, was not hearth and home, but rather the affectionate relationships she cultivated with the two principal adepts of her "sacred society of Friendship," Mary Aubrey (her "Rosania") and especially Mrs. Anne Owen *née* Lewis of Orielton, another family relation, and the beloved "Lucasia" of Katherine Philips's most expressive lyrics. Mrs. Owen lived in Llandshipping, southeast of Picton Castle and only twenty-five miles from Katherine's new home, The Priory in Cardigan. While Philips's verse is ostensibly innocent of explicit sapphic sentiment, a subtle psychosexual subtext sometimes appears to operate in her wooing and courtship poems to women, and probably merits some attention from Philips scholars.

Philips's juvenilia, if not her entire canon, display a broad, eclectic reading in English and especially French literature, as *préciosité* had been brought into vogue by Henrietta Maria, the French queen-consort of Charles I. Essentially derivative in imagery and technique, Philips's early verse also displays the influence of William Cartwright, a Cavalier poet, playwright, and divine, who enjoyed a high reputation in his day. Philips paid homage to her English master (whom she soon would replace with a French one) in a poem beginning, "Stay, Prince of Phansie," prefixed to Cartwright's *Poems* (1651). This minor publication was Philips's first literary credit, and it gave her immediate local visibility. As in Cartwright's verse, Philips's poems are heavily freighted with the poetic effects of three traditions: (1) Classical and Renaissance traditions of platonic love and platonic friendship (Hageman 1986, 573); (2) *préciosité*, abundantly represented in the French *élégie* and the mannered salon verse of Voiture and other devotées of the Hôtel de Ramboüillet; and (3) English "wit," as displayed in the poetic ingenuities of Donne and others of the "metaphysical" school. But Philips wisely distinguished her adaptations of these traditions by introducing into her verse a decidedly feminine feature: ardent friendship between women. By in effect "feminizing" the existing traditions in love-poetry formulated by male poets, Philips founded the first English school of an explicitly feminine poetic, a worthy facet of her work that should be explored.

It was in 1662, during an extended visit to Dublin with the newly-married "Lucasia," that Katherine Philips's life and literary aspirations took the sudden turn that catapulted her from the enclosure of Cardigan to the public light of celebrity: Enter Roger Boyle, first Baron Broghill and first Earl of Orrery.

3. Dublin. It was Dublin, not London or Cardigan, that was the site of Philips's career. In Dublin, Philips was "discovered" and her career launched. There, she met several influential Irish and transplanted English nobles and literary bosses who fostered her talent and materially made her career possible.

Two, perhaps three, matters prompted Philips to leave Cardigan for Dublin in 1662. First, she refused to part with her beloved "Lucasia." Mrs. Owen, newly widowed, had recently married the royalist Welsh colonel Marcus Trevor, first Viscount Dungannon and Baron Trevor of Rostrevor. Philips insisted she accompany the new Lady Dungannon in her journey from Llandshipping, Wales to Dublin to see "Lucasia" happily installed in Manor Rostrevor. Second, Philips had serious family business in Ireland. At the Restoration, her husband, a staunch supporter of Cromwell, had suffered significant financial losses. She hoped to salvage their resources by prosecuting a claim of her husband's to certain properties in Ireland. These legal and civil negotiations extended her visit to well over a year (to her delight). Yet, a third reason for the Dublin visit was quite possibly Philips's developing professional yearnings. Her literary apprenticeship was in Wales, in the 1640s and '50s; by the time of the Restoration in 1660, she was understandably eager to test her potential in a literary climate less competitive than London's and more hospitable certainly to untitled newcomers.

During Philips's stay in Dublin, it was Roger Boyle (familiarly "Orrery") who came forward as her patron. Orrery, an influential power in the Irish peerage and ten years Philips's senior, was the son of Richard Boyle, first Earl of Cork, and a notable figure in Irish affairs, second only to Dublin's Lord Mayor, James Butler Duke Ormande. Like so many pivotal figures in Philips's career, Orrery had close ties to many of Philips's new Welsh relatives (Souers 1931, 167). As she wrote in August 1663: "My good friend ["Lucasia"] has favor'd me with the Acquaintance of my Lord Orrery: He is indeed a Man of Parts." And so he was. Hardly the frivolous man Bishop Burnet thought him to be, Orrery was a man of broad talent and achievement, as soldier, statesman, poet, French translator, and dramatist.[16] William Smith Clark, the principal editor of Orrery's work and a leading scholar of the early Irish theater, identified Orrery as Restoration Dublin's most important literary figure and a generous patron of several minor writers, including Philips (1955, 52–53).

Orrery's literary credits show that he and Philips enjoyed intersecting interests. Like Philips, Orrery was an enthusiast in French literature, platonic friendship, and rhymed heroic drama, particularly tragedy, in which he preceded Dryden and Dryden's brother-in-law Sir Robert Howard (Payne 1925, 173). Clark suggests that "the always vain Orrery" promoted Katherine Philips's work in heroic tragedy to aggrandize his own success in the genre. Regardless, by the time Orrery had "discovered" Philips, he had established himself as a literary lion, principally through an early work, *Parthenissa*, a six-volume French romance he produced during the Interregnum. When he met Philips, Orrery was at work on his most successful play, *The General*, a heroic tragedy which premièred at John Ogilby's new Theatre Royal in Smock Alley, Dublin, in February 1663 and later in London at Lincoln's Inn Fields in September 1664. The vogue ushered in by Orrery's *General* may have steered Philips in the direction of heroic tragedy. When she writes in her letters that a fragment of her first Corneille translation just happened to find its way into Orrery's hands, we have to smile.

Orrery's interest in the untitled housewife from Wales was not fortuitous. As a former peer of Cromwell's, Orrery certainly knew Welsh Parliamentarians, a group that included Katherine Philips's husband and others of the larger Phillipps clan (though many Welsh Phillippses were royalists and members of The Society of Sea-Serjeants, a secret Stuart conclave flourishing in southwest Wales after the disgrace of 1649 [Jones 1967, 59; Phillips 1862, 71]). In her poem "To the Countess of Roscommon, with a Copy of *Pompey*," Philips coyly states that it was not personal ambition but Orrery's prodding that led her to translate Corneille:

> But when you wonder at my bold design,
> Remember who did that high Task enjoin;
> Th' Illustrious *Orrery*, whose least Command,
> You would more wonder if I could withstand.[17]

But Orrery in Dublin had a companion Philips-booster in London, Sir Charles Cotterell. This man, whom Philips affectionately called her "Poliarchus," figured just as prominently in her career as did Orrery. Cotterell was more than Philips's correspondent and confidant: he was her literary editor and royal agent. A Master of Ceremonies at the courts of both Charles I and Charles II, Cotterell was a loyal Stuart, expert diplomat, and seasoned specialist in royal protocol. When the time was most propitious, it was Cotterell who brought Katherine Philips's success in Dublin to the attention of the English court and its prestigious literary circles. Moreover, as a cousin of Sir Thomas Phillipps's sister, Cotterell was related by marriage to Katherine Philips's Welsh relatives (Munby 1951–60, 4:210). Philips probably consolidated her familial links to Cotterell in London at the Restoration, which she attended and celebrated in several panegyrics to the Stuarts (*Poems*, 1678, 2–9).

Katherine Philips's ambitious decision to render a strict couplet-by-couplet translation of Corneille's heroic tragedy *Pompée*, and later his *Horace*, was correct, both for Philips and for the historical moment. No fledgling in French translation, Philips was more than up to the task. In addition to her work in Corneille, she had translated his paraphrase of Thomas à Kempis's *Imitations*, Madeleine de Scudéry's pastoral *Almahide*, and St. Amant's *La Solitude*. Philips's facility in French literature was publicly acknowledged by John Davies of Kidwelly, a Welsh contemporary, who dedicated to Philips a section of his translation of La Calprende's romance *Cleopatra* (1659–68). Philips also was familiar with the mannered verse of the *précieuses* and with the *élégies* of Henrietta Coligny de la Suze. The Ramboüillet circle, it should be noted, included Pierre Corneille, who figured so largely in Philips's dramatic career.

But Philips's attraction to Corneille was more than literary good sense, it was commercially savvy. As a native Londoner with strong literary leanings and influential relatives, foremostly Dryden and Cotterell, Philips naturally kept abreast of literary markets. In her Cardigan-Dublin-London letters, she frequently presses correspondents for information on theatrical vogues. In 1660, when Charles II opened the theaters, which had been legally closed by Parliament since 1642, the climate was indeed overripe for a high-spirited, full-blooded drama. Such was the temper of the times. Philips correctly anticipated that the heroic plays of Corneille, with their oversize tragic heroes, melodramatic plots, lofty ethical arguments, and exotic effects, had exactly what Restoration playgoers wanted. In fact, it is likely that Philips's success in Corneille pointed the way for a run in rhymed heroic drama, especially tragedy, which was rapidly being produced by her contemporaries Orrery, Howard, Dryden, Lee and Otway. Philips's success in Dublin and within months in London brought much attention to French heroic drama by ushering

"Orinda" engraved by William Faithhorne from the Vander Gucht portrait
bust of Katherine Philips. Reproduced with permission from the author's
copy of Philips's **Poems** (3rd ed., 1678)

in a Corneille fad throughout the 1660s (Mambretti 1985, 233–34; 1977, 443–44). This vogue surely gave the lie to Dryden's claim in 1668 that French drama did not have an audience in the English-speaking world (*Works* 1955–, 17:33). With the necessary hindsight, it was left for Pope in the 1730s to mark the value of French heroic drama in the English plays of the preceding age:

> Late, very late, correctness grew our care,
> When the tir'd nation breath'd from civil war.
> Exact Racine, and Corneille's noble fire
> Show'd us that France had something to admire.
> (*Poems* 1961–69, 4:219, 272–75)

Fortunately for literary historians and Philips scholars, a running account of Philips's *Pompey* is available in her 1662–63 letters from Dublin to Sir Charles Cotterell in London. With precision of detail, Philips discusses with "Poliarchus" her progress on the translation, its revisions, subsequent production, and its publication by John Crooke, the King's Printer in Ireland. But Philips's *Pompey* letters are equally important for what they reveal about the politics of female authorship and about Philips herself. We notice, for example, the significant literary and material support she received from male allies in the actual translation and mounting of the play; and we also observe in her letters the emergence of a strong authorial ego in this most "modest" of English women writers.

First, let us acknowledge Philips's wide network of male allies in the *Pompey* project. As she informs Cotterell, her plans for a Corneille translation began only casually, with a translation of a single scene in act 2. The translation was done in Dublin, and circulated (most strategically, one expects) among Philips's new Irish friends—the Butlers, Dungannons, Ogilbys, Orrerys, Roscommons, Temples, and Tyrells. Amusingly, Philips admits to Cotterell:

> By some Accident or another, my Scene of *Pompey* fell into his [Orrery's] hands and he was pleas'd to like it so well, that he sent me the *French* Original; and the next time I saw him, [he] so earnestly importion'd me to pursue that translation that to avoid the Shame of seeing him who had so lately commanded a Kingdom, become a Petitioner to me for such a Trifle, I obey'd him so far as to finish the Act in which that Scene is; so that the whole Third Act is now *English*.[18]

POEMS

By the most deservedly Admired

Mrs Katherine Philips,

The Matchless

ORINDA.

To which is added

MONSIEUR CORNEILLES

POMPEY

&   TRAGEDIES.

HORACE,

With several other Translations out of

FRENCH.

LONDON,

Printed by *T. N.* for *Henry Herringman* at the Sign of
the *Blew Anchor* in the *Lower Walk* of the
New Exchange.   1 6 7 8.

Title-page of the collected works of Katherine Philips.
Reproduced with permission from the author's copy (3rd ed., 1678)

So impressed was Orrery with Philips's ability to translate Corneille's French alexandrines into neat English heroic couplets that he encouraged her to complete the remaining four acts. He judiciously postponed any premature mention of a stage production and subsequent publication. Again Philips wrote to Cotterell: "[Orrery] enjoin'd me to go on; and not only so, but brib'd me to be contented with the Pains, by sending me an excellent copy of Verses" (*Letters*, 61). Orrery's eighty-two-line encomium to Philips, published in her posthumous *Poems* (1667), was the final gesture that spurred Philips to complete the translation. Thus Orrery's compliment to Philips:

> You English *Corneil's Pompey* with such flame,
> That you both raise our wonder and his fame;
> If he could read it, he like us would call
> The copy greater than th' Original;
>   You cannot mend what is already done,
> Unless you'll finish what you have begun:
> Who your Translation see, cannot but say,
> That 'tis Orinda's Work, and but his Play.
> (*Poems*, Sig.A1)

Within just two months, Orrery had what he wanted of Philips: An entirely producible, faithfully-translated heroic tragedy, written by an attractive young English talent with prestigious social and literary connections. His extravagant tribute to Philips was necessary due to her ostensible reticence at the outset of her career. (Brashear would say "feigned" reticence, and she may be correct.) But time was of the essence. Both Orrery and Philips knew that a rival translation of Corneille's play was in progress in London by a competing network, headed up by Sir Edmund Waller with collaborators Sir Charles Sedley, Sir Edward Filmore, Sir Charles Sackville, and Sir Sidney Godolphin. This new urgency attending Philips's translation—from Orrery's first encouragements down to the revisions and last-minute staging details—is dramatically laid out in her correspondence.

A flurry of letters passes between Philips in Dublin and Cotterell in London during the fall and winter of 1662–63. Philips, eager to precede the "Persons of Honour" translation, presses Cotterell to respond to her revisions and to add corrections of his own. They quibble over fine points of grammar and phrasing, the play's inter-act songs, and the appropriateness of the play's prose dedication to Anne Duchess of York. Philips's letters also document her reliance on Sir Edward Dering (the "Silvander" of her poems), a loyal English friend and the husband of Mary Harvey, one of Philips's former classmates at Hackney. Like Cotterell and Orrery, Dering was more than an influential politician: he was a consummate man of letters, member of the Duke of Ormande's Dublin circle, and, as his diaries show, an avid playgoer.[19] After Orrery persuaded Philips to a Dublin production of her play in Ogilby's new Theatre Royal in Smock Alley (a real playhouse, finer than D'Avenant's theater in London, which, after all, was only a remodelled tennis court), Dering contributed to the project by writing the play's epilogue. The prologue was written by another literary lion, Wentworth Dillon, Earl of Roscommon, an established authority on dramatic translation (*Essay on Translated Verse*, 1684). Roscommon's participation in the *Pompey* project was important, as it gave a literary cachet to Philips's translation.

Orrery's role in the project was formidable. Not only did he initially encourage the project, he also financed it. Acting in effect as Philips's producer, Orrery put up £100 to cover the production's elaborate Roman and Egyptian costumes; he probably paid for the scenery, as well. Operatic in presentation, Philips's *Pompey* was performed and staged in the latest heroic mode, with a good deal of special effects. Orrery, drawing upon impressive resources, did everything to ensure a resplendent production. He even engaged the services of his own French composer to score the play's music. Also assisting with the music were Sir Peter Pett, John Ogilby, the unidentified "Philaster" (Colonel Jeffries of Abercynrig?), and Le Grand (the Duchess of Ormande's personal French composer) (Souers 1931, 234n).

And, so, on Tuesday evening, 10 February 1663, with Joseph Ashbury, a professional actor and theater-manager in the title role, Katherine Philips's *Pompey* premièred in Dublin's newest playhouse. Sumptuously mounted, it was a historic production and it pulled in a celebrity audience. Moreover, attendance at matinee performances proved that Philips's translation was also good family entertainment, a rare thing in the Restoration theatre. Not only did her *Pompey* beat Waller's team to the boards by almost an entire year, it also succeeded as a popular favorite for some fifteen years after its début. Its latest recorded London production was at the Duke of York's theater in 1678. Efforts by jealous contemporaries to undermine Philips's success, such as D'Avenant's burlesque of the play in act 5 of his *Play-house To Be Lett* (1663), were obviously fruitless (Milhous and Hume 1977, 18–19). Philips's *Pompey* was widely praised, especially by female playgoers and writers, such as Anne Finch, Lady Winchilsea, also a distant relation of the larger Phillipps group, who acknowledged Philips's achievement in two blank-verse plays of her own.[20]

As fame often has it, Philips became a celebrity in a single evening. It must have been the grandest night of her life. But even with her facility in French translation and her instinctive flair for stage-production, Philips's extravaganza could never have been mounted without the backing of the old boys' network. The stunning success of the English *Pompey* was attributable to many factors well beyond Katherine Philips's talent. The play was not a first-rate dramatic translation because Philips herself was not a first-rate poet; but the play succeeded quite nicely nonetheless because it was a lavish stage production in the contemporary heroic mode and because it effectively conveyed the high spirit of its original. It also was the first English-language rhymed heroic tragedy produced in the history of the Anglo-Irish theater. And if all of this wasn't novel enough, it was the product of a female pen.

Throughout the several weeks of intensive editorial revision and negotiation preceding *Pompey's* première, a less obvious aspect of the project begins to emerge with increasing force: *the rising authorial ego of Katherine Philips*. Biographical notices on Philips have traditionally identified her along the lines of the literary persona she and her coterie carefully constructed. In such English literary surveys as Aubrey's *Lives* (1898), Edward Phillips's *Theatrum Poetarum* (1675) (the first such survey to include a dedicated section on women poets), George Ballard's *Memoirs* (1752), Louisa Stuart Costello's *Eminent Englishwomen* (1844), Sir Edmund Gosse's *Seventeenth-century Studies* (1883), and George Saintsbury's *Minor Poets of the Caroline Period* (1905), Katherine Philips is consistently presented as "the Matchless Orinda," a modest writer of chaste lines. Only Gosse perceived that she was "full of literary ambition" (1883, 249). Philips's interest in fame and her strong desire to closely monitor the printing of her work are almost never mentioned by literary chroniclers. In fact, it would appear to be an amusing blunder of literary history that Philips's "sharp Fit of Sickness" over a so-called pirated edition of her poems printed in Fleet Street by Richard Marriot on 25 November 1663 (*Letters*, 29 January 1664, 110), long construed by "Orinda" devotées as hard evidence of her modesty and authorial reticence, was more likely an acute anxiety attack, resulting from Philips's frustration at not being able to *control* the printing of the first public appearance of her work. Quite understandably we find Philips in her letter of 29 January 1664 in a state of high pique. As she writes to Cotterell from Cardigan, Philips attempted to suppress Marriot's "false Edition." In fact, her dilemma was the talk of the town (*Intelligencer*, 18 January 1664). She complains that Marriot's unauthorized "false Book" is based on "false Copies" of her poems and "bad Verses." His is a "villainous Impression," flawed by production errors ("abominably printed," *Letters*, 235). Marriot's greatest sin was the inclusion of verses which were not hers. As Paul Elmen points out, some of Henry More's poems were included in this surreptitious edition (1951, 55–56). Philips had good reason to become ill, but not for the reason usually given.

Philips's public self-presentation is that of her persona "Orinda," the shy, self-effacing literary personality behind such lines as "[I] never writ any line in my life with an intention to have it printed. . . . I am so little concerned for the reputation of writing [and] I am so far from expecting applause for anything I scribble" (*Letters* 227–228; see also 220–21, 224–25). This is the same voice which routinely evaluates her own work as mere "rags of Paper." The pose of modest amateur was supported by Philips's male backers. The anonymous author of the preface to the first authorized edition of Philips's collected work in 1667, probably Cotterell, mentions "how little she desired the fame of being in Print . . . how much she was troubled to be exposed" (Sig. A4). But as Philips's *Letters* reveal, the woman behind the "Orinda" mask was a wholly different individual. We sometimes see the mask slip in the *Pompey* letters to Cotterell when Philips discloses a sincere interest in fame and when she even boldly positions herself superior to her celebrated contemporaries. Philips's recorded thoughts during the *Pompey* project give us a wholly different reading on her as compared to the traditional Philips hagiography. The *Letters* reveal an aggressive new talent

POMPEY.

A

Tragœdy.

DUBLIN,
Printed by *John Crooke*, Printer to the Kings
Moſt Excellent Majeſty, for *Samuel
Dancer*, next Door to the *Bear*
and *Ragged-Staff* in Caſtle-
ſtreet. 1663.

Title-page of Katherine Philips's *Pompey* (Dublin, 1663).
Reproduced with permission from the National Library of Ireland.

who is very much on the climb. Philips is strident, imposing, sometimes an out-and-out scold. She *must* surpass Waller's rival translation, Philips insists to Cotterell. She *must* present a corrected, bound manuscript copy of *Pompey* to the Duchess of York before Waller's *Pompeius* is printed. Cotterell *must* act as her agent at the English court. "The other translation," she fairly wails to Cotterell on 23 December 1662, "done by so many eminent Hands, will otherwise appear first, *and throw this* [her *Pompey*] *into everlasting Obscurity*" (*Letters*, 94; emphasis added). This statement, above all others, along with similar sentiments in subsequent letters to Cotterell of 27 December 1662 and later, are striking revelations because they bring into focus the authentic artistic personality of "the Matchless Orinda." Under the tensions and accelerated pace of the *Pompey* race against Waller's team, Philips's pride of authorship and explicit desire for fame had finally been articulated.

Evidence of Philip's developing egotism throughout the project also exists in her need to make literary decisions independent of Cotterell and Orrery. In the matter of the play's Dedication to Anne Duchess of York, Philips chooses prose over verse. With an unconcealed eye to her (anticipated) readership, she confidently justifies her decision to Cotterell: "Believe me, Poliarchus, I write the Letter [of Dedication] to the Duchess in Prose, neither out of Laziness or Disrespect, but merely because I thought it would have looked more pedantik and affected to have address'd myself to her in Verse. . . . I thought Prose would savour less of Ostentation" (*Letters*, 140). Then there is the matter of the songs in *Pompey*. Philips wrote the lyrics for five new inter-act songs; she also contributed to the play's incidental tunes, dances, and the grand masque in act 5. Her musical additions to Corneille's text illustrate both original participation in the project and musical talent. The first song, "Since Affairs of the State," was a popular hit about town, and later included in *Choice Ayres* (1675), a successful collection of contemporary songs compiled by John Playford, a leading London music publisher. Philips cleverly brings attention to her song in a poetic tribute to Elizabeth Boyle of the distinguished Cork family and later wife of Nicholas Tufton, Earl of Thanet, in a poem entitled "To my Lady Elizabeth Boyle, Singing now affairs &c." and in these lines to Cotterell of 10 January 1663: "I was so puff'd up with the Honour of [the dutchess of York's] Protection, that I have ventur'd to lengthen the Play by adding Songs in the

Intervals of each Act, which they flatter me here are not amiss. . . .
Philaster has already set one of them agreeably, and [an] abundance
of People are learning it" (*Letters*, 110). As one critic persuasively
demonstrates, Philips's five inter-act songs were quite unlike the
purely transitional tunes in most English drama up to that time.
Hers were integrally linked to the action in *Pompey*, and they also
commented on the play's political intricacies, thereby assisting playgoers' interpretation of the play (Price 1979, 62).

Philips's rising ego is never more apparent than when she takes on
the competition. The *Pompeius* of Waller and his team—many
senior literary men who surely would have regarded the ruddy-faced
housewife from Wales an amusing interloper—was thought to be
unfaithful to Corneille, according to Philips. Her criticism of the
rival translation is severe, even condescending. In a letter to Cotterell
of 17 September 1663, she is harsh: "There is room in several places
for an ordinary Critick to shew his Skill. But I cannot but be surprised at the great Liberty they have taken in adding, omitting, and
altering the Original as they please themselves: This I take to be a
Liberty not pardonable in Translators, and unbecoming the Modesty
of the Attempt" (*Letters*, 178). She also complains that the Waller
team has "garbl'd" Corneille's text. In assuming "so great a
License," the Waller translation is a weak imitation of the original,
she judges; and it is marred, moreover, by "bad" rhymes. "But what
chiefly disgusts me," Philips goes on, "is that the Sence most commonly languishes. . . . I really think the best of their lines equal to
the worst in my translation" (*Letters*, 179–80).

Epilogue: Posthumous Philips

When Katherine Philips left Dublin in mid-June 1663 to return to
the isolation of Cardigan, Wales, little did she know that her career
was essentially over. Never again would she hear the applause of her
contemporaries or work with Orrery and Cotterell on a new play.
Philips's aspirations for a second success equal to if not surpassing
her *Pompey* were dashed by circumstance. Her timing, as always,
was perfect; she simply was unlucky.

The last year of Philips's life was sheer anticlimax compared to the
gay round of her Dublin visit. Not that Philips's enthusiasm had
waned any. If anything, she returned to Cardigan heady with celeb-

rity. Now back on Welsh soil she wasted little time parlaying her maiden success into a second theatrical vehicle. With the success of *Pompey*, Philips became discernibly different from the imposing personality of the Cotterell letters. Evidently validated by the acclaim of 1663, her post-*Pompey* correspondence gives us a relaxed, confident voice. At this stage in her career, Philips had become a self-conscious, professional writer with a product to sell, a commercial market to cultivate, and a reputation to maintain and aggrandize. Unlike her Tudor female predecessors, who circulated their writings in private, Katherine Philips was now a published author and a celebrity. By 1663, she had a public to please, and she was eager to delight again.

Philips peaked very early in her career, and she was keen to build on her notoriety. Moving rapidly, she wisely solidified her position by (safely) continuing with material she could manage. Again, she turned to her French master Corneille and selected his *Horace*, a heroic tragedy of early Rome. Like his *Pompée*, Corneille's *Horace* carried strong nationalistic applications for Restoration playgoers. The existence of an earlier English translation by Sir William Lower (*Horatius*, 1656), did not temper her zeal any more than Waller's competing translation of Corneille's *Pompée* daunted her progress in 1662–63. Philips writes Cotterell on 8 January 1664 that she has begun a second Corneillean translation (*Letters*, 217). This time, she requires no direction from Dublin and London allies. Like her *Pompey*, Philips's *Horace* was intended to be a lavish spectacle; and what is more Philips evidently was planning a London première of *Horace* under her own personal direction. A seasoned tactician by this time, Philips enlisted Cotterell in London and "Lucasia" and Elizabeth Boyle in Dublin to help her arrange a trip to London, where she would stay with her brother-in-law Hector Philips. Ostensibly, Philips had to make the trip to help negotiate a civil post in London for her husband. But what a fine opportunity, she must have thought, to be back on native English soil, in the city of my birth, and *there* put forward my new play!

But only three months into the visit, Philips contracted the fatal smallpox, then at near-epidemic levels. The most celebrated English woman writer of the seventeenth century died quietly and unremarkably in a house in Fleet Street on 22 June 1664, attended in her final hours by her dear "Rosania" (Mary Aubrey).[21] Philips was not quite thirty-three years old. She was buried in the churchyard of St. Benet-Sherehog, at the end of Syth's Lane in London, alongside the graves of her infant son Hector, her father John Fowler, and two grandparents (Aubrey, 1898, 2:154). Ironically, several months before her own death, Philips had composed an elegy on the death of Lord Rich, heir of the Earl of Warwick, who had died of smallpox that same year. In lines presaging her own untimely death, the poem begins, "Have not so many lives of late / suffic'd to quench the greedy thirst of Fate?" (*Poems*, 135).

Philips's *Horace* was produced posthumously at London's Theatre Royal during the 1668–69 Season, based on the four acts Philips completed before her death (her work on the play ended with act 4, scene 6) and the remaining translation done by Sir John Denham (scene 7 of act 4 and all of act 5). The Duke of Monmouth, whose manuscript notebook, taken from him after Sedgemoor, included lines from Philips's verses, delivered the play's prologue. It included high praise for its deceased author:

> So soft, that to our Shame we understand
> They could not fall but from a Ladies hand.
> Thus while a Woman *HORACE* did translate,
> *HORACE* did rise above the Roman fate.[22]

Philips's *Horace* was a favorite at the court of Charles II. It saw an amateur court production on 4 February 1668 with Barbara Villiers, Charles's most rapacious mistress, in a leading role (she borrowed the Crown jewels from the Tower of London just for the occasion) (Van Lennep, Avery, and Scouten 1960–68, 1:128–29). The four acts of Philips's *Horace* were first published in London in 1667 by Henry Herringman. The complete translation, with Denham's contribution, appeared in a subsequent publication by Herringman in 1669, under the title *Horace. A Tragedy. Translated from Monsieur Corneille. The Fifth Act translated by Sir John Denham.* Interestingly, Jacob Tonson selected Charles Cotton's translation of act 5 (1671) over Denham's in his (Tonson's) edition of Philips's work in 1710.

It is regrettable that Philips did not live to complete *Horace*, as she never would have authorized the production it received in London. Like her *Pompey, Horace* was operatic; but its exotic effects and overall intent were severely compromised. Samuel Pepys, an informed theater enthusiast, attended a production of the play on 19

January 1669, and judged it a low "silly Tragedy" (*Diary*, 1970–83 ed., 9:420). The play's entertainments (its songs, masques, incidental tunes) were not any of Philips's doing, but ill-advised additions by John Lacy, a professional English actor-playwright whose forte was not tragedy but comedy. The levity Lacy introduced into the play seriously muddled and unbalanced the play's tragic ethos. "Lacy hath made a farce of several dances," Pepys observed. "[I am] not much pleas'd with the play" (9:240). Properly produced, Philips's *Horace* might have surpassed her first effort, had she lived to see the play through production. It certainly outdistanced *Pompey* as a translation. By 1664, Philips had become a confident translator, and Corneille an old friend. Her *Horace* was far less literal and strenuous a translation than *Pompey*, since Philips's original procedure (strict line-for-line translation) is not as apparent in the second play. But instead of being the culmination of her work during the 1660s, Philip's *Horace* was merely an entertainment for the court and, moreover, a surprising embarrassment to serious playgoers.

Philips's sudden death at the height of her celebrity was a devastating blow to the literary community. But before long, the "Orinda" machine was in full swing. First came Herringman's edition of Philips's work in 1667, a tall handsome folio graced with an engraved frontispiece portrait by William Faithorne of the Vander Gucht portrait-bust of Philips. This first authorized edition of her collected work, reissued by Herringman in 1669 and in 1678, and by Tonson in 1710, was initiated by Sir Charles Cotterell, Philips's literary executor. It consisted of an anonymous preface (probably by Cotterell); commendatory verses by Abraham Cowley, Thomas Flatman, Cotterell, a pseudonymous Irishwoman poet "Philo-Phillipa" (Elizabeth Boyle?), Roscommon, and James Tyrell; 116 original poems and five verse-translations; and the two Corneille translations. Then, Philips's letters to Cotterell were gathered, selected, and certainly edited. Forty-eight were published in 1710 by Bernard Lintot (who may have obtained them through his son) under the title *Letters from Orinda to Poliarchus*.[23] Philips's correspondence was reissued by Lintot, with one additional letter, in 1729. As the chronological gaps in the letters suggest, some of Philips's correspondence to Cotterell have either been lost or surpressed.

Curiously, Philips scholars have yet to raise a most obvious question: had Philips lived to full creative maturity, what direction might her work have taken? Two contemporaries close to the "Orinda" myth, namely Cotterell and "Philo-Phillipa," provide clues that allow us to envision Philips in her later years as an author of serious cultural engagement. First, Cotterell (if, in fact, the author of the preface to Philips's collected work) discloses important information about a body of "lost" work by Philips, being many "excellent discourses . . . on several subjects" (*Poems*, Sig. A4). He has seen these essays, and he reports that they would comprise a volume much larger than Philips's published folio of 1667, 124 pages. Perhaps today's recovery work in feminist studies will locate some of Philips's "lost" essays. Certainly they would be valuable to the history of English feminism, as Philips's essays preceded the published essays of such important turn-of-the-century feminist writers as Bathsua Makin (*Essay to Revive the Antient Education of Gentlewomen*, 1673), Mary Astell (*A Serious Proposal to the Ladies*, 1694), and Mary Lady Chudleigh (*Essays upon Several Subjects*, 1710). Furthermore, given Philips's life and times, her prose writings may offer fresh perspectives on French literature, dramatic translation, and the turbulent political setting of the day. As one who lived through three administrations, Philips may have recorded in these "lost" pieces some important topical information.

The elusive "Philo-Phillipa," clearly a female Irish intimate of Philips's (possibly, a Boyle), gives us further insight into Philips's projected literary maturity. In her rousing tribute to Philips, "Philo" expresses the hope that one day Philips will discover her own voice, and then produce original not translated material:

> But if your fetter'd Muse thus praised be,
> What great Things do you write when it is free?
> When it is free to chuse both sence and words,
> Or any subject the vast World affords?
> (*Poems*, Sig. B2)

Had her *Horace* received the success it deserved, Katherine Philips would have had two major theatrical successes to her credit. Surely she would have gone on to produce original drama of her own in the mid-1660s. And it is entirely likely that she would have become involved in feminist issues, especially in light of the rise of feminist drama by Behn and her lesser contemporaries "Ephelia," Polwhele,

Boothby, and "Ariadne." While it is true that Philips never displayed overt feminist leanings, the woman was ambitious. Understandably, she would have moved her career forward along commercially attractive lines.

At full maturity, an impressive Katherine Philips steps forward. Even as a young, underdeveloped writer of slight life experience and cloying sentimentality, Philips succeeded in becoming the most celebrated English woman writer of the seventeenth century. Had she lived through the 1670s and '80s, Philips might have been as versatile as Behn. Writing Katherine Philips into her future is to observe a career of remarkable development: the adolescent bagatelle of Cardigan and the early friendship lyrics; the dramatic translations from Corneille; the prose-essays Cotterell mentions; and, then, perhaps a historical chronicle, some original drama, even some feminist writings. Philips at full maturity emerges as a significant, eclectic talent in an exuberant age of English literature. Had she grown to a plane of relative artistic independence (Behn's achievement), Katherine Philips could have put aside the "Orinda" myth and the old boys' network that welded and promoted it as mere theatrical props of her past.

Notes

The author is grateful to Lord Sackville, Knole, England, for permission to publish a photograph of the Philips portrait in his collection; the National Library of Ireland, Dublin, for permission to publish a photograph of the title-page of the Dublin edition of Philips's *Pompey;* and to the staffs respectively of the College of Arms, London, the National Library of Wales, the British Library, the Bodleian Library, the University of Cincinnati Library, and the University of Texas Library at Austin for prompt assistance with factual information and manuscript materials requried in this essay. Arthur Scouten generously refined my information on the prologue to *Horace* and on D'Avenant's burlesque of *Pompey* in 1663.

1. Bodleian MS, Rawlinson poet 195, ff 49–78. See Milhous and Hume, "Two Plays by Elizabeth Polwhele," PBSA 71 (1977) and their edition of Polwhele's *The Frolicks* (New York, 1977).
2. See Elizabeth Hageman, "The Matchless Orinda," *Women Writers*, ed. K.M. Wilson (Georgia, 1987); Claudia Limbert, "Two Poems and a Prose Receipt," ELR 16 (1986); Patrick H.B. Thomas, "An Edition of . . . Philips" (unpubl. Ph.D. dissertation, University of Wales, 1982); Lucy Brashear, "The Forgotten

Legacy of 'the Matchless Orinda'," *Anglo-Welsh Review* 65 (1979); C.C. Mambretti, "Orinda and the Restoration Stage," CL 37 (1985).

3. "Saint-Amant, Orinda and Dryden's *Miscellany*," ELN 1 (1964); Thomas, "Introduction," lix.

4. Brashear, 68–70.

5. Phillipps pedigree, NLW MS 12359D.

6. Maureen E. Mulvihill, "Essential Studies of Restoration Women Writers," *Restoration* (Fall 1987), with statistical table of published writings 1660–1700. See also Mulvihill, "Feminism and the Rare-book Market," *Scriblerian* (Autumn 1989).

7. Patricia Crawford, "Women's Published Writings 1600–1700," in *Women in English Society*, ed. Mary Prior (New York, 1985); see Crawford's table of data, 269.

8. Dryden's female elegists were Sarah Egerton, a Mrs. D.E., Sarah Piers, Mary Pix, Elizabeth Thomas, Catherine Trotter, and Delariviére Manley, the collection's compiler. Unarguably, *The Nine Muses* was an unprecedented instance of feminist *esprit de corps* in English publication history.

9. For Dryden's remarks on "Corinna," see *The Letters of John Dryden*, ed. Charles E. Ward (North Carolina, 1942), 125, 127, 132. For Dryden's remarks on Lady Chudleigh, see Ward, 98 and James M. Osborn, *John Dryden* (New York, 1940), 217.

10. Dunton's *Athenian Mercury* of 1694 and 1695 featured Rowe's verse. Swift employed Manley as interim editor of his *Examiner*. Johnson employed Wollstonecraft as translator, reviewer, and editorial assistant of his *Analytical Review*. Hickes directed some Saxon researches of Elstob.

11. *Lives of the Queens of England*, ed. Agnes [and Elizabeth] Strickland (London, 1840–48), 5:285; R.P. Trywhitt, *Notices* (London, 1862), 83; Anne Somerset, *Ladies-in-Waiting* (New York, 1984), 45.

12. John Aubrey, *Brief Lives*, ed. Andrew Clark (Oxford, 1898), 2:153; Souers, 13; Thomas, xviii.

13. "Lady Phillip[p]s made her [Anna Williams] a small allowance, and some other Welsh ladies, to all of whom she was related," Boswell, *Johnson*, ed. E. Malone (London, 1851), 1:297, n.2.

14. James Philips, Katherine Philips's husband, was first married to Frances Phillipps, the youngest daughter of Sir Richard Phillips, Katherine's second stepfather (NLW MS 12359D).

15. Public verse in Philips's poetic canon includes poems to Charles II; Elizabeth, Queen of Bohemia; Gilbert Sheldon, Archbishop of Canterbury; James Butler, Lord Mayor of Dublin; et al.

16. Orrery was Lord President of Munster, Lord Chief Justice, and he held a seat in the Privy Councils of Ireland and England. His heroic tragedies are listed in F.W. Payne, "The Question of Precedence between Dryden and Orrery," RES 1 (1925):173–81.

17. *Poems* (London, 1667; 3d ed., 1678), 151. Author's copy. Hereafter cited parenthetically in text as *Poems*.

18. *Letters from Orinda to Poliarchus* (London, 1705), 66. NYPL copy. Hereafter, cited parenthetically in text as *Letters*.

19. R. Jordan, "Some Restoration Playgoers," TN 35 (1981): 51–57. Also Dering published songs in Henry Lawes's *Ayres* (1675) and verses in Cartwright's *Poems* (1651). The Ransom Research Center, Austin, Texas, has acquired from the resplendent manuscript collection of Sir Thomas Phillipps seventy-six poems by "Orinda" in Dering's hand. Dering's manuscript letterbook, containing six letters to "Orinda," has been acquired by the University of Cincinnati Library.

20. Leo M.J. Manglaviti, "Winchilsea," in *Dictionary*, ed. Janet Todd (New Jersey, 1985), 328. Anne Kingsmill married into the Finch line, relations of the larger Phillipps group, NLW MS 12359D.

21. NLW MS 776, 6–7, note 71.

22. *Covent Garden Drolery* (London, 1672), 80. The prologue did not appear in early editions of Philips's work. The Duchess of Monmouth delivered the prologue to *Horace* at the court production of the play; yet, Ballard (*Memoirs*, 1752:290), Baker (*Biographica Dramatica*, 1764; 1782 ed. I:157), Costello (*Memoirs*, 1844:III, 248), and Wiley (*Rare Prologues* (1940, 339) credit the Duke of Monmouth with delivering it.

23. For evidence of stylistic editing of Philips's letters to Cotterell, compare the version of her letter dated 29 January 1663/4, Cardigan, published in the preface to her *Poems* (1667), with the version published in Lintot's edition of her letters in 1705.

Works Cited

Aubrey, John. 1898. *Brief Lives*. Ed. Andrew Clark. 2 vols., Oxford.

Baker, David Erskine. 1764. *Biographica Dramatica*. London.

Ballard, George. 1752. "Memoirs of Katherine Philips." *Memoirs of Several Ladies of Great Britain*. London.

Barnes, Ambrose. 1867. *Memoirs*. Ed. W.H.D. Longstaffe. Durham, England.

Boswell, James. 1851. *The Life of Samuel Johnson*. Ed. Edmond Malone. 4 vols., London.

Brashear, Lucy. 1979. "The Forgotten Legacy of the 'Matchless Orinda.' " *Anglo-Welsh Review* 65:68–79.

Chester, J.L., ed. 1887. *Allegations for Marriage Licenses 1520–1828*. 2 vols., London.

Clark, William Smith. 1925. *The Early Irish Stage: The Beginnings to 1720*. Oxford.

Crawford, Patricia. 1985. "Women's Published Writings 1660–1700." *Women in English Society 1500–1800*. Ed. Mary Prior. New York.

Dryden, John. 1956–. *The Works of John Dryden*. Edward Niles Hooker and H.T. Swedenberg, Jr., General Editors. 19 vols., Berkeley.

Elmen, Paul. 1951. "Some Manuscript Poems by the 'Matchless Orinda'." *PQ* 30: 53–57.

Goreau, Angeline. 1980. *Reconstructing Aphra*. New York.

Gosse, Sir Edmund. 1883. "The Matchless Orinda." *Seventeenth-century Studies*. London.

[Gould, Robert]. 1691. *A Satyrical Epistle to the Female Author of the a Poem call'd Silvia's Revenge. By the Author of the Satyr against Women.* London.

Greer, Germaine, Susan Hastings, Jeslyn Medoff, Melinda Sansone, eds. 1989. *Kissing The Rod.* New York.

Hageman, Elizabeth. 1987. "The Matchless Orinda: Katherine Philips." *Women Writers of the Renaissance and Reformation.* Ed. Katherine Wilson. Athens, GA.

Jones, Francis. 1907. "The Society of Sea-Serjeants." *Trans. Hon. Soc. of Cymmorodorians.* Sessions, I:57–91.

Jordan, R. 1981. "Some Restoration Playgoers." *Theatre Notebook* 35:51–57.

Kunitz, S.J. and Howard Haycraft. 1952. "Katherine Philips." *British Authors Before 1800.* New York.

Limbert, Claudia. 1989. "Katherine Philips." *Restoration* 13:2–6.

Macdonald, Hugh. 1939. *John Dryden: A Bibliography of Early Editions and of Drydeniana.* Oxford.

Mambretti, Catherine Cole. 1985. "Orinda on the Restoration Stage." *Comparative Literature* 37:233–51.

Manglaviti, Leo M.J. 1985. "Anne Finch, Countess of Winchilsea." *A Dictionary of British and American Women Writers 1660–1800.* Ed. Janet Todd. New Jersey.

Milhous, Judith and Robert D. Hume. 1977. "Two Plays by Elizabeth Polwhele." *PBSA* 71:1–9.

———. 1988. " 'Lost' Plays of the Restoration." *Harvard Library Bulletin* 25 (1977): 5–33.

Mormon International Genealogical Index. 2nd ed., Salt Lake City, Utah.

Mulvihill, Maureen E. 1987. "Essential Studies of Restoration Women Writers: Reclaiming a Heritage, 1913–1986." *Restoration* 2:122–32.

———. 1989. "Feminism and the Rare Book Market." *The Scriblerian* 22, No. 1:1–5.

Munby, A.N.L. 1951–1960. *Phillipps Studies.* 5 vols., Cambridge, England.

O'Donnell, Mary Ann. 1986. *Aphra Behn: An Annotated Bibliography of Primary and Secondary Sources.* New York.

Osborn, James M. 1940. *John Dryden: Some Biographical Facts and Problems.* New York.

Payne, F.W. 1925. "The Question of Precedence between Dryden and Orrery with Regard to the English Heroic Plays." *RES* 1:173–181.

Pepys, Samuel. 1970–1983. *The Diary of Samuel Pepys.* Eds. Robert Latham and William Matthews. 11 vols. London.

Philipps, Mary Margaret. 1906. *The History of the Family of Phillips of Picton.* London.

Philips, Katherine. 1678. *Poems. By the Most Deservedly Admired Mrs. Katherine Philips, the Matchless Orinda. To Which Is Added, Monsieur Corneille's Pompey and Horace, Tragedies. With Several Other Translations out of French.* London, 3rd ed.

———. 1705. *Letters from Orinda to Poliarchus.* London.

Phillips, John Pavin. March 18, 1858. "The 'Matchless Orinda' and Her Descendants." *N & Q,* Sec. Ser., 202–203.

———. 1862. "The Society of Sea Serjeants." *N & Q*, Third Ser., 2:1–2.

Poovey, Mary. 1984. *The Proper Lady and the Woman Writer*. Chicago.

Pope, Alexander. 1961–1969. *The Twickenham Edition of the Poems of Alexander Pope*. John Butt, General Editor. 11 vols., London.

Price, Curtis, A. 1979. "The Songs for Katherine Philips' *Pompey* (1663)." *Theatre Notebook* 33:61–66.

Roberts, William. 1964. "Saint-Amant, Orinda, and Dryden's *Miscellany*." *ELN* 1:191–195.

Smith, Hilda. 1982. *Reason's Disciples*. Ubana.

Somerset, Anne. 1984. *Ladies-in-Waiting: From the Tudors to the Present Day*. New York.

Souers, Philip Webster. 1931. *The Matchless Orinda*. Cambridge, MA.

Strickland, Agnes. 1840–48. *The Lives of the Queens of England from the Norman Conquest*. 12 vols., London. 1902–1903. Victoria Edition, 12 vols., London.

Thomas, Patrick Hungerford Bryan Rev. 1982. "An Edition of the Poems and Letters of Katherine Philips 1632–1664." PhD dissertation, University College of Wales.

Thorn-Drury, Sir George, ed. 1928. *Covent Garden Drolery*. London. (Rpt. of 1672 edition, attributed to Aphra Behn as compiler/editor.)

Trywhitt, Robert Philips. 1862. *Notices and Remains of . . . the Family of Trywhitt*. London.

Van Lennep, William, Emmett L. Avery and Arthur H. Scouten, eds. 1962–1968. *The London Stage* 1660–1800. 11 vols., Carbondale.

Vieth, David M. See Wilmot, John, 2d Earl of Rochester, below.

Ward, Charles E., ed. 1942. *The Letters of John Dryden*. Durham, No. Carolina.

Wilmot, John, 2d Earl of Rochester. 1968. *The Complete Poems*. Ed. David M. Vieth. New Haven.

Winn, James Anderson. 1987. *John Dryden and His World*. New Haven.

Manuscripts:

National Library of Wales MSS. 12359D, 775B, 776B, 21867B.

Bodleian Library MS., Rawlinson Poet 195, ff. 49–78.

"And Poets Shall by Patron-Princes Live": Aphra Behn and Patronage

DEBORAH C. PAYNE

I

Charles II revived patronage as a cultural project soon after the restoration of the Stuart monarchy; in doing so, he made evident an ideological and filial connection to his father's munificent support of the arts thirty years previously (Pickel 1936, 1–16). As with other forms of artistic patronage, the protection of plays was to be read in public spaces as a display of royalist authority. That it was interpreted as such in both the playhouse and the library is borne out in the enthralled tones of the private diary entry and in the obsequious addresses of the printed dedication. Pepys, for one, spent many a night at the theater redirecting his gaze from the stage to the luminaries in the audience; often, he filters his aesthetic response to a play through an aristocratic lens (1974, 8:72). During the Restoration, the relationship between viewing subject and scrutinized object is dynamic, mutable. By the sheer ability to alter the viewer's reception of spectacle, the aristocrat helps to constitute the aesthetic status of the literary artifact. The authority of the aristocracy was such during this time that the public approval of a Lady Castlemaine or the Duke of York could rescue the rapidly diminishing fortunes of a new play.

Nor should we take the Restoration's obsessive fascination with their aristocracy to be mere "royal watching" in the manner of Fleet Street paparazzi. The dynamism of the relationship between spectator and peer, often interpreted as mere "influence" in standard histories of the drama, is perhaps difficult for us to grasp since we rarely have the opportunity to see our own postmodern aristocrats viewing entertainment in a public space. We would be hard-pressed to attribute the success of a Hollywood blockbuster to the president's visible approval, or the acclaim of a West End musical to the queen's smiling assent. Significantly, our leaders are given to viewing spectacle in isolation, thus prohibiting our curious gaze even if we were inclined to watch them watching. But when the king attends the theater in the 1660s and 1670s, that very attendance becomes part of the theatricality of the performing space. Court and aristocratic reaction are virtually inseparable from the dramatic fiction proper.

Yet for all this display of royalist authority, by the late 1660s a note of discernible bitterness can be detected, both in the panegyrics addressed to notable personages and in the dedications themselves (Jose 1984, 24–30). The cultural machinery was in place, but the wheels were not turning smoothly, largely due to an impecunious court. Patronage may very well have been revived as part of a project of royalist myth-making which helped to shore up that cultural oxymoron—a divine right kingship "restored" by common consent of the populace—but the gap between professed aristocratic munificence and actual material practice was far too apparent to improverished writers and other artists. A number of worthy causes taken up early in Charles's reign, such as the Office of Works, the King's Musick, the Chapel Royal, and the Royal Society, soon faltered because of the court's lavish and inopportune expenditures. Individual artists suffered as well. Three years after his appointment as poet laureate, Dryden had difficulty collecting the £500 owed on his salary; he could not collect on the £500 loaned to the king in 1667 until June of 1673. By the time of Charles's death, the arrears on Dryden's salary came to a daunting £1,075 (Foss 1971, 48, 62).

II

It was during this period of tension between patronage as a compelling cultural symbol and enfeebled material practice that the Duke's company produced Behn's first play, *The Forc'd Marriage*, in 1670. She lacked a patron for that first play, not an uncommon occurrence for a new playwright who had yet to catch the eye of a powerful man or woman in court circles. But if we compare the shape of her career to Dryden's, the particular exigencies to which she was subject become apparent. Dryden began a campaign for royal patronage in the outer reaches of the royal family with a dedication to the Duchess of Monmouth affixed to *The Indian Emperor* in 1665; dedications to the Duke of Monmouth and the Duke of York followed in 1668 and 1669, respectively. He secured the laureateship in 1668 (Foss 1971, 68). But whereas Dryden was able to move quickly through increasingly important patrons, as so many stepping stones to his rapid acclaim, Behn wrote for seven years without patronage. All of her first seven plays, produced between 1670 and 1677, lack dedications, and her correspondence, scant though it may be, fails to mention any kind of support.

Even the circumstances surrounding her affiliation with the Duke's company are notable in this respect. Given her prior acquaintance with Thomas Killigrew, patentee of the King's Company and former contact from her spying days in Holland, one would have predicted her debut in his company. Instead, Behn proved a mainstay of the Duke's Company from 1670 until 1682; the United Company produced two of her plays in 1687. Why she failed to make use of such an important contact, particularly given the restricted marketplace of Restoration theater, remains something of a mystery. Whatever the reason, the usual system of contacts and patronage so necessary to the economic and cultural survival of the Restoration playwright simply did not work for Behn early in her career.

What could patronage have secured for Behn during her first seven years as a playwright? To the modern eye, the material benefits to be reaped from patron/client relations appear somewhat tenuous. However, we must keep in mind that such things as payment for epistolary dedications are relative to their culture. For a dramatist worried about her third-night box office proceeds, the customary £10 to £50 awarded for a dedication was a nice way to bolster income (Korshin 1970–71, 1806). Then, too, if we remember that £40 annually kept a family of five out of debt in 1688, the urgency with which playwrights besieged potential patrons with dedications can be better appreciated (Porter 1982, 28). Support may have been sporadic, but for a single woman like Behn—even given the untoward expenses of such feminine items as gloves and stockings during the Restoration—a cash payment of £20 must have seemed a windfall (Maus 1979, 600–01). And throughout her adult life, Behn was dogged by money problems, largely because of her impulsive and generous nature.[1] Even late in her career, after many years of successful publications and productions, she was strapped for funds; an extant autograph letter empowers one Zachary Baggs on 1 August 1685 "to stop what money he shall hereafter have in his hands, of mine upon the playing my first play till this aforesaid debt of six pound be discharged" (Folger MS c.c.1 [4]). Under circumstances such as these, any financial remuneration, however spotty, was clearly welcome.

In addition to money for a nicely turned dedication, a few peers provided the kind of support once typical of earlier seventeenth-century literary patronage (Tennenhouse 1981, 236). A handful of generous men like the Earl of Dorset provided regular stipends or a country retreat to authors. Dorset, for example, not only invited Dryden to be a guest at Knole House one Christmas, but he also placed a £100 note under Dryden's dinner plate (Foss 1971, 36). One suspects that patrons like Dorset were besieged by dedications requesting support simply because there were so few truly munificent benefactors available. Unfulfilled promises, such as those encountered by poets and playwrights, were far more common. Paul Korshin claims that "official patronage" from the crown was slight during the Restoration, and that the Treasury Books reveal as many discontented as rewarded authors (1973–74, 457). Behn herself suffered debtor's prison, probably late in 1668, because of a £150 debt incurred while spying in Holland for the court (Goreau 1980, 115). If the court could not pay for much needed intelligence work during the Second Dutch War, then it certainly could not afford the luxury of maintaining artists. Nonetheless, however infrequent patronal support may have been, its occasional benefits were such that artists still clamored and hoped.

One of the other privileges Aphra Behn might have enjoyed from a patron in those early years of her career was the assumption of debt incurred for publication (Belanger 1982, 6). All of her plays were published, but whether at her expense or that of her printer's, we simply do not know. Although the publication of plays was often correlated to the length of a run to maximize profits—Richard Steele in 1705 was asked not to publish *The Tender Husband* until a month after the premiere—the dramatist usually made little from the transaction (Kenny 1980, 314). Even earlier in the period, when lapse time between performance and publication in the late 1670s could be up to six months, the dramatist often failed to benefit (Milhous and Hume 1974). The demands of the marketplace had little to do with the profit margin for the playwright; she sold her rights directly to the bookseller. If we are to judge from Jacob Tonson's success in luring Dryden away from Henry Herringman by offering him £20 for *Troilus and Cressida*, copyright was not richly rewarded. An influential patron, though, could be of some help in securing prompt or fair payment from a bookseller, or in securing an introduction (Belanger 1982, 5–6).

In Behn's own career there might be a connection between the patronage she secured later on and the quality of the bookseller available to her. Prior to 1679, in her pre-patronage period, Behn was most frequently published by James Magnus, Thomas Dering, and other booksellers known for the publication of low-cost items. The best-known name on that early roster of publishers is that of Richard Bentley, who, while representing a number of playwrights, had a brief and unhappy arrangement with Dryden in the mid-seventies (Roberts 1967, 111–12). After Behn in the post-1679 period began to secure the support of such court luminaries as Nell Gwyn, the Duke of York, the Duke of Grafton, and the Earl of Arundel, she began publishing with the ambitious Tonson brothers, first Richard and then Jacob. By Restoration standards Jacob Tonson was fairly even-handed in his treatment of writers (despite Dryden's grumbling to the contrary), and such a connection may have been far more lucrative than previous ones. Jacob especially was anxious to add popular writers to his ever-increasing stable—thus his pursuit of Dryden—and Behn was a proven box office hit by the end of the seventies. By this time too her own circle of friends included a number of people also known to Tonson: Nell Gwyn, Thomas Otway, even William D'Avenant, fourth son of Sir William, the dramatist and patentee for the Duke's company (Lynch 1971, 13). Any number of people could have intervened on her behalf, although Gwyn and the court would have had the particular influence with booksellers like Tonson (Papali 1968, 13).

However sporadic the material benefits from the patronage system, the economics of writing and publishing during the Restoration ensured that dependent playwrights would continue clamoring in print for recognition from notable peers and even the upper fraction of the gentry. Like a few other dramatists who fell outside the system, Behn managed to get a start in the theater without the intervention of a patron; however, fresh out of debtor's prison because of the court's inability to make good on promised wages, Behn must have appreciated the precariousness of her position. Revealingly, her first two plays recycle the usual D'Avenant plot out of romantic tragicomedy. Lack of a powerful patron may have necessitated adherence to an outworn dramatic formula. At the very least, pleasing the aging patentee for the Duke's Company by emulating his dated style of comedy would have been a smart survival tactic for that odd creature, the professional woman playwright.

III

Whether or not patronage would have protected Behn from the vicissitudes of audience taste, thus enabling her to debut with more innovative scripts in the early 1670s, cannot be determined absolutely. But the tone of the "Epistle to the Reader" prefacing *The Dutch Lover* in 1673 provides a clue. She initially addresses her audience as "Good, Sweet, Honey, Sugar-Candied Reader," but despite several self-deprecating maneuvers (she belittles her lack of education) her annoyance at being held hostage by audience taste is apparent:

> Indeed that day 'twas Acted first, there comes into the Pit, a long, lither, phlegmatick, white, ill-favour'd, wretched Fop, an Officer in Masquerade newly transported with a Scarf & Feather out of France, a sorry Animal . . . A thing, Reader—but no more of such a Smelt: This thing, I tell ye, opening that which serves it for a mouth, out issued such a noise as this to those that sate about it, that they were to expect a woful Play, God damn him, for it was a woman's.[2]

Her next four plays lack any sort of dedicatory or prefatory material until the appearance of *Sir Patient Fancy* in 1678, where she once again takes up issues of bawdiness, audience expectation (this time the "ladies" are answered), and gender. These last two issues are especially important for understanding Behn's problematic position within the patronage system. First, she defends her play from charges of immorality, declaring that if she had put a man's name to the piece "it had been a most admirable Play" (*Works* 4:7). That the criticism

issues from women in the audience especially stings her; male antag-
onism is to be expected, not female. Second, Behn asserts that her
position as a professional, one who must write "for Bread" rather
than "for Glory," should induce more sympathy in the audience, not
less. From both of these defensive charges, we can see how Behn felt
herself to be on the periphery of the system. As a woman, a working
playwright, and a patronless writer, she was especially susceptible to
the vagaries of audience taste.

Furthermore, Behn, like Dryden, Shadwell, Lee, Otway, and other
professional playwrights, found herself in the uneasy position of
competing with aristocrats and "gentlemen writers" who could not
decide themselves whether to play at patronage or letters. Just as we
hear an edge to her voice when she declares that she "is forced to write
for Bread and not ashamed to owne it . . . though it is a way too
cheap for men of wit to pursue who write for Glory," we also hear a
similar edge to Dryden's elegant compliment to John Wilmot, the
Earl of Rochester, in the dedication to *Marriage A-la-Mode:*

> for my own part, I must confess, that I have so much of self-
> interest, as to be content with reading some Papers of your
> Verses, without desiring you should proceed to a Scene or Play:
> with the common prudence of those, who are worsted in a Duel,
> and declare they are satisfied when they are first wounded. Your
> Lordship has but another step to make, and from the Patron of
> Wit, you may become its Tyrant: and Oppress our little Reputa-
> tions with more ease than you now protect them. (1978,
> 11:223–24)

For this generation of writers, caught between a regressive system of
patronage and an emergent marketplace of print at the close of the
seventeenth century, the relationship of dramatist to patron was difficult indeed. Was the patron to be implored, emulated, or surpassed?

Little wonder that when Behn finally does prefix a dedication to a
play in 1679, some nine years after her debut, it displays nothing of
the usual tropes. If anything, both the dedication to *The Young King*
and to *The Feign'd Curtezans* display Bakhtin's sense of the "carnivalesque." Behn undercuts the propriety and decorum of the artist-
patron social contract with a sly sense of humor. The dedication to
The Young King addresses one "Philaster" (perhaps a pastoral
pseudonym for her lover of that period, John Hoyle, a student at

Gray's Inn) from "Astera," a *nom de plume* Behn often used in her poetry. That she would address a lover in a dedication is notable in itself; she goes on to make that private relationship the very stuff of the dedication. The play which she bequeathes into the hands of her lover is a shy virgin who, because "she knew she cou'd not appear on the too-critical English stage without making choice of some Noble Personage, she waited long, look'd round the judging world, and fix't on you" (*Workes* 2:105). By recasting the obligation between dramatist and patron in sexual terms, the speaker subverts the legitimacy of that relationship. The conceit of being lovers both familiarizes and equalizes the footing between "Philaster" and "Astera": one cannot be a faithful client *and* a teasingly independent lover simultaneously. Not only does the speaker's intimate tone undercut the formality demanded by the rhetoric of the dedication, but that private, knowing voice also questions the very characterization of her play as a virgin in need of male protection. The sexual innuendo diminishes the play's virginal status, just as the familiar address to the patron reduces his distanced authority in suggesting that this virgin-token will also be "enjoyed" by the patron. So much for aristocratic—and artistic—distance.

Even more parodic and carnivalesque in tone is Behn's dedication to *The Feign'd Curtezans*, also produced that year. Whereas the first dedication spoofs an eyelash-fluttering femininity to undermine the patriarchal dominance encoded within the patron/client relationship, this piece parodies Cavalier courtliness to subvert the political authority also inscribed within patron/client relations. She dedicates the play to "Mrs. Ellen Guin" from "A. Behn"—no hint of the speaker's female identity here—and the mock-formality of the address smacks of a cavalier saluting his idealized "lady." Behn reinforces the speaker's supposed masculine identity by differentiating herself from Gwyn via the use of pronouns: "for besides Madam, all the Charms and attractions and powers of your Sex, you have Beauties peculiar to yourself," or " 'Tis this that ought to make your Sex vain enough to despise the malicious world that will allow a woman no wit," or "But how much in vain Madam, I endeavor to tell you the sense of all mankinds with mine" (*Works* 2: 305–6). If the exaggerated language is not cause enough for humor, the notoriety of Gwyn's public persona makes the servility of the compliment ludicrous (Maus 1979, 599–600). The lady addressed here is a delicate flower, not the king's "protestant whore" of popular fame, yet the speaker makes his/her "Sacrifice with infinite fear and trembling, well knowing that so Excellent and perfect a Creature as your self differs only from the Divine Powers in this." She has "the pattent from heaven to ingross all hearts" and the smug knowledge of "those that have the blessing of being wounded by your Eyes." The marked disparity between Gwyn's public persona and the ethereal creature hovering in these lines mocks the speaker's courtly pretense to Platonic love. Moreover, the levelling effect of the humor here derives from the implied analogy between the client's praise of the patron and the cavalier's praise of his lady. In both instances the "fit" between panegyrical language and the object of the discourse is askew. Literary clients, like Platonic lovers, should not appear self-interested, if the praise is to have any validity. By writing a dedication to Nell Gwyn, the rowdiest and best known of the king's mistresses, Behn discloses the exchange value (rather than the agapic value) at the heart of both transactions. Praise substitutes for currency, earning, on the one level, sex from the king's mistress, and, on the other, preferment from the patron. By 1679 the two women had known each other for some time; Gwyn had attended Behn's plays from at least 1676 on. How fitting that two outsiders, a woman playwright and a forthright prostitute, should parody that most sacrosanct of relationships between the cavalier and his lady, and in so doing make a mockery of the obeisance customarily shown to patronal authority.

These two dedications raise an interesting question as to why Behn would even bother with mocking the patronage system. By 1679 she had become one of the mainstays of the Duke's company; the following year the court requested performances of at least two of her plays. Obviously, she had succeeded without the help of a patron. Two possible explanations for Behn's disdainful attitude exist. Perhaps as an outsider who had finally achieved success on her own terms, Behn wanted to flaunt the conventional symbols of status. Certainly, having a patron and displaying that support publicly in a dedication serves as cultural validation, especially when the mere presence of the peerage helps to constitute the aesthetic status of the literary artifact, as I have argued earlier. By mocking that relationship in *outré* dedications, Behn both denies the social contract between patron and client, and declares her own independence from it—sort of. It is rather like the rock star who buys a Rolls-Royce and then paints it fluorescent green. In both instances, the Menippean terms of the respective discourses call into question the satiric intent. Although Behn's parody seeks to repudiate its own role in the representation of dedication, ultimately it remains incapable of detaching itself, a strategy typical of the ambivalent structure of carnival (Kristeva 1986, 50). Behn's liminal status within the Restoration theater, that sense of briefly occupying an independent space between the ordered worlds of aristocratic patronage and professional letters, permits her to stand aside in these dedications and flout the conventions of the *ancient régime*. Since the dedication functions as one of the "arenas" in which patronage is transformed into a powerful cultural metaphor, it becomes a fitting vehicle for Behn's sense of burlesque (Turner 1974, 15, 17). But as her subsequent career reveals, she was incapable of living permanently in that liminal state.

I V

Despite her indifferent treatment by the court, Behn was and always had been a committed Tory playwright; even her early plays contain insulting caricatures of Puritans and other "city" figures. But after the command performances at court in 1680 of *The Rover* (11 February) and *The Feign'd Curtezans* (6 May), Behn began writing overtly political comedies. Even more revealing of her political allegiances are the true-blue Tory dedications that accompany the plays. From the time of *The Rover*, Part II, a play which she claims to have written at the behest of the Duke of York, to her last plays in 1678, Behn vows party fealty and asserts the political tenets of an absolute monarchy. Unlike her earlier epistles to the reader, or her mock dedications, these heartfelt pledges remain notably silent on questions of gender, audience taste, or the uneasy relationship between the dramatist and patron. Nor are they at all funny or self-consciously critical. Behn salutes her newly acquired roster of patrons—the Duke of York, the Earl of Arundel, the Earl of Rochester—in the most humorless and sanctimonious of tones.

Perhaps given the political crises in the aftermath of the Popish Plot and the Exclusion Crisis, we should not be surprised that Behn, a Tory from her early years, joined in the fray. Certainly, many other

dramatists did (Canfield 1985). What surprises in reading these dedications is the overwhelming sense of relief in the authorial voice.
Behn does more here than pledge party loyalty; she willingly loses all
sense of a critical, liminal self. Behn's distinctively feisty, often bawdy
voice becomes transformed here into the generic voice of the pane-
gyric. And although the recent memory of the Cromwellian Revolution rendered paradoxical any claim to the timelessness and verity of
royalism, Behn proceeds to do just that in dedication after dedication
(Jose 1984, 24–30). In all four pieces she associates the virtues of
patronage with the ahistoricity of the royalist cause. Power in part
derives from the very timelessness of the patron; since he is outside of
time and flux, his virtues (like those of royalism) are especially
valued in legitimating the dramatic artifact. The patron's gaze,
objective and universal, by extension transforms the play he beholds.
Thus, the Earl of Rochester remains "by your generous Candor, your
unbyast Justice, your Sweetness, Affability, and Condescending
Goodness . . . above the Envy which reigns in Courts" (*Works*
3:183–84). The Earl of Arundel, despite "these troublesome times,
this Age of Lying, Preaching, and Swearing," shows with "what
Loyalty and Conduct you have evaded the Snare" (*Works* 2:199–200).
The Duke of Grafton displays "such power . . . to calm the soul,
and will in spight of You plead for me to the disaffected" (*Works*
1:337–40).

A political melee like the Popish Plot or the Exclusion Crisis not
only constituted a legitimate rhetorical situation for patronage, with
all of the accompanying tropes, but it also provided the dramatist
with very practical reasons for rehearsing that relationship in print.
Because patronage was so intimately associated with the court and
royalist politics during this time, a public show of strength by a
patron could save a dramatist from allegations of political subver-
sion. On the surface, then, it could be said that Behn wrote straight-
forward, patriotic dedications because the politics of the times
confirmed the form. She really did need the protection of the royalist
faction in the playhouse, as she testifies in the dedication to *The
Roundheads:* "This Play . . . was carried in the House *nemine
contra dicente,* by the Royal Party, and under your Grace's illustrious
Patronage is safe from any new Seditious affronts abroad" (*Works*
1:337). But her political enthusiasms become so extreme—she is
imprisoned briefly in August 1682 for an epilogue against Mon-

mouth—as to invite further inquiry, especially given her prior ill treatment by the court in the late 1660s (Mendelson 1987, 151).

There have been recent attempts to claim Aphra Behn as a proto-feminist writer, or to question her political allegiances, since the absolutist male hierarchy implied by royalist ideology ill accords with incipient feminist sensibilities.[3] But even this account should make apparent the necessity for factoring in such variables as class and culture in any consideration of gender. Above all else, patronage, by definition, is a male metaphor: the patron functions as a figural father to the artist/client. That Behn herself understood how, as a self-represented woman, she did not fit this royalist/patronal/male dynamic is all too clear in her send-up dedications to her lover, John Hoyle, and to Nell Gwyn; revealingly, once she secures patronage from the court, she adopts the voice of the grateful male playwright. Maybe a familiar cultural script like royalism, however dislocated it was on the verge of becoming, provided just the necessary camouflage for the only prolific female dramatist writing for the Restoration stage.

Perhaps, too, there is a parable here for feminist critics eager to reclaim their foremothers from the detritus of a masculinist history. When examining a life such as Behn's, it is all too easy to overlook the ease—the very eagerness—with which she embraces patriarchal, royalist ideology. Two important events converged for Behn in 1680: court patronage and political crisis, both of which permitted her to lay aside the issue of her sex once and for all in prefatory writings. Nor was the search for a means of self-representation as a dramatist singular to the second half of Behn's career. Catherine Gallagher has recently argued on the basis of Behn's first prologue that she adopted the guise of the "playwright as whore," a gender-specific version of Locke and Hobbes's theory of possessive individualism:

> a woman who, like Aphra Behn, embraced possessive individualism, even if she were single and never bartered her sexual favors, could only do so with a consciousness that she thus contradicted the notion of female identity on which legitimate property relations rested. Publication, then, quite apart from the contents of what was published, ipso facto implied the divided, doubled, and ultimately unavailable person whose female prototype was the prostitute. By flaunting her self-sale,

Aphra Behn embraced the title of whore; by writing bawdy comedies, which she then partly disclaimed, she capitalized on her supposed handicap. (1988, 29)

Gallagher, however, fails to note that once Behn secured patronage and renown, she quickly abandoned this role, thus suggesting that the complex intersection of patronal support, professional identity, and male camaraderie that comprised the Restoration theater afforded her an opportunity for self-fashioning that in some senses seemed more authentic, more "real" than this self-abnegating pose. After all, the role of "playwright as whore" posits a representation in which the real self must remain unavailable and ultimately un-knowable—a series of endlessly multiple exchanges. By contrast, the representation of a known entity, the male playwright, must have seemed an overwhelming psychological relief. Additionally, as a professional dramatist, Behn could only constitute herself through available cultural discourses, and patronage, above all else, enabled the Restoration writer's paradoxical sense of him/herself as being *both* a working professional and a patronized aesthete. One could not secure patronage, as we have seen with Behn's own career, without first being made legitimate by the marketplace; on the other hand, marketplace legitimation alone was insufficient. One's sense of superiority over the marketplace (the mere rabble) was also vali-dated by the patron's superior taste.

In sketching out Behn's relationship within the larger reaches of the dramatic marketplace, I have attempted to suggest both the mate-rial and cultural reasons for her adoption of the male playwright's voice in the prefatory and dedicatory writings produced during the second half of her career. Perhaps instead of attempting to recuperate Behn as a proto-feminist, we should be examining more closely the construction of gender in cultures that do not offer women means of artistic self-representation outside of patriarchal models. It should not surprise us that the only words available to a seventeenth-century woman such as Behn to describe her writerly self were "my Mascu-line Part the Poet in me" (*Works* 3:187). For the century prior to the bourgeois upheavals that were to traverse Europe (and their concom-itant discussion of "rights," including women's rights), any consid-eration of female artistic self-fashioning will necessarily be contingent upon patriarchal cultural metaphors. For Aphra Behn, patronage

functioned not only as a means toward professional and aesthetic validation, but also as a means toward a represented self.

Notes

1. Of Behn's precarious finances, Sara Heller Mendelson notes: "An habitue of all
   the town amusements, Aphra was not the saving sort. Her tendencies to extravagance were an expression of generosity toward her friends rather than self-
   indulgence." See *The Mental World of Stuart Women: Three Studies* (Amherst:
   Univ. of Massachusetts Press, 1987), 152.
2. Aphra Behn, *Works,* ed. Montague Summers, 6 vols (London: W. Heinemann,
   1915; reprint, New York: Benjamin Blom, 1967), I:223–24. Hereafter cited
   parenthetically as *Works.*
3. See, for instance, Angeline Goreau's attempt to explain away Behn's Tory
   politics by attributing to her a secret longing for a pastoral, depoliticized utopia
   whereby women and men could enjoy each other freely. More recently, Cheri
   Davis Langdell has recuperated Behn as a 1970s feminist by asserting that her
   "very writing and her attitude toward it are acts of sexual politics. . . . If in Kate
   Millett's conception of sexual politics the term implies male domination of
   women in their sexual roles, in feminist and female writers of the Restoration
   sexual politics is the use of power by women to achieve whatever she wants and
   freely chooses." See "Aphra Behn and Sexual Politics: A Dramatists' Discourse
   with her Audience," in *Drama, Sex and Politics,* ed. James Redmond (Cambridge: Cambridge Univ. Press, 1985), 113. For a good refutation of such cul-
   turally and historically naive positions, see the introduction to Sara Heller
   Mendelson's study, *The Mental World of Stuart Women: Three Studies.*

Works Cited

Behn, Aphra. Autograph letter dated 1 August 1685. Folger Shakespeare Library.
    Folger MS c.c.1 (4).
Belanger, Terry. 1982. "Publishers and Wtiters in Eighteenth-Century England." In
    Books and Their Readers in Eighteenth-Century England. Ed. Isabel Rivers.
    Leicester: Leicester Univ. Press.
Canfield, J. Douglas. 1985. "Royalism's Last Dramatic Stand: English Political
    Tragedy, 1679–89." *SP* 82:234–63.
Dryden, John. *Marriage A-la-Mode.* In *Works.* 1956–. Ed. Edward Niles Hooker and
    H.T. Swedenberg, Jr. Berkeley: Univ. of California Press.
Foss, Michael. 1971. *The Age of Patronage: The Arts in England 1660–1750.* Ithaca:
    Cornell Univ. Press.
Gallagher, Catherine. "Who was that masked woman? The prostitute and the play-
    wright in the comedies of Aphra Behn." In *Last Laughs: Perspectives on
    Women and Comedy.* 1988. Ed. Regina Barreca. New York: Gordon and Breach.

Goreau, Angeline. 1980. *Reconstructing Aphra: A Social Biography of Aphra Behn.* New York: Dial Press.

Jose, Nicholas. 1984. *Ideas of the Restoration in English Literature, 1660–71.* Cambridge: Harvard Univ. Press.

Kenny, Shirley Strum. "The Publication of Plays." In *The London Theatre World 1660–1800.* 1980. Ed. Robert D. Hume. Carbondale: Southern Illinois Univ. Press.

Korshin, Paul J. 1970–71. "Johnson and Literary Patronage: A Comment on Jacob Leed's Article." *Studies in Burke and His Time* 12:1804–11.

Korshin, Paul J. 1973–74. "Types of Eighteenth-Century Literary Patronage," *ECS* 7:453–73.

Kristeva, Julia. 1986. *The Kristeva Reader.* Ed. Toril Moi. New York: Columbia Univ. Press.

Lynch, Kathleen M. 1971. *Jacob Tonson, Kit-Cat Publisher.* Knoxville: Univ. of Tennessee Press.

Maus, Katharine Eisaman. 1979. " 'Playhouse Flesh and Blood': Sexual Ideology and the Restoration Actress." *ELH* 46:595–617.

Milhous, Judith and Robert D. Hume. 1974. "Dating Play Premieres from Publication Data, 1660–1700." *Harvard Library Bulletin* 22:374–405.

Papali, G.F. 1968. *Jacob Tonson, Publisher. His Life and Work (1656–1736).* New Zealand: Tonson Publishing House.

Pepys, Samuel. *Diary.* 1970–1983. Ed. Robert Latham and William Matthews. 11 vols. Berkeley: Univ. of California Press.

Pickel, Margaret B. 1936. *Charles I as Patron of Poetry and Drama.* London: Frederick Muller, Ltd.

Porter, Roy. 1982. *English Society in the Eighteenth Century.* Harmondsworth: Penguin.

Roberts, William. 1967. *The Earlier History of English Bookselling.* London, 1889; reprint, Detroit: Gale Research Co.

Tennenhouse, Leonard. 1981. "Sir Walter Raleigh and the Literature of Clientage." In *Patronage in the Renaissance.* Ed. Guy Fitch Lytle and Stephen Orgel. Princeton: Princeton Univ. Press.

Turner, Victor. 1974. *Dramas, Fields and Metaphors: Symbolic Action in Human Society.* Ithaca: Cornell Univ. Press.

"Depressa Resurgam":
Elizabeth Griffith's Playwriting Career

BETTY RIZZO

The gentle FRANCES next put in her claim,
The court found some to praise, and some to blame;
In the dramatic walk, they cou'd not see
The faintest sketch of genuine comedy;
Her sentimental muse can naught display,
But moral lessons, thro' a sleepy play;
Did she but know how hard 'tis to excel
In drawing characters—and writing well,
Her muse wou'd quit the hazard of the stage,
And keep to works which every heart engage.
—William Heard, *The Tryal of Dramatic Genius*, 1773

Elizabeth Griffith's position as a successful eighteenth-century playwright must be granted. In a century when dozens of plays were written for every one mounted, five of her plays were produced at the two London patent theaters between 1765 and 1779. Set the splendid careers of Aphra Behn, Delariviére Manley, Mary Pix, and Catherine Trotter, all of which commenced before 1700, aside, and Griffith's record, compared to those of her peers, is impressive; as produced playwrights only three women outdid her: Susannah Centlivre, who also wrote in that early golden period for women dramatists (sixteen plays), Elizabeth Inchbald (eleven), and Griffith's friend, Hannah Cowley (ten).[1]

Apart from Centlivre, Griffith, Inchbald, and the four brilliant women whose careers began before 1700, thirteen women during the century wrote one full-length play produced at a major London theatre.[2] Six wrote two each: Frances Brooke, Elizabeth Cooper,

Sophia Lee, Charlotte Lennox, Hannah More, and Frances Sheridan. Eliza Haywood had three plays produced. Thus Griffith, with her five productions (two hits, two disappointments, one disaster) is fourth in rank in terms of number of produced plays. Of these four she may well have had the greatest writing skill and drive but the least talent for crafting a play. She was an adept learner, though, and shaped each new play to correct the defects attacked in the preceding one. An analysis of her successes, which rested rather more upon her persistence, her adaptability, and her use of her "weakness" to manipulate men than upon her fine writing capabilities, reveals much about the forces that shaped the writing careers of women by rewarding excursions in some directions but not in others. Griffith's playwriting career differed from the careers of men in two ways. She had to give up her own point of view to adopt that of males, i.e., had to put aside the themes and attitudes and emphases she found natural; and she had to exploit her real helplessness to render male assistance obligatory. Both tactics were costly and degrading to her; but the second was a guerilla tactic in a war she recognized.

Getting one's plays profitably produced in the third quarter of the eighteenth century was no easier matter than it is today. There were only two patent theaters, Drury Lane and Covent Garden. Because of the expense, labor, and risk involved in mounting new productions, the managers of both usually took no more than two or three new full-length plays each season, and previously successful playwrights of course had preference. Such playwrights—Bickerstaff, Colman, Murphy—knew both the art of writing plays and that of cosseting managers. An author, it was generally believed, must appease both Garrick's vanity (by flattery) and his cupidity (by allowing him to edit one's manuscript for a fee) before his play could be accepted. Griffith flattered Garrick shamelessly, acknowledged his collaboration in her plays more than once in writing, and also both played defenseless and, when she could, heaped guilt upon him for having failed in chivalry. It became more dangerous to him to fail or criticize her than to aid her. This final twist, which involved Griffith's charging Garrick more than once with kicking her when she was down, was her own invention.

Griffith was not a born playwright. Though her produced plays were comedies, she was no wit; jests are infrequent in her work, and the comedy characters she interpolated for laughs were borrowed

from other playwrights. She was in all her work as in her life a proponent of the sentimental, of fine feeling. Luckily for her, sentimental
comedy was in vogue during her playwriting career, but she was still
indicted often enough for failing to evoke laughter. As an actress she
had been more successful in tragedy and probably preferred to write
it, but no tragedy of hers (she wrote at least two) was produced. In her
novels, written during the period from 1769 to 1776 after she had
learned that the public liked works in which women were passive
and masochistic, she excelled at placing a refined woman in an
extended, miserable situation and at displaying the subtle, elevated,
exquisite permutations of her responses.

But she was the daughter of Thomas Griffith (1680?–1744), in his
day Ireland's most popular comic actor and a Dublin theater manager, and if she never grasped how to control the structure of a play,
she was always at home in a theater. Her father died when she was
sixteen, leaving his wife and daughter slenderly provided for. Her
careful education in the reading, writing, and speaking of verse, in
graceful movement and the expression of fine sentiment in English
and in French, fitted her for a rich man's wife—a hard position to get
without a dowry—or an actress. From 1749 to 1751 Griffith played
leading roles in Dublin's Smock-Alley Theatre under Thomas
Sheridan (including Juliet to his aging Romeo) and from 1753 to
1755, spoiled for London by Sheridan's stilted, overwrought style of
acting, she played secondary roles at Covent Garden. She had every
opportunity to learn stagecraft and yet her plays tend to be structured
like novels, long narratives without sufficient strong and consistent
conflict that resolves itself climactically through significant action.
Her plotting is timid. As if the play itself is a house to be built and the
characters and language are its occupants and their lives, she excelled
at the latter and wanted the former provided for her, either through a
model that she adopted or translated or through male advice. She
failed herself to seize control of her dramatic structure, and her forte
was the transference to the stage of pathetic situations expressed in
affecting language.

As Griffith wrote for the stage, she simultaneously wrote in many
other forms, translating works from the French, producing three
novels and many novellas, editing, contributing to magazines,
writing criticism and moral advice to women. Considering her frag-
ile health and delicate nerves, her weak eyes, which often failed her

entirely, and her domestic cares, her output is incredible. But the reason she persisted in writing for the stage is that if all went well, the theater paid best. A novel might sell for anything from £5 to one or two hundred, but the playwright, if the play ran, got the house proceeds (expenses deducted) for the third, sixth, and ninth performances. The copyright for a produced play sold for £100. Lucky playwrights had profited from a single play by as much as £700—or $70,000, perhaps, in today's currency. Griffith therefore never ceased struggling to get her plays produced because the prize was so considerable.

Elizabeth Griffith was diminutive, lively, charming, and attractive rather than beautiful: very appealing to men, though in compensating for her Irishness by careful fine manners and diction, she was later in life sometimes thought to be affected. In 1746, while still in Ireland, she had the ill luck to meet Richard Griffith (1716?–88), in his own words an "honorable libertine," meaning that he was honorable in all respects except to women, whom, however, he treated with all possible indulgence and delicacy. He was handsome and charming, high-born but poor, the son of a military man whose only legacy to his son was the suggestion that he had better do as his father did, marry (if only to waste) a fortune. Though ill-educated, Griffith was intelligent, well-read, had literary pretensions, and was a great maker and binder of useful acquaintance. His earliest object was to make Elizabeth his mistress. Like Scheherazade she extricated herself from this danger through a long series of fascinating letters, and he became so addicted to his successful response to the challenge of answering them appropriately that the lovers fell in love with their own correspondence, married one another, and published it.

During their courtship the two worked out an unusual system that made possible the perpetuation of both the letters and the nobility of their authors: he should always treat her as an equal, never allowing her to dwindle into a wife, and would behave to her forever with that courtesy and politeness with which she would behave to him. Warmed by such encouragement, Elizabeth Griffith was often very candid, and on her lover's remarking that he respected her as a male friend, she revealed the guidelines she would use with Garrick:

It is the charter of our sex, to be fools; and the numberless weak-
nessess, which intitle us to your regard and protection, create a

Elizabeth Griffith. Harvard Theatre Collection.

peculiar kind of affection, which it is natural for us to feel for creatures in our power. But should we once disclaim that *powerful* weakness, which renders us alike objects of love and pity, we are no longer intitled to that indulgence and partiality, which the wisest of us want, and the simplest have a claim to. Let me therefore intreat my dearest Harry, to look on my friendship for him as truly masculine; but let my understanding still claim all the privileges of the feminine gender. (Griffith 1757, 1:177)

The Griffiths published the first two volumes of *A Series of Genuine Letters between Henry and Frances* in 1757, the second two in 1767, and the final two in 1770. Known familiarly as Henry and Frances, they were from 1757 revered for their delicate, refined, elevated sentiments and behavior; besides money and fame their letters procured them powerful friends, some preferment, and publishers for subsequent works. But after the failure of his one great project, a linen manufactory, in the early 1750s, Richard Griffith never did much more than eke out a subsistence as political manager in Ireland for such friends as Henry Flood and Lord Charlemont. He wrote, edited, and managed his wife's productions. It was Elizabeth Griffith who decided in 1764, when she had two finished plays and he a finished novel, to move to London. Her establishment there and Richard Griffith's extended stays in Ireland helped to perpetuate both their correspondence and their politeness for some years longer.

Because she had been poor and dowerless, Elizabeth Griffith always felt responsible for the deprivations her family suffered, and in order to repair them she labored far beyond what seemed to be the limits of her physical and mental strength. Her husband's withdrawal to Ireland, where he leaned upon his friends instead of supporting her, and the talents and helplessness of her two children, Richard (born c. 1752) and Kitty (born c. 1756), made her an author and above all a playwright, and made her literally ruthless in her pursuit of theatrical success.

There were undoubtedly even earlier efforts, but her first acknowledged play was *Amana* (1764), a blank verse tragedy adapted from *Adventurer* papers 72–73. The tale of a beautiful Egyptian middle-class maiden who loves the merchant Nouradin and when chosen for the Sultan's seraglio prefers death to dishonor, it had its precursors in such romances as *Oroonoko* and *Aureng-Zebe*. Never produced, and published by subscription, the tragedy exhibits the virtues and faults of Griffith's subsequent work. Exalted sentiments and fine expression are supported by barely adequate verse; the action moves evenly like a narrative in dialogue. But in this early play Griffith makes the heroine's point of view the primary one. Amana is first on stage and interprets the action, inviting us to empathize almost entirely with her. Her lover Nouradin is a merchant, not a great military hero, and cannot signify as do Oroonoko and Aureng-Zebe. Puzzled and disoriented male readers may have found compensation in the standard sadistic treatment Amana suffers, but then she makes disconcerting remarks (honestly though they reflected Griffith's own strategies):

> She who would please proud man, must not disdain
> The lowest methods to attain her purpose:
> Humility's the garb in which their sex
> The most delight to see us dressed—By this
> Their vain superiority is shewn,
> And our dependent state upon their wills.

This is insulting to males; Griffith had much to learn about popular opinion on the subject of women's place before her plays could be successfully produced. She was to learn, though not immediately, that she could not both succeed as a playwright and support the improved status of women.

Those who rejected *Amana* for production probably suggested to Griffith that she try her hand at comedy. Her next play, *The Platonic Wife*, produced at Drury Lane in January 1765, was adapted from Marmontel's sentimental story "L'Heureux Divorce"; in her heroine Griffith seems to have combined the idealized Frances of the *Genuine Letters* with the resourceful Restoration female wit. Neither of these models, as it transpired, was calculated to please the theater-goer of 1765.

Marmontel's tale is of a young girl fresh from the convent and married by arrangement to a considerate husband who wishes first to gain her friendship while she yearns for passionate romance. Their mutual dissatisfaction leads to a separation during which three lovers fail to breach her virtue. In the end she recognizes her husband's superiority and tells him so through the refined expedient of having the portrait of herself, which he has kept, retouched to show on its features her misery and repentance. Husband and wife, re-united, are happy because she has learned to appreciate his character and, her virtue tested, he can safely trust and esteem her.

In Griffith's play what the heroine, Lady Frankland, wants is what Richard Griffith promised in the *Genuine Letters*—continued courtship after marriage, consideration, tenderness, discreet flattery of the wife. Here as in *Amana* Griffith, still riding high on the public adulation of Frances, thought she could propagandize for a better treatment of wives. What Griffith failed to see was that in the *Genuine Letters* Frances, though independent-minded, was always gratifyingly checked, overseen, and overridden by the paternal Henry, while in her play the heroine in charge leaves her husband and returns at will, is always independent, entertaining the proposi-tions of three other men, does just as she likes, and in the end converts her husband to her own point of view. Frankland begins, like any proper English husband, by finding his wife's pretensions ridicu-lous, but in the end recognizes her virtue, falls in love with her, and promises her all the sentimental admiration she craves. Griffith's implicit scheme, then, is that a wife should trade her devotion and sexual fidelity for her husband's love and admiration rather than for the usual return of nothing but lodging and board.

While Lady Frankland's capitulation might have made the play tolerable, her husband's rendered it insufferable. And though Lady Frankland promises at the play's end to obey her reformed husband, likening her former independent self to an unguided skiff in need of a pilot, Griffith also let herself go in speeches like Lady Fanshaw's "Next to the felicity of widowhood is that of being separated. How-ever, there are, my dear, some material differences: While the tyrant lives to whom we have been bound, we never can forget we have been slaves."

The play was therefore condemned for other reasons than for its structure, which one reviewer thought was better fitted for a narra-tive.[3] Tom Davies later claimed that a cabal was got up against the play in advance, that in the unusual disturbance that greeted it, the popular actors Holland and Powell, unused to catcalls and hisses (and feminist doctrine), put their heads out from behind the curtain and begged the town to curtail their mortifications that very night by closing down the play (Davies 1802,2:2). Griffith had given up the cause for lost, but a brilliant rendition of the epilogue by her great friend Mrs. Clive procured the play another trial. Murphy, a rival playwright, noted that the actors labored through hisses and groans for six performances, until Griffith had obtained her second benefit night, before they laid down their arms, apparently suggesting that the lady playwright had received special consideration (Murphy 1801,2:10–11). One review refused to condemn work by a lady, but another called the play the "unfortunate production of a female pen," and suggested that now all deficiencies of plot, character, sentiment, language, and moral should be forgotten. A third review found Griffith a mistress of sensibility and agreeable dialogue but deficient in knowledge of stagecraft; a fourth thought it would have been indelicate had *any* woman been a skilled playwright but also found her frequent use of French phrases affected.[4]

These reviews were devastating to a playwright suffering from chronic depression during which she could not face visitors. But she did well on the play; depending on the value and number of the benefit tickets her friends took, she could have realized £300 on her two nights in addition to the copyright of £100.[5] Despite the problem —damned if she didn't master dramatic structure and stagecraft, damned if she did—she determined to go on as a playwright.

Griffith now released the publication of *Amana* to bookshops and the critics. Subsequent efforts at playwriting demonstrate that she studied her reviews closely. She could do nothing in response to the refusal to criticize a lady's efforts, or to the conclusion that she suffered from that disease of fine ladies, the vapors, and that her play's most valuable pages were those listing its elegant subscribers, but she could learn from a repeated charge that she borrowed too much from the French, in the knowledge of which ladies "are apt to boast themselves with a kind of female pedantry."[6] In future Griffith no longer used French expressions to indicate the refinement of the speaker, reserving them instead to indicate pretentiousness.

She was already at work on a new comedy, *The Double Mistake*, produced at Covent Garden on 9 January 1766. Once again she used old friends to good purpose; *The Platonic Wife* had been taken at Drury Lane while Garrick was away in France, probably through the good offices of her old friend the playhouse treasurer, Benjamin Victor. *The Double Mistake* was probably urged at Covent Garden by her friend Thomas Hull, an acting and playwriting bulwark of that company. This time Griffith built on a previous play and rather disingenuously did not say so, and the *Critical* reviewer pointed out her peccadillo (common enough at the time) with some satisfaction.[7] If Griffith's title was not a subtle apology for her sins of the past (and it probably was), her plot now made open amends. *The Double Mistake* has two heroines. The sensible one, slandered and maligned, loses her lover because her character has been wrongly assassinated. She remains passive and long-suffering, contrives no expedients to vindicate herself, and is finally saved only by the unravelling of the subplot. The silly heroine, a romantic girl who prefers amusement to sober occupation and fops to worthy young men—and who indulges in French expressions—is barely saved, again by the plot rather than by the sensible heroine, from eloping with a fortune hunter. The exemplary girl takes no initiative even to avoid ruin, and the initiative of the nonexemplary girl is shown to be potentially disastrous. Griffith for good measure added two very derivative humors characters to the play, a virtuoso and a lady pedant, the second as ridiculous as any character Fielding could have rendered. For good measure the exemplary heroine prefers "working" with her needle to reading, writing, or the acquisition of languages, while the silly heroine has tastes precisely opposite.

Having done what she could to placate male critics, even to the adoption of a male's structure for her play, Griffith did not rest, but continued to bestir herself. The Griffiths this time guarded against adverse factions by making up supporting parties of their own.[8] Their friends pushed benefit tickets; Gibbon had to take one. (Norton 1956,1:202). And so the play succeeded, running thirteen nights in January and ceasing then only so that the theater could "vary the Entertainments." There was a performance on 17 February by royal command. Griffith had at last—at what a considerable cost only she herself could have known—achieved a popular and financial success. On 10 January the play was published with the author's motto on the title page, "Depressa resurgam." She must have realized at least £500 from the play and she knew exactly what the public wanted; further, she would use these unhappy insights to advantage in her novels.

The reviews were in general complimentary, except for the *Critical Review*, which deemed her alterations an injury to the original, and the *Monthly*, which found the work without novelty and hackneyed—but ah! polite in language and moral in purport.[9]

In response, Griffith determined to essay for the first time an original play. She worked with speed, finishing it by 31 May, and then began her prolonged battle with Garrick. That same day she approached him uncharacteristically directly, without the mediation of friends; no intermediary could have reproached him, as she did, for having injured her by having pronounced publicly against her last play. Her opening sally was inspired:

> The favourable reception that the town gave to "The Double Mistake" has encouraged me to essay their indulgence again, by writing another comedy. Notwithstanding your severe censure upon my last, I most earnestly wish to present my instant performance to the public through your hands. If, therefore, Sir, it may be agreeable to you to receive the comedy I mention, it shall be sent to you immediately, upon this condition, that if you should reject it, you will never mention your having seen it to any person. If I should be happy enough to have my comedy received and approved by you, I shall be truly thankful to you for any observations or alterations you may think proper to make.[10]

She has made the points (1) that she has already written a successful play and has earned a reading; (2) that she has heard his aspersions of her play; (3) that he has injured her and owes her reparation; (4) that she is willing to accept his alterations (and presumably to pay his charges) without complaint. Her approach was successful, so successful that Garrick did not free himself from her trap until he had produced for her (at considerable cost to himself) a hit play. He would choose that play, edit her translation, and stage it with every possible advantage.

It is by turns amusing, edifying, and horrifying to follow their subsequent dealings, in which Griffith is almost always in charge. Garrick responded to her first letter that he was sorry she had seen his remarks on her play, assured her that he never abused the confidence of those who gave him plays to read, but told her he already had three if not four mainpieces chosen for the coming season. Griffith replied on 4 June that it would not suit her to wait an entire season for production, but sent Garrick the comedy, assuring him of its complete originality and of the grateful acknowledgment with which she would receive any mending of its faults or heightening of its merits

(*Correspondence* 1:230). In August Garrick sent a devastating rejection. He found the characters unsatisfactory, unnatural, and not in the least comic, the fable exceptionable, the structure of the play unmendable. "It is my Opinion that notwithstanding there are many good things said, the Whole together would not answer your or our wishes, nor answer the Expectations which the Public may have conceiv'd of its Author" (*Letters* 2:532–33). So much for originality!

Garrick never suffered fools gladly, and probably he expected Griffith to take her rebuff and cease to trouble him. But on 17 August she wrote from Weymouth (the cruelty of his rejection perhaps having necessitated a course of seabathing) assuring him that she would persist. No, she would not appeal his sentence, but it would gratify her utmost wish to write a performance approved by him, and she would not yet despair but that this pleasing event might happen. "Let me at least stand justified in attempting to wear the sock, though I may fail to make it fit me: it was not vanity that led me to the trial, but a young family and a small fortune called for the assistance of a fond mother, who would hazard much more than her fame—her life for their service" (*Correspondence* 1:235).

What could he do, though her writings were in every way the antithesis of his own? His capitulation was abject; he abased himself before her. On 23 August he thanked her for her "very polite, generous, and very affecting letter," and assured her he should think himself happy whenever it was in his power to serve her (*Letters* 2:535). She understood that she could never hope to persuade Garrick to produce a play he did not believe in, but that almost certainly he could now be induced to help her write one he would accept.

By 11 September she was writing from her new home in Hyde Street (financed by *The Double Mistake?*) to assure him that she intended in this matter to rely entirely upon his judgment and friendship. The disagreeable situation of her circumstances, she admitted, might tempt her to precipitation, but she would do as he thought best with Diderot's *Le Père de Famille* (1758), which she was translating at his suggestion, or indeed with any of her theatrical productions. She would positively set about finishing the French comedy—just as soon as her physician permitted her once more to wield a pen (*Correspondence* 1:240–41).

Probably in a visit in March 1767 Garrick promised Griffith both his continuing friendship and a production (*Correspondence* 1:288).

But he remained inconveniently uncompromising in professional judgment, and wrote Griffith on 16 June 1767 that he was greatly disappointed in the fable and characters of her first three acts (*Letters* 2:577–78). Her circumstances, Griffith responded, allowed for no delay in production. For the comedy she had neglected other means of earning. If the play must be rewritten, "I am perfectly convinced of the great advantages it would receive from the masterly strokes of your judicious hand: but alas, Sir! my situation will not admit of delay . . . I must therefore entreat you, by the regard you have been so good to profess for me, that you will consent to bring out the 'pere de Famille' this next winter" (*Correspondence* 1:268–69).

Garrick could not be maneuvered into completely rewriting her translation in time for a winter production and never did produce *Le Père de Famille,* though Griffith's persistent labors on it continued to harass him at least through 1771. He kept copies of most of his correspondence, but his more wounding rejections of Griffith are not now on record; perhaps he either carried bad news in person or considered his attempts to discourage her too ungallant for transmission to posterity. Griffith meanwhile labored over a tragedy, finished her first novel, *The Double Distress* (which "profited" from the lessons she had learned about woman's role), and struggled on with Diderot's play. On 14 March 1768, she reminds Garrick that a year has passed since he promised his friendship and help in producing a play. But the two (unidentified) French plays he has sent her she thinks unfit for the English stage, and although *Le Père de Famille* needs much alteration, she still believes it the firmest prospect and begs him once again to look it over and suggest both deficiencies and improvements. He has mentioned Beaumarchais's recent play *Eugénie* (1767) to her; if he has it, will he send it to her? (*Correspondence* 1:288).

Then with *Eugénie* all went well and swiftly. Griffith wrote to Garrick on 14 May that she intended to proceed without guidance right to the end and submit to him the whole by July. Then she took herself off to lodgings at Windsor to work (*Correspondence* 1:299–300). She was in luck all round that summer. At Windsor she met John Manship, a director of the East India Company, susceptible enough to present her son Richard—a very likely boy—with the post of writer (or clerk) for the company in India, a post worth £1,500 on the market. Joyfully Griffith wrote on. Her great problem lay in

adapting the Spanish customs of the original to her English characters, for she adhered as closely as possible to the original play's structure. On 18 July she had completed a first draft; amendments
followed. A terrifying obstacle developed: on 14 September Griffith
arrived home in London to meet Victor, Garrick's emissary, who
asked her to accept a postponement of production to the 1769–70
season. "Oh! my dear Sir," she wrote, "think what a mortifying disappointment it must be to me to have it now delayed. But were only
my pride at stake, I would readily sacrifice it to your inclination; but,
indeed, Sir, I have better and stronger motives for entreating you to
bring it out this year."[12]

Outfitting a prospective nabob for India was a costly business and
the more assets he took with him to invest in commercial opportunity the better. When Griffith delicately reminded Garrick of his
promise that the play should be produced without delay, he had no
other choice than to produce it. The final revisions were made and
there was great joy in Hyde Street.

Griffith now busied herself about the right title, the right actors,
and the dedication to Garrick.[13] Garrick himself had a request; as
Griffith had so frequently acknowledged to him her obligations for
his providing the subject of the play and his advice, alterations, and
additions to the plot, scenes, language, etc., would she and her husband now write a note repeating their opinion that what he had done
to the play was to its advantage? They could and they did, the indignant playwright begging to be informed who had insinuated anything to the contrary (*Letters* 2:630–31; *Correspondence* 1:322).

The School for Rakes opened on 4 February 1769, with a fine cast,
new scenes, costumes, decorations, and a prologue by Garrick. Mrs.
Clive interrupted her plans for retirement to learn the role of Mrs.
Winifred, the heroine's misguided aunt. The plot was not contrived
to raise the conceit of the ladies. The self-indulgent Sir Eustace,
with the connivance of Harriet's silly aunt, has lured Harriet into a
false marriage. Now, though he adores his supposed wife, he dares
not oppose his father's plan to marry him to an heiress. Harriet and
her aunt arrive in town in pursuit of Sir Eustace at the critical point,
but she is saved only by the complications of the plot, for she does
nothing clever, nor does she display any resourcefulness beyond a
willingness to die. Nor does Sir Eustace reform and claim her; he is
quite as passive as she is. Harriet in the end is dependent for her

disposition on male decisions and takes all the blame upon herself for their selfishness.

But the characters, as Griffith herself acknowledged to Garrick, profited much from his advice (*Correspondence* 1:310) and are the best realized of any in her plays. The structure Beaumarchais provided was secure. The play was an outstanding success. It played unabated for the crucial nine nights and continued to play for seven years. The reviews were many, lengthy, and in general laudatory, though all, in differing ways, took the author's sex into account. The moral (a detestation for gallantry) was generally praised. *The Theatrical Memoirs of the Times* concluded of the epilogue that "a bad commodity, like a negative quantity in algebra, is so much worse than none at all. But . . . how can it be expected that a lady should understand algebra?" (1769, 254–55). *The Court Miscellany* was also equal to dealing with a woman playwright: "Mrs. Griffith, the ingenious writer, is indeed remarkable for that delicacy of expression and softness of stile, which the more masculine of our feminine writers affect to condemn as bordering on quaintness and insipidity" (Feb. 1769, 100).

With Harriot's masochistic sufferings which that heroine dared neither refute nor avenge, Griffith made her final amends for the gallant and independent platonic wife. Her rewards were the profits of three author's nights and the copyright. She may have earned £600. Her dilemma was comic: in order to function as principal family provider she had to exploit men through playing up her own weakness and to exhibit sickly images of dependent women in a condition which she knew to be positively dangerous.

Sadly differing were Garrick's and Griffith's attitudes toward their great success. Garrick felt his obligation to be discharged; he had helped Griffith to launch her son although probably he could more easily have translated *Eugénie* himself. Griffith, on the other hand, purported to believe that now that she had justified Garrick's belief in her, now that their friendship was firmer than ever, they would continue to collaborate in the same profitable way. Each was firm: *he* never again produced one of her plays, and *she* never ceased to beleaguer him.

He avoided her. She wrote a new comedy, badgered him to make up his mind about it, and pushed him into returning it to her (*Cor-*

respondence 1:365-65; *Letters* 2:663-64). He ceased to be in when she called. In June 1770 she appealed to his humane heart:

> When I had first the honour of corresponding with you, I frankly informed you of my motives for writing: your humanity was affected, and you became my friend! Alas! those motives still subsist,—a narrow income, an aged mother, a family to support who have ever lived decently, and debts contracted by providing for a beloved and deserving son! From these painful circumstances it is in your power to relieve me, by saying that you will be kind enough to assist me in bringing on a play, either the next season or the following one. (*Correspondence* 1:386)

Garrick must have remained adamant; a month later George Colman at Covent Garden undertook to produce Griffith's *A Wife in the Right,* the title perhaps a touch of miscalculated hubris. Colman would produce the play—with disastrous results—only in March 1772.

Meanwhile Griffith, before mid-1771, learned from a mutual friend that Garrick had solemnly declared he would never on any condition bring out any piece of hers, adding "many expressions of dislike and disregard" (*Correspondence* 1:534). This time she was afraid to reproach him; she left him alone for two years. But in late 1771 Garrick himself had to write to her because another playwright had begun work on the troublesome *Père de Famille;* it would never have done for him to produce someone else's translation while she might claim she was still translating it for him (*Letters* 2:718-19). And so, on 6 December 1771, she delightedly sent him the play: "If your leisure, Sir, would but permit your considering this work, and pointing out what you think necessary to its improvement, I should have no doubt of its *success*" (*Correspondence* 1:445). She added news of her own ill health and her husband's departure for Ireland but this time Garrick endorsed her note: "I see your tears, and hear your sighs, / Which ever female craft supplies, / To move a hard obdurate block." He was positively on to her, and his rejection must have been definite enough, for she did not broach the subject of this play to him again nor did she approach Garrick until made desperate by Colman.

The title of *The Wife in the Right* may have been calculated to rouse interest, but the plot was entirely safe. The wife's husband has fallen in love, soon after his marriage, with his wife's own virtuous friend and companion; at the same time he has a conniving mistress (for the woman with resource and initiative is now villainous). The friend's own love affair is threatened when it is thought she has fled the house to further her affair with the husband. In the end, without the good women having made one move to save themselves, the mistress's plots are overthrown, the friend vindicated, the husband reclaimed. And the play is once again like a novel told in dialogue.

The play's debacle, however, stemmed from production problems: the popular low comic Ned Shuter was too drunk to learn his lines, to open the play as announced on 5 March 1772, or to remember his part when he finally played it on 9 March; apparently he made it up as he went along. The epilogue was applauded but when the play was announced again, apples were aimed at the chandelier and Colman withdrew the play forever. He subsequently refused Griffith a third night or any compensation whatsoever, and she swore never to deal with him again. Griffith published the play ($£100$) but the reviews concentrated on the details of her misfortune.

Difficult though it must have been for Griffith to approach Garrick again, approach him she did in the spring of 1773 with the draft of a new comedy which he promptly rejected. She used her old ploy; she reproached him for having been *predetermined* never to accept a play of hers again.[14] Garrick fell into her trap by seizing, cleverly, he thought, on her "one expression . . . which cancels every expression of kindness and regard" to justify his refusal. "If I was *predetermined* to refuse your play, I am a very unjust manager and a very dishonest man" (*Letters* 2:870–71).

Now she had him. "It is now above two years since a person . . . informed me . . . he had heard you declare, in the most solemn manner, 'that you would never, on any condition, bring out any piece of mine,' . . . This, Sir, has, for the time mentioned, prevented even my paying my respects to Mrs. Garrick and you; as I would rather submit to the self-denial of not seeing you, than obtrude where I had reason to fear my visits might not be agreeable" (*Correspondence* 2:534).

Garrick had probably sent the heavy message with deliberation, but now he paid for it; for if she were to submit any manuscript to him and he were to refuse it, his refusal *must* seem predetermined. He had never realized that despite the message, she might submit a play again. He must have soothed Griffith, for in 1775 she dedicated her *Morality of Shakespeare's Drama Illustrated* fulsomely to him as a tribute of her friendship and esteem.

And on 30 May 1775—her husband all but nonexistent, her son struggling but still alive in India—she wrote again, with a scheme in mind despite despair at several fruitless dramatic attempts.[15] "If you would be so good as to point out any plan for me to go upon, I should have no doubt of its success. You have read and know everything, and the quickness of your genius can with a single glance discover what is, and what is not, likely to succeed upon the stage. . . . Give but a hint . . . and I will exert my utmost powers . . ."(*Correspondence* 2:56). Garrick perceived the female playwright as a separate species and operated on a quota system. He responded that he was already overloaded with the commodity, having received plays from both Charlotte Lennox and Hannah Cowley (*Letters* 2:1010). Could she not, we can imagine him musing, understand that she had *had* her turn? But, he added, if he were to find a play to be profitably imitated from the French or revived, he would at once let her know.

On 21 August 1777, after Garrick's retirement from the theater, Griffith wrote to say she had two comedies finished, both of them familiar to him, and asked if he could not help her make one fit for representation and then recommend it "as from a nameless author" to Richard Sheridan, Garrick's successor at Drury Lane.[16] Garrick must have taken pity and instead suggested she translate a play by Garrick's protégé, the French actor Anthony Le Texier; and for Le Texier's sake he oversaw the work. "Patience and shuffle the cards, you *fancy*, is my motto," she jests, but adds unhappily that she is able to find neither Garrick nor Sheridan at home (*Correspondence* 2:316).

And here ends what survives of the Garrick-Griffith correspondence. The Le Texier translation came to nothing. But after Garrick's death in 1779 Sheridan did produce Griffith's last play, *The Times,* an adaptation of Goldoni's *Bourru Bienfaisant* (1770). It was Garrick's suggestion, she said in her advertisement to the published play, and had he only lived to afford her that friendly assistance which he had given on former occasions, her comedy would have been more worthy of the reception with which it was honored.

The Times took as its theme the growing extravagance of the upper classes, and depicted the dissolute life of the fashionable Mr. Woodley, reformed in the end by his wife, Lady Mary. Lady Mary put her efforts into a proper channel—social reform; the play pleased, ran for the hoped-for nine performances, and probably earned Griffith at least £300.[17]

Colman was vindictive; in the *Monthly Review* he complained that Griffith had viewed with too much delicacy the frailties of her own sex and was too little acquainted with the irregularities of the other, but at the same time found the rout scene too coarse (March 1780, 245–46). Other reviewers found her morality her strong point—this was what one said about Mrs. Griffith by this time. Fanny Burney, though, thought the play, which she saw in Bath, "very feeble and mawkish,"[18] and in 1796 in *The History of the Theatre of London* the play was reported to be more of a sentimental novel than comedy. So, in regard to her control of the form, Griffith's playwriting career ended as it began.

But now, like one of the happiest strokes in her own comedies, in 1780, just ten years after his departure, her son Richard Griffith reappeared from India not even thirty and a nabob, rich enough to buy an estate in County Kildare, marry two heiresses (serially), establish an important family, sit in the Irish parliament, and adopt his parents in the decline of their years. This must in her own mind have justified all her efforts, and yet. . . .

Griffith knew, as we know, that in her a splendid spokeswoman for women's rights was corrupted. The wonderful platonic wife who demanded equal regard and treatment was replaced in Griffith's work by a model woman perfectly patient beneath the afflictions rained on her by tyrant man and hoping only one day to claim through perfect passivity and virtue what she had never enjoyed, a husband's devotion and esteem. In a period when men still treasured their rakish prerogatives, Griffith was rewarded only when she wrote as keeper of the feminine moral flame. No one listened to (or paid for) the voice that wanted to show how it really was with women. It might be said that her manipulation of Garrick through the wiles that society forced upon women was her revenge. Perhaps. But Griffith's best triumph, as her best revenge, was her knowledge that she herself had never yielded the initiative, never ceased plotting and ploying in the best of Restoration comedy traditions, in order to attain her first objective—the successful establishment of her children. And she did attain it.[19] And she did win many battles. If the dissemination of ideas about the lot of women had been her primary purpose, she would have found ways to win that struggle too, but she couldn't have won both. Garrick might have complained that her aggressive behavior differed from the passive courses she advised for women. Her knowledge that this was so was the wreath of victory which she took with her to her comfortable retirement in Kildare.

Notes

1. My count is based on data in *The London Stage, 1660–1800* (Carbondale: Southern Illinois University Press, 1965–68), 11 vols. Before the Licensing Act of 1737, plays produced in any major London theater have been counted; after the act, plays produced only in the two patent theaters—the Haymarket is excluded. Only full-length plays have been counted. As a result, my calculations, made with these imposed limits, produce very different data from the calculations on a much grander scale of Judith Stanton, elsewhere in this volume. *The London Stage* is also the source of all data on performance dates of Griffith's plays.

2. These were Joanna Baillie, Hannah Brand, Dorothea Celisia, Charlotte Charke, Lady Elizabeth Craven, Catherine Cuthbertson, Mary Davys, Marie Theresa de Camp, Elizabeth Richardson, Jane Robe, Mary Robinson, Charlotte Smith, and Mariana Starke.

3. *Candid Review* (February 1765): 41–45.

4. *Critical Review* (February 1765): 153; *Monthly Review* (February 1765) 155; *London Chronicle*, 26 January 1765; *Candid Review* (February 1765): 41–45.

5. The editors of *The London Stage* have given the house receipts of a play, wherever they survive, but these are available only for Griffith's last play. £400 could be worth about $40,000 today. At that time a printer earned £50 a year, and the average yearly government stipend for a clerk was £200.

6. *Candid Review* (March 1765): 169–72. The other conclusions about the play are from *Gentleman's Magazine* (May 1765): 234; *Critical Review* (March 1765).

7. Her model was *Elvira; or, The worst not always true* (1667) by George Digby, Earl of Bristol, republished in Dodsley's *A Select Collection of Old Plays*, vol. 12, 1744.

8. *Critical Review* (January 1766): 55.

9. *Monthly Review* (January 1766): 78.

10. *The Private Correspondence of David Garrick, Esq.* ed. James Boaden (London: H. Colburn and R. Bentley, 1831–32), 2:226. Hereafter cited parenthetically in text as *Correspondence*.

11. *Letters of David Garrick*, ed. David Mason Little and George Kahrl (Cambridge,

Mass.: Belknap Press of Harvard University, 1963), 2:515. Hereafter cited parenthetically in text as *Letters*.

12. *Correspondence* 1:366. Boaden has misdated this letter 15 September 1769 instead of 1768 and has accordingly misplaced it.

13. Boaden has misdated and misplaced Griffith's letter to Garrick begging him to accept the dedication and suggesting actors, and has placed it in Garrick's 1766 correspondence (2:226–27). Her second letter about casting and Garrick's response to it, dating from December 1768, are properly placed (*Correspondence* 2:321).

14. *Correspondence* 2:539–41. Boaden has correctly placed this letter according to date, but has published earlier (pp. 533–34) the two letters which should follow. Garrick's was undated; Griffith's, probably dated 31 May, is wrongly dated 3 May.

15. It is possible to compile at least a partial list of Griffith's unproduced plays, of which I know seven or eight. Those published but unproduced include *Amana*, Beaumarchais's *The Barber of Seville* (probably her translation), possibly *Dorval*, another translation from Diderot (see bibliography at conclusion of this essay). Unpublished plays include the comedy Griffith sent Garrick in the summer of 1766; the translation of *Le Pere de Famille;* the tragedy Griffith was writing in 1767; the comedy given Garrick in spring 1773; and the translation of Le Texier's play she worked on in November 1778. There were almost certainly others.

16. *Correspondence* 2:258. The younger Sheridans, Richard and his sisters, did not like their father's former leading lady and friend, and Richard Sheridan may already have refused both *The Barber of Seville* and others of her plays.

17. *The London Stage* provides the house receipts for the author's nights, from which must be subtracted the house fee of £105 a night. Griffith was also given tickets valued at £17.11.0 on her third night, which, like her tickets for the first two nights could have been disposed of for considerably more. Attendance at this play was good but not unusually so.

18. Frances Burney, MS Diary and Letters, vol 1, pt. 2, f. 1143 (Berg Collection, New York Public Library).

19. Griffith's daughter Catherine, or Kitty, married John Buck, B.A., M.A. and Fellow, B.D. and D.D. of Trinity College, Dublin and rector of Desertcreat from 1787 to 1842.

Works Cited

Griffith, Elizabeth. 1764. *Amana. A Dramatic Poem. By a Lady*. London: T. Harrison.

———— 1776. *The Barber of Seville. By the Author of Eugènie, or The School for Rakes*. London: For the Author, sold by J. Bew. Second edition, London: J. Chouquet, 1776.

———— 1767. *Dorval; or, The Test of Virtue*. London: Dodsley.

———— 1766. *The Double Mistake. A Comedy*. London: J. Almon.

———— 1775. *The Morality of Shakespeare's Drama Illustrated.* By Mrs. Griffiths. London: T. Cadell.

———— 1765. *The Platonic Wife, A Comedy. By a Lady.* London: W. Johnston, J. Dodsley, and T. Davies.

———— 1769. *The School for Rakes: A Comedy.* London: T. Becket and P.A DeHondt.

————. *A Series of Genuine Letters between Henry and Frances.* Vols. 1 and 2. London: W. Johnston, 1757.

  ————. Vols 3 and 4. London: W. Johnston, 1767.

  ————. Vols. 5 and 6. London: W. Richardson and L. Urquhart, 1770.

———— 1780. *The Times: A Comedy.* London : Fielding and Walker.

———— 1772. *A Wife in the Right: A Comedy.* London: For the Author.

The Delicate Distress. In Two Novels. In Letters. By the Authors of Henry and Frances. In Four Volumes. The first and second, intitled The Delicate Distress by Frances; the third and fourth intitled, The Gordian Knot, or Dignus Vindice Nodus, by Henry. London: Becket, 1769.

Works By Others

Boaden, James, ed. 1832. *The Private Correspondence of David Garrick, Esq.* 2 vols. London: H. Colburn and R. Bentley.

The British Magazine, January 1766.

Burney, Frances. Ms Diary and Letters. Berg Collection, New York Public Library.

The Candid Review, and Literary Repository, Feb 1765; March 1765.

The Court Miscellany, February 1769.

The Critical Memoirs of the Times, No. 3, February 25, 1769.

The Critical Review, February 1765; March 1765; January 1766; March 1769; January 1780.

Davies, Thomas. 1802. *Memoirs of the Life of David Garrick.* 2 vols. London.

Digby, George, 2nd Earl of Bristol. 1744. *Elvira; or, the worst not always true,* in Dodsley, Robert. *A. Select Collection of Old Plays. In Twelve Volumes.* Vol. 12. London.

Genest, John. 1832. *Some Account of the English Stage From the Restoration in 1660 to 1830.* 10 vols. Bath: H. E. Carrington.

The Gentleman's Magazine, May 1765.

Gibbon, Edward. 1956. *The Letters of Edward Gibbon,* ed. J.E. Norton. 3 vols. New York: Macmillan.

The Historical, Political, and Literary Register. London: S. Bladon, 1770.

The History of the Theatres of London From the Year 1771 to 1795. 2 vols. London: Martin, et al. 1796.

Little, David Mason and George Kahrl, eds. 1963. *Letters of David Garrick.* 3 vols. Cambridge, Mass.: Belknap Press of Harvard University.

The London Chronicle, January 26, 1765; January 14, 1766.

The London Evening Post, March 12, 1772.

The London Magazine, January 1766.

The London Stage, 1660–1800. 11 vols. Carbondale, Ill.: Southern Illinois University Press, 1965–68.

The Monthly Review, February 1765; March 1765; January 1766; February 1769;
   August 1772; March 1780.
Murphy, Arthur. 1801. *The Life of David Garrick, Esq.* 2 vols. London: J. Wright.
The St. James's Chronicle, January 26, 1765.
Theatrical Memoirs of the Times, 1769.
The Theatrical Review; or, New Companion to the Play-House in 2 Vols. London: S.
   Crowder, J. Wilkie, and J. Walter, 1772.

The Paper War of Hannah Cowley
and Hannah More

ELLEN DONKIN

In January of 1779 David Garrick died, leaving in his wake a group of women playwrights who suddenly found themselves without a mentor. In the vacuum created by his death, a brief but violent controversy erupted between the two most prominent of these playwrights, Hannah Cowley (1743–1809) and Hannah More (1745–1833), both of whom had made successful theater debuts as the result of Garrick's careful sponsorship. In the summer of 1779, Hannah Cowley accused Hannah More of having plagiarized. She stated in the press that More's production of *Fatal Falsehood*, which had opened in May of 1779, had borrowed substantially from Cowley's play *Albina*, which opened in July of 1779 but allegedly had been written some three years before.

The debate was much publicized, both in the London papers and in the preface to Hannah Cowley's printed edition of *Albina*. There were charges and counter-charges. Eventually the controversy died down, largely because a new theater season was under way, but it was never satisfactorily resolved. Hannah More subsequently quit playwrighting altogether; by contrast Hannah Cowley continued a successful and productive career as a professional playwright until 1792, when she retired of her own volition. More's biographers have tended to treat Mrs. Cowley as a crank, and the entire sequence of events as the accusations of a desperate and failing playwright. In one version, Cowley is reported to have stood up in the theater on the second night of *Fatal Falsehood* and shouted "That's mine! That's mine!" before fainting dead away (Jones 1952, 52). But Mrs. Cowley was neither failing nor desperate, and the profile which emerges of her long and successful career does not suggest a paranoid crank, but points toward a larger and graver explanation. In part, Mrs. Cowley's accusations must be understood as a kind of barometer by which we may gauge the degree to which women playwrights suddenly felt endangered in their chosen profession, without the support and access to that profession which had been provided them by Garrick's mentoring.[1] But it is also important to understand that Garrick's mentoring was a part of the problem: that his style of mentoring had a darker side that did not show itself until after his retirement and death. This mentoring took the form of creating a competitive daughter syndrome. The pattern was reminiscent of the famous opening scene in *King Lear,* in which each daughter is called upon publicly to name her love and loyalty for Lear as greater than that of her sisters. As in *Lear,* the legacy of this dynamic did not show itself fully until the retirement of the patriarch, at which time incipient hostilities became manifest among the literary sisters.[2] In the case of the paper war, Cowley identified the source of the trouble as another woman playwright, instead of Garrick's mentoring and its relationship to theater in eighteenth-century England.

Garrick's role in assisting women playwrights has never been adequately acknowledged. To dismiss his efforts as wholly manipulative or self-interested would unbalance what is admittedly a complex picture. From the letters, prefaces, prologues and epilogues, he emerges as a benign and canny mentor to virtually every playwright whose work he decided to produce, but for a significant number of women playwrights, this kind of assistance constituted their only point of access into the profession. It would be difficult to argue that Garrick showed women playwrights any special consideration or that he actively sought them out; however, it can be argued persuasively that he gave them the same painstaking care in the middle process from rewrites to actual production that he did male playwrights, and in this he stands alone in his generation. The statistics are revealing here: between 1747 and 1776 (the duration of his tenure as manager of Drury Lane), Garrick produced nine contemporary women playwrights (not counting Hannah More, whose first play opened the year after he retired), for a total of 128 performances. By contrast, Covent Garden produced three contemporary women playwrights in the same span of time for a total of twenty performances (Pedicord 1954, 198–237). The ratio of performances is

Hannah Cowley. (Engraved for the *Ladies Magazine*.)
Reproduced by permission of the Henry E. Huntington Library,
San Marino, California.

approximately five to one. One of the three women produced at
Covent Garden, Elizabeth Griffith, had already been produced by
Garrick, and thus constituted a lesser risk. If we include plays by
women of earlier periods, specifically Behn, Centlivre and Pix, the
ratio of performances by women playwrights from 1747–76 is 292 for
Drury Lane as compared to 111 for Covent Garden for the same
period, which narrows the ratio to three to one, and suggests that
Covent Garden might produce women playwrights once they were
tried and true, but was unlikely to take a chance on an unknown.
Garrick, by contrast, appears to have taken chances on unknown
women playwrights, successfully sponsoring two women who were
to become career professionals (Hannah Cowley and Elizabeth Griffith), and engineering short-term successes for a number of others.

One wonders why Garrick made efforts on behalf of women in an
age that was often ruthlessly critical of women's literary efforts. One

Hannah More. W. Finden, sc. from Roberts, William, *Memoirs of the Life and Correspondence of Mrs. Hannah More*, V.1, London 1834. Reproduced by permission of the Henry E. Huntington Library, San Marino, California.

explanation is altruism, but the larger picture suggests something more practical. Given the size of the collective theater audience in London, it was to the manager's advantage to have a large number of new scripts within a season's repertory, so as to keep audience interest alive and the percentage of repeating attenders high. By this encouragement and receptivity to the work of women, Garrick was maximizing the submissions of new scripts and increasing his chances of finding a good one. It is also true that the women he took under his wing were so grateful for the opportunity to be produced by him that they were anxious to please him, to be molded by his tastes and wisdom. It was a kind of dependency that exactly suited Garrick, whose long experience in playwrighting, performing, and producing made him an excellent judge of what would succeed with his audiences. The relationship that developed between him and these women tended to give him access to a maximum amount of new material with a minimum amount of resistance to his editorial advice and guidance.

Garrick's advice and guidance emerge in a variety of ways from letters and other records. Dorothy Celisia, in her advertisement for *Almida,* referred to "the judicious and friendly hand of Mr. Garrick," and reports that "he spared neither pains nor expense to please the public in the respect of decoration," by which she meant not only new scenery and stage decor but also new costumes (Celisia 1771, n.p.). Garrick also wrote for his new playwrights: for Hannah More's maiden production of *Percy* he wrote the prologue, and for Hannah Cowley's *Runaway* he wrote the epilogue. He was concerned financially: for Hannah More he carefully invested her profit of £600 after *Percy* closed; to Mrs. Griffith, who was in financial straits, he wrote that he would personally seek a bookseller for her play, since the publication of her play depended largely upon a guarantee of production from him (Little and Kahrl 1963, 2:582–583, no. 472). Another letter from him to Mrs. Griffith indicates that she had anxiously tried to dictate casting for her upcoming production of *School for Rakes,* and that here Garrick had gently but firmly insisted that she trust his judgment in the matter (Little and Kahrl 1963, 2:630–631, no. 524). She relented, and the result was a major success. In this case, Mrs. Griffith also was indebted to Garrick for the very subject matter of her play; it was he who had suggested a script by Beaumarchais as the basis for her English adaptation. A similar kind of solicitude emerged in his development of More's *Percy* after his retirement from Drury Lane; his assistance to her included getting her an entrée to Thomas Harris at Covent Garden, since Garrick's own producing days were over.

One of the most subtle and important kinds of help that Garrick was able to offer was in the fine art of timing a production's opening advantageously. For example, he deliberately delayed Griffith's opening of *Père de Famille,* despite her anxious protests (Little and Kahrl 1963, 2:583, no. 472), and allowed More's *Percy* to go up relatively early in the 1777–78 season. In spite of More's dire predictions, the play had an extremely successful run of nineteen nights; similarly Cowley's *Runaway* played for seventeen nights when it opened in the 1775–76 season, an outstanding run for a new play by a novice playwright.

But it was in the areas of editing and shaping dramatic texts that Garrick made his most significant contributions to these women. Neither Cowley nor More was an actress, and so their practical experience of the production and rehearsal process was limited, experience that might have played an important part in developing playwrighting skills. Garrick's wide experience as manager, director, playwright, and actor constituted a crucial missing link in their transition from writer to playwright. His alterations and suggestions on their plays consistently point in the direction of performability, that is, of creating roles for actors that offer possibilities for vigorous characterization and action, instead of endless speechifying. One particularly valuable piece of evidence is the manuscript of Hannah Cowley's first play, *The Runaway*, which bears approximately sixty different additions, deletions, and alterations in Garrick's handwriting to the fair copy submitted to Larpent on 5 February 1776. For example, the opening lines of the play are a speech by George, who has just come home on college vacation: "Oh, for the luxury of Night Gown and Slippers! No poor jaded Hack of Parnassus can be more tired than I am. The Roads so dusty and the sun so hot—'two'd be less tolerable riding post in Africa" (Cowley 1776). Garrick's rewrite of the same line reads simply: "Oh, for the luxury of Night Gown and Slippers! No poor jaded Hack of Parnassus can be more tired than I am." Here Garrick cut away unnecessary exposition and forced the length of the speech down to a size manageable for someone who is too hot and tired to talk. Later, in the climactic moment of the play, it is revealed that old Mr. Hargrave, George's father, intends Lady Dinah, a woman of fortune in her fifties, not for himself but for George, his college-aged son. George and his friends have all been laboring under the misconception that old Hargrave has intended to marry Lady Dinah himself. In a scene between George and his father, the stage directions at the moment of revelation read: "A long pause, staring at each other." Then George's line as it was originally written by Cowley, read: "Then I hope we shall soon be awakened. I was never in so horrible a dream in my life." Garrick cut the entire line and replaced it with "Wife! Lady Dinah my wife!" Again, Garrick insisted on less text and more subtext; his line for George heightened the moment of shock and disbelief where Cowley's had inadvertently flattened it.

Overall what is most striking about Garrick's work on *The Runaway* is the way he tightened the text without damaging the charm and ingenuousness of the characters and situations, and helped Cowley structure into the text moments that are clearly *performable*. One very early letter (probably 1775) to Garrick from Cowley suggests the strain of trying to adjust her script to his expectations, but her effort and willingness paid off (Cowley n.d.). Later she would learn from adapting the work of earlier playwrights like Aphra Behn (*The Lucky Chance*) and Susanna Centlivre (*The Salamanca Doctor Outwitted*), but where she initially learned to craft a dramatic moment was from David Garrick.

Garrick's work on More's *Percy* and *The Fatal Falsehood* appears to have been more broadly structural in nature. The work on Cowley's script left the larger movement of the plot intact and concentrated on restructuring small comic moments; in More's plays Garrick characteristically challenged the basic structure of the plot itself. Unlike Cowley's work, the fair copies of More's *Percy* and *The Fatal Falsehood* are virtually untouched, so we have to rely on the letters that passed between them to understand Garrick's work on these two manuscripts (and, significantly, Mrs. Garrick's as well: the revisions on More's play were to become a family affair). As usual, Garrick's letters indicate a finely tuned sense of his audiences. Of *Percy*, which resolves around the meeting of two estranged lovers, he wrote More that her first draft of the third act "raises such Expectation from the Circumstances, that a great deal more must be done, to content ye Spectators and Readers—I am rather vex'd that Nothing More is produc'd by that Meeting, which is the Groundwork of the Tragedy, & from which so much will be required, because such an Alarm is given to the heart & the Mind—" (Little and Kahrl 1963, 3:1126, no. 1043). The final version ended with Percy throwing Elwina to the ground, suggesting that More took Garrick's advice to heart and forced the scene up to a climactic ending. To judge from the correspondence, More tended to round off the ends of her acts, instead of grinding them to a fine pitch of excitement and creating a natural appetite for the next act. A good deal of More's other writing, like *Sir Eldred and the Bower*, was in verse, some of it taken from ballads, and most of it less concerned with dramatic situation than with language and narrative. Garrick's suggestions acted to counter a tendency in her work to create cantos with a downward inflection rather than acts and scenes with a rising inflection.

As a whole, one is repeatedly struck by the sagacity and good will of Garrick's editorial efforts for these women, and at the same time by a certain paternal concern which extended well past the normal call of duty. Nor was Garrick unaware of his impact upon women playwrights. In a letter to Frances Cadogan, he wrote with some heat about Mrs. Brookes, who published a novel in 1777 called *Excursion* in which his integrity was impugned (Mrs. Brookes had an axe to grind because Garrick had rejected a play of hers for production). Garrick complained that Brookes

> has invented a Tale about a Tragedy which is all a Lie, from beginning to ye End—she Even says, that I should reject a Play, if it should be a Woman's—there's brutal Malignity for you— have not ye Ladies—Mesdames Griffith, Cowley & Cilesia spoke of me before their Plays with an Over-Enthusastick Encomium? What says the divine Hannah More? (Little and Kahrl 1963, 3:1172, no. 1109).

There are even faint resonances with *Lear:* "What says our second daughter, our dearest Regan . . .?" (1.1.68).

Whatever the ambiguities, the extent to which these women playwrights had been nourished and promoted by Garrick would make itself sadly clear in the period following his retirement and death. In all areas they experienced disastrous change. Editorial assistance was nonexistent. In the production and timing of openings it was difficult to distinguish between flagrant carelessness and deliberate sabotage. For example, Cowley's first produced play after Garrick's retirement, a small gem called *Who's the Dupe?*, was promised a good mid-season opening by Richard Brinsley Sheridan, Garrick's successor at Drury Lane. Instead it was allowed to languish, opening late in the season (mid-April), by which time it could not have a regular run because of end-of-season benefits. Mrs. Cowley was then to pay 100 guineas to the management "(Thirty of which had been added by the present Managers) for the chance of a Benefit, at a time when the current business of the Theatre would not produce that Sum" (Cowley 1779). In other words, far from making money on

Who's the Dupe?, she actually stood to lose substantially. In another instance, her tragedy *Albina* went unperformed for three years after its original completion in 1776 while it got passed from Sheridan to Harris with spurious promises of production. When George Colman the Elder finally agreed to produce it at the Haymarket in July of 1779, the timing was so conspicuously bad that even the prologue made jest of it: "Hang these authors and their airs! . . . What right has She upon our *Summer* stage?" (Cowley 1779).

In addition to being badly timed, *Albina* suffered from wretched miscasting. Robert Palmer, an actor noted for his large stature, was cast as Gondibert, the dwarf lover. The novice Miss Montagu made a hash of the villainous Editha, and after the reviews went against her, burst into tears on stage in mid-performance, and made a moving plea for audience sympathy (a performance ludicrously inconsistent with the behavior of the character she was supposed to be playing). Ultimately she was replaced by a Miss Sherry, who did admirable work, but not in time to save the show from closing. Colman at least had a conscience; he scheduled Cowley's third benefit night for the seventh instead of the normal ninth evening of the run, perhaps to make sure she received some compensation in case the show closed prematurely.

Hannah More's fate at the hands of Thomas Harris with *Fatal Falsehood* in 1779 was no better. She and Garrick had worked hard on the play in its early stages, and the two of them believed that another summer of work on it would make it a good prospect for the fall of 1779. Unfortunately, Garrick's death in January made these revisions impossible. Shortly after Garrick's death, Harris "no sooner understood that the play was in readiness, than he solicited her with so much earnestness to let him bring it out the very next month, that she yielded to his persuasions, against the better judgement of herself and her friends, and suffered it to appear at an unfavourable season" (Roberts 1834, 1:163). So *Fatal Falsehood* opened in May of 1779, an astonishingly late date for a new mainpiece to be introduced into a season. It was harshly reviewed, in spite of a fine performance by Miss Younge as Emmelina, and lasted only three nights, just long enough for a single benefit night, instead of the three More must have hoped for.

Nor were the difficulties limited to mismanagement. The literary climate for women playwrights, which had been tempered by Garrick's efforts on their behalf, became positively acidic after his death. Colman the Elder, for example, took the opportunity to lampoon women playwrights in a comedy called *The Separate Maintenance,* which was produced at the Haymarket simultaneously with *Albina.* His play featured a lady playwright named Mrs. Fustian, a "strange, ranting, crazy being" (*Morning Post,* 9 September 1779), and an indignant reader wrote to demand if the satire was pointed directly either at Mrs. Cowley or at Miss More (*Morning Post,* 9 September 1779). In a later play by his son George Colman the Younger, called *The Female Dramatist,* the central character was a Madam Melpomene Metaphor, whose young nephew Beverley determines that her passion for scribbling needs to be cured: "You shall see me transform her into a downright housewife—and by a Single Stroke of my Art, turn her pen into a Needle, and her Tragedies into thread papers" (Colman the Younger, 1782). Sheridan's epilogue to More's *Fatal Falsehood* reinforces the same familiar theme of the lady scribbler, surrounded by evidence of domestic irresponsibility and literary pretensions. Although it was by no means unusual for an epilogue to humorously denigrate the play preceding it in order to solicit warm compensatory applause from the audience, this epilogue was so astringent that one critic reported: "The audience evidently did not relish the jest, for it certainly wore a strong appearance of a severe and illiberal attack on female genius" (*The Gazetteer,* 18 May 1779).

Attacks on women playwrights were by no means limited to "envious bards" or new managers, but appeared also in the press. In a direct shot at Garrick's patronage of women playwrights, the *St. James Chronicle* (8 May 1779) complained: "we are tired of indulging Authours [*sic*] because they are Females. The Success of these Amazonian leaders brought forward a Mrs. Griffith, a Mrs. Cowley, and a Miss More. Some well-timed flattery to a late Manager and Actor brought on the Tragedy of *Percy,* the most interesting parts of which were borrowed from a French Play, without the common good manners of acknowledging it." It was an old and familiar theme: if a woman playwright had a conspicuous success like *Percy,* it could only be explained by her having lifted her material from some other (male) source. The epilogue for More's *Percy,* written by Garrick himself in 1777, constituted a startling contrast to the spiteful irritability of his colleagues:

Tho' I'm female, . . .
I come, the *friend* and *champion* of my sex;
I'll prove, ye fair, that let us have our swing,
We can, as well as men, do any thing. . . .

It was in this negatively charged atmosphere that Hannah Cowley and Hannah More came to grief in the summer of 1779, just six months after Garrick's death, in the wake of both women's productions having been severely mismanaged. What is striking about this so-called "paper war" is that in fact only two relatively polite volleys were fired by the protagonists; the battle was in large part fought and promoted by other parties and by the newspapers themselves. At some point during the summer, the voyeuristic thrill of this altercation surpassed the excitement of what was being offered onstage, and the paper war became a substitute for theater. The flavor of the exchanges in the newspapers suggests a kind of meta-theater, a mud hen wrestling match into which Cowley and More had been reluctantly pressed. Dibdin best expressed the unhealthy pleasure a bored and restless London found in watching two women go at it: "Had these foolish ladies no friend to prevent their making themselves a town talk? What were they cavilling about after all?" (Dibdin n.d., 5:303-4).

The paper war actually began as early as May 7, when a review of More's *Fatal Falsehood* stated that the play was "astonishingly similar" to a manuscript as yet unpublished by Mrs. Cowley (*Morning Chronicle*, 7 May 1779). This same reviewer on August 2 (in the review for Cowley's *Albina*, which had opened July 31) stated that the reader would discern a strong resemblance to *Fatal Falsehood*, but suggested that in fairness to Mrs. Cowley, "we feel ourselves bound to declare that we read the play of *Albina* four years ago, and that it was essentially the same piece that it is now." In the *St. James Chronicle* (August 5-7) the position shifted subtly from a defense of Mrs. Cowley's originality to an accusation of plagiarism directed at More. An open letter to the paper (which may have been a plant by Cowley's husband, who was himself the theater critic for the *Gazetteer*), relates that the writer overheard a conversation at Haymarket in which it was hotly debated whether More stole from Cowley or Cowley from More, and implies that Garrick himself may have been implicated in assisting More to steal from Cowley (*St. James Chronicle*, 5–7 August 1779). Hannah More, in a letter to the *Morning Post*, responded directly for the first and last time in language that clearly indicates her anxiety about voyeurism: "It is with the deepest regret I find myself compelled to take a step repugnant to my own Feelings, and to the delicacy of my Sex; a step as *new* to me as it is disagreeable; for I never, till this moment, directly or indirectly, was concerned in any paragraph in any London paper. . . . I am under the necessity of solemnly declaring, that I never saw, heard, or read, a single line of Mrs. Cowley's tragedy . . ." (*St. James Chronicle*, 12–14 August 1779). To which Mrs. Cowley replied, in language that indicates similar anxieties about voyeurism: "I wish Miss More had been still more sensible of the indelicacy of a newspaper altercation between women, and the ideas of ridicule which the world are apt to attach to such unsexual hardiness . . ." (*St. James Chronicle*, 14–17 August 1779). She promised to explain herself more fully in the upcoming publication of the preface to *Albina*.

The preface, which was published later that August, gives our best account of Cowley's version of the dispute. She began by recounting her early success with *Runaway* in 1776 as a novice playwright working under Garrick, "but this success closed with the unfortunate period in which Mr. Garrick resigned the management of Drury Lane" (Cowley 1779). Following his retirement, Cowley sought Sheridan's help in producing *Runaway* for a second season at Drury Lane, but discovered, after a demoralizing series of broken appointments, delays, and reports of mislaid manuscripts, that she had been "shelf'd" (Cowley 1779). *Albina*, which by this time had already been returned by Garrick and by Harris, was then offered to Sheridan, who deflected it back to Harris, but promised to produce her third play, the aforementioned *Who's the Dupe?*, which as we know also got badly delayed until it became a financial liability. In the meantime, More's *Percy* had come out in 1777, bearing some likeness to *Albina* but nothing provable. The *Albina* manuscript at this point was still circulating among managers.

The final disaster was the opening of *The Fatal Falsehood* in May of 1779. This time, stated Cowley, the similarities were so striking that they were impossible to ignore, because by the time *Albina* finally straggled to a late July opening the same year, the public impression was that Cowley had borrowed from More instead of the reverse. Cowley was careful not to accuse More outright of having plagiarized, but she left the reader little doubt about her own opinion, that "by some wonderful coincidence, Miss More and I have but one common stock of ideas between us" (Cowley 1779). She states that while the play was in Mr. Garrick's possession at Hampton (his country home), "Miss More was a visitant at Hampton," but softens the implications by adding that the managers may have inadvertently communicated the ideas of Cowley's script in the process of editing and advising More. However the information traveled though, directly or indirectly, Cowley felt robbed of ideas, reputation, and remuneration.

Cowley and More never directly confronted one another again, although the debate continued in the newspapers through various editorials and letters. On 19 August 1779, the *Gazetteer* took the solemn step of initiating a public inquiry by committee, which came down (predictably, because of Captain Cowley's affiliation with the paper) on the side of Mrs. Cowley. With the advent of the new September season, the controversy finally died out completely. But the questions raised by the allegations were never completely resolved. The question of whether or not More deliberately borrowed from Cowley is a complex one and deserves careful examination.

Briefly, the similarities between the two plays, *Fatal Falsehood* and *Albina,* can by summarized as follows: The most striking one, which so upset Cowley, was that in both plays, a villain/villainess [Bertrand/Editha], plots to destroy a romance [Rivers and Julia, Edward and Albina] in order to better his/her own position. This plotting takes the form of convincing a gullible character [Orlando/Gondibert] that his affections are returned by the lady in question [Julia/Albina], when in fact nothing could be further from the truth. It is the hope of each villain that the duped suitor [Orlando/Gondibert] will kill or defeat his "rival" [Rivers/Edward]. In a startling plot reversal at the end, Orlando accidentally kills Bertrand, whom he mistakes for Rivers, and Gondibert accidentally stabs Editha, mistaking her for Albina. The resolution in *Fatal Falsehood* is somewhat contrived and unsuccessful: Orlando's betrothed, now abandoned and thinking that Orlando has killed her brother Rivers, enters the stage "distracted" and dies for no accountable reason; in remorse, Orlando kills himself. Julia and Rivers, the original romantic pair, are thereby left intact and unencumbered. In *Albina,*

Gondibert—upon killing the woman he thinks to be Albina—kills himself before realizing that Albina lives, and that it is Editha he has killed. Again, Albina and Edward, the central couple, are left intact.

In reading the plays, it is easy to see why Cowley was angered. In her preface, she claimed that her play was entirely original (although she had obviously borrowed a character name from Davenant). More makes no such claims, but the surviving letters between her and Garrick make no mention of outside sources and show evidence of the plot having evolved and changed over a period of many months. So in spite of startling similarities, the evidence points towards More's innocence, although there is nothing conclusive.

Other evidence is equally circumstantial. The only common link between Cowley and More that might have constituted a leak during the writing of *Fatal Falsehood* (which took place from July 1778 through January of 1779), was Garrick himself. According to Cowley's preface, her script of *Albina* went first to Garrick, with the title *Edwina,* early in the summer of 1776, and then to Mr. Harris in the summer of 1777, after which it bounced back and forth between Harris and Sheridan to no effect until the summer of 1779, when it was at long last picked up by Colman for the Haymarket. We know with some certainty that Hannah More received no editing or advice from either Sheridan or Harris; in fact, she is quoted as saying that Harris was so anxious to get his hands on *Fatal Falsehood* that he would hardly give her time to finish it. The logical conclusion is that when Garrick and More were working on *Fatal Falsehood,* it had been two years already since he had seen the early versions of *Albina,* if indeed he ever read it at all (since by the time she submitted it to him, he had already retired from management.) No letters survive to prove that Garrick ever read *Edwina/Albina* or that he made any editorial suggestions to Cowley. On the contrary, the letters from this period indicate that his work with playwrights as a whole radically diminished, with the striking exception of Hannah More, who must be seen as a personal family friend rather than as a developing commercial playwright. If Garrick did indeed 'leak' any of Cowley's ideas for *Albina* to More, it would probably have been unconscious; as Cowley herself says, "Amidst the croud of Plots, and Stage Contrivances, in which a Manager is involv'd, *recollection* is too frequently mistaken for the suggestions of the *imagination*" (Cowley 1779).

In an alternative scenario, Cowley said in her preface that she had been informed that Hannah More was a "visitant" at Hampton during the period in which Garrick was holding Cowley's play, the clear implication being that More might herself have happened upon the manuscript and helped herself to its contents. But here Cowley appears to have been misinformed: More did not visit the Garricks for about a year after his final performance on 10 June 1776, and the correspondence bears this out (Stone and Kahrl 1979, 434). So we may conclude that More could not have seen the script on her own, because by the time she was visiting the Garricks again in the summer of 1777, the script had already been forwarded to Thomas Harris.

Another important bit of evidence is a letter about *Fatal Falsehood* written by More to Garrick on 10 October 1778, which reads; "Be so good as to treat me with your usual candour, and tell me how I have failed or succeeded in unfolding the story and characters; and above all, *if you can recollect any other tragedy that it is like, as I shall be most careful of that*" (Boaden 1832, 2:315; emphasis added). More was making indirect reference to her earlier failure to adequately acknowledge her sources for *Percy*, which had gotten her in some minor difficulties with the press in 1777 and which later were resolved. What is striking about her letters from this earlier period is the care with which she discusses and weighs each source with Garrick, from a French play by Belloy to Percy's *Reliques*. The overall impression is of a rather academic and scholarly process, rather than the furtive gleanings one might expect from a career plagiarist. Garrick, in a much earlier letter to Mrs. Griffith, wrote on the subject of borrowing "that there can be no Objection to the introducing Circumstances, Incidents, Characters, and Even Scenes, that may bear some resemblance to other Plays; Authors should only take care that Such incidents, Characters & Scenes are not too nearly imitated or ill-chosen" (Little and Kahrl 1963, 2:535, no. 424). But Garrick is speaking in the context of a play that had already long since had its run and was in the public domain; the ethics of dipping into an unproduced and unpublished script whose author still hoped for remuneration were another matter entirely.

The final piece of evidence is the most circumstantial and indeed the most subjective of all, and that is the cumulative impression arising out of the correspondence that More's real reason for involving herself in commercial playwrighting was because it created a structure within which she could legitimate and prolong her contact with David Garrick. As her later work was to bear out, she did not really approve either of theater or of theater people (with the singular exception of Garrick himself), except in the service of religion. The writing of *Percy* and *Fatal Falsehood* were a kind of slum adventure for her, not the foundations of a playwrighting career. For Garrick's part, playwrighting and producing, the two things he most needed to get away from after his retirement, were his gift to her as an adopted literary daughter, a Cordelia to his old age.[3] They were a way of structuring the relationship, which fell into a strangely gray area and required the legitimating presence of Mrs. Garrick in the form of an additional editor. This scenario is consistent with More's strikingly indifferent attitude toward the success or failure of *Fatal Falsehood* after Garrick's death, and an early letter to one of her sisters dated sometime in 1776: "I find my dislike of what are called public diversions greater than ever, except a play; and when Garrick has left the stage, I could be very well contented to relinquish plays also. . . ." (Roberts 1834, 1:72).

The evidence on the whole, although largely circumstantial, tends to suggest two things: first, that plagiarism had probably not occurred. The logistics of manuscript access, combined with the professional integrity in all parties concerned (Cowley, More, and Garrick), together with More's lack of ambition in commercial playwrighting, makes the case for plagiarism a thin one. Furthermore, the logic of Hannah More's having borrowed from Mrs. Cowley when she already had a strong literary advisor and critic in Garrick, is strained. Second, whatever else the evidence suggests, it does prove conclusively that Mrs. Cowley was not the crackpot that More's biographers have tended to portray. Her grievances, both artistic and financial, were in all cases rational and legitimate ones. But if there in fact was no plagiarism, and Mrs. Cowley was not a crank, how then may we account for these charges?

Two documents resonate throughout this narrative and may help point to an explanation. The first is a letter to Garrick written by Mrs. Cowley in 1777, the year after his retirement, and one year after their successful collaboration on *The Runaway*. Mrs. Cowley describes a fruitless effort to reestablish contact with him and the rebuffs by his servants, and says with heart-rending simplicity: "I have lost your friendship!" (Boaden 1832, 2:223). Subsequently, Garrick replies to her with great solicitude, explaining that he has been desperately ill, and that she and Captain Cowley are welcome guests (Little and Kahrl 1963, 3:1165, no. 1101). One final letter survives to Mrs. Garrick, in which mention is made of an unnamed Lord H— (likely Harrowby), and the implication is that the Garricks attempted to find her some sort of patronage (Boaden 1832, 2:224–225). But what is striking about the correspondence is Mrs. Cowley's desolation about her perceived abandonment by Garrick. Evidently the combination of his retreat into private life and his illness had played havoc with her sense of his protection. This sense of loss must have been peculiarly complicated by the fact that Hannah More, whose claims to a playwrighting career were comparatively slender, was the sole and conspicuous recipient of Garrick's limited energies after his retirement. To add insult to injury, More's friendship with the Garricks gave her an easy mobility in distinguished literary circles that included Johnson and Sheridan. The fact that the intercourse between Garrick and More was less a professional exchange than a way to construct a family would probably have been cold comfort to Hannah Cowley. She has been displaced as the favored daughter, when in fact her skills were far superior.

The second document that throws light on the situation is Cowley's preface to *Albina*, which oscillates curiously between her charges of plagiarism, and her accounts of repeated failure to find a foothold with the new winter managers, Harris and Sheridan.

> Should it, after all, appear to the Public, that there is nothing more in these repeated resemblances, than what may be accounted for supposing a similarity in our minds; and that, by some WONDERFUL coincidence, Miss More and I have but one common stock of ideas between us, I have only to lament that the whole misfortune of this similarity has fallen upon me. Now, as in this case, we must continue writing in the same track, it seems reasonable that we should have our productions brought forward in turn; instead of which Miss More has had TWO tragedies brought out, both of which were written since mine, whilst I struggled for the representation of ONE in vain. But, as there seems to be little hope of my obtaining this, or any other favour from the Winter Managers, I presume at least, that, as I do not pretend to prove—what is impossible for me to

know—that Miss More ever read, or copied me, it will be admitted that I have not copied her. . . ." (Cowley 1779)

The charges and counter-charges of plagiarism, above and beyond the impugnment of personal integrity, were inextricable from the issue of profit: "by the conduct of the Winter Managers, I have been deprived of a reasonable prospect of several hundred pounds, and have spent years of fruitless anxiety and trouble." She closes grimly: "My productions have been uniformly received by the Public with applause; yet I find the doors of the Winter Theatres shut against me.—To this severe fate I most reluctantly submit" (Cowley 1779).

Ultimately, we must understand the preface to *Albina,* and the paper war as a whole, as having had less to do with plagiarism than with a deep-seated anxiety about authorship itself; that Cowley's and More's dependence upon Garrick's editorial and production assistance had raised unconscious questions after his departure, questions about who the real author of their successes was. Had they written their plays, or had Garrick? This anxiety about authorship took the form of a very public debate that sought to persuade London that *in both cases,* More's and Cowley's, one playwright had generated original work, and the other had borrowed or stolen her ideas. Unable to name Garrick, they named one another. It was a form of burial: they were both participating in an effort to distance themselves from the presence of the male mentor. Both women, but Cowley in particular, felt robbed, and both women sought to reclaim their texts. The peculiarity and complexity of their story is that they sought redress through one another, rather than from the canonized patron whose memory they were socially and politically constrained to honor.

It is particularly striking that Cowley is at pains to make a disclaimer for Garrick when she says that any cross-fertilizing of plot material by Garrick must have been an "accident" of Garrick's memory. In other words, she carefully names Garrick as *conduit* rather than as *source.* Both women, by naming each other as thief, distance themselves from the far more frightening possibility that their material, their success, and their futures had been wholly dependent upon the presence of the father.

Cowley's conspicuous success after Garrick's death suggests that, for her, the separating and healing process was ultimately successful.

In More's case the departure of the mentor and the end of her commercial playwrighting efforts were co-extensive, although her literary efforts continued to be successful in other areas, with other male mentors.

In retrospect, the paper war had the unfortunate side effect of further imperiling the precarious position of women playwrights generally by inviting all of London to witness divisiveness among them. This divisiveness had the special complication of gender: it added to the crime of writing and public speaking the crime of public acrimony. It further succeeded in successfully shifting the focus of the debate from the similarity between the two plays, to the questionable wisdom of allowing women playwrights in the theater at all. As Charles Dibdin wrote for all posterity on the subject of this paper war: "Nothing can be more ridiculous than literary quarrels even among men, but when ladies, fearful lest their poetic offspring should crawl through life unheeded, publicly expose themselves to the world, in order to ascertain their beauty and legitimacy, who does not wish they had occupied their time with a needle instead of a pen," (Dibdin n.d., 5:303–34). But the underlying issue was invisible not only to the public but also to the principals themselves: that Garrick's praiseworthy guidance and help to women playwrights during his career as manager had created in them a correspondingly strong need to distance themselves and their work from the power of his authority and authorship in order to continue working after his death.

Notes

Funding for the research of this article was provided by the William Andrews Clark Memorial Library in Los Angeles. Permission to quote from the Larpent manuscripts of *Albina* (LA 486) and *The Runaway* (LA 402) by Hannah Cowley, from George Colman the Younger's *The Female Dramatist* (LA 598), George Colman the Elder's *The Separate Maintenance* (LA 490), and from Hannah More's *Percy* (LA 440), has been graciously extended by the Huntington Library, San Marino, California.

1. See Penina Glazer and Miriam Slater's *Unequal Colleagues* for a useful discussion of professional access for women through male mentors in the late nineteenth and early twentieth centuries.
2. Beth Kowaleski-Wallace discusses the complexities of literary mentoring for

middle-class women in eighteenth-century England, and coins the very useful term "imposter syndrome" to describe the resulting uneasiness felt by literary daughters about claiming their own work. See her article, "Milton's Daughters: The Education of Eighteenth-Century Women Writers" in *Feminist Studies*.

3. Lest the repeated parallels to *Lear* appear to be purely literary, it is helpful to recollect that Lear was one of Garrick's most successful roles, and one with which he was personally identified, both by his public and by other actors. See Leigh Woods's *Garrick claims the Stage*, 42, in which Woods describes an actress who knelt backstage to receive Garrick's benediction *in character as Lear*.

Works Cited

Boaden, James, ed. 1832. *The Private Correspondence of David Garrick*. 2 vols. London: Henry Colburn and Richard Bentley.

Celisia, Dorothy. 1771. *Almida*. London: T. Becket & Co.

Colman, George (the Elder). 1779. *The Separate Maintenance*. Manuscript LA 490, Larpent Collection, Huntington Library, San Marino, Calif.

Colman, George (the Younger). 1782. *The Female Dramatist*. Manuscript LA 598. Larpent Collection.

Cowley, Hannah. 1779. *Albina*. Manuscript LA 486, Larpent Collection.

———. Letter to David Garrick, n.d. Manuscript y. c. 646 (1). The Folger Library, Washington, D.C.

———. 1776. *The Runaway*. Manuscript LA 402. Larpent Collection.

Dibdin, Charles, n.d. *A Complete History of the Stage*. Vol. 5. London: printed by C. Dibdin.

Glazer, Penina, and Miriam Slater. 1987. *Unequal Colleagues: the Entrance of Women into the Professions, 1890–1940*. New Brunswick: Rutgers Univ. Press.

Jones, M. G. 1952. *Hannah More*. Cambridge: Cambridge Univ. Press.

Kowaleski-Wallace, Beth. 1986. "Milton's Daughters: The Education of Eighteenth-Century Women Writers." *Feminist Studies* 12, no. 2 (Summer), 275–293.

Little, David M., and George M. Kahrl. 1963. 3 vols. *The Letters of David Garrick*. Cambridge, MA: Belknap Press at Harvard Univ.

More, Hannah. 1779. *The Fatal Falsehood*. London: T. Cadell in the Strand.

———. 1777. *Percy*. Manuscript LA 440. Larpent Collection.

Pedicord, Harry William. 1954. *The Theatrical Public in the Time of Garrick*. Carbondale: Southern Illinois Univ. Press.

Roberts, William. 1834. *Memoirs of the Life and Correspondence of Mrs. Hannah More*. 2 vols. 2d edition. London: R. B. Seeley and Burnside.

Stone, George Winchester, and George M. Kahrl. 1979. *David Garrick: A Critical Biography*. Carbondale: Southern Illinois Univ. Press.

Woods, Leigh. 1984. *Garrick Claims the Stage*. Westport, Conn.: Greenwood Press.

3

The Dresser

"*An Actress at her Toilet.*" *Courtesy of the Print Collection,*
The Lewis Walpole Library, Yale University.

Finding the Good Parts:
Sexuality in Women's Tragedies in
the Time of Queen Anne
KENDALL

E nglish theater has long been not just a business but a competitive, often cut-throat business. While private patronage and
networks aided Katherine Philips substantially and were of
some help to Aphra Behn, there is no evidence that Catharine Trotter
or Mary Pix slept any easier for the pittances their patrons doled out.
Trotter, a teen-aged prodigy, attempted to support herself as well as
her impoverished mother and sister by writing plays; and some need
goaded Mary Pix to produce at least twelve plays (possibly more) over
the course of ten years. Later in the eighteenth century, as the special-
ization of Elizabeth Griffith and the struggles of Hannah Cowley
and Hannah More attest, hard times continued for women who dared
to venture into the play-market. Yet the women who wrote in the
shadow of Jeremy Collier at the time of Queen Anne were caught in a
peculiar bind.

As women, the playwrights were subject to ridicule and moral cas-
tigation for even associating with theater folk. They named Behn
and Philips as their models in numerous poems and prefaces published with their plays, but neither provided a model they could
actually emulate. Behn's reputation had been spattered with a good
deal of Puritanical mud, though her bawdry continued successful at
the box office long after her death; "the matchless Orinda," on the
other hand, kept her good name, though her plays were never competitive at the box office. How might a new generation of women
craft plays that were "warm" enough to seduce the public into
buying tickets but "chaste" enough to pass Puritan scrutiny and
allow the playwrights' reputations to remain intact?

One possibility was to focus on the "chaste" but passionate yearnings of two noble women for each other. This might now be described as "lesbian" eroticism, though there is a mutability of sexual expression in these plays that almost defies modern analysis. In fact we need new language to talk about old sex. Our language and our way of thinking about sex and sexuality has been polluted since early in this century when such sexologists as Havelock Ellis burst upon the face of history like a boil smelling of Sigmund Freud (see Faderman 1981 for a landmark study of how nineteenth-century sexologists labeled lesbianism as deviant). Since then it has been commonplace to speak of "sexual identity" as if it were innate, like color of eyes or shape of nose. We sympathize with adolescents who experience a "crisis" of "sexual identity," but it is customarily accepted that people should know, by the end of adolescence, whether they are homosexual or heterosexual, and if there is any question, declare themselves. The evidence of theater history is that there was no such rite of labeling in the eighteenth century, for reasons both liberating and confining to women of the time.

I'm not suggesting that strong sexual identities did not exist then as now. Certainly there have always been people whose sexual preferences were specific and specifically delimited. Six years ago, when I started my study of women playwrights in the time of Queen Anne, I thought I had found the birthplace of lesbian theater—among white people. With a hoot of delight, I discovered the overt expression of erotic feeling between women; nowhere in all dramatic literature prior to the twentieth century had I read anything like this, and I was hungry for it. Of course the word "lesbian" was not in use in the eighteenth century as it is now. But there is a heat, a passion, a distinctly erotic flavour to certain speeches between women in these plays—a heat which I at first called "lesbian."

This interpretation was strengthened by the lack of criticism of these plays in the nineteenth to mid-twentieth centuries. Blind or insensitive to the "good parts" in these plays, heterosexual critics found them without interest. Once the plays were rediscovered, scholars failed to note the presence of eroticism between women in them (Cotton 1980, Morgan 1981, and Steeves 1962 all comment on the plays without mentioning what seemed to me most unusual about them).

I know of no moment in dramatic history when women's sexuality has been explored with more obvious delight and whimsy than in

Queen Anne. Studio of J. Closterman.
Courtesy of the National Portrait Gallery, London.

plays by women in the time of Queen Anne. Early in my researches I learned that the queen herself, according to the woman who knew her most intimately for the longest time, was what would now be called a lesbian. She had, Sarah Churchill wrote, "noe inclenation for any but of one's own sex" (Green 1967, 318). Nonetheless, Anne apparently had a sincere affection for her husband, with whom she conceived about twenty children, all of whom died. I found this pattern repeated in the plays: women might love other women passionately and sensually, yet cherish a kind of dogged loyalty, perhaps even love or erotic attraction, for their husbands. Was this, then, lesbianism? Was it bisexuality? How might one speak of it?

The queen's sexual behavior, like that of many characters in plays by women in her time, cannot be labeled neatly in the language bequeathed by Ellis and his ilk to Kinsey, Masters and Johnson, or even lesbian sexologist Joann Loulan. I was forced to imagine another sexual universe than the one I was accustomed to, a universe in which lines were not clearly drawn; in which sexual identity was blurred; in which eroticism was a language transcending the naming of parts or the claiming of identity. This eroticism helped women playwrights depict forms of "heat" that might attract audiences without offending their sense of propriety and decency.

The world revealed in the erotic passages that pepper women's plays of the early eighteenth century is a world seething with sexual interest that defies the notion of sexual identity. There are women pining for men while resting their heads on the tender and loving breasts of other women who "pant" for them; men lusting for other men but pursuing women in the marriage-market; women married to men but in love with women who may or may not move in and live with the married couple; and men toying with other men's interests while longing for the comfort of a woman's arms. All of these permutations of sexual desire occurred in a social context which is foreign to us now and requires some examination; in this essay I concentrate on revelations of love between women in three women's plays.

Queen Anne and Sexuality in Her Time

The second daughter of England's Roman Catholic monarch, James II, was the devoutly Protestant Anne, born in 1665 and called "the glory of her sex" by playwright Susanna Centlivre. Others called her "poor Queen Anne." She suffered ill-health, obesity, and pregnancy throughout her adult life (yielding no living heirs despite the numerous pregnancies, many carried to full term). She also enjoyed a short, glorious, prosperous, yet troubled and finally scandalous reign, from 1702 to 1714.

As a girl Anne was a tomboy who rejected feminine finery and pastimes, inclined to be more interested in politics and history than most young women, played the guitar, enjoyed horseback riding, had an unusually low speaking voice, and was indifferent to male suitors (see Abel Boyer's account of the personal and social aspects of Anne's development). Anne's indifference to men was interpreted as "shyness"; however, she was anything but shy in developing passionate attachments to girls during her adolescence. Anne conducted an epistolary love affair with Frances Apsley in which she-who-would-be-queen posed as "Ziphares," a man pining for his beloved "Semandra" (Gregg 1980, 21). The other adolescent girl who won Anne's heart was Sarah Jennings, later Churchill. Their attachment continued into their adult lives and was disturbing to some members of Anne's family, including her brother-in-law, William of Orange. He described the attachment in 1687 as "an immoderate passion" and told Anne it should be terminated (Hamilton 1975,86n). Anne refused.

Sarah was five years older than Anne and married John Churchill when she was seventeen. Anne repeatedly wrote Sarah of her hope that "next to Lord Churchill I may claim ye first place in your heart" (Gregg 1980, 30), and the letters written almost daily by Anne to her beloved Sarah over the next twenty-five years are tender, erotic, and devoted (see Green 1967, appendix, for examples). These include the years when John Churchill was abroad, waging war with Louis XIV at Anne's behest. I might now be writing this essay in French rather than English were it not for the fact that it was in Anne's personal interest to keep Sarah's husband stationed in France, where he would not demand the attentions of his wife, attentions Anne chose to reserve for herself.

Since about 1691, the princess and Sarah had used pen names to address each other by mail, Mrs. Morley for Anne and Mrs. Freeman for Sarah, both suggested by Anne so there would be "nothing of Distinction of Rank between us" (Gregg 1980, 81–82). Both women understood that Anne's chief duty was to bear the nation a Stuart heir. The tragedy of her miscarriages and the deaths of her many babies in childbirth or youth was the source not only of personal despair and physical wear and tear to Anne but also of great sadness to the nation; the consensus of modern historians is that Anne's children died because of her husband's syphilis (Bevan 1964, 434). But the years when John Churchill was away making war and Mrs. Morley and Mrs. Freeman were harmoniously exchanging letters, holding hands in public, sleeping together, and addressing each other as "my dearest," "my sweet," and "my beloved" were banner years for women playwrights, and for female friendship themes, sometimes erotic in flavor, in women's plays.

Agnes de Castro

Catharine Trotter's *Agnes de Castro* (first performed 1695, printed 1696) features a heroine who claims she was not "made for Love" except the love of Constantia; and Constantia (identified in the script as "The Princess," which was also how Anne was known in 1695) loves her husband and Agnes "equally." Because Constantia's husband is in love with Agnes, the whole action of the play involves a test of the friendship of the two women. Their love passes the test, for Constantia never blames Agnes for the situation, and Agnes remains immune to the rapturous longings of Constantia's husband until the last moments of the fifth act; even then her faint words of praise for him are an expression of her loyalty to Constantia, whose dying wish was that Agnes accept his love.

The first scene between the two women takes place in Constantia's bedroom, as the Princess says, "My Agnes! Art thou come! My Souls best/ Comfort, Thou dear Relief to my oppressing Cares" (Steeves 1982, 2:3; subsequent quotations are identified only by page number). In a long but well-crafted scene, Agnes declares she loves Constantia and "to serve you wou'd abandon Life" (7), though she envies Constantia's husband for his "blessings" in a wife (7). Constantia reassures Agnes that their love will overcome all obstacles, but when Agnes leaves the room and Constantia faces her husband, the princess appears painfully torn between him and Agnes. Constantia says she understands why he loves Agnes, as she shares that obsession with him; and yet "Oh Dear Prince! there's not a part of me,/ That is not fill'd with softest Love for thee,/ My Soul's all thine,

I languish for thy Love" (9), though she adds, "Fear not for Agnes, Sir,/ I love her, and her being dear you you,/ More strongly recommends her to my care" (9). This portrait is of a much more complex sensual identity than we are accustomed to finding in twentieth-century literature.

Much later in the play a minor female character describes with amazed and voyeuristic fascination how the princess and Agnes behave when alone together: "I found/ The Princess leaning on her Rivals Neck;/ They mingled Kisses with the tend'rest Words,/ As if their Rivalship had made 'em dear" (20). The peak of passion between the two women comes in Constantia's death scene. Agnes tells Constantia she is "my Light, my Guard, my All" (25); Constantia begs Agnes, "Be less transported; they too moving Grief,/ Had almost forc'd from me a Wish to live" (26); and then with her last dying breath Constantia commends her son to Agnes's care and begs Agnes to marry the prince (26), a dying request which Agnes finds unbearable. Instead Agnes begs to be "intomb'd alive, with my dead Friend" (30) and moans, "Ah miserable Agnes! shun Mankind;/ There's nothing vertuous, since Constantia's gone,/ No Life without her; I'll go find her out,/ And breathe my Soul into her Lifeless Corps" (31). Agnes imagines her own death and hopes, "But I shall meet my Princess where I go,/ And our unspotted Souls, in Bliss above,/ Will know each other, and again will love" (34). This language is scarcely that of ordinary friendship; the very choice of words betrays an intermingling of sense and spirit.

Trotter leans heavily on her source for this play, a novel translated from the French by Aphra Behn, published in 1688, but Trotter shapes her scenes to intensify the relationship between the two women and to contrast the depth of emotion in the passion of the two women with the shallowness of men's passions. Trotter's Agnes is more indifferent to men than Behn's Agnes was, and Trotter's story makes the erotic energy between the two women more palpable than Behn's did (see Kendall 1986a for a full comparison of Trotter's Agnes with Behn's).

Queen Catherine

The play by Mary Pix which most resembles *Agnes de Castro* is also the one that features a character audiences might have associated

Mary Pix. Unknown artist.
Courtesy of the National Portrait Gallery, London.

with Anne. That is *Queen Catherine* (1698). Interestingly, Trotter wrote the epilogue to this play. She and Pix were so closely associated at this time that there can be no doubt they discussed their work and apparently came to some of the same conclusions about how to include eroticism without being branded as bawdy.

At first Pix's Queen Catherine and her companion Isabella seem but traditional friends, gossiping with each other about the men in their lives. Catherine longs for her husband, Tudor, and Isabella calls him "the Masterpiece of Heaven,/ And wonder of the Earth" (Steeves 1982, 1:9; all quotations are subsequently identified only by page numbers). Catherine observes Isabella's fondness for Clarence but warns Isabella (too late) that Clarence is untrustworthy and treacherous. Isabella's heart is torn between the Queen and Clarence, for whom she expresses strong erotic feeling. Isabella says his "God-like form" and his respect for her have made it impossible for her to rebel against the "awfull power" of her attraction to him.

Pix's queen tells the man she loves that her friend Isabella "almost rivals" him in her heart; for the queen, the existence of simultaneous love for a woman and a man is less troubling than it is for Isabella, who is unsure where her primary loyalty should lie. Finally though, when Isabella is fatally stabbed, it is the queen she returns to. Her dying wish is to be laid at the queen's feet. The central action of the play, for Isabella, involves a conflict between her love for the queen and her love for a man. Isabella casts her lot with the man, and on that decision (shown to be the wrong one) hangs the tragic denouement of the play, including the deaths of Isabella and Tudor. Pix provides an interesting variant on the love vs. duty theme so common in heroic tragedy, and the moral of the tale seems to be that women are wiser to focus their passions on each other than to risk life, love, and country for heterosexual attraction, which is somehow more vulgar. Women's love is not only safer and more dependable than men's; in this dramatic universe it is a little closer to the angels.

The Double Distress

Pix's *The Double Distress* (1701), a five-act tragicomedy set in ancient Persia, is replete with "good parts." It opens with a revelation of attraction between Leamira, Princess of Persia (played by Elizabeth Barry) and the gentle Cytheria, a Medean princess (played by Anne Bracegirdle). Leamira says,

> Let haughty statesmen at a distance treat,
> My Arms shall raise her to my tender Heart;
> And while I hold thee thus, my Cytheria,
> The Crown upon my Father's Head is not
> So priz'd, as is this Gemm within my Bosom.
> What Monster, bred beneath the frigid Zone,
> But wou'd, like me, thus open wide its Arms,
> And burn with ardent Fires for her Reception
> (Steeves 1982, 1:11; subsequent references
> to page numbers only).

Cytheria responds to Leamira in like fashion, but both women are in love with men as well. Cytheria, in fact, has conceived a frightening passion for her brother, Cyraxes, and Pix milks this for every ounce of titillation it offers. Cytheria, in a long and passionate scene with Cyraxes, recoils at her own feelings. After an embrace, Cytheria cries out in horror, "Fly, fly Cyraxes, Cytheria fly" (32). She croons sweetly, racked by longing and guilt, "What change is this my trembling Heart allarms!/Starts ev'ry Pulse, and unknown Wishes warms, Kindles my Blood, and with delightful Pains./And killing Pleasure thrills thro' all my Veins" (31).

The play is heavily erotic throughout and features numerous scenes in which Leamira and Cytheria embrace and kiss, rest their cheeks against each other's panting breasts, and discuss their apparently doomed loves. Sudden fifth-act revelations confirm that Cyraxes is not *really* Cytheria's brother; the two women marry the two men they have loved from the start, become sisters-in-law, and continue their relationship after marriage, making this a play with a happy ending for everybody.

This is almost how things worked out at Kensington Palace. Queen Anne, Sarah Churchill, their marriages, and their relationship all flourished in the years between 1695 and 1708, when thirty-one women's plays were staged on London's two professional stages. However, around 1704, the queen and Sarah began to suffer disharmonies. There was another woman involved. By 1708 Sarah had brewed a major scandal, accusing the queen of unreasonable passion for Abigail Hill Masham, who replaced Sarah as the queen's intimate companion. Broadsides likened Queen Anne to Edward II, and Abigail to Gaveston; and Sarah felt her former lover should be dethroned for loss of reason (see Kendall 1986b for amplification and documentation of these events). The issue was never whether or not the queen was homosexual; the issue was whether a queen who loved the company of other women might be subject to a loss of reason owing to this fact. It is ironic that the only person in Britain who seemed to feel the queen had lost her reason was the woman she was rejecting. Nonetheless, erotic female friendships, which are rare enough in English drama and had only surfaced in women's plays between 1695 and 1706, disappear altogether after this scandal.

It appears that the queen's behavior, coupled with Puritanical views of heterosexual passion, contributed to a temporary fashion for the public expression of eroticism between women, until the scandal fanned by Sarah Churchill called the queen's reason into question. While the presence of eroticism between women in women's plays would not alone establish such a fashion, Delariviére Manley's key novel *Atalantis* (1709) refers to a "cabal" of fashionable women who cherished erotic attachments for each other, many of them ladies of the court. The novel, published at the height of the scandal, alludes to a situation which has presumably been going on for quite some time. These scraps of evidence, taken with the well-known homosexual exploits of Anne's brother-in-law, the tradition of the effeminate fop, and other romping expressions of multi-sexuality or romantic same-sex friendship suggest that the sexual scene in eighteenth-century England cannot be described in modern psychosexual terms.

While these plays offer a treasure house of erotic imagery and certainly the roots of what has become a lesbian tradition in literature, it is simplistic to call them "lesbian." That word implies the existence of an option that was not available to eighteenth-century women in the sense that it is available now. Marriage was compulsory for middle- and upper-class women who didn't take to the nunnery, and there was almost no chance a pair of female lovers might set up housekeeping together and avoid sex with men. So nothing like monogamous, committed lesbian relationships appears in the literature of the time. While in some women's plays it is possible for a widow to choose to remain single, there is no representation of two women who make a life together.

The plays offer us a glimpse at a world in which women were both more and less free than we have language to describe. They were more free to explore expressions of love for each other without having to cross dangerous lines of sexual identity; there was no lesbian threat. They were less free to create lives together without the interference and domination of men; there was no lesbian option. We are forced, finally, to enjoy all the "good parts" of these plays as their audiences must have enjoyed them: as expressions of a free-flowing erotic energy and passion that was never vulgar.

Works Cited

Bevan, Bryan. 1964. "Queen Anne 1665–1714." *Contemporary Review* 205: 432–435.

Boyer, Abel. 1722. *The History of the Life and Reign of Queen Anne*. London.

Clark, Constance. 1984. *The Female Wits: Catherine Trotter, Delariviére Manley, and Mary Pix—Three Women Playwrights Who Made Their Debuts in the London Season of 1695–96*. Ann Arbor, Mich. University Microfilm International. No. 8409389.

[Cockburn], Catharine Trotter. 1696. *Agnes de Castro*. London.

Cotton, Nancy. 1980. *Women Playwrights in England c. 1363–1750*. Lewisburg, Pa.: Bucknell Univ. Press.

Faderman, Lillian. 1981. *Surpassing the Love of Men: Romantic Friendship and Love Between Women from the Renaissance to the Present*. New York: William Morrow.

Green, David. 1967. *Sarah, Duchess of Marlborough*. New York: Scribner.

Gregg, Edward. 1980. *Queen Anne*. London: Routledge.

Hamilton, David. 1975. *The Diary of Sir David Hamilton 1709–1714*. Ed. Philip Roberts. Oxford: Clarendon.

Kendall, [Kathryn M.]. 1986. "From Lesbian Heroine to Devoted Wife: Or, What the Stage Would Allow." *Journal of Homosexuality* 12 (May): 9–22.

———. 1986. *Theatre, Society, and Women Playwrights in London from 1695 through the Queen Anne Era*. Ann Arbor, Mich.: University Microfilm International. No. 8618505.

Manley, [Mary] Delariviére. 1971. *The Novels of Mary Delariviére Manley*. Ed. Patricia Koster. 2 vols. Gainesville, Fla.: Scholars' Facsimiles and Reprints.

Morgan, Fidelis. 1981. *The Female Wits: Women Playwrights on the London Stage 1660–1720*. London: Virago.

Pix, Mary. 1701. *The Double Distress*. London.

———. 1698. *Queen Catherine*. London.

Steeves, Edna L., ed. 1982. *The Plays of Mary Pix and Catharine Trotter*. 2 vols. New York: Garland.

Aphra Behn: The Playwright as "Breeches Part"

FRANCES M. KAVENIK

I t is tempting to consider Britain's first professional woman playwright, Aphra Behn, a feminist, and to find qualities in her plays which distinguish them from those written by her male counterparts (see, for example, Langdell). But the truth about Behn is both simpler and more complex, deeply rooted in the times during which she prospered. From the moment she first began writing for the stage in 1670 until her death in 1689, Behn was the consummate professional. In the preface to *Sir Patient Fancy* (1678), among others, she acknowledges the fact that she writes "for Bread, and not ashamed to owne it, and consequently ought to write to please (if she can) an Age which has given severall proofs it was by this way of writing to be obliged" (1915, 4:7). This fact, of course, does not make Behn any less imaginative than her fellows—Wycherly, Dryden, Etherege, or Shadwell—but it does mean that her creativity, like theirs, was tempered and bounded by public taste, dramatic convention, and theatrical conditions. Because these external factors altered, sometimes radically, during the two decades Behn wrote for the theater, her writing changed with them, at the same time retaining certain distinctive patterns set during her earliest years as a playwright.

Some ten years before her debut, Restoration drama itself began in a climate far from ideal for theatrical enterprises, without trained actors, playwrights, or audiences, and without theaters (Van Lennep 1965, xxi–xxii). A few years later, most of these problems had been solved, but managers were still forced to scrounge for plays, Killigrew in particular relying on Jacobean and Caroline plays which he claimed on behalf of the pre-Commonwealth King's Men (see Free-hafer 1965, 7-8; Hume 1980, 156–72; Milhous 1980, 1-34). Because the most popular plays of this older repertory were by John Fletcher, either alone or in collaboration, and by Jacobean and Caroline dramatists, like Massinger and Middleton, who imitated his style, one can see why, in the sharply competitive atmosphere of two rival houses vying for the same audiences, the first new, untried play-wrights chose to write their plays in a modified fletcherian style. Behn was no exception.

The "fletcherian mode," whether in comedy, "mongrel" tragi-comedy, or tragedy, had distinctive and recognizable characteristics. Based on affective, rather than internal directives, it elicited audience response by a variety of means: near-simultaneous, independent ac-tions which sometimes attain the status of separate plots; energetic and episodic movement through surprising revelations; twists of for-tune; and character reversals, discoveries, and peripeteias. Actions and characters are balanced and counterpointed to complicate the dynamics of the play, without much regard for verisimilitude, narra-tive coherence, or cognitive development. The plots of these plays, keyed higher or lower, depending on genre, repeat a few well-worn situations: courtships obstructed by rivals, parents, or other author-ity figures, and/or the wilfulness or folly of the lovers themselves. But the plays sustain their audiences' interest by the intricate and unforeseen means to the obvious end, and by unpredictable charac-ters who change "shape from moment to moment" (Waith 1952, 38) and can be manipulated at will by the playwright.

During the 1660s, the new Restoration playwrights altered this fletcherian pattern to suit the tastes of contemporary audiences, by updating settings and characters into modern "types," by making better use of the new movable scenery. Exploiting the possibilities inherent in female actresses playing female roles enabled these playwrights to take fuller advantage of Fletcher's balanced male and female parts to create the "gay couple" first identified by John Har-rington Smith. By the late sixties, confrontations between well-matched male and female antagonists were common fare on-stage in both comic and serious actions, as, for example, in the two plots of Dryden's *Secret Love* (1667). The final alteration, occurring just be-fore Behn's first play appeared, was a new freedom in exploring this inherently licentious material, seen in Thomas Betterton's *The*

Amorous Widow,[1] one of whose plots, derived from Molière's *George Dandin,* graphically demonstrates the perils of unequal marriage.

Thus Behn appeared as a playwright at a crucial juncture in Restoration comic development, after initial production problems had been solved, and comedy was set to "take off" into a period of virtually unchecked activity. Her first two plays, *The Forc'd Marriage* (1670) and *The Amorous Prince* (February 1671), explore sexual issues somewhat tentatively, but by the time of *The Dutch Lover* (February 1673), *The Town-Fopp* (September 1676), *The Counterfeit Bridegroom* (Fall 1677), *The Debauchee* (c. February 1677), *The Rover* (March 1677), and *Sir Patient Fancy* (January 1678), she was "one of the boys," so to speak, in her forthright presentation of the perils and delights of unleashed sexuality.

From the first, Behn chose to adapt the more exotic, usually tragicomic, version of the fletcherian mode in her own plays, often borrowing from Jacobean or Caroline sources.[2] Such plays were often set abroad, sometimes in past or vaguely undefined times, to establish a comfortable distance between the action on stage and the audience and give the playwright latitude for elaborate plot contrivances. Behn uses foreign settings for the first time in her first two plays— *The Amorous Prince, or, the Curious Husband* (Florence) and *The Forc'd Marriage, or, the Jealous Bridegroom* (France)—both appearing in the 1670–71 season. Both are also set at court and peopled with princes and princesses, nobles, hangers-on, and servants. As in such Fletcher plays as *The Maid's Tragedy* and *Philaster,* the court setting introduces a level of political machination to the intrigue plot, and Behn uses those court settings to establish conflicts between various kinds of authority and a more meritorious set of values—honor, friendship, love—which ultimately prevails.

Both plays are based on standard fletcherian romantic dilemmas. In *The Forc'd Marriage,* the king of France rewards his favorite warrior with his choice of bride, despite her prior attachment to the prince. In proper fletcherian style, Behn offers not just one but several comparable misalliances in subsidiary actions that involve climactic swordfights, jealous encounters, a near-death, and mistakes of all kinds before the mismatched young people are finally sorted out satisfactorily. In the double plot structure of *The Amorous Prince,* one action centers on Frederick, the amorous prince of the title, who has an insatiable appetite for young and innocent women, not excluding his best friend's sister or bride-to-be, while the other focuses on Antonio, so jealous of his wife he makes his friend Alberto "test" her virtue. More concerned with the sexual activities of its principals than *The Forc'd Marriage, The Amorous Prince* calls attention to Frederick's excesses throughout the play and sets up his "conversion" at the end by having characters continually remind each other that he's just spoiled and over-indulged.

If meant to placate the more staid members of the audience, such excuses were probably unnecessary even at this time; other Restoration dramatists were allowing their characters even more indulgence without explanations. At any rate, by February 1673, when *The Dutch Lover* premiered, the stage had already been exploiting greater sexual explicitness in plays like Wycherleys' *Love in a Wood* (March 1671), Dryden's *Marriage-à-la-Mode* (April 1672, possibly November 1671), Ravenscroft's *The Citizen Turn'd Gentleman* (July 1672), and Shadwell's *Epsom Wells* (December 1672), and Behn was in tune with such developments. What these comedies share with each other, and with Behn's up to the Exclusion Crisis, is a readiness to test the limits of all forms of received authority against the demands of basic human desires, specifically for money, power, and sexual release. Because the audience these comedies entertained was heterogeneous, and because individual members of it might wish to be titillated and yet also preserve their sense of moral superiority, these comedies were designed to deliver their radical messages "safely" by means of various adaptations of the fletcherian mode. In the comedies above, Wycherley and Shadwell offer balanced pairs of lovers within the same play who recognize different goals, identify different systems of values, and follow different paths to their respective conclusions. (Generally an immoral hero[ine] or couple is counterweighted with a recognizably moral one or one who "converts" to morality at the end.) In *The Citizen Turn'd Gentleman,* Ravenscroft locates all the baser forms of trickery in secondary characters and keeps the play relatively chaste otherwise. And Dryden's *Marriage-à-la-Mode* toys through four-and-a-half acts with suggestions of adultery, cuckolding, and even a *ménage a quatre,* only to retreat into relatively conventional marriages and betrothals at the end. Behn used several of these patterns in her own plays, but also, from *The Amorous Prince* on, adapted a type usually seen in the more romantic fletcherian plays, the "breeches part," for her own ends.

The "breeches part" or "woman drest in man's cloaths" already had a long and honorable stage tradition prior to the Restoration. Derived from Plautine and Italian Renaissance comedy, the girl dressed as a boy, what Victor Oscar Freeburg calls the "female page," was a popular figure in Elizabethan and Jacobean drama, and he identifies its four basic elements: "First, the disguised heroine seeks her husband or lover; second, she serves this man unrecognized; third, she acts as love messenger to a rival mistress; and fourth, some lady who believes that the disguised person really is a man becomes the victim of a mistaken wooing" (1951, 40). His list of plays featuring such disguises (61–99) includes a number of Jacobean dramas that were popular in the early Restoration repertory, among them Shirley's *Love in a Maze* and *The Grateful Servant*, Middleton's *The Widow*, Fletcher's *The Maid's Tragedy*, *Philaster*, *The Coxcomb*, and *The Night Walker*. During the 1660s, one finds numerous restoration imitations of these kinds of plays, like Glapthorne's *Argalus and Parthenia* (1661), Stapylton's *The Slighted Maid* (1663), Dryden's *The Rival Ladies* (1664), Killigrew's *The Siege of Urbin* (1665), Boyle's *Guzman* (1669), and many more. John Harold Wilson (73) counts eighty-nine plays first performed on the Restoration stage between 1660 and 1700 which have breeches parts.

In the traditional romance or romantic comedy, the breeches part is used to break down the basic courtship motif—active men intriguing for passive women—by exploiting the role's potential for comic or pathetic effects: a woman dons breeches to escape guardian or unwanted suitor and finds herself in dangerous or ridiculous situations. By the late sixties a more combative sexual element was being introduced; for example, in Dryden's *Secret Love* Florimell (played by Nell Gwyn) dons breeches to humiliate Celadon by acting as his rival, and succeeds with panache. Operating in a more serious tragicomic mode, Behn effects much the same transformation a few years later in *The Dutch Lover*. Debauched by Antonio and abandoned by her family, Hippolita decides to seek her own revenge, girding her loins for it in a set-speech worthy of the most extravagant heroic hero.

> Methinks I am not what I was,
> My Soul too is all Man;
> Where dwells no Tenderness, no womanish Passions.

I cannot sigh, nor weep, nor think of Love,
But as a foolish Dream that's gone and past.
Revenge has took possession of my Soul,
And drove those Shadows thence; and shows me now
Love, in so poor, so despicable a Shape,
So quite devested of his Artful Beauty,
That I'm asham'd I ever was his Votary.
(4.2. 293‒4).

Although the action ends predictably—Antonio wounds her, repents, and they marry—for a short time there is on stage a blurring of male/female role distinctions which is highly suggestive.

This altered use of the breeches part by Behn and other dramatists was but one facet of a greater conceptual shift taking place during the period, where "the idea of authority . . . was detached from the hierarchical structure of feudal society . . . secularized" (Staves 1979, xi). This process shows up in 1660s comedies like *The Committee* (1662), but dominates 1670s drama, where one regularly sees power transferred from the older to the younger generation, from rules of conduct or honor to license, from vested political authority to meritocracy. Indeed, all the "sex comedy" of the seventies served up fare whose challenge to orthodoxy went well beyond sex to present a severely weakened form of traditional authority. Moreover, in most of these comedies such displays of freedom, of expanded choices, are no longer, as in 1660s comedies, responses to externally produced situations (e.g., obstructive parents), but are enacted by characters purely to serve their own ends. Yet 1670s heroes and heroines are not presented nor do they see themselves as rebels, with or without causes; instead, acting in response to inner drives and calculating social costs, they concentrate their energies on circumventing obstacles to their will and pleasure. As Harold Weber puts it, rake heroes (and heroines) "prefer to manipulate their society in order to fulfill their own desires rather than to reform it" (Weber 1986, 116).

The three Behn plays which premiered during the 1675–76 season—*The Debauchee, The Town-Fopp,* and *The Rover*—clearly illustrate this shift, and while the first two are set in London and *The Rover* in Naples, all three contain important breeches part roles. While *The Town-Fopp* is almost a reenactment of the plot of *The Forc'd Marriage* with appropriate domestic substitutions—including the use of prose instead of verse and the addition of a fop, Sir Timothy Tawdry—*The Debauchee* is genuinely new and takes advantage of the freedom of the stage and the age. The titular character, Careless, goes his merry way through the plot, getting drunk, casting aside his mistress, and attempting to cuckold his uncle, who has forgiven and reinstated him countless times. Loveless, his rival for the hand of a rich widow, has meanwhile inspired the love of a young woman who acts as his page and must sort out their tangled love affair. Both plays contain rake heroes and assertive heroines in a relatively nonjudgmental environment that includes cuckolding and multiple love affairs. But Behn also provides conclusions involving conventional marriages so that individual members of the audience may choose whatever "ending" they prefer and can assume, for example, that Careless's reformation and marriage are purely temporary and that he will continue his libertine course, or that he has truly reformed and that the Widow is clever enough to curtail his further amours.

The Rover pushes the boundaries of this format even further, thereby testing the limits of acceptable social behavior. First, it exploits more fully than Behn's previous comedies the juxtaposition of English and foreign characters, juggling a broad range of tone and character adroitly. In Willmore, the "rover" of the title, Behn individuates the archetypal rake-hero; dispossessed since the interregnum, he has few ties beyond the occasional male friend and a deep-rooted loyalty to king and country. Consequently, his relationships with women are brief, peripatetic, and pragmatic rather than romantic; as he explains to Hellena at their first meeting: "I am come from Sea, Child; and *Venus* not being propitious to me in her own Element, I have a world of Love in store—Wou'd you would be good-natur'd, and take some on't off my Hands."[3] The humor of this odd "courtship" speech perfectly embodies the character Behn wants to establish; blunt to the point of vulgarity, Willmore's attractiveness lies in his open, almost childlike licentiousness, as when he yearns "Oh, for my Arms full of soft, white, kind—Woman" (2.1.27).

Though balanced by three other pairs of lovers, from the serious Belvile and Florinda to the farcical Blunt and Lucetta, the triangle of Willmore, Hellena, and Angellica Bianca is the focal point of the play. On the surface, the action seems conventional Restoration comic fare: Willmore, tempted by both the virginal Hellena and the courtesan Angellica Bianca, follows his lustful urges at first but eventually succumbs to the lure of virtue and matrimony. But neither these relationships nor the female characters that fix them are so polarized as they first appear; furthermore, the male and female roles are sufficiently unconventional as to give the play a fresh, piquant air.

Hellena, the breeches part, is the more familiar figure, but, as with Willmore, Behn creates a distinct personality within the stock type. Hellena is first portrayed as beset, along with her sister Florinda, by parental authority and designated for the nunnery, but she shows her true aspirations in her first speech:

> And dost thou think that ever I'll be a Nun? Or at least till I'm so old, I'm fit for nothing else. Faith no, Sister; and that which makes me long to know whether you love *Belvile*, is because I hope he has some mad Companion or other, that will spoil my Devotion; nay I'm resolv'd to provide myself this Carnival, if there be e'er a handsom Fellow of my Humour above Ground, tho I ask first. (1.1.11).

The carnival environment of the play—where all roles, classes, and values are subsumed in anarchy—becomes Hellena's playground and testing-ground. From her first encounter with Willmore, she matches him, pique and riposte, first exciting his interest and then testing his constancy in various guises, including breeches. Finally she wins his admiration and a proposal of marriage based on their shared dispositions: "we are so of one Humour, it must be a Bargain" (5.1.101). Indeed, in their curious mixture of innocence and earthiness and their dedication to promiscuity, Willmore and Hellena are as one. Thus, with Hellena, Behn fully extends the capabilities of the breeches part beyond the assumption of more ordinary masculine prerogatives to include sexuality. Hellena repeatedly asserts that she will rid herself of her troublesome virginity during the carnival, even if she has to take the initiative ("tho I ask first"). She lights on Willmore as her spiritual twin early on, and though she remains technically chaste throughout the play, she is firmly committed to his ethos throughout.

Another woman who takes on masculine assertiveness is Angellica Bianca, the courtesan, and her tempestuous relationship with Willmore ventures into new comic territory. Our first sight of her is,

appropriately enough, of her picture being hung outside her lodgings as an advertisement of her favors. From her appearance, however, Angellica Bianca begins to reveal a complex personality and a
clear understanding of power relationships: "He that wishes to buy,
gives me more Pride, than he that gives my Price can make me Pleasure" (2.1.31). On the one hand she vows that "nothing but Gold
shall charm my Heart" (2.1.31); yet she is so taken with Willmore's
flagrant appreciation, railing, and honorable poverty that she dis-
penses her favors gratis and gives him money, thus relinquishing her
power and setting up her own later humiliation.

In the course of their brief but torrid affair, their confrontations
show their likeness and, more important, their recognition of it. At
their first meeting, Willmore reviles her not on moral but on intensely personal grounds. Assuming that they are equals—people who
have no resources, family, money, or position to fall back on—he
condemns her for doing what he would despise in himself: "Yes, I am
poor—but I'm a Gentleman,/And one that scorns this Baseness
which you practice./Poor as I am, I would not sell my self"
(2.2.38–40). Angellica Bianca responds by criticizing male practices:
"Pray, tell me, Sir, are not you guilty of the same mercenary Crime?
When a Lady is proposed to you for a Wife, you never ask, how fair,
discreet, or virtuous she is; but what's her Fortune—which if but
small, you cry—She will not do my business—and basely leave her,
tho she languish for you" (2.2.40). His response—"It is a barbarous
Custom, which I will scorn to defend in our Sex, and do despise in
yours"—only begs the question. Thus Behn uses a rather conventional encounter between social outcasts to explore the mercenary
and self-interested motives underlying modern sexual relations.
Both characters acknowledge that the cost of maintaining personal
integrity without the finances to indulge it can be too high, and that
prostitution—of the male or female variety—may be the only answer,
tacitly acknowledged when Willmore accepts money from her.

Yet, by their second encounter (4.2) the balance of power has
shifted, as Angellica Bianca berates Willmore for his inconstancy
and accuses him of chasing a "virtuous mistress." Denying the
charge, he is nonetheless ready when Hellena appears in male garb as
her own servant pleading "his mistress' " case, to listen with interest
to the offer of "some kind young Sinner, one that has Generosity
enough to give a favour handsomely to one that can ask it discreetly,

one that has Wit enough to manage an Intrigue of Love" (4.2.77). Reappearing once more in act 5, Angellica is vengeance personified; among Willmore's crimes are teaching her to love, taking away her pride, and replacing it with a "mean submissive passion," i.e., making her a slave. When she assumes the ultimate male role and threatens him with a pistol, she also ironically speaks in the accents of a romantic hero[ine]: "Traitor./Does not thy guilty Blood run shivering thro thy Veins?/Hast thou no Horrour at this Sight, that tells thee,/Thou hast not long to boast thy shameful Conquest?" (5.94–95). But Willmore, predictably, refuses to respond in kind, and replies in prose: "Faith, no Child, my Blood keeps its old Ebbs and Flows still, and that usual Heat too, that cou'd oblige thee with a Kindness, had I but opportunity" (5.94). By the time Angellica leaves, scorning Willmore and ready to resume her former role as inviolate love-goddess, Willmore is ready to arrange a modern-style liaison with Hellena, his alter ego: "I was never claw'd away with Broad-Sides from any Female before, thou hast one Virtue I adore, good-Nature; I hate a coy demure Mistress, she's as troublesom as a Colt, I'll break none; no, give me a mad Mistress when mew'd, and in flying on I dare trust upon the Wing, that whilst she's kind will come to the Lure" (5.100).

Graphically and humorously in this series of confrontations, Behn exposes the underside of contemporary manners, balancing her defense of the libertine ethos with the auxiliary plots, where Blunt's self-interest achieves only his humiliation and Belvile and Florinda's romantic love is rewarded. Willmore and Hellena are a lively and attractive pair playing a delightful sexual power game, but Angellica's presence, her words, her very existence add an extra dimension to the play. Behn's configuration of the rake, the breeches part, and the courtesan in *The Rover* enables her to clarify certain basic truths about human and social nature for the audience in a new and exciting way, truths which her later plays assert only covertly, if at all.

The Exclusion Crisis, beginning with the Popish Plot in October 1678, induced a number of changes in Restoration comedy. For almost three years, the city of London was wracked with the kind of political upheaval and uncertainty that had not existed since the closing years of the interregnum, and the theaters were affected directly and immediately. One piece of evidence the *London Stage* editors muster is the epilogue to Behn's *The Feign'd Courtesans* (March 1679), which begins "So hard the times are, and so thin the Town,/Though but one Playhouse, that too must lie down" (Summers 2:411). The "one Playhouse" refers to the demise of the King's Company, so long plagued by internal dissension that it welcomed its union with the Duke's Company in 1682 (Milhouse 1980, 1–34; Hume 1976, 341).

The political climate could not but affect the writing of new plays. Most obvious was the appearance in the 1681–82 season of a group of political comedies, among them Behn's *The Roundheads* (c. December 1681), clearly intended to placate the town and the censor. Like Crowne's *City Politiques* and D'Urfey's *The Royalist,* also produced in the same season, *The Roundheads* (based on John Tatham's *The Rump,* 1660) takes a firm pro-Tory position, mitigating it only by a setting of the last days of the interregnum.[4] The more conventional forms of comedy also responded to the needs of a restless and uncertain populace hungering for social cohesion. Whereas playwrights had earlier basked in the liberty of writing for an audience secure in itself and tolerant of deviance on stage, those same playwrights now accepted the popular need to fix value. Comedies written after 1678, therefore, tend to divorce the rake hero[ine] from the position of authority s/he had attained during the 1670s, often by a retreat into morality or a structural devaluation of libertinism. Behn's comedies, as usual, are part of this process; many of them simply beg the question by spending far more time on farce and satire than on the conflict between well-matched sexual antagonists.

It was impossible, of course, for author or audience to restore fully the relative innocence of the 1660s; too much had intervened. One of Behn's solutions was to explore the consequences of the libertine ideology, thus creating a moral conclusion. *The Revenge* (late June 1680), for example, alters the ending of the Willmore/Angellica confrontation and turns comedy into potential tragedy. A discarded mistress, instead of retreating to lick her wounds in private, decides to kill her erstwhile lover, enlisting the aid of his best friend, who is besotted with her. Though the ploy fails, the play, with its multiple betrayals and Newgate scenes, exposes the darker implications of passion, transforming the carnival atmosphere of *The Rover* into a nightmare world where lies, mistakes, and false appearances can have serious consequences. And *The Revenge,* like *The False Court,*

The Roundheads, The City Heiress (May 1682), and *The Emperor of the Moon* (March 1687), has no breeches part to mitigate its tone.

Two other plays of this post-1678 period have such roles but use them in such a way as to deny their formal validity, particularly noticeable since both plays strongly resemble Behn's 1670s comedies. The plot of *The Feign'd Courtesans* (March 1679) is even more complicated than that of *The Rover*, with three love pairs, a villain, a couple of fools, and enough disguises to keep the wardrobe mistress in a frenzy. The two English lovers, Fillamour and Galliard, are respectively romantic and libertine, but attracted alike to a pair of "courtesans" who turn out to be only "feigned" (young gentlewomen, in fact, escaping their guardian-brother). Confrontations between the lovers are likewise feigned, as in act 4, scene 2, where Galliard and Cornelia, in her courtesan's role, argue the advantages of a foolish over a witty lover. Because the audience knows that she will bed neither suitor and that all this heat and activity will end in matrimony (though Cornelia promises to be a "Mistress-like Wife"), there is, in effect, no real assertion of libertine values in the play. The breeches part figure (Laura Lucretia) does not get her man, and the quasi-libertine Galliard is overpowered and outnumbered by the moral characters.

The Second Part of the Rover (January 1681) initially seems prepared to reprise the Hellena/Willmore/Angellica Bianca triangle in Ariadne/Willmore/La Nuche. Despite this resemblance, the carryover of Willmore and Blunt, and its foreign setting (Madrid this time), *Rover II* shows its differences most obviously in its use of the breeches part and courtesan roles. (Our first clue is that Elizabeth Barry, who played Hellena in *Rover I*, plays La Nuche in the sequel.) The play begins with Willmore celebrating his freedom, Hellena having conveniently died at sea, and being attracted to two women—Ariadne and La Nuche—and they to him. The plot is more complicated and more farcical than that of *Rover I*; Blunt is joined by a counterpart, Fetherfool, and together they pursue two unusual heiresses, a giantess and a dwarf. The love triangle turns into a quadrangle when Willmore's friend Beaumond, betrothed to Ariadne, is attracted to La Nuche. Behn keeps the audience guessing about the outcome, but leaves hints along the way that Beaumond is really an "honest" lover ("nay, a very Husband" La Nuche scorns him [4.1.176]), that La Nuche has succumbed to "Tyrant Love" for Will-

more, and that Ariadne is plagued by second thoughts. Only Willmore remains in character, though more passive in his role as lover
than as Mountebank in the farcial plot, but succumbs to romance in
the end, though "without the Formal Foppery of Marriage"
(5.3.208).

Both these comedies generally avoid the kind of sexual confrontations which comedies and their audiences of the 1670s thrived on.
The Willmore of *Rover II* and Galliard pose no threat to social
order; still less do their female counterparts; the reign of anarchy is
past. This alteration is further clarified by the group of 1680s comedies in which Behn makes adultery palatable. In *The False Court*
(November 1681), for example, a rich nobleman's betrothed is forced
by her father to marry a jealous old man. Disguised as "the Grand
Turk," the young man kidnaps the newlyweds and gives the husband
the choice of becoming a cuckold or a eunuch, with predictable
results. Marital infidelity is also treated sympathetically in *The
Younger Brother* (probably written about this time, though not produced until 1696) *The Roundheads,* and *The Lucky Chance* (April
1686). In all these plays, young women are forced or tricked into marrying old husbands. All have former lovers to whom they were
betrothed and who reappear to "rescue" them, sometimes with the
husband's consent and presumably with the audience's forbearance,
and the plays end with talk of "divorce."

These plots replace what happened in Behn's 1670s comedies—
wild young men and women finding mutual satisfaction somewhere
between freedom and commitment—with actions that may seem
more immoral but aren't. None of the young lovers in these four
plays is licentious; his/her passion is focused on a single, suitable
lover. Having taken vows of marriage, the women often feel guilty
about their own adultery, but Behn salves their qualms, and the audience's, by creating husbands who are seditious, cowardly, or avaricious. The crafty, lively young men are wit heroes but not rakes, the
women are more passive than active, and the plays ask no difficult
questions about freedom, sex, or individual behavior. Thus Aphra
Behn ended her career as she had begun it, in tune with the demands
of the theater-going public, though not the same public with the
same demands of a decade before.

Robert L. Root Jr. has suggested of Behn that "The 'genuine problem in her comedies' was the central issue of Restoration comedy—

the problem of arranged marriage—and hers was the clearest articulation of it before the great culminating treatment in the 1690s" (1977, 3). A recent biographer, Angeline Goreau, thinks that Behn espoused a feminist philosophy which contradicted the leading conventional and unconventional positions of her time. "The vision of free love that Aphra opposed to the wits' libertinism was based on a philosophical system that underlies much of her writing: social convention, she held—whether the convention of modesty or that of liberated conformity—had denatured instinct. Aphra's moral system defined what was right as what came naturally. Society and its morality, based on false assumptions, were responsible for the corruption of relations between the sexes" (1980, 187). Both these assessments are based—no less than those of the nineteenth-century critics who were scandalized by Behn's plays—on assumptions about women and women writers. Had these comedies come to us unsigned, they would, I suspect, be seen as no more or less feminist than *The Country-Wife*, a play that has a good deal to say about the condition of women.

As a writer, Behn's legacy is a body of work which depicts the social expectations and unconscious desires of men and women of her time as played out on stage. Her prejudices were those of her peers and her audience, tempered by dramatic convention. Along with her fellows, she lauded wit, style, and beauty over incongruity of behavior and expectation. In Behn's comic world, man and woman, rake, whore, and virgin, all respond to the same basic needs but meet with differential success, owing to a combination of capability, personality, circumstance, and luck, and those who deny their own desires or try to restrict others' freedom fare badly. But these plays are "moral" or even thematic only insofar as—and when—the audience wanted or needed them to be; as entertainment, their primary function was to respond—much as today's television programs do—rather than assert. Under these constraints, Aphra Behn mastered her craft, turning out lively, popular comedies which, often enough, slice through convention to unveil nature as her age chose to see it. Her particular ability was for choreographing a wide range of characters and actions, and for juxtaposing personalities and ideologies to create vivid dramatic conflicts. In her use of the breeches part, she showed that women could share the libertine philosophy with men and experience its liberating effects, in much the same way as she was able to compete on relatively equal terms with the best male playwrights of her time.

Notes

1. Hume calls *Amorous* "the first real comedy of sex and cuckoldry" (1976, 90) and suggests a date of c. 1670; the *London Stage* identifies the first known production as late as November 1670, some two months after the probable premiere of Behn's *The Forc'd Marriage* and three months before the first known production of her *Amorous Prince*.
2. For example, *Abdelazer* from *Lust's Dominion* (c. 1600); *The Debauchee* from Brome's *A Mad Couple Well Matched* (1635–37); *The Revenge* from Marston's *The Dutch Courtesan* (c. 1604); *The Rover* from Killigrew's *Thomaso, the Wanderer* (1654); *The Town-Fopp* from Wilkin's *The Miseries of Enforced Marriage* (1607); *The Amorous Prince* from Davenport's *The City Night-Cap* (1624). See Link (1968, 91–101) and Meredith (1976).
3. Behn, *Works*, vol. 1. act 1, scene 2, page 21. All the plays discussed here are in volume 1 of the *Works* and will subsequently be cited parenthetically in the text.
4. Behn's caution was well-founded; witness the production problems which beset Crowne's *City Politiques* in July 1682 and after (see John Harold Wilson ed. ix).

Works Cited

Behn, Aphra. 1915. *The Works of Aphra Behn*. Ed. Montague Summers. 6 vols. Reprint. New York: Phaeton, 1967.

Freeburg, Victor Oscar. 1951. *Disguise Plots in Elizabethan Drama: A Study in Stage Tradition*. Reprint. New York: Benjamin Blom, 1965.

Freehafer, John. 1965. "The Formation of the London Patent Companies in 1660." *Theatre Notebook* 20 (Autumn): 6–30.

Goreau, Angeline. 1980. *Reconstructing Aphra: A Social Biography of Aphra Behn*. New York: Dial.

Hume, Robert D. 1976. *The Development of English Drama in the Late Seventeenth Century*. Oxford: Clarendon.

——————. 1980. "Securing a Repertory." In *The London Theatre World, 1660–1800*. Carbondale: Southern Illinois Univ. Press. 156–72.

Langdell, Cheri Davis. 1985. "Aphra Behn and Sexual Politics: A Dramatist's Discourse with her Audience." In *Drama, Sex and Politics*. Ed. James Redmond. London: Cambridge Univ. Press, 109–28.

Link, Frederick M. 1968. *Aphra Behn*. New York: Twayne.

Meredith, David Wilfred. 1976. "Borrowing and Innovation in Five Plays by Aphra Behn." Unpublished dissertation. Kent State University.

Milhouse, Judith. 1980. "Company Management." In *The London Theatre World, 1660–1800*. Ed. Robert D. Hume. Carbondale: Southern Illinois Univ. Press. 1–34.

Root, Jr., Robert L. 1977. "Aphra Behn, Arranged Marriage, and Restoration Comedy." *Women and Literature* 5 (Spring): 3–14.

Smith, John Harrington. 1948. *The Gay Couple in Restoration Comedy*. Cambridge, Mass.: Harvard Univ. Press.

Staves, Susan. 1979. *Players' Scepters: Fictions of Authority in the Restoration*. Lincoln: Univ. of Nebraska Press.

Van Lennep, William, ed. 1965. *The London Stage, 1660–1800: A Calendar of Plays, Entertainments & Afterpieces Together with Casts, Box-Receipts and Contemporary Comment Compiled from the Playbills, Newspapers, and Theatrical Diaries of the Period. Part I: 1660–1700*. Intro. Emmett L. Avery and Arthur H. Scouten. Carbondale: Southern Illinois Univ. Press.

Waith, Eugene M. 1952. *The Pattern of Tragicomedy in Beaumont and Fletcher*. New Haven: Yale Univ. Press.

Weber, Harold. 1986. *The Restoration Rake-Hero: Transformations in Sexual Understanding in Seventeenth-Century England*. Madison: Univ. of Wisconsin Press.

Wilson, John Harold. 1958. *All the King's Ladies: Actresses of the Restoration*. Chicago: Univ. of Chicago Press.

―――. Introduction. *City Politiques*. By John Crowne. 1967. Lincoln: Univ. of Nebraska Press, ix–xix.

"I by a Double Right Thy Bounties Claim":
Aphra Behn and Sexual Space

JESSICA MUNNS

I, by a double Right thy Bounties claim,
Both from my Sex and in *Apollo*'s Name:
Let me with *Sappho* and *Orinda* be,
Oh ! ever sacred Nymph [Daphne], adorn'd by thee,
And give my verses Immortality.[1]
(orig. italics)

Aphra Behn was a prolific and successful writer who between 1670 and 1678 wrote at least seventeen plays. She also wrote a considerable body of verse, a large number of prose tales, made a number of translations, and pioneered the narrative and epistolary novel forms in England with *Oroonoko* (1688) and *Love Letters Between a Nobleman and His Sister* (1684–87). She was the first professional woman writer, and vigorously sought acknowledgment and "Fame as much as if I had been born a *Hero*" (1915, preface, *The Lucky Chance*, 3:187; emphasis in original). Fame, if not heroism, was accorded to her but her fame was tinged with infamy and her detractors drew attention to the anomaly of her being a writer and a woman.

In "Women's Published Writings 1600–1700," Patricia Crawford points out that "In writing for publication women risked their reputations. . . . Silence was an essential component of modesty" (1985, 216). Behn not only wrote for publication and money, not private circulation and friends, but she also wrote, as Frances Kavenik puts it in this collection, as "one of the boys," that is, immodestly and with license. In asserting access to her poetic "Masculine Part," Behn faced double censure, and contemporary writers, even when admitting her talent and wit, deplored her style. Crawford notes that Dryden advised a woman writer to avoid Behn's license, which gave "some scandall to the modesty of her sex" (217). Women writers urged caution and modesty on Behn. Anne Wharton recommended that she "Scorn meaner themes, declining low desire, / And bid your Muse maintain a Vestal Fire" (1695, 244). Anne Finch, Countess of Winchilsea, a talented poet who felt the constraints of sexual typing, praised Behn's talents—but with reservations. In her poem, "The Circuit of Apollo," itself an interesting feminization of a Restoration poetic form, the god refrains from handing the laurels to Behn. He admires her work and

> said amongst Femens [*sic*] was not on the earth
> Her superior in fancy, in language, or witt,
> Yet own'd that a little too loosely she writt;
> Since the art of the Muse is to stir up soft thoughts,
> Yett to make all hearts beat, without blushes or
> faults.
> (Finch 1979, 24. 12–16)

Most women writers were well aware of the hostile audience that awaited their verses and were anxious to deny any eagerness to publish and be damned. In Anne Finch's preface to the only collection of her poems published in her lifetime (1713), she expresses hesitation and doubt over the value of her works, which she does not even refer to as poetry or verses but deprecatingly as "Rimes": "For I have writt, and expos'd my uncorrected Rimes, and immediately repented; and yet have writt again, and again suffer'd them to be seen" (Finch (ed. Rogers) 1979, 9). Finch's verbs indicate the sexual nature of writing; her act of writing becomes an act of exposure, which demands repentance. And "yet"—the adverb carries the weight of insistent female desire—"again and again" she has not only written but has also revealed her writings and "suffer'd" the pleasure/pain of scrutiny. Finch's preface is a flirtation, even a titillation, a giving and then a taking away, an admission and a denial of access to and congress with the writer and the page and the writer and the public.

Katherine Philips, the "matchless Orinda," was also dubious over publication. When an unauthorized edition of her poems was published, she wrote to her friend and mentor Sir Charles Cotterell that

Sometimes I think that to make verses is so much above my
reach and a diversion so unfit for the sex to which I belong, that I
am about to resolve against it forever, and could I have recovered
the fugitive papers that have escaped from my hands, I had long
since, I believe, made a sacrifice of them to the flames. (Philips
1705, 127–28).

Philips's style is more shrinking than Finch's but equally ambiguous. "Sometimes" she wonders about the fitness of a woman writing
verse; she is "about" to give up writing, but has not ("yet"); and she
can only "believe" that she might have burnt her papers, and, as with
repentance, undergone purification. In these women's prefaces and
letters the act of writing is equivocal: like virgins in Restoration
drama, they do and they don't want the experience; they desire and
fear the consequences of their impulses. They situate their works on
the margins of literary production screened by playful, "feminine"
and modest disclaimers that seek to minimize the effrontery of
publication.[2]

Compared to these virginal flirtations with words, Behn's style
and approach are pugnacious. Behn neither hides her sex under a
masculine name, cross-dressing nomenclatures to slip across the barrier of gender, nor in admitting her gender does she abide by the
unwritten rules that limit female experience. Rather than cross-
dressing, Behn double-dresses and insists that her audience/readers
accept her female gender and her right to a freedom of expression and
range of topics hitherto limited to male literary production. Indeed,
in the lines quoted at the beginning of this chapter, Behn does not
merely refuse to apologize for being a woman and a writer, but boldly
claims a *double* privilege from female nymph and male god for being
so. It is the doubleness of her claims and the doubleness of her vision
that characterizes not merely Behn's "feminism" but her creation of a
new sexual space from which to speak. In claiming her double rights,
Behn assaults her reader's identity, as well as undoing and remaking
her own as she marks out a territory from which to operate.

In her prefaces Behn does not flirt, she asserts; she does not hesitate,
she threatens:

All I ask is the Priviledge for my Masculine Part the Poet in me
(if any such you will allow me) to tread in those successful paths

my Predecessors have so long thriv'd in, to take those Measures
that both the Ancient and Modern Writers have set me, and by
which they have pleas'd the World so well: If I must not because
of my Sex, have this Freedom, but that you will usurp all to your
selves; I lay down my Quill . . . for I am not content to write
for a Third day only. I value Fame as much as if I had been born
a *hero.* (1915, *The Lucky Chance,* 3:187).

In this passage Behn carries out her double act; she asserts both her
femaleness and her maleness. She insists she has a male part, not a
private part, but a public part; her "Quill" with which she writes
herself as poet. Far from shrinking from public attention, she
demands her place in the limelight. In defining the poet in her as
masculine, Behn does not deny that women can write verse. She is
pointing to the cultural tradition of her male "Predecessors," but she
sees this tradition as setting standards and precedents rather than
excluding her. She demands the right to enter the dance ("measures"), spaces and places where men tread, but nowhere does she
deny that she is also a woman, a member of "my Sex." Maleness is
only a "part," not the whole. The Quill/pen/penis with which Behn
writes is not a borrowed tool; it is *her* "Quill," and rightly belongs to
her. She will only lay it down if men refuse to acknowledge her right
to that which has been constituted to figure male supremacy. Men
"usurp all" to themselves and deny wo/man access to the variety of
parts that constitute the whole. Behn does not deny that penning
verse is male; she denies that poetic maleness is an exclusive category.

   In asserting her "Masculine Part the Poet in me," Behn trans-
gresses repressive literary boundaries. To use Jonathan Dollimore's
term in his essay "Subjectivity, Sexuality and Transgression," this is
a "subversive reinscription" of terms of literary discourse (1986, 57).
If writing is male, then as a woman and a writer Behn claims a male
part, too. Behn does not want to be a genteel lady poetess, nor does
she just want money, "Third day" house takings; she wants "Fame,"
and her place in the central literary tradition, which, inevitably, is a
male tradition. To take that place, without concealing her sex, she
must insist on a kind of literary androgyny; she will be a poet and a
hero, and, unequivocally, she lets everyone know she is also a
woman. Behn refuses to be marginalized; men "usurp all to your-
selves" and she reappropriates territory at the center and reinvests it.

Two-and-a-half centuries later in *A Room of One's Own* (1929), Virginia Woolf was to praise Behn's entry into the male-dominated realm of professional writing and also (in the voice of Mary Beton) to assert the need for literary androgyny: "one must be woman-manly or man-womanly" (Woolf 1929, 108). The androgyny Woolf postulates here and elsewhere is not actual and biological, nor is it, surely, a denial of difference. In *Orlando,* Woolf, using the image of dress, speculates that "In every human being a vacillation from one sex to another takes place, and often it is only the clothes that keep the male or female likeness, while underneath the sex is the very opposite of what is above" (1929, 186). Behn's texts are like Woolf's strip-teasing image; the preface is one thing, the play is another. But with further acts of undressing the assertive female preface signals male aggression while the bawdy male play delineates female sensibility. Genders slip and change places before our eyes, for in what Julia Kristeva has delineated as a new "signifying space, a both corporeal and desiring mental space" (Kristeva 1981, 33), there is room for free play as the speaker works with, through, and above the old classificatory system. It is Behn's free play in a space neither allowed nor defined by her culture which has the power to disrupt and disturb. Woolf's position is still controversial and it is not surprising that Behn's assertions of her fe/maleness can still lead to critical denunciations and assertions that her work is merely imitatively masculine and even antifeminist.[3] Despite the sharp rise in Behn studies, Behn's battles are not yet over and her claims to heroism have not yet been accepted.

Behn's double-dressing can be found throughout her works. Prologues and prefaces inform audiences and readers of the author's sex. *The Rover* (1677), Behn's most popular play, is an apparent exception insofar as the first two issues were printed without the author's name. Indeed, the prologue, which was not written by Behn, refers to the author by male pronouns (1967, *Prologue, lines* 38–40). However, in a postscript to the play, Behn asserts her gender and specifically addresses women readers as she defends her play from the (justifiable) criticism that it is heavily indebted to Thomas Killigrew's *Thomaso, or, The Wanderer* (1654). She notes ironically that had the play been a failure,

> I should have had no need of imploring that justice from the critics, who are naturally so kind to any that pretend to usurp

their dominion, *especially of our sex:* they would doubtless have given me the whole honour on't. (1967, xvi)

This postscript appears only in the first quarto editions of the play and the italicized passage is omitted in the first issue and in some of the second issues. The anonymous "Person of Quality" who provided the prologue, and Behn's printer, John Amery, presumably had more qualms than she had about her assertion of female authorship.

Behn's open and often angry insistence on her gender and her authorship has been seen by Katharine Rogers in *Feminism in Eighteenth-Century England* as incidental to her actual literary production:

> "The poet in Behn" was indeed masculine: her consciousness of herself as a woman appears almost entirely in these explicit defenses of the woman author, which are in no way integrated into her creative works. These show values and perceptions hardly distinguishable from those of the male writers with whom she competed. (Rogers 1982, 58).

It is undoubtedly true that Behn *does* write like other (male) Restoration dramatists in terms of her genres, styles, plot materials and topics. She writes with brio about promiscuous young men, impotent old men, hot-blooded virgins, cuckolding city wives, and bold courtesans. It is also possible, as Nancy Cotton suggests in her essay in this collection, that Behn's femaleness is signalled by her cheery depictions of an untroubled masculinity such as Willmore's in the *Rover* plays. It is male dramatists who have given us some of the most strongly androgynous male characters, such as Etherege's feline and seductive Dorimant in *The Man of Mode* or Wycherley's metaphoric eunuch, Horner, in *The Country Wife.*[4] Understandably, Behn is less concerned than a male dramatist with confusions in male identity than with asserting that there are no territories marked off from her fe/male access.

The drama of the day, influenced by popularized Hobbesian theories of human nature, presented bold and aggressive heroes and heroines who alike exhibit that "generall inclination of all mankind, a perpetuall and restless desire for Power after power, that ceaseth only in death." (Hobbes 1968, 161). Behn's characters share in this general restlessness and pursue their desires vigorously. Nevertheless, for all their conventionality and topicality, Behn's plays are not the mere products of gender reversal. Behn rarely loses sight of the difference between men's and women's experience as they struggle for their goals. Less concerned than a man with onslaughts on phallic supremacy, Behn is more aware than men of the realities of the womb and the social consequences of male supremacy. As Jacqueline Pearson has pointed out in her recent book, *The Prostituted Muse: Images of Women and Women Dramatics, 1642–1737*, Behn's interventions are subtle and to be found in her sympathy for outsiders, her depictions of strong, independent women, and her intense interest in the operations of the double sexual standard (1988, 143–68). Ironically, it is only by writing about such topics with the freedom of a man that Behn can express the constraints of a woman.

In *The Rover I*, the heroine, Hellena, asks her lover, who suggests they freely enter into an open affair, "What shall I get? A cradle full of noise and mischief, with a pack of repentance at my back?" (1967, 5.5.453–54). Behn is a realist about marriage and the choices most women have in life. At the end of *The Town-Fop* (1677) the unfortunate Phillis, who has married the brothel-crawling town-fop of the title, explains her choice bleakly enough to her brother: "Sir, you deny'd me my Portion, and my Uncle design'd to turn me out of doors, and in my Despair I accepted of him" (1915, 3:V,4). Few dramatists of the period portray sexual disgust more explicitly than Behn, or more tightly link arranged marriage with prostitution. In *Rover I*, for instance, Hellena instructs her sister on the horrors of her approaching arranged marriage to an elderly suitor:

> the giant stretches itself, yawns and sighs a belch or two loud as a musket, throws himself into bed, and expects you in his foul sheets; and ere you can get undressed, calls you with a snore or two. And are not these fine blessings to a young lady?
> . . . And this man you must kiss, nay kiss none but him too, and nuzzle through his beard to find his lips. And this you must submit to for threescore years, and all for a jointure. (1967, 1.1.119–28).

A less sexually graphic but equally depressing picture is painted in *Sir Patient Fancy* (1678):

> Custom is unkind to our Sex, not to allow us free Choice; but we above all creatures must be forced to endure the formal Recommendations of a Parent, and the more insupportable Addresses of an odious Fop; whilst the Obedient Daughter stands—thus—with her hands pinn'd before her, a set Look, a few Words, and a Mein that Cries—Come marry me. (1915, 4:1,1).

Behn's plays offer sympathetic portraits of women choosing their own mates and devastating portraits of the frustrations and humiliations of unhappy marriages. Ruth Perry has noted in her recent biography of Mary Astell that Behn was not "philosophically interested in the power relations between men and women," but that she did assert "her sense of her own power and sexual independence in images of lust between women or in portraits of impotent men" (1968, 17). Perhaps Behn was not "philosophically interested," but she was certainly practically conscious of the power relations between men and women in a society in which women were the objects of masculine exchange and signs of male power. Her dramas, stories, and verses explore female strategies to assert choice and to balance that power but they also recognize the limits to these strategies.

Behn's women characters are often sadly realistic about their situations and their options. In *The Rover I*, Angellica Bianca, a courtesan, tries to substitute power and money for love but discovers that she is capable of "a mean submissive passion" (1967, 5.252) for the promiscuous Willmore. She violates her own rules and gives herself to him freely but cannot keep him. Her anger and humiliation as she watches him pair off with the wealthy and virginal heroine, Hellena, are unforgettable and cast a shadow over the marriages that conclude the play. The male characters may triumph over the female characters but the women's submission can be "mean" and bitter. In *The City Heiress, or, Sir Timothy Treat-All* (1682), Lady Galliard, who has been bullied and tricked into marriage with Sir Charles Merriwill, detaches herself painfully from Wilding, whom she loves and has slept with but who has married another young heiress. At the end as the couples pair off, words and stage directions combine to present an uncomfortable moment as the defeated Lady Galliard moves to her unwanted husband:

Here, be as happy as a Wife can make ye—one last look more,
and then—be gone fond love. [*sighing and looking on* Wilding,
giving Sir Charles *her hand*] (1915: 2:V, 5).

This strain of sadness and the inclusion of uncomfortable moments
that throw off-balance the move toward a conventionally happy conclusion are fairly usual in Behn's work. At times, however, Behn ad-
justs law to reward her lovers, allowing divorce when divorce was
almost impossible (*The Town Fop*, 1676) or, occasionally, she packs
lovers off to bed together without regard to the social consequences
(*The False Count*, 1682, *The Lucky Chance*, 1686). Behn asserted
female rights when there were few social structures to support those
rights. She writes like a man in that she frequently gives her females
energies, powers, and possibilities that were only allowed to men. By
the same token, she writes as a woman in presenting images of
women released from the constraints of a male-inscribed femininity.
Rarely, however, does she neglect that such release takes its toll or is,
like Hellena, the embodiment of such release, short-lived.

Claiming equality in intellect, energy, sexual desire, and literary
creativity does not involve denying difference in terms of either biology or social reality. In a recent essay, "Deconstructing Equality-
Versus-Difference: or, the uses of Poststructuralist Theory for Feminists," Joan W. Scott has drawn attention to what Martha Minow has
called "the difference dilemma." The problem is that "both focusing
on and ignoring difference risk recreating it." Minow suggests that
instead "a new way of thinking about difference" is required, which

> involves rejecting the idea that equality-versus-difference con-
> stitutes an opposition. Instead of framing analyses and strate-
> gies as if such binary pairs were timeless and true, we need to ask
> how the dichotomous pairing of equality and difference itself
> works. (Scott 1988: 33–50, 39).

In its way and in her day, what I have termed Behn's "double-
dressing," that is, her agreement on both sameness/equality *and*
difference—masculine freedom and female identity—insistence de-
stabilized the fixed opposition of "binary pairs."

That such endeavors were at all possible for Behn is partly because
her atypicality defied definition and because her solitary stance min-
imized the threat of women as writers. Moreover, the two literary

genres she used most often, drama and the novel, were popular, "low," and innovative forms, which did not confer great status on their producers and which were not yet fully sexually inscribed. Had Behn sought fame as an epic poet, a theologian, or a philosopher, her education, which lacked Latin and Greek, and her sex (which determined her education), would have undermined her authority. As it is, the popular forms Behn utilized were relatively open and her claim to equal rights, if not unchallenged, was tenable. Behn points this out in her preface to *The Dutch Lover* (1673): "Plays have no great room for that which is men's great advantage over women, that is Learning" (1915, 1:224).[5]

Moreover, Behn staked her claim for literary equality at one of the few moments when a woman could make such a claim without provoking instant derision. Repressive and authoritarian though the actual social mores of the period were, in works of fiction and in theory it was possible to imagine new and freer forms of human nature and human sexuality. The work of the cartesian rationalist, Poulaine de la Barre, *De l'egalite des deux sexes* (1673), was published in England in 1677 with the rousing title, *The Woman as Good as the Man*, and argued forcefully for mental equality. For a short time, it became possible to discuss the sociology of marriage, the nature of sexual satisfaction, homoerotic love and to reconsider the boundaries of gender.

Restoration "libertine" poets delighted in pointing out that it was custom/hypocrisy and not Nature or truth which prescribed female modesty. The Earl of Rochester frequently, if ironically, encouraged the Phyllises and Chlorises of his lyrics to be true to their nature and inclinations and act out, like him, the promiscuous promptings of desire. On stage, not only sexual license but female intelligence was celebrated. Wycherley's Horner, for instance, proclaimed, "Methinks wit is more necessary than beauty, and I think no young woman ugly that has it, and no handsome woman agreeable without it" (1981, *The Country Wife*, 1.1.469–72). Bisexuality was rather fashionable in court circles, and on stage, drag scenes were popular, with women dressed as men, displaying in their masculine part their delectable female parts.[6] As Frances Kavenik demonstrates, various of Behn's heroines don breeches (for instance, Hellena in *The Rover* and Celinda in *The Town Fop*) and, while it is possible to dismiss this cross-dressing simply as sexy display, the popularity of the combination of female sexuality with masculine freedom suggests that there was a need (and ability) to imagine a new identity for women. This temporary mood of tolerance was usually only one of theoretical freedom, being largely confined to the publication and performance of works by men. But it matched Behn's tastes and aspirations and she embraced this freedom not only in her public writings but also in her private life. Behn's long-time lover, John Hoyle, was bisexual and in her verses "To Fair Chlorinda" (1915, 6:page 363) she coquettes as a woman with another woman:

> In pity to our Sex sure thou wer't sent
> That we might Love, and yet be Innocent.
> For sure no Crime with thee we can commit:
> Or if we should—thy Form excuses it.

Libertine promiscuity and bisexuality represent the extreme edge of seventeenth-century sexual discourse. More moderately, in plays, verses and pamphlets a new liberty is frequently proposed for women, and that liberty is usually associated with demands for better female education,[7] assertions of female mental abilities, and denunciations of arranged marriages—topics which Behn made very much her own.

Typically, Behn is forthright and optimistic over women's access to education. In her verses to Thomas Creech on his translation of part of Lucretius' *De Rerum Natura,* (1915, 6:220) she sees translations as empowering women. Again she uses spatial/territorial images as she celebrates women's movement into hitherto forbidden male preserves:

> Till now, I curst my Birth, my Education,
> And more the scanted Customes of the Nation:
> Permitting not the Female Sex to tread,
> The mighty Paths of Learned Heroes dead.
> The God-like *Virgil,* and great *Homers* Verse,
> Like Divine Mysteries are conceal'd from us.
>   We are forbid all greateful theams
>   No ravishing thoughts approach our Ear,
>   The Fulsome Gingle of the times,
> Is all we are allow'd to understand or hear. . .
> So thou by this Translation dost advance

> Our Knowledge from the State of Ignorance,
> And equals us to Man! . . .
> (1915, 6:page 167)

For Behn neither reading (Classics) nor writing is necessarily a gendered activity. Reading and writing have become gendered merely through conscious acts of appropriation aimed at denying women access to areas of thought and activity. Translation becomes a means of removing the barrier erected to figure difference in terms of absence of mind. In the course of the lines cited above, Behn moves from Job-like abject curses at her condition to become a new Eve released from a male dominated Eden. Reading is woman's fortunate fall; learning is the forbidden fruit that gives knowledge of equality. In these views and claims Behn can be seen as part of a wider movement that both informed and enabled her work. She was unique but she was lucky in living at one of the few times before the present century in which literature was seriously (if often wittily) engaged in reassessing gender typing.[8]

Behn's position, however, was always precarious and she outlived the era of reassessment and cultural exploration. Her status as a professional was odd rather than admirable and the bawdy and erotic nature of her plays and verses made her vulnerable to attack. Energetic, intelligent, highly sexed, and passionate, Behn's women were not the image of womanhood most contemporary women wanted to see. Nor were Behn's poxy whore-mongering rakes and roistering cavaliers the kind of men women wanted to see on the stage—even if they sat surrounded by them in the pit. By the later 1670s the women in the audience had stopped reeling under the barrage of sexual language and activity on stage and started reacting to it.[9] Women boycotted Thomas Otway's sexual farce *Friendship in Fashion* (1677), which he rather feebly defended by saying Mrs. Behn liked it, and they bitterly attacked Wycherley's *The Country Wife* (1678), which he sulks about in the preface to his next play, *The Plain Dealer*. They hissed Edward Ravenscroft's *The London Cuckolds* (1681), they boycotted Sedley's outspoken *Bellamira* (1687), and, by petitioning the court, they got Tom Durfey's *A Fool's Preferment* (1688) stopped.

Behn seems to have been most sensitive to the attacks on her work by her own sex. In the preface to *Sir Patient Fancy* she complains that women have damned her play. Behn's arguments are varied and contradictory as she denies her play is "baudy" (which it is) but also complains that no one minds if a man's play is bawdy. She strikes a self-pitying and pathetic note as she depicts herself as obliged to write for a living but also denies that there is any shame in so doing: "They [other women] ought to have had the good Nature and justice enough to have attributed its faults to the Authors unhappiness, who is forced to write for Bread and not ashamed to owne it" (1915, 4:7). In the same preface she is also aggressive and angry, asserting that the play's "loss of Fame with the Ladies" has not hurt the work and accusing her female detractors of picking on her precisely because she is a woman:

> I printed this play with all the impatient haste one ought to do, who would be vindicated from the most unjust and silly asper-sion, Woman could invent to cast on Woman, and which only my being a Woman had procured me. *That it was baudy,* the least and most Excusable fault in the Men writers, to whose Plays they all crowd, as if they came to no other end than to hear what they condemn in this; *but from a Woman it was unnatu-rall* (1915, 4:7; emphasis in original)

The woman with a "Masculine Part," who claims to be a poet, not a poetess and a hero, not a heroine is emerging as a freak of nature rather than the product of the new "Customes" and wider learning celebrated in "To Mr. Creech."

Society was not moving in the direction of integration and androg-yny. Free play between the signs of gender, which for a short time opened up the system, ceased. What power women could accrue to themselves was the power to elevate womanhood in terms of its con-ventional attributes: domesticity, softness, chastity, modesty and fi-delity.[10] As the seventies wore on, Behn's position became more iso-lated. She was both before and behind her times. The claims to professionalism and equality which she makes belong either to the earlier revolutionary period, when issues of gender were open to re-consideration, or to later periods, when women's entry into literary fields was established. The pathos and anger, and the claims for fe-male solidarity and haughty rejection of feminine morality found in the preface to *Sir Patient Fancy* indicate the problematics of her position.

By the end of the century, in *A Short View of the Immorality and Profaneness of the English Stage,* Jeremy Collier invokes nature, not nurture, to define women. He propounds a moral biology that makes writing like Behn's not merely immodest but simply impossible for a woman. "Modesty," he assures us, "is the distinguishing virtue of that sex," and "that it might always be at hand, 'tis wrought into the mechanism of the body" (1698, 11). The next century sees the emergence of many female authors and, increasingly, their acceptance as a normal part of the literary scene. Rarely, however, do they write with Behn's freedom or wit about love, sex, and marriage. Their gain is won at the cost of open access to "masculine" styles and topics. The territories Behn reappropriated are lost; the male usurpation of wide areas of common experience is largely unchallenged. There is no "Priviledge for the Masculine Part" in a woman because there are no masculine parts in a woman.

Aphra Behn's struggles and assertions are relevant to contemporary feminist critical theory and practice. In *The Madwoman in the Attic,* Gilbert and Gubar ask rhetorically, "If the pen is a metaphorical penis, from what organ can women generate texts?" (1979, 7). Behn clearly feels quite comfortable with a pen/quill between her fingers and this is not because she writes as a woman seducing a man or as a woman pretending to be a man. Rather it is because she asserts a confident literary androgyny that crosses boundaries set by a patriarchal biology which defines women in terms of mechanisms of repression and exclusion. Behn is not prepared to write on the margins, to cede territories to masculine imperialism or to collapse biological woman into constructed femininity—as Collier and his many followers did. Behn's strategies of appropriation are inclusive, not collusive, and they merit our attention as the arguments over "essentialism" either reassert or entirely deny difference. It is seductive to retreat to the margins and deny our "Masculine Part" and continue the sterile dance of the signs of binary opposition. It simplifies life to embrace blithely the belief that all are equal and the best will rise. Behn's assertions of a "double right" take her to a third position, to a place which does not exist, from which she can imagine parallel existences: woman as other and woman as the one, woman as object and herself as subject. If Behn had simply asserted female rights, or if she had rejected all the works and signs of men, her position would be radical but unproblematic. It is her claim to a male part and a double right that takes her to the point where the categories of gender deconstruct themselves. It brings her stance close to that advocated by Kristeva when she writes:

In the third attitude, which I strongly advocate—which I imagine?—the very dichotomy man/woman as an opposition between two rival entities may be understood as belonging to *metaphysics*. What can 'identity,' even 'sexual identity,' mean in a new theoretical and scientific space where the very notion of identity is challenged? (1981, 33–34; emphasis in original)

In our contexts it is salutary to study a seventeenth-century woman's precarious yet satisfying double act—an act that put her socially and mentally into the virgin territory of a new sexual space.

Notes

1. Behn's lines inserted into her translation of the sixth book of Abraham Cowley's *History Of Plants*, cited by Jane Spencer in *The Rise of the Women Novelist: From Aphra Behn to Jane Austen* (1986, 52).

2. Margaret Cavendish, Duchess of Newcastle, is an obvious exception to this sort of bashful modesty. Her situation as a great aristocrat, as well as her undoubted eccentricity, make her a special case. For further discussion of contemporary attitudes toward female publication see Patricia Crawford (1985) and, with particular reference to Behn, Angeline Goreau (1980).

3. See, for instance, Toril Moi's discussion of modern feminist reactions to and rejections of Woolf's theory of androgyny in *Sexual/Textual Politics* (1985, 2–18).

4. See Helen M. Burke's discussion of the significance of Horner's imaginary castration in "Wycherley's 'Tendentious Joke': The Discourse of Alterity in *The Country Wife*," (1988; 227–41).

5. Robert Adams Day has pointed out that there were advantages as well as disadvantages for Behn in moving into new literary genres free of the weight of masculine tradition. He also notes that "the playhouse was a social limbo, wholly alien to the conventions that governed the conduct of gentlefolk and nobility" (1986, 372). *Fetter'd or Free? British Women Novelists 1670–1815.*

6. In a "Tentative List of Plays Using Breeches Parts" between 1665–1707, compiled by Laura Morrow with help from Arthur H. Scouten and distributed at the South-Central Society for Eighteenth-Century Studies, Fayetteville, Arkansas, 1988, eighty-one plays are listed, along with fourteen plays adapted for breeches parts and three plays performed with all-female casts. Of the eighty-one breeches parts plays, twenty-nine were produced in the 1670s.

7. See Anne Finch's poem, The Introduction,

Good breeding, fassion, dancing, dressing, play
Are the accomplishments we shou'd desire;
To write, to read, or think, or to enquire
Wou'd cloud our beauty, and exhaust our time,
And interrupt the Conquests of our prime;
Whilst the dull manage, of a servile house
Is held by some, our utmost art, and use.
(ll. 14–20)

The civil war produced such feminist tracts as *The Woman's Sharpe Revenge* (London, 1640), which deplored and ridiculed the inadequacy of the education given to women. In 1675 a Mrs. Woolly published a pamphlet in which she attacked contemporary attitudes toward women with bitter irony: "by their leaves, had we the same literature, he would find our brains as fruitful as our bodies . . . " (cited in Lawrence Stone, *The Family, Sex and Marriage in England 1500–1800* (1979, 228. By the end of the century Mary Astell's *A Serious Proposal to the Ladies for the Advancement of their True and Greatest Interest* (London, 1694) vigorously argues the need to educate women.

8. See Peter Malekin's discussion of late seventeenth-century sexual attitudes in *Liberty and Love: English Literature and Society, 1640–1688* (1981), especially, "Love, Sex and Attitudes to Women in Poetry," 134–48.

9. This draws on John Harrington Smith's essay, "Shadwell, the Ladies and the Change in Comedy," in *Restoration Drama: Modern Essays in Criticism* (1966, 236–52).

10. For a discussion of gains and losses as women novelists gained acceptance and respect, see Jane Spender's *The Rise of the Woman Novelist*, especially the first chapter, "Wit's Mild Empire: The Rise of Women's Writing."

Works Cited

Adams, Robert Day. 1986. "Aphra Behn and the Works of the Intellect." In *Fetter'd or Free: British Women Novelists 1670–1815*. Ed. Mary Anne Schofield and Cecilia Macheski. Athens, Ohio: Ohio Univ. Press.

Astell, Mary. 1694. *A Serious Proposal to the Ladies for the Advancement of their True and Greatest Interest*, London.

Barre, Poulaine de la. 1677. *The Woman as Good as the Man*, London.

Behn, Aphra. 1915. *The Works of Aphra Behn*. Ed. Montague Summers. 1915, 6 vols. Reprint New York: Benjamin Blom, 1967.

———. 1967. *The Rover*. Ed. Frederick M. Link, London: Edward Arnold.

Burke, Helen. 1988. "Wycherley's 'Tendentious Joke': The Discourse of Alterity in *The Country Wife*." *The Eighteenth Century: Theory and Interpretation* 29, no. 3: 227–41.

Collier, Jeremy. 1698. *A Short View of the Immorality and Profaneness of the English Stage*, London.

Cowley, Abraham. 1795. *History Of Plants*. Trans. N. Tate et al. London.

Crawford, Patricia. 1985. "Women's Published Writings 1600–1700." In *Women in English Society*. Ed. Mary Prior. London and New York: Methuen, 211–82.

Dollimore, Jonathan. 1986. "Subjectivity, Sexuality and Transgression: The Jacobean Connection." In *Renaissance Drama*. Ed. Mary Beth Rose, N.S. 17, Evanston: Northwestern Univ. Press and Newberry Library Center for Renaissance Studies, 53–81.

Finch, Anne. 1979. *Selected Poems of Ann Finch, Countess of Winchilsea*. Ed. Katharine M. Rogers. New York: Frederick Ungar.

Gilbert, Sandra M., and Susan Gubar. 1979. *The Madwoman in the Attic: The Woman Writer and the Nineteenth-Century Literary Imagination*. New Haven: Yale Univ. Press.

Goreau, Angeline. 1980. *Reconstructing Aphra: A Social Biography of Aphra Behn*. New York: Dial.

Hobbes, Thomas. 1968. *Leviathan*. Ed. C. B. Macpherson. Middlesex: Penguin.

Kristeva, Julia. 1981. "Women's Time." Trans. Alice Jardine and Harry Blake. *Signs* 7, no. 1: 13–35.

Malekin, Peter. 1981. *Love and Liberty: English Literature and Society, 1640–1688*. London: Hutchinson.

"Mary Tattle-Well and Joane-Hit-Him-Home, Spinsters." 1640. *The Woman's Sharpe Revenge*. London.

Moi, Toril. 1985. *Sexual/Textual Politics: Feminist Literary Theory*. London and New York: Methuen.

Pearson, Jacqueline. 1988. *The Prostituted Muse: Images of Women and Women Dramatists 1642–1737*. New York: St. Martin's.

Perry, Ruth. 1986. *The Celebrated Mrs. Astell: An Early English Feminist*. Chicago: Univ. of Chicago Press.

Philips, Katherine. 1705. *Letters from Orinda to Poliarchus*. London.

Rogers, Katharine M. 1982. *Feminism in Eighteenth-Century England*. Urbana: Univ. of Illinois Press.

Scott, Joan. 1988. "Deconstructing Equality-Versus-Difference: or, the Uses of Poststructuralist Theory for Feminism." *Feminist Studies* 14, no. 1 (Spring): 33–50.

Smith, John Harrington. 1966. "Shadwell, the Ladies and the Change in Comedy." In *Restoration Drama: Modern Essays in Criticism*. Ed. John Loftis. London, Oxford, New York: Oxford Univ. Press, 236–52.

Spencer, Jane. 1986. *The Rise of the Woman Novelist: From Aphra Behn to Jane Austen*, Oxford: Basil Blackwell.

Stone, Lawrence. 1979. *The Family, Sex, and Marriage in England*, 1500–1800, New York, Cambridge: Harper Torchbooks.

Wharton, Anne. 1695. "To Mrs. A. Behn on What She Writ of the Earl of Rochester." In *The Temple of Death a Poem written by the Marquess of Normanby . . . To which is added Several Poems by the Honourable Madam Wharton*. London.

Woolf, Virginia. 1929. *A Room of One's Own*. Reprint New York and London: Harvest, Harcourt Brace Jovanovich, n.d.

———. 1928. *Orlando*. Reprint New York and London: Harvest, Harcourt Brace Jovanovich, n.d.

Wycherley, William, 1981. *The Plays of William Wycherley*. Ed. Peter Holland. Cambridge: Cambridge Univ. Press.

Aphra Behn and the Pattern Hero

NANCY COTTON

Differences in Restoration attitudes toward the comic hero generally rest on differences in class and politics. Thomas Shadwell, for example, from his Whig point of view, called the aristocratic dramatic hero "a Swearing, Drinking, Whoring, Ruffian" in the preface to his *Sullen Lovers* (1668, I:11), and wrote *The Squire of Alsatia* (1688) to illustrate his idea of a pattern hero, Belfond Junior, who, although not a swearer or drinker, does considerable whoring. Similarly, Richard Steele, writing in *The Spectator* in May of 1711, expressed his detestation of Etherege's Dorimant as "a direct knave," while admitting that *The Man of Mode* was considered "the pattern of genteel comedy: (1850, I:108). Steele, like Shadwell, offered his own version of the pattern hero, the deadly dull Bevil Junior in *The Conscious Lovers* (1722), demonstrating the shift in dramatic taste toward sentimentalism and middle-class values. The recent recovery for the canon of Restoration drama of plays by women suggests that we ought to consider whether gender was a factor, like politics and class, in the presentation of the comic hero.

Aphra Behn's *Rover* (1677) is a good place to begin because she is the most important woman writer of the Restoration and *The Rover* is a major play. Nothing in the play struck its original audience as distinctively feminine in outlook; it was produced anonymously and believed to be the work of a man. To isolate what, if anything, from the perspective of hindsight might depend on Behn's point of view as a woman, we can compare her with two close contemporaries, George Etherege and William Wycherley, because these three writers have so much in common that variation in their attitudes toward the hero may be in part determined by gender.

Indeed, the similarities among the three playwrights are striking. All three were born in the country, Etherege in the mid-1630s and Wycherley in 1640, the year traditionally given for Behn's birth, which means that all three were children and adolescents during the upheavals of the English Civil War and the Commonwealth.[1] As adults they all became Londoners and won the friendship of the leading court wits, the Earl of Rochester and the Duke of Buckingham, along with establishing reputations as wits in their own right. All were personally attractive and won the admiration of the opposite sex. All three were loyalists, Tories, personal adherents of King Charles II and his brother James, Duke of York, later James II. All three playwrights could view London society from an exotic perspective because of sophisticated and unusual experiences abroad. Behn went to South America as a young woman and then worked as an English spy in Antwerp. Wycherley, about the age of fifteen, went to France to live for several years under the influence of the Marquise de Montausier and her *precieux* circle. Etherege lived in Constantinople for several years as secretary to the English ambassador to Turkey. All three were routinely strapped for funds; Etherege eventually married for money and was knighted to please his rich wife.

All were enormously talented playwrights who wrote for the public theater with great success, although only Behn was a professional writer; Wycherley and Etherege fashionably affected to be gentlemen amateurs. In spite of her profession, Behn shared with Wycherley and Etherege aristocratic attitudes, if not aristocratic status. The plays of all three stayed in the theatrical repertory until the changes in taste embodied in the movements toward reform and sentimentalism, after which all three were ignored or reviled by Victorian critics, then rehabilitated by twentieth-century scholars.

These three all wrote pattern hero plays, which, interestingly, appeared within the same year: Etherege's *The Man of Mode; or, Sir Fopling Flutter*, first produced in March, 1676; Wycherley's *The Plain Dealer*, produced December 1676; and Behn's *The Rover; or, the Banished Cavaliers*, produced in March 1677.[2] These three plays, oddly enough, are never compared, although each is a major play by a major Restoration dramatist: *The Man of Mode* and *The Plain*

Dealer are discussed as comedies of manners, while *The Rover* is treated separately as a woman's play or as a comedy of intrigue.[3]

Nonetheless, the three plays are strikingly similar. To begin with, each is named for the chief male character, and the title suggests that he is to be perceived and understood as a type: the man of fashion, the honest man, the cavalier-in-exile. Wycherley's plain dealer, a naval captain named Manly, plans to emigrate to the Indies, seeking a less hypocritical place to live than London. Behn's rover, named Willmore, is also a captain, an officer in the royalist army, personally and politically loyal to the exiled Charles II, sharing his king's European travels and hardships. Etherege's man of mode is Dorimant, London rake and man about town; the title has a variety of ironic implications, and it is used in the play in a joking reference to the foolish Frenchified fop, Sir Fopling Flutter. In spite of Etherege's irony, to which we will return, his title and his play suggest that Dorimant is "the mold of fashion and the glass of form." Similarly, Wycherley's title and the name of his protagonist also suggest a pattern hero, especially in view of the fact that after the success of the play Wycherley himself was in compliment called "manly" Wycherley and "the plain dealer" for the rest of his life. Behn's subtitle and the play's political attitudes suggest the banished cavalier as a pattern hero, at the very minimum a pattern of loyalty to his king. All three plays are pattern hero plays—of sorts—although only *The Man of Mode* is generally considered in this light.

While some critics continue to argue that Dorimant, Manly and Willmore are objects of satire, the concluding act in each case rewards the protagonist with the most desirable woman in the play and her large fortune; in each case the woman has picked out the man after having observed his behavior in some public place and admired him. Dorimant pairs off with the charming Harriet, who has a dowry of unspecified size, but described as "hugeous" (1.1.48). The penniless rover marries the witty maiden Hellena, who brings him 300,000 crowns. And Manly is served devotedly by the disguised Fidelia, who "followed him to sea in man's clothes" ("The Persona", 12) and brings him £2,000 a year. Those who are satirized in Restoration drama are not given these kinds of romantic and monetary rewards, which are reserved for the hero. Moreover, in each play the virtues and faults of the title character are a central interest and a major topic of discus-

sion for the other characters, who desire his acquaintance and cultivate his friendship.

The plays propose different kinds of pattern heroes, who therefore
naturally inhabit different kinds of dramatic worlds. *The Man of
Mode* depicts the world of fashion in an essentially realistic mode.
The Plain Dealer criticizes the world of fashion; its mode is satiric.
The Rover is romantic, glamorizing the days of royalist exile. The
important difference regarding the portrayal of the hero is not genre,
however, but authorial attitude: Etherege and Wycherley, but not
Behn, depict their heroes ambiguously; a critique of the pattern protagonist is built into the language and structure of these plays.

Etherege's method of critique is irony. As so often in Restoration
comedy of manners, the fop in the play, the wonderful Sir Fopling
Flutter, is a parodic version of the beau, a commentary by way of
excess on the foibles of the man of fashion. Both Dorimant and Sir
Fopling, for example, pride themselves on being well dressed—but
Sir Fopling is ridiculously overdressed. Both Dorimant and Sir
Fopling write songs—but Sir Fopling's is terrible. Both make court
to all women and involve themselves in fashionable amours—but the
women laugh at Sir Fopling. Each is essentially engrossed in
himself—but Dorimant is self-possessed while Sir Fopling is self-
deceived. Dorimant, in short, excels with negligent ease; Sir Fopling
works too hard at everything.

The values that Sir Fopling espouses and tries to embody, however, are precisely those that Dorimant does embody, and Sir
Fopling's admiration of Dorimant is itself a critique of the pattern of
fashion—it enchants fools. In one way the play contrasts the true
man of fashion and the false pretender, but in another way it reminds
us that fashion alone, as an end in life, is foolish.

Ambiguity is even more pronounced in the portrayal of the plain
dealer. Manly's false mistress Olivia and his false friend Vernish trick
and exploit him, which makes him look gullible, but he fails here in
judgment, not in honesty and bravery, which are the pattern virtues
he represents. In fact, the tricksters use his good qualities to dupe
him. Vernish refers to him matter-of-factly as "brave" (5.2.346) and
"honest" (4.2.153), and Olivia counts on "his great spirit" (4.2.147)
to make him behave well to her in spite of her cruel treatment of him.
Moreover, Wycherley allows Vernish and Olivia to heap verbal abuse
on the hero, some of it rather acute. Olivia ridicules his military

manner and naval dress, which are too rough for the salon and bou-
doir. But Olivia and Vernish are the villains of the play. Wycherley
portrays Manly in the opening scene as a man of blunt speech and
unmatched bravery and prowess, a captain who sank his own ship
carrying "five or six thousand pounds of his own" (1.1.113) rather
than let her fall into the hands of the Dutch; Wycherley then shows
Manly ridiculed by a London society that does not value these good
qualities as much as it does fashionable dress and polished demeanor.
The problem is in the society, not the hero.

Behn's hero, Captain Willmore, is not criticized in these ways. He
combines the good qualities of the civilian hero, Dorimant, and the
military hero, Manly. Like Manly, he is a fighting fool, a military
officer of courage and prowess; he is a true friend, and he despises a
woman who trades sex for money. Like Dorimant, he is young,
amorous, impudent, inconstant, irresistible to women, and determined to avoid marriage; he pursues a number of women in the
course of the play, all of them pretty, but he loves the heroine and is
willing to marry her for her wit. Willmore is more good-natured and
fun-loving than Dorimant and Manly, a man always ready to enjoy
women, wine, and swordplay. His penniless condition is a sign of his
virtue; like many a real-life cavalier, he lost his estate in the service of
his prince.

In contrast, the butt of the play, Ned Blunt, is the "banker"
(1.2.297) for the English exiles; he has plenty of money because, as he
boasts, he "had more grace than to forfeit my estate by cavaliering"
(1.2.51–52). Blunt is to Willmore as Sir Fopling is to Dorimant. Like
Willmore, Blunt becomes involved with a prostitute, but, while Willmore attracts a beautiful, wealthy courtesan who dotes on him and
gives him money, Blunt is tricked and robbed by a whore. Here the
contrast between the hero and his imitator works differently than in
The Man of Mode: the play implies not that whoring is foolish, but
that Blunt is simply not the man that Willmore is, that he just can't
measure up. Blunt's humiliation enhances rather than undercuts the
hero.

This lack of undercutting is what sets Behn's portrayal of the hero
apart from those of Etherege and Wycherley. I should acknowledge
that it is at least possible that the distancing of the rover in time and
space—to the continent in the 1650s—might imply a critique of the
hero by suggesting that he existed only in the good old days. I men-

tion this possibility because remote and exotic setting is the strategy of the Restoration heroic play in depicting an exaggerated heroic ideal. Feats of derring-do were possible at the conquest of Granada that were not given to the London rake of the 1670s. The European exile of the cavaliers, however, was alive in the memory of many in Behn's audience, especially and including the king. It seems unlikely, therefore, that Behn intended the setting as an implied critique of the rover.

The reason for the undercutting of the hero in Etherege and Wycherley is, perhaps, the same as the reason for the distancing of the heroic play—the expectation of criticism. The built-in critique of the hero anticipates and thus attempts to defuse criticism, a strategy common in traditional English dramaturgy. Shakespeare abounds in examples, notably Falstaff's running commentary on his own bulk and Hamlet's self-laceration for delay in killing the king. That Etherege and Wycherley use this strategy suggests that they antici-pate the sorts of criticism they incorporate, that Dorimant is a fop and that Manly is an uncivilized brute.

Etherege and Wycherley are uneasy about their pattern heroes because changes in seventeenth-century life were changing the nature of the masculine ideal—the reason the Restoration spawned so many pattern heroes in the first place. The changing technology of war, in particular, caused a decline in the prestige of brawn and a corresponding confusion about appropriate roles for men. Hamlet, for example, is a cerebral rather than a physical hero, uncertain about meeting the demands of his dead warrior father and partly envious of Fortinbras's military career. Because of a ninety-eight pound weakling with a gun is stronger than Mark Antony with a sword, Antony appears in Shakespeare primarily, and in Dryden exclusively, as a lover. In the eighteenth century, duelling becomes problematic for the civilian hero. Steele said that he wrote *The Con-scious Lovers* "for the sake of the Scene of the Fourth Act, wherein Mr. Bevil evades the Quarrel with his Friend" (1971, 299); his insis-tence that his pattern hero may refuse to duel without losing his mas-culine honor shows how crucial for him is the question of physical courage. The military hero also changes on the eighteenth-century stage, becoming a figure of fun, a Macheath or a Tom Thumb. The warrior-king was disappearing from life as well as from the stage: William III, rulers from 1688 to 1702, was the last king of England whose official portrait depicted him in armor, and George II was the last English king to lead his troops in battle, in 1743 (Folkenflik 1982, 19).

It is the declining prestige of brawn that is Wycherley's hidden agenda in *The Plain Dealer*. The faithful heroine, who in her disguise as a wandering boy has seemed to many critics a figure from the past, loves Manly for his physical courage; the villainess, who represents the trivial and fashionable contemporary Town, scorns his military manner as uncouth. Wycherley's choice of a man for his hero means that physical strength and courage are part of his definition of manliness. Etherege deals exclusively with civilian life, the fashionable world that Olivia represents, and his implied critique of Dorimant suggests that purely civilian man, urban and urbane, may be a bit of a fop.

Behn seems unconcerned about these masculine doubts. Willmore is forthrightly presented as a military hero, a fighter of courage and prowess, and this is part of what makes him attractive and dashing. Wycherley also exalts physical prowess, but he allows a striking amount of criticism, which, even though it comes from the villains, nonetheless pervades the verbal texture of his play. Behn's unambiguous portrayal of the masculine pattern might be affected by her gender in that a woman might worry less about masculine roles than a man trying to fulfill them; perhaps she was, as a woman, less sensitive to changes in attitude toward heroic brawn.

Because the term "petticoat author" was oxymoronic in the Restoration, my colleagues in this section see Behn as necessarily androgynous in her public, professional role as a writer, a role that asserts the "masculine part" of her self, a role analogous to the "breeches part." While this may be true, a comparison of the pattern heroes of Behn, Wycherley, and Etherege suggests that Behn wrote from her own gender perspective rather than aping the attitudes or genres of her nearest male counterparts. We might even speculate that she deliberately chose to avoid manners comedy because of lack of interest in its pervasive concern with refinement and over-refinement in the hero. Because the hindsight of history has made us value the comedy of manners as the outstanding artistic innovation of the Restoration theater, we somehow feel uneasy about those authors who chose not to write in this new genre, as though there must have been something wrong with their taste. It is equally possible that Behn found the masculinist preoccupations of manners comedy uninteresting and preferred to use romantic comedy to pursue her own interest in unhappy and forced marriage as a trap for women.

Notes

1. Biographical information on Behn in this paragraph is taken from Cotton (1980), Duffy (1977), Goreau (1980); on Wycherley, from McCarthy (1979) and Rogers (1972); on Etherege, Cordner (1982).
2. Plays are dated according to *The London Stage 1660–1800*.
3. An interesting example of this occurs in Robert Hume's "Concepts of the Hero in Comic Drama, 1660–1710." In the middle of the essay he dismisses the leads in *The Rover* as unimportant to his discussion because, in spite of his title, he makes an *ad hoc* claim of exclusive concern with comedy set in London.

Works Cited

Behn, Aphra. 1967. *The Rover*. Ed. Frederick M. Link. Regents Restoration Drama Series. Lincoln: Univ. of Nebraska Press.

Cordner, Michael. 1982. Introduction. *Plays*. By Sir George Etherege. Ed. Michael Cordner. Cambridge: Cambridge Univ. Press.

Cotton, Nancy. 1980. *Women Playwrights in England c. 1363–1750*. Lewisburg, Pa.: Bucknell Univ. Press.

Duffy, Maureen. 1977. *The Passionate Shepherdess: Aphra Behn 1640–89*. London: Jonathan Cape.

Etherege, George. 1966. *The Man of Mode*. Ed. W. B. Carnochan. Regents Restoration Drama Series. Lincoln: Univ. of Nebraska Press.

Folkenflik, Robert. 1982. Introduction. *The English Hero, 1660–1800*. Ed. Robert Folkenflik. Newark: Univ. of Delaware Press.

Goreau, Angeline. 1988. *Reconstructing Aphra: A Social Biography of Aphra Behn*. New York: Dial.

Hume, Robert D. 1982. "Concepts of the Hero in Comic Drama, 1660–1710." *The English Hero, 1660–1800*. Ed. Robert Folkenflik. Newark: Univ. of Delaware Press.

The London Stage 1600–1800. 1960–68. Ed. Emmett L. Avery et al. 11 vols. Carbondale: Southern Illinois Univ. Press.

McCarthy, Eugene. 1979. *William Wycherley: A Biography*. Athens: Ohio Univ. Press.

Rogers, Katharine M. 1972. *William Wycherley*. Twayne's English Authors Series. New York: Twayne.

Shadwell, Thomas. 1927. *The Complete Works*. Ed. Montague Summers. Vol. 1. London: Fortune Press.

Steele, Richard. 1971. *Plays*. Ed. Shirley Strum Kenny. Oxford: Clarendon.

_____, and Joseph Addison, 1850. *The Spectator*, No. 65. *Works*. Vol. 1. New York: Harpers.

Wycherley, William. 1967. *The Plain Dealer*. Regents Restoration Drama Series. Ed. Leo Hughes. Lincoln: Univ. of Nebraska Press.

Dressing to Deceive

EDNA L. STEEVES

Ever since Rosalind donned men's clothes and induced the shy
Orlando to practice the courtship routine on her, pert young
actresses have enjoyed cavorting about the stage in breeches.
The breeches role was popular, especially in Restoration comedy,
and it is interesting to consider the ways in which dress as disguise is
used as a major plot device by a little-known Restoration playwright,
Mary Pix, who had a dozen plays performed on the London stage
from 1696 to 1706.

One can argue to little purpose about the lack of merit in minor
literary works, particularly drama, which of necessity must appeal to
the state of a contemporary audience. Of the hundreds of plays produced on the Restoration stage, few are known and read today, fewer
still revived. Such minor plays, however, may be more representative
of what pleased the audience than more notable dramas that have
better stood the test of time. Although some of Mrs. Pix's plays are, in
fact, a pretty good "read," as a dramatist she is far from major league.
What her plays well illustrate is what theater-goers in the late years of
the Restoration and the early years of the eighteenth century liked to
see presented on the boards. Here one observes faithfully reflected the
taste for heroic bombast just perceptively becoming softened by
romantic passion; for complicated plots involving a great variety of
disguise; for racy, smutty dialogue; and for song, dance, and spectacle. More pertinent to my purposes here, her plays, like those of her
contemporaries, reflect the growing importance of women on the
stage, in the audience, and as playwrights. As one might expect,
Mary Pix created female characters more realistically than male

characters. And she was fond of all kinds of disguise, especially the breeches disguise.

Although disguise is as old as fiction itself, Restoration drama made extensive use of this narrative device, and Mrs. Pix followed the trend. Dress as disguise forms a major motif in her plots. Dressing to deceive is particularly prominent in two of her comedies which I wish to consider in some detail here: *The Innocent Mistress* (1697) and *The Adventures in Madrid* (1706). These are not the only plays in which Mrs. Pix disguised a female character in men's clothes; but in these two comedies, the major plot complication revolves around a breeches role.

The complicated plot of *The Innocent Mistress* involves three couples who will be happily married as the curtain falls. Sir Charles Beauclair, a younger brother, has been married in his youth at his family's insistence to a rich, ill-favored widow whom he abhors. He has since fallen heir to his family estate and title, and has also fallen in love with Bellinda, a virtuous young lady who, assuming a disguised name, has fled her father's home to escape a forced marriage. These two are the romantic leads. The second couple is Sir Francis Wildlove, a rake and a womanizer as his name indicates, and Miss Beauclair, the spirited and witty niece of Sir Charles. The third couple is a country gentleman, Beaumont, and the young lady he loves, Arabella, who at the death of her parents has been left to the care of Cheatall, a merchant, and brother to Sir Charles's wife. Cheatall has forged a will depriving Arabella of her inheritance. The entangling and disentangling of the affairs of these three couples form the main plot strands of this comedy, strands cleverly interwoven by Mrs. Pix.

The problem to be solved for Sir Charles and Bellinda consists of his being able to rid himself of his termagant wife. When Sir Charles married her, she was the supposed widow of a wealthy merchant in the Indies trade, one Flywife, alias Allen. As his name implies, Flywife had flown his plague of a wife and assumed a new name. Their daughter, Peggy, a chip off the maternal block, lives with her mother, Lady Beauclair. Meanwhile, Flywife has provided himself with a kept mistress, who goes by his name. Spendall, a sharper and hanger-on to Sir Charles, plans with the aid of his accomplice, Lyewell, to feather his nest by marrying Peggy. The plot makes use of various servants: Searchwell, Wildlove's man; Gentil, Cheatall's man; Eugenia, Lady Beauclair's woman; Dresswell, Miss Beauclair's woman; Betty, Bellinda's maid; and Jenny, Mrs. Flywife's maid.

Performed by His Majesty's Servants (Betterton's company) at the New Theater in Little-Lincolns-Inn-Fields, the comedy had some famous actors and actresses in the featured roles: Betterton as Sir Charles, Verbruggen as Wildlove, Hodgson as Beaumont, Underhill as Flywife, Bowen as Cheatall, Mrs. Barry as Bellinda, Miss Brace-girdle as Miss Beauclair, Mrs. Prince as Arabella, Mrs. Lee as Lady Beauclair, Mrs. Howard as Peggy.

In order to provide the requisite happy ending, Mrs. Pix must enable Sir Charles to rid himself of his wife so that he can marry Bellinda; the rake Wildlove must be tamed into a proper husband for the witty but discreet Miss Beauclair; and Beaumont must succeed in freeing Arabella and her fortune from the clutches of her scheming guardian. To bring about these changes, Flywife's true identity must be revealed. And the randy Peggy must be helped to a husband.

Mrs. Pix resolves these complications largely through the use of disguise of various kinds. Her characters assume aliases, change their residences, and in particular dress to conceal their true identities. One of the most interesting of these disguises, and one integral to the plot, is Miss Beauclair's dressing in men's clothes for the purpose of discovering Wildlove's rakish habits. This breeches role is here nicely handled by the actress Anne Bracegirdle.

Wildlove has been courting Miss Beauclair, but she has good reason to suspect that he pursues every skirt in town. At the opening of act I, Wildlove informs his friend Beaumont, in town from the country, that there are only three kinds of women: first, the common whore, who obliges everybody; second, the kept mistress; and third, one whom he describes as "not a whore, but

> a brisk, airy, noisy coquette that lives upon treating, one spark has her to the play, another to the Park, a third to Windsor, a fourth to some other place of diversion; she has not the heart to grant 'em all favours, for that's their design at the bottom of the treats, and they have not the heart to marry her, for that's her design, poor creature. So perhaps a year, or it may be two, the gaudy butterfly flutters around the kingdom, then if a foolish Citt does not take compassion, sneaks into a corner, dies an old maid, despised and forgotten. The men that fit those ladies are

your rake, your cully, and your beaux (1982, I, pages 1–2, opening scene).

Wildlove considers such women fair game. But with a woman of honour, like Miss Beauclair, his manner is modest, respectful, and, since he thinks matrimony a noose about the neck, even wary.

Miss Beauclair subjects Wildlove to two tests. In the first test (act 2, pages 17–18) as she strolls in St. James Park with Sir Charles and Bellinda, she spies Wildlove at a distance, leaves her companions, dons a courtesan's mask, and induces Wildlove to follow her. Assuming her available, he talks familiarly to her, confessing that he loves a virtuous young lady whose modesty prevents his proposing. She suggests he practise on her. The scene is, of course, reminiscent of one in *As You Like It* (act 4, scene 1); and although the badinage does not equal Shakespeare's, the dialogue has verve and wit. As Wildlove warms to his wooing, he throws off the respectful suitor's manner and rushes her; whereupon she unmasks and calls loudly for her uncle. Recognizing her, Wildlove stands abashed and begs her pardon. In this first attempt to test his character, Miss Beauclair has assumed the identity of a common woman-about-town by donning a mask and talking and acting immodestly.

In the second testing of Wildlove's intentions (act 4, pages 27–28), Miss Beauclair dresses in men's clothes and bounces into a room at Locket's where Wildlove and Mrs. Flywife are enjoying an assignation. When a message calls Wildlove away, young breeches makes up to Mrs. Flywife, who values a neat pair of legs. Giving him a ring to pay his debts, Mrs. Flywife tells him where she lives. The breeches-clad Miss Beauclair follows Mrs. Flywife, only to discover that the Flywifes live in the same house where Bellinda lodges, and Miss Beauclair fears meeting her uncle there and having her disguise penetrated. She returns home, but before she can shed her breeches attire, Wildlove arrives, seeking revenge on the young spark who has stolen Mrs. Flywife from him. Wildlove challenges young breeches to a duel. She twits him, then throws off her disguise, declaring she will have nothing more to do with him. He swears reform. "That's hard to believe," she retorts, "but I must beg your pardon, I'm in haste to unrig" (act 4, page 31).

In her breeches disguise Miss Beauclair has determined that her suitor is indeed a rambler; yet she is convinced that with a woman of honour he will conduct himself like a perfect gentleman. As one last trial, however, she directs her maid to inform Wildlove that she has, in disgust at his whoring habits, married Spendall. When Wildlove challenges Spendall, Miss Beauclair reveals this final trick; whereupon Wildlove proposes and swears eternal fidelity. That Miss Beauclair can consider marrying this rake may seem psychologically unsound to us; but the fact is that she, the sprightly, witty, unromantic type, hankers for the same kind of husband. They are well matched. In the final scene she says to him: "If you can give me your heart, I can allow you great liberties: but when we have played the fool and married, don't you when you have been pleased abroad, come home surly: let your looks be kind, your conversation easy, and though I should know you have been with a mistress, I'd meet you with a smile" (act 5, page 46).

Resolution of the Beaumont-Arabella plot also involves a disguise of dress. Beaumont dresses like a sailor, pretending to be Arabella's long-lost brother from the Indies. When Cheatall declares Arabella to be an only child, Beaumont says he is her bastard brother. Gentil and Eugenia, who espouse Arabella's cause, spread the rumor that she has been murdered by Cheatall. When Beaumont threatens Cheatall with death, Cheatall confesses to the forged will and gives up the documents proving Arabella's identity and her right to her dead father's estate. Since she had promised to marry Beaumont once her inheritance was assured, the Beaumont-Arabella marriage can now take place. Beaumont's disguise in seaman's dress has effected this untangling.

Mrs. Flywife has become so enamoured of the breeches-clad Miss Beauclair that she follows young breeches all over town, at length tracking him to Sir Charles's house. As the principals come together here, the jealous Flywife, in pursuit of his wife, arrives and is recognized by Cheatall as Lady Beauclair's first husband, the merchant Allen, supposedly dead. Flywife must now choose between his legal wife, Lady Beauclair, and his mistress, Mrs. Flywife. He chooses his plaguey wife over his cheating jilt. This frees Sir Charles of his wife, and chief complication of the main plot. Hence at the close of the play, the three couples find all their difficulties solved.

A further disguise has led to a faked marriage between Spendall and Peggy. Spendall induces Lyewell to dress in lawyer's robes and to pretend that Spendall is heir to a large estate, thus tricking Lady

Beauclair into permitting a marriage between Spendall and Peggy. In the closing scene, Sir Charles reveals Spendall for the sharper he is, to Lady Beauclair's chagrin, and Flywife, now in the role of Peggy's father, threatens to look into the legality of that marriage. But Peggy, now that she has a husband, refuses to give him up. The plot leaves the strumpet, Mrs. Flywife, as odd-one-out. She appears, however, to deserve her fate, for it was her assignation with Wildlove which induced Miss Beauclair to adopt the breeches disguise to investigate Wildlove's rambling. Miss Beauclair's adoption of the breeches role, then, has led to the resolution of the plot entanglements and to the resulting happy ending.

The second play by Mary Pix to be considered here is her three-act comedy entitled *The Adventures in Madrid,* performed at the Queens Theatre in the Hay-Market in the summer of 1706, and published later in the same year. Although the play bears no author's name on the title page, it was generally attributed to her by contemporaries and has been so attributed by later historians of the drama. It bears all the earmarks of her style.

The scene is Madrid, making it the second comedy in which Pix used a Spanish setting. Important to the plot is the location of the two houses in which the events of the story take place: Don Gomez's palace and the English Ambassador's residence adjoin each other. A piazza on the street front serves both houses, and in the rear a walled garden is attached to Gomez's palace. Unknown to the owners of the two houses is a secret passageway, constructed through the rafters, which opens Gomez's house to that of the Ambassador. The proximity of the two residences and the existence of the secret passageway are essential to the plot.

Like most Restoration comedies, this comedy has a complicated plot, and in it Mrs. Pix employs several disguises in dress. Two young Englishmen, Bellmour and Gaylove, have come to Spain seeking adventure, and are living in the Ambassador's house. Soon after their arrival, they see at church two Spanish ladies, Clarinda and Laura, both veiled as the Spanish custom demands for ladies of quality. The two Englishmen immediately fall in love with the two young ladies, veil or no veil. Bellmour is the romantic type; Gaylove the witty rake.

The villain is old Don Gomez, whose half-brother, now dead, has left his son, Don Philip, and his daughter, Clarinda, to Gomez's guardianship. To get his hands on the fortunes of the brother and sister, Gomez shipped Philip off to the Indies, reported him dead, and forced Clarinda on threat of death to marry him. The marriage has not been consummated, and is of course incestuous, being between an uncle and his niece. Clarinda, closely guarded, has no one to rescue her from a husband she abhors. Her friend Laura also has a brother who, in cahoots with Gomez, schemes to seize his sister's fortune and marry her to Gomez's twin brother. Incarcerated in Gomez's house, Laura has managed to escape and has taken refuge in the Ambassador's house. In fact it is Laura, seeking escape for herself and Clarinda, who has contrived to get the secret passageway constructed between the two houses. This is the situation as the play opens.

The first dress disguise, a Spanish habit, is adopted by Bellmour. As an Englishman, he is suspected by Gomez as a pursuer of women, and his Spanish dress hides his identity. Bellmour also dresses his servant Jo in a Spanish habit and charges him to find a go-between to further his romance. This go-between is a Spaniard named Gusman, in love with Lisset, a female servant to Gomez. Lisset has befriended Clarinda and Laura, for which reason she has incurred Gomez's displeasure and has been imprisoned by him. The ingenious Laura, by bribing the prison guards, has gotten Lisset released. To aid in freeing Clarinda and Laura of Gomez's villainous designs, Lisset adopts men's clothes, assuming the name of Licias and pretending to be a eunuch. Gomez is delighted to put a eunuch as guard over the two girls. This breeches role is the major disguise in the play and is essential to the resolution of the plot.

We have here a woman dressed in breeches playing the role of a eunuch. Eunuchs appear in numerous Restoration plays, with actresses usually taking the role. Apparently the idea of a harem stocked with luscious virgins available for a one-night stand and guarded by a man-no-man titillated the taste of the audience. Such a taste is not, indeed, confined to the period; witness modern comics who still joke about Joseph Smith and the Mormons, and the delight with which the harem-pants fashion of a few years ago struck the twentieth-century male.

Philip arrives in Madrid to free his sister and retrieve his fortune. He meets and falls in love with Gaylove's sister, Emilia, who is also visiting Spain and staying in the Ambassador's residence. In the final scene, Philip brings the Inquisitor General to the Ambassador's house to pass judgment on Gomez. At the trial, evidence is strong against Gomez, who is led away to prison. Lisset now divests herself of her breeches disguise, revealing that she has masterminded the plot to free Clarinda and Laura. By playing the role of a eunuch, she has gained Gomez's confidence and thus has been able to defeat his villainies. The two sets of lovers have been able to court their lady-loves with the aid of Lisset the "eunuch," whom Gomez has placed as guard over them. Furthermore, Lisset is aware of the secret passageway and makes frequent use of it, not only to spy upon Gomez and thus defeat his machinations, but also to ferry both young men to trysts with their mistresses. When in fact Gaylove discovers that by means of the secret passageway Laura has been, unknown to him, frequently in his bedroom, he remarks: "Well, well, you have been so often in my bedchamber that after a little church ceremony I shall certainly claim you for a bedfellow" (3. closing scene). This is his manner of proposing.

The breeches disguise then, which Lisset assumes until the final scene, is the device by means of which all plot complications are resolved. It is Lisset who vouches for the truth of Clarinda's tale of ill usage by Gomez, and of Laura's story of betrayal by her avaricious brother. It is also Lisset-in-breeches who has witnessed the faithfulness of Gusman's love for her by his many attempts to get himself imprisoned because he mistakenly thinks she is there. Although in Restoration comedies the breeches disguise was often assumed by an actress for plot purposes, and was particularly popular for pert young actresses speaking the epilogues, it was not often a disguise on which the entire plot revolved, as it is in this comedy by Mary Pix.

The comedy ends with four pairings: Bellmour and Clarinda, Gaylove and Laura, Philip and Emilia, and Gusman and Lisset. Even Jo and Clarinda's maid are looking sweet on each other. Everyone plans to set sail for England. Jo, who has been frightened out of his wits by various Spanish bustanados, declares that only in England do peace and prosperity prevail. Lisset, however, though agreeing to marry Gusman, maintains that she liked wearing the breeches very well. "I have gotten such a smack of liberty," she says, "and such a taste of wearing the breeches, that I shall never make a good Spanish wife nor indure to be locked up" (3. page 69).

The play had a distinguished cast: Freeman as Gomez, Booth as

Gaylove, Husbands as Bellmour, Bowan as Gusman, Cory as Philip, the inimitable comic actor Pack as the servant Jo, Mrs. Barry as the romantic Clarinda, Miss Bracegirdle as the witty and daring Laura, Mrs. Bowman as Emilia, and Mrs. Bicknell in the lively breeches role.

The epilogue was spoken by Miss Porter, "the Little Girl" as she was often listed in the casts of Restoration plays. In the comedy she had played the role of Laura's page and had therefore worn men's clothes. When this play was performed, Miss Porter was then a very young girl, yet the epilogue has her speaking words more befitting an orange wench than a child barely out of pinafores. But the daredevilishness of a young actress wearing breeches and speaking smut charmed the Restoration audience, as Mrs. Pix well knew.

Mary Pix's plays, produced on the London stage between 1697 and 1706, perfectly illustrate the theatrical taste of the audience. That taste was of course changing (indeed, Collier's attack merely pointed to what was already in the air), and the trend toward sentimentalism would produce a very different kind of play in the new century, all but banishing the sparkling wit of the earlier comedy and altering the heroic to the pathetic. The early years of the eighteenth century evidence significant change in the composition of the audience, which in turn affected the nature of the theater itself, the acting companies, and the plays written for the stage. One practice, however, continued popular: that of saucy young actresses dressed in breeches romping about the stage. The idea was too entertaining to be readily abandoned.

Works Cited

Pix, Mary. 1982. *The Plays of Mary Pix and Catharine Trotter.* Ed. Edna L. Steeves, New York: Garland.

4

Set Change:
The Colonial Scene

"Scrub." Courtesy of the Print Collection,
The Lewis Walpole Library, Yale University.

Susanna Rowson: Feminist
and Democrat

DOREEN ALVAREZ SAAR

Although she was the author of America's first best-seller, *Charlotte: A Tale of Truth* in 1791, Susanna Haswell Rowson and her novels were forgotten by literary critics for almost a century and a half. In 1966, in *Love and Death in the American Novel*, Leslie Fiedler sparked a revival of interest in Rowson's novels by using *Charlotte* as a model for the female distortions of the sentimental novel of analysis (93–98). A few years later, when feminist critics challenged the male-defined canon of American literature, they reinterpreted Rowson's novels and saw them as part of the development of a women's tradition of American writing. Over the past two decades, Rowson's contribution to the novel has been affirmed: it is time to recognize her contribution as a playwright to the developing American theater.

Between 1794 and 1810, Rowson wrote at least five original plays that were produced on the American stage: *Slaves in Algiers, or a Struggle for Freedom; The Volunteers; The American Tar, or The Press Gang Defeated; Americans in England, or Lessons for Daughters;* and *Hearts of Oak.* The impact of Rowson's work on the American theater is suggested by the fact that of the approximately forty plays written by Americans before 1787, fewer than six were intended for production on the professional stage (Spiller 1953, 185). During the post-Revolutionary period (1783–1800), "plays written by Americans occupied an exceedingly small part of the offering in any theater" (Meserve 1977, 127). Of the few American women writing for the stage, Mercy Otis Warren wrote plays to be read to family and friends (Meserve 1977, 73–74) and Judith Sargent Murray published anonymously (Meserve 1977, 154).

Slaves was Mrs. Rowson's most important play: it was printed, a relatively rare event, and became a stock piece in the repertory of the New Theater Company. It was the work of the tendentious English critic, William Cobbett, known as "Peter Porcupine," that would bring *Slaves in Algiers* to the attention of a wider audience. In his pamphlet *A Kick for a Bite,* Cobbett denounced Rowson and her play for her feminism and republicanism. Cobbett was offended by Rowson's outspoken advocacy of women's rights throughout *Slaves,* particularly in her epilogue:

> Well, Ladies, tell me—how d'ye like my play?
> "The creature has some sense," methinks you say
> "She says that we should have supreme dominion,
> And in good truth, we're all of her opinion.
> "Women were born for universal sway,
> "Men to adore, be silent and obey."
> (Rowson 1794, 10–15)

Beyond this historical significance, *Slaves in Algiers* should be recognized as an important feminist transcription of the ideas of the American Revolution. In *Slaves,* Rowson explores the interrelationship between three themes: slavery, women's rights, and republican concepts of liberty. While manipulating republican outrage at the injustice of slavery to express radical ideas about the condition of women, she carefully contrasts the oriental conditions of female oppression with the liberties and equalities guaranteed by democracy, and in doing so, turn the notions of the Revolution to protofeminist ends. This exploration of the relationship between republican ideals and the reality of the situation of American women in the last half of the eighteenth century makes *Slaves in Algiers* a landmark in the development of feminist political ideology in American drama.

I

Susanna Rowson was born Susanna Haswell in England on 25 February, 1762. Her mother died shortly after giving birth. While the young Susanna remained in England, her father, Lt. William Haswell, a revenue collector, was sent to the American colonies where, in 1765, he married a Massachusetts woman, Rachael Woodward. Susanna was brought to Massachusetts in 1767. Susanna's life in America was peaceful until the outbreak of the American Revolution when the Haswells found themselves imprisoned by the Revolutionary army. In 1778, they were exchanged for American prisoners and sent back to England.

Once in England, both her father and stepmother fell ill. At sixteen, Susanna became the chief support of the family, which now included three younger half-brothers. In 1786, she published her first work of fiction, *Victoria, A Novel*, and married William Rowson, a hardware merchant. For the rest of her life, she turned her hand to whatever would support her alcoholic husband and the relatives who became part of the extended Rowson household.

Although most of her earnings came from her novels, she and her husband also worked in British theaters. Between 1786 and 1792, the Rowsons appeared on the English provincial stage. At the same time, it seems that William Rowson maintained some connection with Covent Garden. In 1788, Susanna published a long poem, *A Trip to Parnassus; or a Critique of Authors and Performers*, which was a commentary on the performers and playwrights of the English stage. While continuing to work as an actress, she published *The Inquisitor, or the Invisible Rambler*, a collection of tales, and *Poems on Various Subjects* in 1788, *A Test of Honor* in 1789, *Mentoria, or the Young Ladies' Friend* and *Charlotte: A Tale of Truth* in 1791; *Rebecca; or, the Fille de Chambre* followed in 1792. *Charlotte* became a best-seller in America and in 1793, Thomas Wignell signed the Rowsons for his American company,[1] considered "the finest dramatic and operatic corps that America had seen" (Pollack 1933, 55). Because of an outbreak of yellow fever, the company did not arrive in Philadelphia until 1794.

It is likely that Rowson's roles were an important preparation for her playwriting.[2] George Seilhamer, in *History of the American Theater* (1891), records her many American roles, including Audrey in *As You Like It*, Mrs. Placid in *Every One Has His Fault*, Lucy in *The Rivals* and Lady Sneerwell in *The School for Scandal* (351–53). A contemporary review reveals that Rowson was a competent actress: "I must confess myself very well satisfied with Mrs. Rowson's performance of the part. . . . She displayed a thorough knowledge of her author, and his subject. . . . I do not pretend to bring this lady forward as a first rate actress, but she is always perfect, and attentive to the business of the scene" (Vail 1933, 82).

While performing, Rowson continued to write plays and songs: *Slaves in Algiers* was produced in 1794; *The Volunteers* in 1794; *The Female Patriot*, an adaptation of Massinger's *Bondsman*, in 1795; "America, Commerce and Freedom," a popular song, and *Americans in England* in 1796; *The American Tar, or the Press Gang Defeated* in 1797; and *Hearts of Oak* in 1810. *Slaves in Algiers, or a Struggle for Freedom* was first performed by the New Theatre in Philadelphia on June 30. It was an immediate success and was later performed in both New York and Baltimore. Her other plays were also warmly received; unfortunately, only a fragment of one play exists.

In 1796, Rowson left the Philadelphia Company to join the Federal Street Theatre in Boston. In 1797, she made her farewell stage appearance. She subsequently opened a "Young Ladies' Academy" in Boston. Because of her work as an educator of women, she would later be called one of the "central architects of the new female ideology" of the new republic (Kerber 1980, 11). Rowson continued to write novels and textbooks and became a contributor to magazines. She died, a respected educator and journalist, in Boston in 1842.[3]

II

Slaves in Algiers, or a Struggle for Freedom was written in response to public outrage about Algerian piracies which included the capture of some fifteen American ships and 180 American sailors who were pressed into slavery (Quinn 1923, 121–2; Seilhammer 1891, 155). Rowson's play was among the first of an outpouring of literary responses to this indignity; most of these narratives about Algiers were "a new kind of captivity narrative, one that added to the charms of outraged Christian morality, the piquancy of insulted American patriotism" (Cook 1970, 18).

While her preface to *Slaves* credits Cervantes' story of the Captive in *Don Quijote* as her inspiration, Rowson probably borrowed the plot of *Slaves* from a subplot of her novel, *A Test of Honor*. The motifs of the earlier version are reworked so that the flavor of the original sentimental and didactive novel remains.[4] Among the important motifs which Rowson carried over are those of filial piety, virtue rewarded, and seduction. In order to understand the central plot mechanism, the escape attempt of foreign captives in Algiers, the reader must understand the complex family histories of the captives. A beautiful young Englishwoman, Olivia, her father, Constant, and her fiancè, Henry, have all been captured by Algerian pirates and sold to Muley Moloc, the Dey, who has designs on Olivia's honor. However, Olivia and her father do not know that Henry was captured during a rescue attempt and has been in Algiers actively working to organize an escape for all foreign captives. In addition, Olivia's long-lost mother, Rebecca, and brother, Augustus, are slaves in Algiers; separated from her husband and daughter by the American Revolution, Rebecca believed them both to be dead but rumor of their existence led her to renew the search for them. During her search, Rebecca was also captured by the Algerians. Although her captor, Ben Hassan, a Jew, has promised Rebecca freedom if and when her ransom money arrives, he already has received the ransom and is only holding her in hopes that she can be persuaded to marry him. Meanwhile, Rebecca has spent her captivity instructing Ben Hassan's daughter, Fetnah, about the rights of women, America, and liberty.

Because of Rebecca's teachings, Fetnah, who is a concubine of the Dey, is passionately interested in obtaining her freedom. During the prelude to the escape, she falls in love with a freed Christian slave, Frederick, who is planning, with Henry, to help the captives escape. Their plotting is aided by the Dey's daughter, Zoriana, who has been secretly converted to Christianity, has fallen in love with Henry, and serves as the unwitting link between the separated family members. When Zoriana informs Olivia of the plans for escape, Olivia discovers that Henry is also a prisoner in Algiers and that Zoriana loves him. In a noble gesture, Olivia makes secret plans to stay behind and offer herself to the Dey so that the others may make their escape. She plans to temporarily appease the Dey with a promise of marriage and then to kill herself before the marriage ceremony. Unfortunately, when the escape takes place, it fails and most are recaptured. Olivia, as she has planned, offers herself to the Dey in return for the lives of Henry and Constant, but at the same moment, slaves in the city rebel against the Dey. The slave revolt convinces the Dey of the error of his ways and he agrees to release all his prisoners. The play ends with a recognition scene in which Rebecca, Olivia, Augustus and Constant are reunited and Olivia proclaims: "Long, long may that prosperity continue—may Freedom spread her benign influence thro' every nation, till the bright Eagle, united with the dove and olive-branch, waves high, the acknowledged standard of the world" (3.7.203–7).

III

While it is clear that the Algerian piracies provided the immediate spark for *Slaves,* it is also clear that *Slaves* goes beyond this theme and that the play is about "tyranny in general and . . . tyranny of men over women in particular" (Parker 1986, 68). Its critique of male tyranny is made powerful by the identification of women's rights with the new liberating forces of republicanism in America. Rowson's unconscious tapping of the ambient rhetoric of the American Revolution begins in the prologue. The first half of the prologue expresses general patriotic sentiments about the enslavement of America's sons but the message couched in a metaphor which identifies the American symbol of the eagle with female and maternal qualities: "shall the noble eagle see her brood,/Beneath the pirate kite's fell claw subdued?/View her dear sons of liberty enslaved/Nor let them share the blessings which they sav'd?" The second half hints at Rowson's vision of women's rights as an extension of human (i.e., male) rights:

> Some say—the Comic muse, with watchful eye,
> Should catch the reigning *vices* as they fly,
> Our author boldly has reverse'd that plan,
> The reigning virtues she has dare'd to scan,
> And tho' a woman, plead the Right of Man.

As we read *Slaves,* we must bear in mind the cultural constraints on Rowson's feminist leanings. We must look for the expression of her challenges to the masculine order in the disjunctures of traditional dramatic structure. Bound by the conventions of plot, Rowson most directly shows her interest in women's rights in her development of character and her treatment of slavery. Of the four scenes in act one, the first three are entirely devoted to the depiction of women in slavery. In this play as in the rest of Rowson's work, slavery is "a symbol of the arbitrary subordination of the female as endorsed by various social systems and organizations" (Weil 1976, 99).

The first act does not even hint at the conditions of American sailors held in Algerian dungeons but gives a completely female meaning to slavery. The audience is introduced to slavery through the character of Fetnah, daughter of Ben Hassan, and an unwilling concubine to the Dey. The whole action of the scene consists of a dialogue between Fetnah and her maid in which Fetnah complains about her enslavement and describes her longings for freedom. To Selima, her maid, who sees Fetnah's position as a privileged one, Fetnah defends liberty as an abstract need that goes beyond the need for mere physical comfort.

> In the first place I wish for liberty. Why do you talk of my being a favorite; is the poor bird that is confined in a cage (because a favorite with its enslaver) consoled for the loss of freedom. No! Tho' its prison is of golden wire, its food delicious, and it is overwhelm'd with caresses, its little heart still pants for liberty: gladly would it seek the fields of air, and even perched upon a naked bough, exulting carrol forth its song, nor once regret the splendid house of bondage. (1.1.6–15)

Fetnah has been taught the joys of freedom by Rebecca, a female representative of American liberty: "It was she who nourished in my mind the love of liberty, and taught me woman was never formed to be the abject slave of man. Nature made us equal with them, and gave us the power to render ourselves superior" (1.1.90–92). In the character of Fetnah, Rowson treats slavery not merely as a political problem but as a sexual one; as Parker points out, in *Slaves,* "Rowson joined the love of political liberty with the love of sexual liberty" (1986,70).

Scene two of the first act expands the meaning of female slavery by showing how an American and a Christian woman, Rebecca, reacts to her enslavement. Presented as the spotless image of American motherhood and a monument to the triumph of the female American spirit of liberty over the conditions of tyranny, Rebecca, like the maternal American eagle of the prologue, inspired her son, Augustus, with patriotic fervor while resisting the blandishments of her captor. Rebecca embodies the spirit of the captive who, as the prologue suggests, "While . . . enchain'd, imprison'd tho' he be, / Who lifts his arm for liberty, is free." In a later scene, after a courageous outburst by her son, Rebecca exclaims: "There burst forth the sacred flame which heaven itself fixed in the human mind; Oh! my brave boy, ever may you preserve that independent spirit, that dares assert the rights of the oppressed, by power unawed, unchecked by servile fear" (3.2.11–15). Here, in the situation of Rebecca, Rowson first connects the situation of the female in slavery with the political implications of republicanism. Although Rebecca identifies her imprisonment with the political ideals of Americans, her imprisonment, like that of Fetnah, an Algerian, and unlike that of the American male prisoners, remains sexual, not political, in nature. She is a captive because she has excited the lust of Ben Hassan, not because she champions American freedom. Her slavery parallels the conditions of social slavery which all women of that period experienced. For women, money (a ransom in Rebecca's case) becomes the only means by which imprisonment in marriage to a powerful male may be avoided. And, as in Rebecca's case, even the best efforts of friends may be defeated by the schemes of ruthless men. Like the heroines of the sentimental novel, Rebecca resists the attacks on her virtue and remains noble and pure.

Scene three opens on a meeting of the two remaining important women, Olivia and Zoriana who, although their situations differ are also captives because of their gender. Like Rebecca and Fetnah, Olivia is a prisoner because she is the object of a man's need to express his sexual power through complete control of women. Olivia's captivity is a more graphic example of the powerless situation of all women and thus, Olivia is more like the female character in traditional seduction plots than Rebecca is: Olivia is unmarried, pledged to another, and thinks of death as an alternative to forced and unhappy marriage. Zoriana is the only woman who is not a slave of the Algerians. Unlike the others, Zoriana is the prisoner of love; she loves, unrequitedly, Henry, who is a Christian and Olivia's fiancé. Further, since Zoriana is a secret convert to Christianity, she is bound by her belief in her filial duty to her father, the Dey.

Rowson treats her male characters as stock figures. Rowson does not spend a scene, as she does with the female characters, in developing any individual intricacies in their characters. The two dominant villains are sketchily drawn. The Dey does not appear until the second act when he does a certain amount of pro-forma grumbling. Introduced as a sly coward, Ben Hassan is allowed to become a comic villain as he seeks to escape in women's clothing. With the exception of Frederick, the captives are also stock types. Henry is simply a romantic lead. Constant does not appear until the last act. Rebecca's son is treated as a child and functions primarily as the object of his mother's fierce patriotism. The part of Sebastian, a Spanish slave involved in the escape, provides only comic relief. Only Frederick grows as a character. Our interest in him derives from his hopeless quest for love and his consequent ability to accept a woman as an equal in matters of love. He wanders through the first part of the play hoping to find a woman who will love him: despairing of ever being loved, he says "Moor or Christian, slave or free woman; 'tis no matter, if she was but young, and in love with me, I'd kneel down and worship her. But I'm a poor miserable dog, the women never say civil things to me" (1.4 32–36).

Rowson's decisions about her character portrayal seem to indicate that Rowson felt that, ultimately, women were powerless. Although her women are courageous and noble, they are trapped by social structures and strictures. They have neither the means nor the training for escape so that their fate lies in the hands of men who are less interesting but more powerful because of gender.

Ironically, the character of Fetnah, an unusual and somewhat unconscious choice of heroine for Rowson, enables Rowson to make the most effective case against male domination. Although the play indicates that Fetnah has been raised a Moslem, she has a Jewish father and an English mother. Having been sold by her father into the Dey's harem, she is a fallen woman. Therefore, in developing Fetnah's character, Rowson was free from the constraints of Christianity and traditional morality; as a non-Christian, Fetnah could be a fallen woman and yet a good one. This freedom allows Fetnah to be heroic in a way that Olivia, Rebecca and even Zoriana can never be. Further, in this character Rowson could deal directly with sexual domination. The dynamic of the sentimental female character requires that the female possess a sense of the mystery of sex. Since Fetnah is already the Dey's concubine, Rowson could be more direct in her exploration of the sexual dynamic of power. For example, Fetnah associates through phallic symbolism the power of the Dey with the power of male gender and underlines the repugnance with which she approaches her sexual relationship: "No—he is old and ugly,—then he wears such tremendous whiskers, and when he makes love, he looks so grave and stately, that I declare, if it was not for his huge scymitar, I shou' burst out a laughing in his face" (I.1, 19–23). While the offers of marriage to Rebecca and Olivia are posed by their captors as alternatives to a long imprisonment, Fetnah makes clear that the Dey's domination of her is based on the threat of physical violence. The explicit physical danger that Fetnah faces makes her the most courageous of all the characters in the play. Describing her attempt to reason with the Dey, she tells us how courage can be gained from fear: "Frightened! I was provoked beyond all patience and thinking he would certainly kill me one day or another, I thought I might as well speak my mind, and be dispatched out of the way at once" (1.1. 53–56). After she escapes from the palace by dressing as the Dey's son, she risks her life to go to the grotto where Frederick and Henry are hiding with their band. She asks to participate as an equal in the escape and rejects Frederick's attempt to shield her from danger: "A woman! Why, so I am; but in the cause of love or friendship, a woman can face danger with as much spirit, and as little fear, as the bravest man amongst you" (3.1.107–11). She is smart as well as courageous. When the Dey discovers her in the garden with Frederick, she saves Frederick with her quick wit. In all her dealings with men, Fetnah proves herself to be any man's equal.

Because of the importance of Christianity to Rowson's world view (Weil 1976, 65), Rowson provides explicit boundaries for the metaphors of freedom and explicitly rejects any association of liberty with licentiousness. When Ben Hassan tries to persuade Rebecca to become one of his wives, he argues that the American love of liberty should allow her to marry him: "our law gives us a great many wives—our law gives us liberty in love; you are an American and must love liberty" (1.2.76–78). While Rebecca's response begs the direct question, Rowson cloaks liberty in Christian virtue: "Hold, Hassan; prostitute not the sacred word by applying it to licentiousness; the sons and daughters of liberty, take justice; truth and mercy, for their leaders, when they live under her glorious banners" (1.2.80–3).

Although most Rowson scholars agree on the feminist sentiments of the play, none have noted its radical plot structure which subverts the bounds of the traditional sentimental plot. In *Slaves*, all the women experience a true throwing off of bonds. Rowson takes the escape out of the hands of the male characters (Olivia's father and fiancè) to whom it might traditionally have been given, and describes a revolt lead by the weakest male character, Frederick, and a comic Spaniard. The captives are freed only because real slaves revolt. Their moment of exultation is strengthened by the fact that the marriage celebrations that traditionally would provide closure for the female characters are not even discussed at the conclusion of the play. In addition to their freedom from marriage as a conclusion of the plot, almost every woman in the play acts to subvert an aspect of the traditional female role. Fetnah rebels against her father and rejects her liaison with the Dey, a traditional form of patriarchal relationship. Zoriana rebels quietly against the patriarchal structure of Algeria by rejecting her oppressive religion. Rebecca works to undermine patriarchal authority by spreading words of freedom. It is she who searches for Constant and not Constant who finds her. Olivia rebels against her fate by planning to sacrifice herself.

Throughout the play, Rowson uses America as the symbol of liberty: indeed, the play is dedicated to "The citizens of North-America." The preface makes clear that the play will contain "no one sentiment, in the least prejudicial, to the moral or political principles of the government under which I live. On the contrary, it has been my endeavour to place the social virtues in the finest point of view, and hold up, to merited contempt and ridicule, their opposite vices" (ii). In an early scene between Rebecca and Augustus, Rebecca laments that their captivity is a denial of their hard-won American birthright of freedom: "Must a boy, born in Columbia, claiming liberty as his birthright, pass all his days in slavery" (1.2. 17–19). Even Augustus, a mere child (but an American child!) claims American citizenship gives him an immunity to fear: "Fear mother, what should I be afraid of? ain't I an American, and I am sure you have often told me, in a right cause, the Americans did not fear anything" (3.2.49–50). After they are liberated by the slave revolt, the characters read their release as a vindication of the American way of life. Constant insists to the Dey that his only hope is to imitate a republican way of life: "Open your prison doors; give freedom to your people; sink the name of subject in the endearing epithet of fellow-citizen;—then you will be loved and reverenced—then you will find in promoting the happiness of others, you have secured your own" (3.7.182–86).

Because America is used as a symbol of liberty and human rights throughout the play, Rowson is able to expand it into a symbol of liberty for women. Describing Rebecca, Fetnah says, "She came from that land, where virtue in either sex is the only mark of superiority. She was an American." In another speech to Frederick, Fetnah, despairing, says of America: "and take me to that charming place, where there are no bolts and bars; no mutes and guards; no bow strings and scymetars—Oh! It must be a dear delightful country where women do just as they please" (2.2 41–44). American notions of equality allow Fetnah to realize the traditional submissiveness of Algerian women and become the strongest and most interesting character in the play. For the women in *Slaves in Algiers,* freedom is the right to have control over the disposal of their own person. The theme of liberty, "the Rights of Man," is defined by the women in the play as the right to love freely, as the signal for the escape from the Dey suggests, "The signal's given, you must obey, / 'Tis liberty and love." The implied connection between American ideals and feminism did not escape the eye of William Cobbett, who wrote sneeringly that "sentiments like these could not be otherwise than well received in a country, where the authority of the wife is so unequivocally acknowledged" (1795, 23–24). In Rowson's later works, America would become her "ultimate symbol of female emancipation" (Weil 1976, 91).

Rowson's use of slavery as a means of arguing for female liberty in an American context has important cultural significance for post-Revolutionary Americans. While the theme of slavery is used in *Slaves* to promote women's rights, it was familiar to Americans as a major ideological description of the Anglo-American Revolutionary controversy. The political rhetoric of the American Revolution traded on the common heritage of English liberty, and during the Revolutionary era, the Americans began to integrate the terms of Whig politics into the language of their revolution. Liberty was not a mere political cry but had a specific political definition for Whigs: it was the "power held by the people" and was always the very antithesis of despotism" (Wood, 1969,23). Slavery was also the opposite of liberty for American Whigs, it was the "absolute political evil" (Bailyn 1967, 232). Slavery was defined as "the condition that followed the loss of freedom, when corruption, classically, had destroyed the desire and capacity of the people to retain their independence: most commonly when the elements of power had destroyed—by bribery, intimidation, or more subtle means—the independence of the 'democratical' elements of the constitution" (Bailyn 1967, 233–34). During the Revolutionary period, Americans used the term slavery to describe their specific political condition and as Bailyn and Wood have shown, the political writings of the period resound with references to slaves and slavery. Although individual women began to connect their situations with the antislavery rhetoric of the new republic (Norton 1980, 235, 481), Americans did not wish to explore "the socially radical implications of their republican ideology" in terms of women nor did they develop "the obvious antislavery implications of egalitarian rhetoric" (Kerber 1980, 269). Thus, Rowson's use of slavery in *Slaves in Algiers* is unusual because it connects American political ideology of liberty with the powerful political image of slavery for the purpose of promoting women's rights.

Mrs. Rowson's portrayal of familial relationships also has some radical implications for post-Revolutionary Americans. As Jay Fliegelman has shown, the excessive interest of both English and American literature of the last half of the eighteenth century reflected an ideological shift in the nature of the family structure (1982,9). The Americans were politically committed to a rejection of the traditional patriarchal family model in favor of a new affectional family model. In *Slaves*, there is an implicit contrast between the accepting, loving family of the Constants and the oppressive patriarchal family of Ben Hassan and the Dey. In each instance, the oppressive family structure leads to a rebellion by women—Fetnah, an outspoken rebellion and Zoriana, a quiet rebellion.

Again, the values placed on the family models reflect their symbolic political use during the Revolution. As Burrows and Wallace have shown, the special language of the family relationship had been used as a symbolic expression of the political relationship between Britain and her colonies (1972,168). At the beginning of the colonial relationship, the image of the parent provided political authority for royal absolutism and obedience of the governed (171). By the 1770's, the meaning of the parental analogy had been changed as contractualism began to stress the mutual obligations between parent and child (186). The colonists began to describe the parental relationship with England in ways that stressed mutual obligation and respect, thus discovering that England "did in fact prefer to think of colonists as slaves rather than as children" (198). Eventually, the American colonists began to use the parental analogy to argue against English rule. While the political rhetoric of the revolutionary period eventually described the overthrow of both the king and the king as father, this domestic revolution did not extend itself to women. Americans adopted the English common law, in which the male was defined as "lord" and the woman as "woman" so that assumption about a wife's identity within her family "was that the husband remained the king." (Kerber 1980, 119–20). In *Slaves,* however, Rowson shows that rebellion against the parent for personal liberty and the right to dispose of one's own person is particularly necessary for females: as Zoriana proclaims at the beginning of act 2, the value of her jewels is "the ransom of love from slavery."

The link between female virtue and American demands for liberty were forged by the Revolutionaries themselves in what Kenneth Silverman has called "Whig sentimentalism," where attacks on female virtue became a symbol of the colonial situation. The motifs of the traditional sentimental novel meshed well with the political aspects of Whig sentimentalism, "a pervasive idiom of groaning, mutilation and rape" (Silverman, 1976, 82). As colonists feminized the image of Liberty, they began to see themselves as "defenders of virtue against an act of rape" and "attached to their cause the full force of the sentimental love tradition that defended the guileless purity of daughters and wives against scheming seducers bent in befouling them" (85, 86). Norton believes that the emphasis on female purity was strengthened by republican notions of civic virtue: "republican theorists . . . invested new meaning in the traditional cliché that women were the source of virtue in a society" (1980, 228).

Rowson's natural literary style may have easily adapted to the sociopolitical consciousness of America. Rowson's fiction had always been what George Petter has called the "novel of victimization" in which interest is developed through "the contrast between the readers' cozy comfort and the heroine's sorrows and insecurity" (1971, 29); chief among these is what Petter calls the mainstay of the eighteenth century novel, "actual or attempted seduction or adultery" (26). Throughout *Slaves,* Rowson implies the potential for rape of all of the woman characters. In the first scene of the first act, Fetnah describes her visit to the Dey and his threat of rape and violence: "I have condescended to request you to love me. And then he gave me such a fierce look, as if he would say, and if you don't love me, I'll cut your head off" (1.1.48–51). Each woman in the play is held precariously in an honorable position only because her virtue is triumphant. Rebecca, the virtuous American, speaks of the way in which the spirit defies the trammels of slavery: "The soul, secure in its existence, smiles / At the drawn dagger, and defies its point." (2.1.1–2). Having vowed to stay behind if the plan of escape fails, Olivia talks lovingly of the possibility of death rather than dishonor: "the thought of standing forth the preserver of my being, of the man who loves me next heaven, of the friend who could sacrifice her own happiness to mine, would fill my soul with such delight" (2.1. 103–108). Thus, Rowson's interest in female virtue complements the American vision of the female as metaphor for the spirit of the nation.

Notes

1. Wignell was an important figure in the early years of the American theater. A cousin of Lewis Hallam, whose family had created the first American touring companies (Silverman 1976, 541), Wignell had been a popular comedian on the American stage and was the original Jonathan of Royall Tyler's *The Contrast*. After the Revolution, he had been a member of the reconstituted American company under the management of Lewis Hallam and John Henry (Vaughn 1981, 40; Quinn 1923, 61).

2. For those who may see the similarity between Rowson's work and that of Mrs. Inchbald, there is evidence that Rowson was influenced by Inchbald's work (Parker 1986, 9,61).

3. The biographical information here was drawn from Parker (1986), Brandt (1975) and Weil (1976). They differ, on occasion, as to some of the facts of Rowson's life.

4. In *A Test of Honor*, the main male character, Frederick, is held captive in Algiers. He tells the story of a woman who saves her father and sister by vowing to marry a Moor. Like Olivia, she intends to kill herself before the ceremony can take place. However, her action moves the Moor to set her and the others free.

Works Cited

Bailyn, Bernard. 1967. *The Ideological Origins of The American Revolution*. Cambridge, Mass.: Harvard Univ. Press.

Brandt, Ellen B. 1975. *Susanna Rowson: America's First Best-Selling Novelist*. Chicago: Serbra Press.

Burrows, Edwin and Gordon Wallace. 1972. "The American Revolution: the Ideological Psychology of National Liberation." *Perspectives in American History* No. 6. 167–306. Cambridge, Mass: Harvard Univ. Press.

Cobbett, William. 1795. *A Kick for a Bite; or Review upon Review.* Philadelphia: Thomas Bradford.

Cook, Daniel, ed. 1971. *The Algerine Captive.* New Haven: College and Univ. Press.

Fiedler, Leslie. 1966. *Love and Death in the American Novel.* New York: Dell.

Fliegelman, Jay. 1982. *Prodigals and Pilgrims.* New York: Cambridge Univ. Press.

Kerber, Linda K. 1980. *Women of the Republic: Intellect and Ideology in Revolutionary America.* Chapel Hill: Univ. of North Carolina Press.

Meserve, Walter J. 1977. *An Emerging Entertainment: The Drama of the American People to 1828.* Bloomington: Indiana Univ. Press.

Norton, Mary Beth. 1980. *Liberty's Daughters.* Boston: Little, Brown.

Parker, Patricia. 1986. *Susanna Rowson.* Boston: Twayne.

Petter, Henri. 1971. *The Early American Novel.* Columbus: Ohio State Univ. Press.

Pollack, Thomas Clark. 1933. *The Philadelphia Theatre in the Eighteenth Century.* Philadelphia: Univ. of Pennsylvania Press.

Quinn, Arthur Hobson. 1923. *A History of American Drama: From the Beginning to the Civil War.* New York: Harper and Bros.

Rowson, Susanna Haswell. 1794. *Slaves in Algiers.* Philadelphia: Wrigley and Berriman.

Seilhamer, George. 1891. *History of the American Theater.* v. III Philadephia: Globe.

Silverman, Kenneth. 1976. *A Cultural History of the American Revolution.* New York: Thomas Crowell.

Spiller, Robert, Willard Thorp, Thomas Johnson, and Henry Seidel Canby. 1953. *Literary History of the United States.* New York: Macmillan.

Vail, R.W.G. 1933. *Susanna Haswell Rowson, The Author of Charlotte Temple, A Bibliographical Study.* Worcester, Mass.: American Antiquarian Society.

Vaughn, Jack, 1981. *Early American Dramatists: From the Beginnings to 1900.* New York: Fredrick Ungar.

Weil, Dorothy. 1976. *In Defense of Women: Susanna Rowson (1762–1824).* University Park: The Pennsylvania State Univ. Press.

Wood, Gordon. 1969. *The Creation of the American Republic, 1776–1787.* Chapel Hill: Univ. of North Carolina Press.

Mercy Otis Warren:
Dramatist of the American Revolution

JEAN B. KERN

Mercy Otis Warren (1728–1814) was not only the first female historian, but also the first woman dramatist of the American Revolution. Her entire life was spent in the colony that later became the state of Massachusetts, yet she had a far better education than most young women in either England or America in her lifetime. She was allowed to attend the tutorial classes of her two older brothers at the home of the Reverend Jonathan Russell near the Otis home in Barnstable and there she received a background in history, literature, philosophy, and theology. When her brother James read Homer and Virgil in the original languages in order to enter Harvard, Mercy read such classics in the translations of Dryden and Pope but she also read Shakespeare, Milton, and Raleigh's *History of the World*. And when James Otis went off to Harvard, he introduced his sister to John Locke's two *Treatises on Government* as the basis for her education in political theory. Thus by the time she married James Warren and settled at Plymouth in 1754, she was well trained to teach her own five sons and to understand the political events leading up to the American Revolution. As the sister of the fiery James Otis, the wife of Gen. James Warren of the 1772 Plymouth Committee of Correspondence, and the friend of such other Patriots as John Adams and Elbridge Gerry, Mercy Warren was aware that her Patriot relatives and friends were on a collision course with the Loyalists in Massachusetts.

Between 1773 and 1779 she wrote five plays, all published anonymously, about the struggle to free the American colonies from English rule, thus becoming a major spokeswoman for the Patriots.

The first two of her plays, *The Adulateur* and *The Defeat,* both appeared in Boston newspapers in 1773 and were widely read and discussed. Despite the fact that she had never seen a play in Puritan Massachusetts, she caught the attention of readers with short satiric skits in which she defined the tensions between Patriots and Loyalists: freedom versus tyranny; home versus mother country. Her appeal for her readers was her bold use of labels of the main characters in the history that was unfolding. Gov. Thomas Hutchinson she named Rapatio, a character who opposed Patriots like her brother James Otis (labeled Brutus), her husband (Rusticus, a gentleman farmer), and the others that included John Adams (Hortensius) and Samuel Adams (Cassius). Her short scenes had no plot because the issues were not yet resolved. Her skits were incomplete and broke off with Servia (her name for the Massachusetts colony) still at risk. However, her satiric labels stuck because they clearly defined the antagonist loyalists as black and the protagonist patriots as white. Her characters were boldly portrayed and her pen was caustic. She was well aware that "Ridicule could reform," as she wrote her friend Abigail Adams (Fritz 1972, 72–73).[1]

In 1775 she published her next play, *The Group,* the only one of her satires that she acknowledged as author. Using the same labels for her characters, Warren now attacked the Mandamus Councillors appointed by Parliament after Hutchinson (Rapatio) was removed from office and left for England. In *The Defeat* Rapatio had been sentenced to the scaffold, but *The Group* drops this idea and changes strategy as Warren concentrates on disagreements among the colonial Loyalists. She also adds a new charge against them for the way they treat their wives. Hateall, for example, who admits he married the dowager Kate only to get his hands on her dower, announces, "I broke her spirits when I'd won her purse" as he recommends green hickory or a willow twig to tame any rebellious wife who dares oppose her lord's superior will (Warren 1980, 2.3, p. 15). Simple Sapling also promises his wife will board any Loyalist troops assigned to him; if she refuses, he will turn her and their children out of his house. The wives, Kate and Silvia, do not appear as characters in the play; we know them only by what Warren has their husbands say about them. Patriot wives, by implication, are not treated with such cruelty. Like the patriot lady described in a stage direction preceding the epilogue as "nearly connected with one of the prin-

Mrs. James Warren (Mercy Otis), painted about 1763. John Singleton Copley. Reproduced by courtesy of the Museum of Fine Arts, Boston.

cipal actors in the group," they know that peace will come to Servia only when "freedom's sons are Masters of the Field" (Warren 1980, 21).[2] This epilogue is as close as Mercy Warren comes in her satiric plays to speaking in her own voice.

Encouraged by the Patriots' successful defense of Dorchester Heights in 1776, Warren labeled as "a Farce" her fourth play *The Blockheads or, The Affrighted Officers* (1776). The play is thought by Benjamin Franklin, her editor (Warren 1980, vxii), to be her answer to General Burgoyne's lost play, "The Blockade of Boston," which had satirized the American patriots. Characters from her previous play reappear: Dupe is still the secretary of state as he was in *The Group;* Rapatio's brother, Meagre, and Simple Sapling are again in the cast; but the language is coarser in this prose farce, a feature that has caused some scholars to doubt her authorship.[3] Franklin convincingly refutes their objections by pointing out the sexual language already used in *The Group* (Warren 1980, xvii), which she had admitted writing. He might have added that as a farm wife, Mercy Warren would also have such inspirations to scatology as privies and excrement within both her experience and vocabulary. Such controversy over whether she was capable of indelicate language in *The Blockheads* obscures the importance of her change of strategy. *The Group* was her pivotal play about the Revolution because in it she assumed the ultimate victory of the Patriots and concentrated on dissension among the Loyalists. By 1776, with the Patriots successful, she could celebrate the blockheads of her title as wooden-headed incompetents unable to defend Boston against the "Yankee dogs" who were breaking the Blockade. The earthiness of her language matches the hardships both the patriots and loyalists were suffering.

She also extended her social satire in *The Blockheads* by including a Loyalist wife and daughter more concerned with escape to Halifax for better food and English fashions than with commitment to the Loyalist cause. By alternative scenes of Loyalist soldiers describing starvation during the Blockade of Boston—food is so scarce that vermin drop off their victims' bodies (1.1, p. 4)—with scenes of their women, Warren presented a grim picture of the demoralized Loyalists in her ironic farce. Simple's wife aspires to British clothes and good roast beef now that she is "a GOVERNMENT LADY" and not a "rusty" farmwife (2.2, p. 10), while her daughter Tabitha plans to elope with a British officer even after she learns from her maid that L--d Dapper is impotent; "he will serve as a *cully* to fleece for my indulgences in *dress* and *fashion*" (2.1, p. 9). In the Epilogue spoken by Simple's wife after her arrival in Halifax, Warren underscores the final irony: Halifax is worse than Boston, with the women finding only a barn for shelter and "paltry fish my food" (Epilogue, 1.5).

Warren's last brief pamphlet play, *The Motley Assembly* (1779), continued her social satire on American women who imitate foreign fashions. In two brief scenes Mrs. Flourish, Mrs. Taxall, and Mrs. Bubble long for the British to return to Boston to restore some social life at assemblies where, as the play's and the women's names suggest, clothes are their primary interest. But in alternate scenes Captains Careless and Aid criticize such frivolous assemblies, where Whigs as well as Tories only dissipate their "patriotic zeal." This brief epitaph to the Revolution was Mrs. Warren's farewell to writing political or social satire in dramatic form, but it hints already at her fear that the hard-won victory of the Patriots might be tainted by corruption of their ideals, a theme she would pursue later in her two heroic tragedies.

As plays, Warren's five early efforts are imperfect. There is more talk than action; they lack plot, sometimes even offering more than one conclusion, as in *The Blockheads,* perhaps an indication that she could not make up her mind what to emphasize. Yet they were effective political propaganda for the Patriots' cause. By carrying over from play to play broad labels like Rapatio, Meagre, and Dull Warren was consistent in reminding her readers of the faults and inadequacies of their Loyalist opponents. Evidently she realized that her dramatic format distanced her characters from mere political statement and was more effective than essays. Hers was a bold strategy reminiscent of the anti-Walpole satires of the London theater of the 1730s, although there is no evidence that she had read such plays as Fielding's *Grub Street Opera* or *The Historical Register,* or that when she included her frivolous "ladies" in *The Blockheads* and *The Motley Assembly,* she knew of Dodsley's *The Toy Shop* as social dramatic satire (Meserve 1977, 38).[4]

What is significant is that Mercy Otis Warren wrote plays at all when even her intelligent friend Abigail Adams confined herself to letters. By contrast Mercy Warren, living as she did on the cutting edge of history, chose drama—the eighteenth-century equivalent of journalism—to enter the arena of politics in the crucial years of 1773 to 1779. Though her satiric pamphlet plays were understandably anonymous because of social strictures against a female daring to write for public consumption, they reflect her sensitivity to and understanding of the major issues of the Patriots' resistance to England. Certainly her five plays were an effective outlet for her frustration with British authority in Massachusetts. In effect, the very act of writing them made her a participant in a war from which her gender excluded her.

With the battle won for the new nation, Mrs. Warren did not forget threats to the newly independent America's survival while the victorious patriots struggled to write a Constitution. By the time she published *Poems Dramatic and Miscellaneous* in 1790, she had already begun work on her history of *The Rise, Progress and Termination of the American Revolution,* published finally in 1805. Thus when she wrote her considerable occasional verse and her two heroic tragedies, *The Ladies of Castile* and *The Sack of Rome,* she simultaneously kept an eye on the progress and trials of her country. Both of her tragedies were ambitious five-act plays in blank verse and occupied the major portion of the 1790 volume.

The suggestion for the subject matter of her two full-length tragedies came from her favorite of her five sons, Winslow Warren.[5] Winslow apparently wrote her during his residence in Europe in the 1780s, urging her to choose history of a more general interest than the American episodes of her satiric plays (Anthony 1958, 148). In her dedication to *The Ladies of Castile* she replied,

> *To a* Young Gentleman in Europe, *at whose Request a regular* DRAMATICK WORK was first attempted: My dear Sir,
> You have never named me a subject, though you prohibited an American, and seemed to have no predilection in favour of British incident, therefore, . . . I have recurred to an ancient story in the annals of Spain, in her last struggles for liberty (1980, 100).

Her dedication reflects, as does her dedication of the entire *Poems Dramatic and Miscellaneous* volume to President George Washington, her preoccupation with the new American republic and her hope "if life is spared" to complete her history of the American Revolution (Warren 1980, v–vi). Thus, if she had private motivation to abandon American subject matter at Winslow's suggestion, she still had public motivation lest the political and social immaturity of her own new country should lead to the "weakness and cruelty" of Valentinian's Rome (Warren 1980, ix), her stated reason for writing

The Sack of Rome. Threats to individual liberty were also present in *The Ladies of Castile* because the defeat of the *communidades* (municipalities) following Charles V's troubled rule led to an absolute monarchy. Cecilia Tichi writes of Mercy Otis Warren as one of the "worried celebrants" of the American Revolution (1977, 275–91),[6] which aptly describes her personal as well as public motivation for writing two heroic tragedies.

Warren's son Winslow was an all-too-clear example of the faults his mother feared would beset the new American nation. His willingness to concentrate on material comfort mirrored the risk of corruption in American business and government. His debts, for which he was imprisoned when he finally returned in 1791 from Europe, were the result not only of his failure as an import merchant but also his personal fondness for gambling and women. Mercy sent him a copy of *The Sack of Rome* with the ringing advice of the upright Aetius to his son:

> Let not ambition, avarice, or love,
> Contaminate thy patriotic worth;
> And as my sword has sav'd the commonwealth,
> Drove back her foes, and given peace to Rome,
> Let thine example teach her to be free.
> (2.4, p. 25)

But Winslow replied with criticism of her lack of unities of time and place, repaying her indulgence in choosing his recommendation for subject matter of more general interest with his own self-indulgence.

There is no evidence that Winslow Warren recommended the format of her heroic tragedies or that he had even seen such plays on the London stage in the 1780s when Dryden and Lee's tragedies, for example, were rarely performed (Meserve 1977, 48).[7] At any rate, his mother avoided the rigidity of rhymed couplets and opted for the more flexible blank verse in her two full-length tragedies. Her dramatic technique had greatly improved over her incomplete, episodic early pamphlet plays. There is more attention to plot drawn from her reading of history. Though her blank verse is not always supple, it, too, shows improvement over the verse of her early satiric drama. Emily Stipes Watt finds her dramatic verse better than any of her occasional poems (1977, 42).[8] But her ability to create and develop characters is the greatest advance in technique in Warren's last plays.

The Sack of Rome has several characters torn by divided loyalties. Aetius, the commander of the Roman army, has tried to defend Rome from both the ruthless Emperor Valentinian and the threat of foreign invasion; he is killed by order of the emperor early in the play, shortly after delivering the advice to his son Gaudentius previously quoted. Gaudentius also is torn between his desire to avenge his father's death and his love for Valentinian's daughter, Eudocia. If he kills the emperor to avenge his father, Eudocia swears she can never marry him. Her mother, Edoxia, is even more torn. Well aware of Valentinian's crimes, she finally opens the gates of Rome to Genseric and his Vandals in a vain attempt to restore order to the nation. Instead she learns that her daughters will be carried off to Africa. Even her suicide attempt is prevented as Genseric's troops lead her, too, off in golden chains. Against this backdrop of rape, pillage, and corruption Gaudentius has no chance to carry out his father's advice to "teach [Rome] to be free."

The Ladies of Castile is a stronger play because its plot is closer to Mercy Warren's public and private motivation for writing her last tragedies. In the prefatory letter to Winslow, she stated clearly why she chose her subject matter:

> The history of Charles the fifth, the tyranny of his successors, and the exertion of the Spanish Cortes, will ever be interesting to an American ear. . . .
>
> The nations have now re-sheathed the sword; the European world is hushed in peace; America stands alone:—May she long stand, independent of every foreign power; superior to the spirit of intrigue, or the corrupt principles of usurpation that may spring from the successful exertions of her own sons:—May their conduct never contradict the professions of the patriots who have asserted the rights of human nature. . . . (Preface, 100–101)

This outright statement of purpose is both a private appeal to her wayward son and a public appeal to the American Federalists as well as to the Order of the Cincinnati, who she feared would restore a monarchy in America. Thus *The Ladies of Castile* has been described as a metaphor of the American Revolution (Kerber 1980, 269–71). Although it was a better tragedy than *The Sack of Rome*—i.e., tighter in structure, and with more tension in the plot, it was the latter play which she sent to John Adams in London to see whether it could be performed there. If she thought a tragedy about the downfall of a once powerful empire "debilitated by the habits of every species of luxury" (Preface to the Public, ix) would be a less irritating subject to a British audience, she was discouraged by Adams's reply after he showed the play to Arthur Murphy and Richard Cumberland: "Nothing American sells here," Adams reported in the aftermath of the American Revolution.[9]

If *The Sack of Rome* had no appeal to a London audience, *The Ladies of Castile,* which was about a revolution in progress, would undoubtedly have appealed even less. Its subject was the resistance of Don Juan Padilla and the *communidades* to their cruel and dictatorial governor, Don Velasco—too close a parallel to the Patriots' resistance to Governor Hutchinson in Massachusetts. Yet it contained two of Warren's best-developed characters in Maria, Don Padilla's wife, and Louisa, Don Velasco's daughter. Maria believes that "virtue must spring from the maternal line" (1.5, p. 115) and this strong statement of the moral force of women is borne out by her actions. She is not afraid to dismantle shrines to pay her husband's restive army. Don Padilla calls her "a firm, heroic, noble soul" (2.4, p. 126), and heroic she becomes when, after her husband is executed by Don Velasco, she rallies the demoralized forces to continue fighting (5.1, pp. 163–64). She is also a rational woman, like Mercy Otis Warren herself. But she tells her brother, "nice distinctions . . . may be discussed in calmer times than these"; necessity now demands action (1.5, p. 114). She is, again like Warren, worried about the future of her young son, who may become a pander to a corrupt prince (5.2, p. 165) instead of defending the rights of man. Thus Maria, like Mercy Warren, has private as well as public motivation to oppose Velasco.

By contrast, Louisa is so in love with her father's enemy that despite her religious scruples, she can only contemplate suicide to avoid being forced to marry a traitor she does not love. Although she is reminiscent of Eudocia in *The Sack of Rome,* who was torn between loving her father's enemy, Gaudentius, and marrying a parricide, Louisa is a stronger character who never questions her love for Francis, the brother of Maria; Louisa finds the courage to stab herself and die in her lover's arms before he, too, commits suicide. The play closes with Conde Haro's prayer that such civil feuds may end and warfare cease. The double suicide thus closes the play with a moral commentary like that in Shakespeare's *Romeo and Juliet*. If Mercy Warren meant the characters of Maria and Louisa to be models for Winslow's choice of a wife, it is probably because he wrote his mother that he hoped to settle down with a woman, "whether handsome or not would be immaterial to me—provided she had at least 5,000 Guineas." For Mercy, the guineas were immaterial; she even crossed them out in the copy she made of Winslow's letter (Brown 1896, 252–53). It was strength of character and love in spite of adversity which she celebrated in both Maria and Louisa.

In arguing for the capabilities of women in her heroic tragedies, Mrs. Warren created characters who were the antitheses of the greedy, frivolous women of her earlier social satires, *The Blockheads* and *The Motley Assembly*. She thus allied herself with the women of the Enlightenment who celebrated their sex as the moral force in eighteenth-century society. She is, therefore, closer to the women dramatists of the Queen Anne period (see Kendall, pt. 5) than to such contemporaries as Mary Wollstonecraft, whose *Vindication of the Rights of Women* was not published until 1792, two years after Warren's *Poems Dramatic and Miscellaneous*. Warren did, however, correspond with the English historian Catherine Macaulay and even entertained her and her much younger husband at the Warrens' Milton home in 1784; and she also defended this marriage in a letter to John Adams by arguing that a woman had as much right to marry without censure a young man less than half her age as an older man to marry a girl of fifteen.[10] A more ideal marriage, like her own, between equals who shared the same principles and belief in freedom was that of Don Juan Padilla and Donna Maria in *The Ladies of Castile*.

All of Mercy Otis Warren's drama illustrated a cultural lag between England and America.[11] Her incomplete satiric plays depend not on vitality of plot as Susanna Centlivre's do (see Butler's discussion elsewhere in this collection) but on the repetition of broad labels to damn the Loyalists and praise the Patriots. By repeating the labels (Rapatio, Spendall, Dupe, and Humbug) from play to play, she used the technique of English dramatic satire against Robert Walpole and the English Whig party of the 1730s and 1740s, writing drama as polemic. When she added Loyalist women to her political satires, she continued her use of broad labels

(Flourish, Taxall, Bubble) to satirize their shallow social values in a nation at war.

Warren's two heroic tragedies, written after America won its independence, show even greater cultural lag since she chose a format popular on the Restoration stage but rarely performed in England in the late eighteenth century. Thus while her tragedies were more ambitious and show her capable of writing full-length drama in blank verse of reasonable metric smoothness, she chose a form of tragedy whose time had passed.

While Warren's dramatic format lagged behind British stage fashions, she was undoubtedly also affected by the prejudice against theater in Puritan Massachusetts. It is idle to speculate what kind of plays she might have written had she lived in Philadelphia, where, despite some Quaker opposition, theaters did exist. And even if she had seen Royall Tyler's comedy, *The Contrast,* performed in New York in 1786, it would have been too late to influence her up-to-the-minute satires of the people and events of 1773–79. What is unique about Mercy Otis Warren is that without the stimulus of seeing a play performed, she found a dramatic voice at all and used it to participate in the public affairs of her male peers. Finally, the ideas and characters of her "closet" drama are more important than its quality, for she alone among American women spoke out publicly for the recognition of her sex as a moral force in an enlightened America.

Notes

1. Fritz establishes that Mercy Warren was a conscious satirist. Kerber discusses how women of this period sublimated a wish to engage directly in political action by using satire (1980, 105–10). Their broadsides, like Warren's satiric plays, thus revise the notion of female passivity in patriotism.

2. All quotes from Warren's plays are from *The Plays and Poems of Mercy Otis Warren,* (1980) ed. Benjamin Franklin V. Because one page of *The Defeat* was illegible, see Franklin's "A Note on Mercy Otis Warren's *The Defeat*" (1982, 17) for accurate text of the page.

3. Fritz (1972, 318–19); Quinn (1923, 46); Ford (1928–29, 15–22); Meserve (1977, 71–72) all declare Warren did not write this play.

4. Meserve gives evidence that a plagiarized version of Robert Dodsley's play was printed in the *Virginia Gazette,* numbers 37–39 (1737), but it is doubtful that Mercy Warren at the age of nine was aware of Dodsley's satire.

5. All her biographers agree that Winslow was her favorite. Anthony traces care-

fully the exchange between mother and son of what should be her subject matter after the Revolution.

6. Mercy Warren's quarrel with John Adams over Shay's Rebellion is another facet of her worry over the new country—especially that the Federalists were leading the new republic astray. However, Norton interprets this quarrel as her resentment of Adams's patronizing manner (1980, 122).

7. Meserve's mention of one historical tragedy by Thomas Godfrey, *The Prince of Parthia,* which was performed briefly in Philadelphia in 1765, indicates Winslow could have heard of heroic tragedy but it is extremely unlikely that he saw the performance in Philadelphia (Meserve 1977, 48).

8. This is high praise, indeed, since Watt finds her devotional poems better than Eliot's *Four Quartets.*

9. For an account of Adams's efforts on behalf of Mercy Warren's request about an English performance of *The Sack of Rome,* see the Warren-Adams Letters (1925, 300–301).

10. Two of her biographers give similar accounts of Catherine Macauley's visit to the Warrens and the comment it caused; Fritz (1972, 25) and Anthony (1958, 126) are the most pertinent.

11. Stone, Jr. estimates the cultural lag between England and America at twenty years (1976, 338–46). For Mercy Otis Warren it was greater, i.e., twenty-five to thirty-five years for her political satires, and a century at least for her heroic tragedies.

Works Cited

Adams, John. 1925. *Warren-Adams Letters, Massachusetts Historical Collections,* 73, vol. 2.

Anthony, Katherine. 1958. *First Lady of the Revolution: The Life of Mercy Otis Warren.* Garden City, N.Y.: Doubleday.

Brown, Alice. 1896. *Mercy Warren.* New York: Charles Scribners.

Ford, Worthington C. 1928–29. "Mrs. Warren's *The Group. Proceedings of the Massachusetts Historical Society* 62:15–22.

Franklin V, Benjamin. 1982. "A Note on Mercy Otis Warren's *The Defeat.*" EAL 17 (Fall): 165.

Fritz, Jean. 1972. *Cast for a Revolution: Some American Friends and Enemies, 1728–1814.* Boston: Houghton Mifflin.

Kerber, Linda. 1980. *Women of the Republic.* Chapel Hill: Univ. of North Carolina Press.

Meserve, Walter J. 1977. *An Emerging Entertainment: The Drama of the American People to 1828.* Bloomington: Indiana Univ. Press.

Norton, Mary Beth. 1980. *Liberty's Daughters.* Boston, Toronto: Little, Brown.

Quinn, Arthur Hobson. 1923. *A History of the American Drama from the Beginning to the Civil War.* New York and London: Harper.

Stone Jr., George Winchester. 1976. "Lag and Changes: Standards of Taste in Early American Drama." *ETJ* 28:338–46.

Tichi, Cecilia. 1977. "Worried Celebrants of the American Revolution." In *American Literature 1764–1789: The Revolutionary Years.* Ed. Everett Emerson. Madison: Univ. of Wisconsin Press.

Warren, Mercy Otis. 1980. *The Plays and Poems of Mercy Otis Warren.* Ed. Benjamin Franklin V. Delmar, N.Y: Scholars Fascimiles and Reprints.

Watt, Emily Stipes. 1977. *The Poetry of American Women from 1632–1945.* Austin: Univ. of Texas Press.

'Quitting the Loom and Distaff': Eighteenth-Century American Women Dramatists

MARY ANNE SCHOFIELD

> I am obnoxious to each carping tongue
> Who says my hand a needle better fits,
> A poets [*sic*] pen all scorn I should thus wrong;
> For such despite they cast on female wits,
> If what I do prove well, it won't advance—
> They'll say it's stolen, or else it was by chance.
> —Anne Bradstreet

Quitting the loom and distaff" as Judith Sargent Murray put it (1798, 3:192), the decision to wield the pen rather than the pin, has been the concern of women writers from the sixteenth century. Geographic location did not retard such decisions, and the women in the newly formed United States found themselves with similar views. In the midst of all the attendant cares—of revolution, of survival—attached to the birth and establishment of a new nation,[1] it is no small wonder that there existed a colonial literature, and even more especially, a colonial, feminine/feminist theater. To be sure, American theater itself was in the most nascent of stages. Yet as historians of American drama tell us (Meserve, Quinn, Seilhamer, et al.), there was, in fact, a burgeoning theater tradition in the colonies, beginning with the first theater in Williamsburg in 1716 (Hornblow 1919, 22). Philadelphia soon became "the most important [theater center] in America" (Pollock 1933, 3). Yet these surveys record the history of the male-dominated colonial theater, with critical investigations of male dramatists; with the exceptions of Mercy Otis Warren (1728–1814) and Susanna Haswell Rowson (1762–1824), the latter known primarily as a novelist, no mention is made of other women playwrights, or, for that matter, actresses.[2]

Clearly, I cannot hope to rewrite the entire theatrical history of the colonial and post-revolutionary theater here; instead, I offer brief notations about the women dramatists of the early years. I would hope that such findings would induce other scholars to continue critical investigations of these dramatists and also of the actresses who performed during this period.[3] Though perhaps only third- or fourth-rate in their own skills as dramatists, they provide invaluable information about the age and the theatrical world of the post-revolutionary period in the states to the War of 1812. These women quit the loom and the distaff for a reason; the twentieth-century scholar needs to record that reason.

The colonial period did not witness the launching of any careers of women dramatists. But once the first wave of political unrest had settled, as Meserve notes, a change in the dramatic profile of America was underway; the citizenry began to yield on anti-theater laws and slowly new theaters opened and old ones were remodeled. The Dramatic Association of Pennsylvania was created "for the purpose of obtaining the entertainment of a Theatre in Philadelphia, under a liberal and properly regulated plan." Progress was slower in Puritan Massachusetts; in Boston, drama enthusiasts took matters into their own hands, opening the "New Exhibition Room" in August 1792. Within four years Boston added the Federal Street and the Haymarket theaters, and by 1796 theaters had been established in Gloucester, Newport, Providence, Hartford, and Portland (Meserve 1977, 126).

Several women playwrights responded to this new impetus, and one of the most popular and productive of this small, select group, which included Warren and Rowson, Murray is the first native-born woman dramatist to have her plays professionally produced.

Judith Sargent Murray was born in Gloucester, Massachusetts. Sharing in her brother's education, Murray was clearly educated beyond the means normally given to the female sex, and she used this education wisely, writing for the *Universalist Quarterly* and the *Massachusetts Magazine*. Her principle literary work was *The Gleaner. A Miscellanous Production* (1798), a compendium including the first "female advice column" (fictitious letters written to help frustrated housewives), as well as short stories and essays on such topics as philanthropy, hospitality, and household economy.[4] *The Gleaner* also contains her two plays, *The Medium or, Happy Tea-Party* (1795) and *The Traveller Returned* (1796); the compendium includes early feminist criticism of literature and the theater. There is a very disarming quality about the essays of *The Gleaner,* and though "assuming the masculine character" (ix),—Murray's own voice is audible:

> I am *rather* a plain man, who, after spending the day in making provision for my little family, sit myself comfortably down by a clean hearth, and a good fire, enjoying, through these long evenings, with an exquisite zest, the pleasures of the hour, whether they happen to be furnished by an amusing tale, a well-written book, or a social friend. (1:13–14)

Murray goes on in this persona to explain that he/she will "give to my materials whatever texture my fancy directs; and, as I said, feeling myself entitled to toleration as a Gleaner, in this expressive name I shall take shelter, standing entirely regardless of every change relative to property, originality, and every thing of this nature, which may be preferred against me" (1:16).

The masculine pseudonym masks her active feminism; (she is greatly influenced by Mary Wollstonecraft); be it for the magazine or the stage, her thoughts focus on women's rights. Her essay, "On the Equality of the Sexes," for example, was first published in the *Massachusetts Magazine* in 1790; the same thoughts are presented dramatically in *Virtue Triumphant* (1795). Murray is very concerned with the woman's position in contemporary society, and she chooses carefully and specifically to concern herself with the theater, the influence of literature and women's position vis-á-vis the arts.

Murray was a strong supporter of the theater. After the ban on dramatic performances in Boston was lifted in 1793, Murray, Field notes, "was one of the earliest to patronize the theatre [Federal Street Theatre in Boston], thereby championing an art branded by many of her contemporaries as an influence for evil" (1931, 32). Murray outspokenly asserts her support, castigating the Commonwealth of Massachusetts and its hypocritical laws on morality:

> The great question which does, and *ought* to occupy the mind of every patriotic moralist, is the *utility* of licensed stage-

playing. Perhaps I may as well withdraw the word *licensed,* for, in the present enlightened era and administration of liberty, the citizen would hardly consent to an abridgment of those amusements, the evil tendency of which could not be unequivocally demonstrated to his understanding; the late struggle in the State of Massachusetts, evinces the futility of erecting barriers, not substantiated by reason. The law in that state was outraged in its very face: the flimsy subterfuge of *moral lectures* deceived no one; and though, as I am informed, the theatrical prohibition is but *partially repealed respecting the Bostonians, and remains in full force upon the rest of the state,* yet it is notorious, that itinerant players are constantly marching and countermarching from town to town, to the no small diversion of the good people of this very respectable member of the Union. (1:225)

In this very same essay, she goes on to repudiate specifically charges made against the theater. For example, to counter the charge that the theatre is a waste of time, she replies:

Prodigality of time, is indeed an irremedial evil; and if it can be proved, that an hour devoted to the theatre would certainly have been appropriated to an beneficial employment, for which no moment of leisure will in future present, I for one, shall be impelled to allow the validity of the allegation. . . . But, with the same breath I contend, that those evenings which are emulated at the shrine of Bacchus, which are loitered in a tavern, in unnecessary gossiping, cards, scandal, and the numerous vagaries of fashion, will be *comparatively redeemed,* if marked by an entertainment so incontrovertibly rational. (1:226)

To the charge of "impudent expenditures," she answers that, if so desired, money should be given to the poor. And to the third charge, "encouragement of idleness," she retorts:

To the third objection I cannot allow the smallest weight: *Who, I would ask, are the Idlers?* Perhaps there is no mode of life which requires more assiduous and laborious application than that of a *good* and *consistent* actor. School exercises are certainly not the most *pleasureable* employments of adolescence; and every adult can tell, how much more easily he could imprint the memory of his early years, than that retention which is the accompaniment of his matured life. But the *ambitious* and *principled* actor hath past the age of flexibility, and still his days are, almost unceasingly, devoted to study: by frequent repetitions, such is the constitution of the mind, the finest sentiments too often pale, and the well-informed, ingenious and meritorious performer is in danger of losing his taste for the highest mental enjoyments; while the entertainment which he produces for others, is the result of unremitted and painful labour to himself. (1:226–27)

Murray saves the severest criticism—that the theater provides a "Relaxation of Morals"—for her last defense:

And I ask, Doth not a *virtuous theatre* exemplify the lessons which this preacher labors to inculcate? I take it for granted, that none but a *virtuous and well regulated theatre* will be tolerated. In the southern and middle states, Philadelphia particularly, no performance can make its appearance upon the stage, without passing under the previous examination of the governor and two other respectable magistrates, who, by their avowed approbation, become responsible for the public for the merit of the piece. (1:227)

She concludes by calling on historical precedent:

The man of firmness, of principle, of worth innate; the mild, the consistent, the regular, the maternal fair one; these shall be rewarded with bursts of heartfelt applause; while the imbecile or irresolute votary of error, the unprincipled betrayer, the fraudulent villain, the licentuous, perverse and abandoned female; these *characters* shall be stigmatized with reproach, exhibited in their native atrocity, and set up as beacons to deter our young people from pursuing a path, which will render them odious to every person possessed of sentiment and virtue. . . .

If it may be presumed, that the stated objections, thus considered, are obviated, I conceive it will not be denied that, from a *chaste and discreetly regulated* theatre, many attendant advantages will indisputably result. Young persons will acquire a refinement of taste and manners; they will learn to think, speak, and act with propriety; a thirst for knowledge will be originated;

and from attentions, at first, perhaps, constituting only the amusement of the hour, they will gradually proceed to more important inquiries. (1:228, 230)

Murray's remarks here are revolutionary. Not only does she support the theater at a time of its least popularity, but she also clearly recognizes the educative possibilities of the theater and of literature. Murray uses both in order to advance and support her unflagging interest in women's education. Novels and theater attendance can increase women's knowledge, though she realizes, for example, the problems inherent in novel-reading (i.e., inflaming the imagination) and limits this activity to children:

> Novels, I think, may very properly and advantageously constitute the *amusement* of a girl from *eight to fourteen years of age, provided always that she pursue her reading under the judicious direction of a guardian family:* By the time she hath completed her fourteenth year. . . . I am mistaken if her understanding will not have made such progress, as to give her to rise from the table with proper ideas of the lightness of the repast; of the frivolity of those scenes to which she hath attended; of their insufficiency, as sources of that kind of information which is the offspring of truth, and of their inability to bestow *real knowledge* on those substantial qualities that nerve the mind, and endow it with the fortitude so necessary in the career of life.
>
> Under the requisite guidance, she will learn properly to appreciate the heroes and heroines of the novelist; repetition will create satiety, and she will have risen from the banquet before the consequence of her intoxication can materially injure her future life. (2:63)

Murray does not openly in this essay or elsewhere in *The Gleaner* offer theater as the post-novel-reading stage for young women, though the perceptive critic/reader can reason that such is her intention.

Clearly, Murray herself found that the drama was educative. In *The Medium, or Happy Tea Party* (later titled *Virtue Triumphant*) she plays upon this notion of female education and women's rights. (The two plays are not presented as works by "the Gleaner" persona, but rather are attributed to the mythical correspondent, Philo Americanus, a strong supporter of the new republic.) The story concerns the fate and fortune of Miss Eliza Clairville, who, unfortunately, falls in love with and is beloved by Charles Maitland. Of course, male opinion á la the senior Maitland sees her only as a "needy adventurer" (3:17), and he refuses to bless such an unequal union.

Male perception is inaccurate throughout the play, and the women take it upon themselves to educate the male properly. Matronia teaches the elder Ralph Maitland the proper way to see a woman, as self-assertive and independent. Eliza explains how she will marry him, and Charles remarks "for, while she has, in the most unequivocal terms, avowed her preference, she has, with the same breath, declared that she will never meet me at the altar, but on equal ground" (3:50).[5]

Eliza is a stock character, "the virtuous damsel of unknown parentage, who succeeds finally in proving herself the social equal of others" (Field 1931, 78). Yet Murray's use of her to support female equality takes her out of the stock characterization, and as Meserve notes: "The issue of the self-assertive woman is clearly stated and occurs very early in the history of America" (1977, 155).

In *The Traveller Returned* (1796), Murray turns to revolutionary themes rather than feminist issues. Rambleton returns to America after a nineteen-year absence; the war between Britain and America continues. He has come, he tells us, in search of the woman who betrayed him: "Angelic loveliness! and could such a form become the receptacle of deliberate vice? Yet she was grossly wanting, both to herself and me, if not absolutely guilty; and this day must decide, whether the portrait or the original shall ever again resume their seat in my bosom" (3:125).

Betrayal and war are the themes, and, though masking her theories in the romance story (i.e., Camden is in love with Emily Lovegrove though affianced to Harriot Montague), it is Lady Liberty who is the true heroine of the piece. Camden remarks:

> I esteem Harriot Montague; but Emily Lovegrove enchants my reason, and triumphs over my dearest sentiments! Yet, the acquisition of broken faith shall not intervene a soldier's laurels—Indeed, these struggles do not well suit with my profession! America, now weeping over her desolated plains and warriors slain in battle, should be my sovereign lady. It is not thus

that Washington inglorious, wastes his hours! Well, well—I'll
haste to your parade, and there forget my weakness. (3:135)

But liberty, like Rambleton, must go disguised in the play; justice
must work undercover.

In the other sections of *The Gleaner,* Murray does not examine the
fate of women so covertly. She forthrightly declares her enthusiasm
for the discarding of the needle and the acquisition of the pen (No.
LXXXVIII):

> I take leave to congratulate my fair country-women on the
> happy revolution which the past few years has made in their
> favor; that in these infant republics, where, within my remem-
> brance, the use of the needle was the principal attainment which
> was then thought *necessary* for a woman, the lovely proficient is
> now permitted to appropriate a moiety of her time to studies of a
> more elevated and elevating nature. Female academies are every
> where establishing. (3:188)

Murray is confident that she is at the brink of a new female era:

> I may be accused of enthusiasm; but such is my confidence in *the
> Sex,* that I expect to see our young women forming a new era in
> female history. They will oppose themselves to every trivial and
> unworthy monopolizer of time; and it will be apparent, that the
> adoring [of] their persons is not with them a *primary* object.
> (3:189)

Yet, she cautions, women have forgotten that they are women, and
so they learn to charm covertly: "Mild with all the modest virtues and
every sexual grace—these they will carefully cultivate; for they will
have *learned,* that in no character they can so effectually charm, as in
that which nature designed them the *pre-eminence*" (3:189).

And as ̣ ̣ ̣ have learned how to use their sex, so too they have
learned how to use literature and the theater to their benefit:

> Acquainted, theoretically, with the nature of their species, and
> experimenting with themselves, they will not expect to meet, in
> wedlock, with those faultless beings, who so frequently issue,
> armed at all points, from the teeming brain of the novelist. They
> will learn properly to estimate; they will look, with pity's softest

eye, on the natural frailties of those whom they elect partners for life. (3:190)

Murray herself is anything but frail in her assessments of the contemporary theater scene and she turns her attentions to the American stage in "Observation on the Tragedies of Mrs. Warner" (No. XCI) (3:260–66), where she stresses the need for American productions. Theater managers are the enemy, she tells us; they search in vain for good foreign productions, neglecting native talent: "Was the American taste decidedly in favor of native works, the superintendents of the Drama would find it for their interest to cherish indigenous abilities, and the influence of patronage would invigorate and rear to maturity the now dropping plant" (3:262–63). She continues:

> The stage is undoubtedly a very powerful engine in forming the opinions and manners of a people. Is it not then of importance to supply the American stage with American scenes? I am aware that very few productions in this line have appeared, and I think the reason is obvious. Writers, especially dramatic writers, are not properly encouraged. Applause, that powerful spring of action . . . is withheld, or sparingly administered. No incentives are furnished. (3:262)

It is to offer such incentives that Murray writes. She is in the vanguard of the feminine, post-revolutionary theater.

Mrs. Marriott (n.d.), identified only as "of the Old American Company," is the author of the 1795 *The Chimera: or Effusions of Fancy: A Farce in Two Acts.*[6] Though not extraordinarily long or intellectually complex, *The Chimera* is paradigmatic of the post-revolutionary, feminine theater experience; it is the story of the ever-resourceful, free-willed Matilda, who disguises herself as one sort of chimera in order to display her "virago" tendencies, voice her independence, and yet still get her man.

Marriott fuses together the romance tradition with the burgeoning interest in feminine, revolutionary themes. For example, Matilda pretends to be "affected," to have lost her senses by a thorough indoctrination into romance reading; she sees footmen as princes, laborers as kings (Marriott 1795, 5). But Matilda uses her romance-reading only as a disguise, for she uses romance to run away from Lord Aberford; not only does she fashion herself a heroine, she also feigns madness. Aberford, typically, assumes that money will solve the problem (Marriott 1795, 8). But when Matilda continues to attack him, Lord Aberford has only one response: to leave. "I am sorry for your misfortune, Sir Lambert," he says;

> she is a fine girl, but she is incurable, she ought to be bled, and put into a cold bath, and kept on water gruel. I must be going, I dare not stop all night with you, for I'm afraid that she will do something to immortalize her name. (9)

Matilda uses her disguise and effectively gains the man she wants. She is well aware of the seriousness of her quest and the frivolousness of her "romance" mask. Miss Martin, a spinster, on the other hand, has not. She seriously writes love letters to her servant, exalts her "dove-like quality," and generally makes a fool of herself. Mrs. Marriott, like Murray, criticizes such behavior and the absurdity of such romantic notions with Miss Martin, and with Dolly, Matilda's secretary, who chastises Mr. Frolic: "I that am as great a virgin as a vestal. . . . Now, if ever you hopes to win my affection, you must imitate the heroine of some great romance, such as *Don Quixote,* for instance" (13).

Unfortunately, Marriott is unable to sustain her feminism to the end, and the denouement is brought about by Rupert, who unmasks Martin and Matilda. He casts himself in the role of teacher and tells her "to lay by these romantic notions, and become a useful member of society" (23). At the end, Matilda casts off her chimera, her virago-disguise, claiming devotion to Rupert (24) and goes off to live happily ever after.

In *The Chimera,* Marriott has provided a useful symbol for this entire feminist impulse. The women dramatists mask their serious concerns in the chimerical, unpretentious disguises of romance, thus hoping to entice a greater audience/readership, while yet educating the same audience to its proper place. Both Marriott and Murray heralded the American, independent spirit. Meserve accurately and succinctly describes the post-revolutionary theater when he notes:

> In the wake of the Revolution, all the major playwrights stressed nationalism while employing the devices and techniques of seventeenth- and eighteenth-century English comedy

and heroic tragedy. Likewise, in the comedies and farces, pantomime-spectacles, and sketches by lesser playwrights, nationalistic gestures seemed mandatory. (145)

Margaretta V. Bleecker Faugeres' tragedy, *Belisarius* (1795), is a historical set-piece that allows her to display her bombastic rhetoric and high-flown sentiments of independence and nationalism. Of the post-revolutionary American women dramatists, Faugeres (1771–1801) is the most cautious and restrained. Though she claims not be be disguised, in her preface she writes that the author

> has endeavored to avoid all that unmeaning *rant* which forms so conspicuous a part in most productions of this kind, together with the awful *asservations and maledictions*. What their effect upon the *stage* may be, she knows not, but to a mere reader they are ever tiresome, and frequently disgusting; for which reason, as *Belisarius* was from its commencement intended for the closet, she has attempted, in its stead, to substitute concise narrative and plain sense.

And yet, this consciousness operates to her detriment, for the characters of *Belisarius* remain flat and two-dimensional. It is a moral polemic, with a protagonist conceived as the mythical all-American hero. The plot revolves around the possible return of Belisarius, the Roman general. Justinian, the Roman emperor, was responsible, for Belisarius's exile, imprisonment, and political fate; his wife, Theodora, was responsible for Belisarius's broken engagement to Julia.[7] The play charts the movement from the exile and banishment of Belisarius and Julia and explores the power of love over hate. As public opinion swells, Justinian repents of his former action, and the two men are reconciled. Their fate is an easy one. Not so that of Julia. Together with Theodora, the empress, she suffers a cruel life and dies. Faugeres cannot relive the torment of the woman's fate; Julia's lines aptly characterize her life: "I, deserted, / Roam round the world in search of envy'd *Peace* / Who still eludes my grasp.—strip of my friends, / I suffer all alone, unheard, unheeded" (12).

Faugeres cannot find the feminine voice that her women characters so desperately need, and at the end, her tragedy, too, remains unheeded, unheard.

Although Madame Gardie, the final post-revolutionary dramatist to be examined here wrote one pantomime in 1796, attempts to locate a copy of it have so far proven futile. Biographical data has been equally sparse, and I can only conclude by sharing these facts gathered from O'Dell and Pollock (passim): Madame Gardie was first celebrated as a dancer. She married the dissipated M. Gardie and moved to St. Domingo with him. They returned to France, but his relatives refused to acknowledge her, and so, they resettled this time, in Philadelphia. Gardie made a living copying music, but when his major patron left the city, Gardie was plunged into despair. He killed his wife and then himself.

In closing, there is, clearly, no final assessment or assertion to make, no conclusion to be drawn. Suffice it to say that there was a post-revolutionary, feminine American theatre. Women did quit the loom, plays were written, and actresses and actors continued to find work.

Notes

1. Meserve points to a social upheaval after the Revolution as "those same people who had demonstrably lacked a homogeneity and had prided themselves on their individuality while succeeding in a revolution" were faced with the problem of trying "to find a common bond." Meserve notes that this "national disharmony" grew to crisis proportions during the period 1783–1800, when Thomas Jefferson was elected president of a disunited nation. "To counterbalance the strain that accompanied the social and political factionalism, there has to be a comforting relaxation, and the theatre, as did the literature of the period, helped to provide the necessary change of pace. But the drama, because it demanded a more immediate reaction, more accurately and more readily reflected the attitudes of the people. . . . The dramatists . . . promote nationalism" (1977, 92–93).

2. Moses' critical remark about representative theater is typical of the lack of attention paid to women dramatists: "The Drama of the period is well represented by Mrs. Mercy Warren's *The Adulateur* (1773) and *The Group* (1775); Brackenridge's *The Battle of Bunker Hill* (1776) and *The Death of General Montgomery* (1777); the Tory satire, *A Cure for the Spleen* (1775); John Leacock's *The Fall of British Tyranny* (1776); and Burgoyne's *The Blockade*" (1815).

3. To date, all that exists is a 1931 dissertation on Judith Sargent Murray; no work has been done on Faugeres, Marriott, or Gardie. The actresses of the period have come in for more scholarly scrutiny with Doty's book on Ann Brunton Merry and the 1925 edition of *Grandmother Tyler's Book. The Recollections of Mary Palmer Tyler*. The new *Biographical Dictionary of Actors, Actresses, Musicians,*

Dancers, Managers, and Other Stage Personnel in London. 1660–1800, edited by Highfill, Burnim, and Langhans, though unfinished, is invaluable.

4. Field describes the contents of the first volume as some thirty-four items including the Margaretta narrative; reflections on philanthropy, justice; comments on medical concerns; and essays on drama, mythology, and religion. Field calls the second volume "truly a miscellany," which contains, among other items, letters and "comments on such subjects as education, bachelor life, and advantages of self-reliance, etc.; an essay on spiritualism; remarks on the virtues, and sketches of the lives of famous kings and queens of England, France and Russia" (1931, 53, 61–2).

5. Eliza remarks to the older Maitland by way of explanation of her position:

I can never wear the envied title of your daughter, except a miracle should render me the equal of your son. . . . You behold the being whom I could challenge as relation! Consider, Sir, is such a female a fit companion for your son? Subordination, rank and degree, are of divine original; the lines are justly drawn; and he who breaks the rank assigned him by his Creator, is surely an aggressor" (3:62).

6. Meserve notes that in December 1794 "a Mr. and Mrs. Marriot appeared with the John Street Theatre Company in New York. Previously, Mr. Marriot had acted at the Theatre Royal in Edinburgh, but in New York both he and his wife played major roles during the 1794–1795 season. By the end of 1796 they were in the company of the Haymarket Theatre in Boston" (135–36). See also Seilhamer, passim.

7. *Belisarius:*

As a state prisoner hath long detain'd her;
She early was betroth'd to Belisarius,
And lov'd him tenderly; but Theodora,
Fearful lest the proud soldier should aspire
One day to wear the royal diadem,
Sent *Julia* off by force, and prison'd her
For many a lingering year (1, p. 11)

Works Cited

Anthony, Katherine. 1958. *First Lady of the Revolution: The Life of Mercy Otis Warren.* Garden City, N.Y.: Doubleday.

Benson, Mary Summer. 1935. *Women in Eighteenth-Century America.* New York: Columbia University Press.

Bleeker, Ann. 1793. *The Posthumous Works of Ann Eliza Bleecker, in Prose and Verse, To Which is Added a Collection of Essays, Prose and Poetical by Margaretta V. Faugeres.* New York: T. and J. Swords.

Bradstreet, Anne. 1867. *The Works of Anne Bradstreet.* Ed. John Harvard Ellis. Charlestown.

Dexter, Elisabeth. 1950. *Career Women of America.* Francestown: Marshall Jones Co.

——. 1924. *Colonial Women of Affairs.* Boston: Houghton.

Doty, Gresdna Ann. 1971. *The Career of Mrs. Ann Brunton Merry in the American Theatre*. Baton Rouge: Louisiana State University Press.

Faugeres, Margaretta V. 1795. *Belisarius: A Tragedy*. New York: T. and J. Swords.

Field, Vena Bernadette. 1931. *Constantia. A Study of the Life and Works of Judith Sargent Murray*. Orono: University of Maine Press.

Hornblow, Arthur. 1919. *A History of the Theatre in America*. New York: J. B. Lippincott.

Marriott, Mrs. 1795. *The Chimera: or Effusions of Fancy: A Farce in Two Acts*. New York: T. and J. Swords.

Meserve, Walter J. 1977. *An Emerging Entertainment. The Drama of the American People to 1828*. Bloomington: Indiana University Press.

Moody, Richard. 1955. *America Takes the Stage*. Bloomington: Indiana University Press.

Moses, Montrose J. 1915. *The American Dramatist*. Boston: Little, Brown.

Murray, Judith Sargent ("Constantia"). 1798. *The Gleaner. A Miscellanous Production. In Three Volumes*. Boston: I. Thomas and E. T. Andrews.

Odell, George C. D. 1927. *Annals of the New York Stage*. New York: Columbia University Press.

Pollock, Thomas Clark. 1933. *The Philadelphia Theatre in the Eighteenth Century*. Philadelphia: University of Pennsylvania Press.

Quinn, Arthur Hobson. 1923. *A History of the American Drama*. New York: Harper.

Rossi, Alice S., ed. 1973. *The Feminist Papers: From Adams to de Beauvoir*. New York: Columbia University Press.

Seilhamer, George O. 1969. *History of the American Theatre: New Foundations*. New York: Haskell House.

Smith, Thelma M. 1944. "Feminism in Philadelphia, 1790–1850." *The Pennsylvania Magazine in History and Biography* 68, no. 3:243–68.

Tupper, Frederick, and Helen Tyler Brown, ed. 1925. *Grandmother Tyler's Book*. New York: G. P. Putnam's Sons.

Vaughn, Jack A. 1981. *Early American Dramatists: From the Beginnings to 1900*. New York: Frederick Ungar.

Weil, Dorothy. 1976. *In Defense of Women: Susanna Rowson*. University Park: The Pennsylvania State University Press.

5

Critical Reviews

"Mrs. Siddons as The Muse of Tragedy." (After Reynolds.)
Courtesy of the Print Collection,
The Lewis Walpole Library, Yale University.

Britain's First Woman Drama Critic:
Elizabeth Inchbald

KATHARINE M. ROGERS

W hen the publisher Longman decided, in October 1805, to
bring out a collection of 125 current acting plays, he
asked the popular dramatist Elizabeth Inchbald to provide biographical-critical prefaces. It was an unconventional request
for the time, for while women were commonly allowed the fancy and
sentiment which produce imaginative literature, they were supposed
to lack the judgment required for criticism. Even though Inchbald
exerted herself to find merit and soften strictures, especially in the
plays of living authors (many of whom were her personal friends),
the mere fact that she criticized the work of men angered them and
caused her anxiety.[1] In 1808, as *The British Theatre* was nearing
completion (it was published over several years), George Colman the
Younger took offense at her mild criticism of several of his plays
(which actually she judged much more favorably than they deserved)
and published an insufferably patronizing letter of reproof.[2] She
reprinted it, together with her reply, before his play *The Heir at Law*
in the ensuing volume of *The British Theatre* (vol. 21). Mortified
that his works have been "somewhat singed, in passing the fiery
ordeal of feminine fingers," Colman charges that she missed their
actual deficiencies only to find fault in the wrong places; why didn't
she apply to him to enlighten her: "I should have been as zealous to
save you trouble, as a beau to pick up your fan." Even worse, she had
ventured to mention that the elder George Colman's dramatic
writing had declined after his initial success: "is this *grateful*" the
son ejaculates, "is it *graceful*, from an ingenious lady, who was originally encouraged, and brought forward, as an authoress, by that *very*

man, on whose tomb she idly plants this poisonous weed of remark, to choke the laurels which justly grace his memory?"[3] The absurd disproportion between Colman's indignation and the mildness of her criticism shows that he was outraged simply by her presuming to judge her male colleagues; his reproach of ingratitude, that he expected a woman to be grateful for being granted any professional opportunity.

Inchbald's answer opens on a distressingly defensive note, as she deplores having let a publisher persuade her to write criticism, which she describes as "the cursory remarks of a female observer." However, she goes on to answer Colman's arguments far more competently than he had answered hers, and to point out that her obligations to his father consisted only of the attention any theater manager would give to the work of a beginning dramatist. Moving to the attack, she hints delicately that insecurity must underlie Colman's touchiness, "a degree of self-contempt, which I may be pardoned for never having supposed, that any one of my 'manly contemporaries in the drama' could have indulged," and adroitly uses his own play to deflate masculine pretensions based on superior formal education, as she yields to men, and to him in particular, "all those scholastic honors" which he "so excellently described" in his own dramatic character, the comic pedant Dr. Pangloss.

Inchbald's prefaces are most interesting for what they reveal about herself—as an individual and as a woman who had achieved great success in a man's world and yet was intent on maintaining femininity as her contemporaries defined it. Sometimes she enlivens her biographical sketches with insights derived from her own experience. In her essay on *Hamlet,* for example, she imagines Shakespeare as a brilliant youth escaping to the city from a stultifying provincial atmosphere, just as she herself had. She uses her biography of Susannah Centlivre to justify a woman's undertaking the masculine profession of playwriting (*The Busy Body*). Her own experience of earning her living by writing makes her sympathize with the hack dramatist John O'Keefe, who wrote more than was good for his reputation. Critics, she observes, censure writers as if they always published for glory works which they were proud of, but actually they may be pressed by financial need to bring out what their own judgment condemns, all the while "sinking under the shame of their puerile works, and discerning in them more faults, from closer attention and laudable timidity, than the most severe of their censurers can point out" (*The Castle of Andalusia*).[4]

As an experienced actress and playwright, Inchbald understood what worked in the theater—why, for example, Centlivre's comedies were more successful than *The Way of the World*. She appreciated good acting roles and recognized the actor's contribution to the creation of character on stage. Thus Thomas Morton's *A Cure for the Heart Ache,* though undistinguished as literature, illustrates fine theatrical craftsmanship because the characters were designed to be embodied by actors: hence they "exactly please upon the stage, the sphere alone for which they were formed." As a playwright, she considered technical problems such as how to devise incidents to develop the basic conceptions of fable and character or how to sustain dramatic probability even when the plot takes an unlikely turn: distracting the audience by fixing their attention "solely upon every beauty which the dramatist displays," as in the masquerade scene in Hannah Cowley's *The Belle's Stratagem,* where the hero improbably falls in love with the heroine after a few hours of conversation.

Starting life as a farmer's daughter, Inchbald could never have accumulated her considerable fortune without rigorous hard work, self-discipline, and economy; her task was doubly hard in light of the limited opportunities open to women. Even after she had achieved success, she lived in modest lodgings and often did her own heavy housework, so as to be sure of maintaining her independence and her ability to help numerous distressed relatives. Accordingly, she had great contempt for financial irresponsibility. Arthur Murphy, she remarks acidly, was accustomed to the comforts of a gentleman and "had not strength of mind to yield up the ease and elegance, which affluence alone should bestow, for the content and pride of freedom and independence. But to reproach" him for this "would be treating him harshly, according to the rules of custom, though with perfect justice, according to the principles of honor and fortitude" (*All in the Wrong*). Her list of Murphy's successive means of support brings out by contrast the resources that were not available to women: after "the powers of invention forsook" him, he translated Tacitus, then got a government sinecure and finally, when he was even more infirm, a generous pension.

Her praise of Richard Cumberland for sympathetically presenting a Jewish hero would be expected from a liberal eighteenth-century humanitarian, but her praise of *The Jew* as a defense of misers as well is distinctively her own: "Mr. Cumberland has in one single part, rescued two unpopular characters from the stigma under which they both innocently suffered." Actually, it is likely that Cumberland emphasized Sheva's penny-pinching in order to give a little comic relief to his noble character and tearful story. But Inchbald makes it an exemplary characteristic; she describes the miser in her own image, as one who stints himself to "preserve a sane and purified mind" and to bestow more upon his neighbor. She goes on to note, accurately, that "indiscriminate profusion has been the dramatic hero's virtue in every comedy." Amiable wastrels like Sheridan's Charles Surface, redeemed by their benevolent impulses and spared the consequences of their thoughtless extravagance, abound in the drama of the period, but are conspicuously absent from her plays.

Though Inchbald was influenced by the sentimentalism of her period, she was consistently hard-headed about money. Thus she was not taken in by the specious morality of Edward Moore's *The Gamester*, which represents as amiable and essentially virtuous a man who ruins his family by gambling. She demolishes the sense and morality of this popular and admired tearjerker, which glorifies the uncritical devotion of the hero's wife. "An audience mostly supposes, that she performs an heroic action as a wife" when she hands over her last piece of property to her husband; "but readers call to mind, she is a mother," who is "yielding up the sole support of her infant child, to gratify the ideal honor of its duped and frantic father." An audience should "be taught, that charity without discrimination is a sensual enjoyment, and, like all sensuality, ought to be restrained" (Colman the Younger's *John Bull*). Though her own plays generally include a little delicate distress, she never confuses well-judged charity with heedless profusion.

Nor does she glorify romantic infatuation. When romantic love appears in her comedies—and it is not a prominent theme—it is a settled or a rationally grounded affection. Love may, as it is supposed, "engage every heart"; but it is conjugal love that raises a really deep interest (*Venice Preserved*). Inchbald sees the passion of Romeo and Juliet as adolescent infatuation rather than ideal love and therefore concludes that the play, however excellent and charming, is not deeply moving. On the other hand, the love of Othello and Desdemona is profoundly so, since Shakespeare convinces us that it was well founded. Congreve's *The Mourning Bride* does not touch the heart because the love on which it centers, "though . . . substantiated by wedlock . . . still . . . is merely bridal; neither cemented by long friendship, [nor] offspring." In her own comedies, she is more concerned with realistic marital problems than with the difficulties of young lovers, which furnished most dramatic plots in her time.

Inchbald's emphasis on marriage over courtship reflects the priorities of a mature, experienced woman, even as her insistence on economy reflects woman's traditional role of conserver. She also expresses an intelligent woman's irritation at men's tendency to idealize folly or insipidity in women: she is disgusted with the hero of Thomas Holcroft's *The Road to Ruin* for falling in love with an arrant fool, and she remarks that "Elegance in Charlotte Rusport, and beauty in Louisa Dudley, are the only qualities which the two actresses, who represent those parts, require" (Cumberland's *The West Indian*). She uses the experience of Sarah Siddons, who succeeded on the London stage only after her judgment was formed, to demonstrate that mature intelligence can make women more attractive (*Isabella, or The Fatal Marriage*). Inchbald finds Sheridan's illiterate Mrs. Malaprop too far-fetched to be funny and attacks the cliché that the life of an unmarried woman must be barren and joyless (Thomas Morton's *The Way to Get Married*). Her woman's viewpoint also appears in her distaste for the aggressively masculine values that male dramatists have traditionally glorified. In Corneille's *Horace* she finds the lover Curiatius, whose courage is "joined with sensibility and tenderness," to be "superior, both as a man and a hero, to Publius Horatius, the brother," whose "rugged bravery, . . . never feels beyond its own selfish glory" (William Whitehead's *The Roman Father*, adapted from *Horace*). She notes that women do not generally like *Henry IV, Part I* and *Cato* because of these plays' predominantly masculine values.

Unfortunately, she was not always so independent. She was self-conscious about daring to be a critic, and perhaps, as a beautiful woman used to charming men, she was particularly reluctant to displease them. In any case, her prefaces do include placatory tributes to conventional ideals and stereotypes of womanhood. Though she justifies Centlivre's professional authorship and even the irregularities of her life, Inchbald condemns the immorality of *A Bold Stroke for A*

Wife (which actually is quite clean), even though she concedes it was no worse than other plays of its time. "Though her temptations, to please the degraded taste of the public, were certainly more vehement" than those of contemporary males who did not write to eat, "yet, the virtue of fortitude is expected from a female, when delicacy is" in question; and she "should have laid down her pen, and taken, in exchange, the meanest implement of labor, rather than have imitated the licentious example" of others. Luckily for herself, Inchbald was not put to this test, since audiences in her time preferred the strict sexual morality and refined speech of her own comedies. On other occasions, she repeated ancient slurs on women: they are naturally deceitful and mischief-making (*Coriolanus*); they are greedy for praise and unable to keep a secret (Beaumont and Fletcher's *Rule a Wife and Have a Wife*). Contrary to the evidence of her own writing, she says women are liable to fall into "bad grammar, false metaphors and similes, with all the usual errors of imperfect diction" (*Lovers' Vows*).

The critical principles of Inchbald's prefaces reflect the assumptions of her time, though she applies them with perceptiveness and flexibility. Late eighteenth-century critics prized interrelated values of naturalness or probability, gentility, and morality. Probability requires incidents which occur in normal life, full of "little touches of refined nature," and passions "such as commonly govern mankind" rather than violent stagy ones (Colley Cibber's *The Careless Husband*). Inchbald praises Murphy's *All in the Wrong* because its dialogue "never in one sentence soars above the proper standard of elegant life; and the incidents . . . are bold without extravagance or apparent artifice." In one particularly skillful scene, "unlooked-for accidents" produce the highest comic effect, and yet all has "arisen from causes consonant with the general events of life."

Probability in character required avoidance of extremes. Though Inchbald greatly admired Congreve's *Love for Love,* she faulted many of its characters for exaggeration (as well as immorality): too heavy insistence on idiosyncrasies produced by temperament or occupation makes characters unbelievable. Holcroft's *The Road to Ruin* is supremely effective theatrically because it represents paternal and filial affection "with infinite power, and yet without one inflated or poetic sentence.—The scenes between Dornton and his son are not like scenes in a play, but like occurrences in the house of a respectable banker, who has a dissipated, though a loving and beloved, son." Characters should also illustrate a realistic mixture of virtues and vices. When Cibber endowed a licentious coxcomb with frankness and valor (Clodio in *Love Makes a Man*), he showed "justice, or rather judgment" unusual among authors. Carlos in the same play might seem unnaturally wise and good, but Cibber makes him so young and studious that "he appears like one whom temptations have yet never reached, rather than" one preternaturally immune to them. Inchbald admires the human reality of Shakespeare's Antony and Cleopatra and points out that this elicits from us "more lenity to their faults—more reverence for their virtues" than we feel for the stilted public figures in Dryden's *All for Love*. Mixed characters are also more useful in providing moral lessons (Murphy's *The Way to Keep Him*).

Inchbald often comments on the difficulty of portraying good characters without making them insipid, and, in her preface to Massinger's *A New Way to Pay Old Debts*, illuminates this problem with the insight of a practicing dramatist. Virtuous people have fewer turbulent passions and more control over those they have, and are not subject "to those grand exhibitions for a theater—remorse, or despair." And yet an author must create situations for them that will excite "sensations which awaken interest." It requires fertile invention to devise "Bold and unlooked for occurrences, [which] will raise conflicts in the most peaceful bosom" and surprise a good person into succumbing to temptation.

In her own plays, Inchbald generally avoided perfect characters. This was wise, since she was not able to make them interesting. Mr. Haswell in *Such Things Are* is colorless, though he derives some force from being based on a real-life hero, the prison reformer John Howard. Lady Eleanor Irwin in *Every One Has His Fault* is defined as a model wife, mother, and daughter, her appeal coming solely from her stock pathetic situation. On the other hand, Mr. Harmony, in the same play, is a successful comic character because he is not perfect: his universal benevolence is just a bit ridiculous because it is powered less by principled philanthropy than by a compulsive need to dispel ill-will and unpleasantness. In general, Inchbald's characters meet her standard of naturalness. They are typically well bred, often intelligent, but not extraordinary—neither preternaturally witty, nor distorted by a prevailing humor.

Yet improbability may be excused if it produces sufficiently beautiful imaginative or emotional effects. Leontes' unfounded jealousy is unbelievable, but it occasions such noble behavior and such affecting suffering in his wife that "the extravagance of the first is soon forgotten, through the deep impression made by the last" (*The Winter's Tale*). Inchbald may have been aiming at an analogous effect by setting her *Such Things Are* in Sumatra. Only in such a place can she show a Sultan, made cruel and self-absorbed by the loss of his beloved wife, keeping that very woman in prison for years because he is too callous to care who may be languishing in his dungeons. Through this melodramatic fable, Inchbald can make vivid her plea for prison reform in England.

Refinement, the second great principle, meant avoidance not only of bawdry, but of anything "low"—vulgar characters or slapstick humor. Inchbald consistenty faulted dialect characters, because they were lower class and because their incorrect English was too easy a source of comedy, and never used them in her own work. She praises Cumberland's *The West Indian* for "wholly refined" language and "perfectly delicate" ideas, for bestowing wit and humor "on persons of pleasing forms and polite manners." This skill "divides, like a gulf, the superior, from the inferior, dramatist." It is easy to raise a laugh by the blunt repartee or comic accidents of characters in low life, "But to exhibit the weak side of wisdom, the occasional foibles which impede the full exertion of good sense; the chance awkwardness of the elegant, and mistakes of the correct . . .—these are efforts of intellect . . . [which] can alone confer the title of a good comic author" (Cumberland's *The Brothers*). Inchbald's dislike of the "low" led her to overvalue the younger Colman's *Inkle and Yarico* and to undervalue his genuinely amusing *The Heir at Law*. The first play is finer in her eyes because it is free of crude, dialect-speaking characters and full of high-flown moral declarations, and its characters are exaggerated in the direction of sentimental virtue rather than comical humors.[5] She can't help enjoying Dr. Pangloss, a caricatured pedant in *The Heir at Law*, but she must justify him on moral grounds: "when solemn sentences and sprightly wit are found ineffectual, the ludicrous will often prove of import."

Fortunately, however, Inchbald's dramatic practice was not so rigorous as her theory. She worried in the preface to *Such Things Are* that Sir Luke and Lady Tremor, two of the most amusing characters, were "low"; and so they are, if marital squabbles and the humble origins of Lady Tremor, whose father was a grocer, make them so. But they are not coarse or crude; their humor comes from their characters rather than from class mannerisms such as vulgar accents; their fighting involves poking at foibles rather than abuse; and they do not jar with the more refined characters, Twineall, Lord Flint, and Haswell. They are very funny, and it is happy for the play that she did not purify them into elevated but insipid gentility.

Inchbald shared in the overpreoccupation with moral teaching typical of her time. Even when she praises a play as light entertainment—for example, Morton's *A Cure for the Heart Ache*—she takes care to point out that it teaches a useful lesson and makes admirable moral reflections along the way.[6] She climaxes her appreciative description of the awe-inspiring Kemble-Siddons production of *Macbeth* by calling it "one of the most impressive moral lessons which the stage exhibits." She is horrified by "that unrestrained contempt of principle which pervades every scene" of *The Beaux' Strategem*, meaning chiefly Mrs. Sullen's adulterous intentions. In her own plays, she approves the good, reproves the bad and sets up edifying scenes; but in general she upholds a sound moral system based on honesty and humanity, and eschews the blatant moral declamations which studded the plays of many contemporaries. She follows sentimental morality by presenting human nature as essentially good and preferring to reform rather than reject misbehaving characters, but she refrains from presenting worthless characters redeemed by benevolent impulses.

Inchbald deviated from the norm only in her relatively enlightened presentation of unhappy fallen women (in serious drama only, where they can suffer adequately for their sins). In the preface to her highly successful adaptation of August von Kotzebue's *Lovers' Vows*, she points out that Agatha, the unwed mother in the play, suffered greatly, and that those who condemn her ultimate reunion with her lover "forget there is a punishment called *conscience,* which, though it seldom troubles the defamer's peace, may weigh heavy on the fallen female and her libertine seducer." The morality of Benjamin Thompson's *The Stranger*, another adaptation from Kotzebue, may not be perfect; but it shines in comparison with that of so-called pious Protestants or patriots who defame their opponents so "that the nation may hate them without offence to brotherly love."

Inchbald's critical principles suggest the limitations of drama in her period, both her own and that of others. There was far too much emphasis on negative virtues: plays must not violate the probability of ordinary life; they must avoid any hint of vulgarity; they must not present any character or action that could possibly provide a bad example.[7] Strongly marked characters may be considered improbable; low-life characters and farcical incidents are vulgar; a cynical view of human nature is unrefined and immoral; wit is apt to challenge accepted standards of morality or propriety. The result of such apprehensions is liable to be insipid correctness. Inchbald was capable of seeing this very fault in her own *To Marry, or Not to Marry*, despite its popular success. Here, she acknowledges, in avoiding farcical incidents, broad jests, dialect, songs and processions, she also avoided wit and humor.[8] She points out that her major characters "are all justly drawn, but not with sufficient force for high dramatic effect." They have neither the psychological depth required to make realistic drama of character interesting, nor the intensity and exaggeration necessary for comic or satiric effects; nor does the play contain any other sources of entertainment.

Drama so concerned with gentility could hardly deal incisively with serious issues. In general, Inchbald seems to have accepted sentimental benevolence as a substitute for social criticism, at least in plays: she takes the younger Colman's *Inkle and Yarico* to be an indictment of slavery, even though all it really teaches is that it is not nice to sell one's Indian common-law wife. Her own radical opinions (she was a friend of Godwin and Holcroft) rarely appear in either plays or prefaces. The only examples are her relatively lenient attitude toward fallen women (if repentant and if found in German drama), her attack on prison abuses in *Such Things Are* (tactfully set in Sumatra, not England), and her acid comment on the complacent patriotic sentiments that were a staple of contemporary plays: "The author tells us truly, that, 'we have in England, palaces for poverty, and princely endowments for calamity'—the English are charitable, but they are too apt to boast of their benevolent endowments: a higher boast would be, to have fewer paupers who require them" (Morton's *The School of Reform*).

A desire to deal seriously with the problems of male-female relationships, together with reluctance actually to do so, may underlie Inchbald's dissatisfaction with her *Wives as They Were, and Maids as They Are* (even though it was, like most of her plays, very successful). Her preface to this comedy is her most detailed analysis of her own work. It has a good fable and characters, she says; but she did not execute her design effectively because she failed to develop it with appropriate incidents: some are insipid and some improbable, and there are jarring shifts in tone. She resorted to farce (though she well knew that its extravagance would be out of keeping with her basically realistic portrayal) and then, successively, to "the serious, the pathetic, and the refined comic." In particular, she failed to devise appropriate incidents to illustrate the extraordinary marriage of Lord and Lady Priory. She did not succeed in "gratifying certain expectations indiscreetly raised."

These accurately noted technical deficiencies result from Inchbald's inability to maintain consistently the realistic manner that suited both her subject and her personal style. *Wives as They Were,* which centers on the relationship between a lively daughter and her dictatorial father and that between a selfish, domineering husband and his resigned wife, raises challenging issues about male authority and female duty. But no dramatist writing for the conventional theater of 1797 could deal realistically with such actual social problems. Accordingly, Inchbald resorts to fantastic situations and easy dramatic effects. She contrives a plot whereby the daughter lives in the same house as her father but does not recognize him as such, so that her refusals to obey him are not a challenge to paternal authority. She indicates that Lady Priory, a cool, sensible woman, has reasons for submitting to her husband, even though she is neither weak nor devoted to him; but she does not analyze the woman's motivation or her situation so as to make her attitude plausible. She leads the couple to a confrontation, but lets it tail off into conventional sentiments. She illustrates the Priory marriage with fantastic detail because presenting it realistically would raise uncomfortable questions about the actual patriarchal marriages of the time. In lieu of developing the serious issues, Inchbald diverts her readers with pointless farcical episodes, such as a confusion between the dignified father and a young rake produced by an unmotivated exchange of coats at the end of act 2, or with factitious pathos, such as Miss Dorrillon's effusive reaction to the false tale that her father is in debtor's prison (5.2). The problem with the play is not so much shifts in tone or fluctuations in quality as it is discrepancy between stimulating ideas and conventional development.[9]

Inchbald did recognize the pressure of convention on the theater, although not explicitly in connection with her own work. In her preface to Colman's *John Bull,* she remarked that the dramatist "must please at first sight, or never be seen more" and therefore must address the audience's "habits, passions, and prejudices, as the only means to gain this sudden conquest of their minds and hearts." Hannah Cowley, her successful contemporary, made the same point in the prefatory "Address" to her own comedy *A School for Greybeards:* unlike a novelist, who can follow nature freely, the dramatist feels "encompassed in chains" when she writes, which check her in her "happiest flights, and force" her "continually to reflect, not, whether *this is just?* but, whether *this is safe?"* (1786, vi–vii). The contrast between possibilities in drama and the novel is strikingly illustrated by Inchbald's own Miss Dorrillon, who, as the author notes in her preface, is of the same type as Miss Milner of her *Simple Story.* Miss Milner is far more affecting and convincing, not only because of the wider scope for development afforded by the novel, but also because of the novelist's greater freedom to present a heroine with obvious faults as an intensely sympathetic character.[10]

Notes

1. The gentleness of Inchbald's criticism appears when we contrast her *British Theatre* prefaces with Richard Cumberland's in a similar collection, *The British Drama* (1817). Cumberland delighted in tearing plays apart on grounds of improbability or immorality. (It is true that he was not dealing with living authors apart from himself.) Nevertheless, even James Boaden, Inchbald's admiring biographer, deplored her writing of criticism, on the grounds that it was to her interest "to conciliate everybody" and that "There is a something unfeminine . . . in a lady's placing herself in the seat of judgment" (1833, 2:84).
2. Inchbald's overestimation of George Colman the Younger was general in the time. E.g., Thomas Gilliland wrote of Colman that "no one stands more prominent, or deserves to rank higher. . . . His works contain great beauties of

thought, neatness of diction, and a potent share of morality . . ." (1808, 1:297–98).

3. All quotations but the last one from Hannah Cowley on p. 288 are from Inchbald's prefaces in *The British Theater* and the two letters printed before *The Heir at Law*. Since all of these are short (no more than five pages) and the volumes are not continuously paged, I have simply indicated in context or parentheses the play to which the relevant preface belongs.

4. Personal experience may also account for her interpretation in the moral she draws from Olivia's infatuation with Viola in *Twelfth Night*, on "the imprudence of women, in placing their affections, their happiness, on men younger than themselves"; this probably reflects her unhappy passion for the actor John Philip Kemble, who was four years younger than she. Her Catholic religious affiliation may be seen in her disgust at the crimes committed by Henry VIII and Cardinal Wolsey "under the pretense of religious duty" and in her unusual sympathy with the deposed Catholic King James II, deserted by his Protestant daughters (*Henry VIII, King Lear*). Her definition of "the grand moral" of *Lovers' Vows* as "to set forth the miserable consequences which arise from the neglect, and to enforce the watchful care, of illegitimate offspring" may reflect her difficult relationship with Mr. Inchbald's illegitimate son.

5. She did occasionally notice excesses in gentility: Richard Steele's Bevil and Indiana "sink into insipidity, through the lifeless weight of mere refinement" (*The Conscious Lovers*).

6. Cf. Gilliland: Morton's "plays carry under the alluring vehicle of pleasure, a potent share of ethics, and when fascinating an audience, the antidote to immorality insensibly steals on the mind, and leaves an indelible impression of some useful lesson" (1808, 1:471). On the emphasis on morality in the drama in general, see Thomas Holcroft in *The English Review* of May 1783: the contemporary theater contributes "to humanize the heart, and correct the manners," by ridiculing follies, giving "the most beautiful precepts for . . . conduct," alluring "to the practice of virtue by declamations conveyed" in poetical thoughts and attractive language, and "exhibiting dreadful examples of the dreadful consequences of vice" (Gray 1931, 298).

7. Charles Lamb astutely recognized that the essential failings of late eighteenth-century comedy as practiced by Inchbald and Holcroft were excessive moralizing and restriction to "common life" ("On the Artificial Comedy," Renwick, 1963, 234).

8. The pressures on Inchbald as a dramatist and her superior penetration as a critic are illustrated by John Genest's unqualified admiration for this play: "This comedy . . . does Mrs. Inchbald great credit—it is chaste and simple—there are no farcical incidents—no songs, nor processions—no broken English—no striking situation—no particular stage effect—in a word, none of those meretricious arts, by which the favor of the public has been so successfully courted" (1832, 7:669).

9. Similarly, in *I'll Tell You What* and *Every One Has His Fault*, she raised the issue of divorce, but abstained from developing it to any conclusion.

10. Genest provides an indication of contemporary audience reaction to Miss Dorrillon: he found her "not a pleasing character" (1832, 7:309).

Works Cited

Boaden, James. 1833. *Memoirs of Mrs. Inchbald.* 2 vols. London: Richard Bentley.

Cowley, Hannah. 1786. *A School for Greybeards: or, the Mourning Bride.* London:
G. G. J. and J. Robinson.

Cumberland, Richard, ed. 1817. *The British Drama: A Collection of the Most
Esteemed Dramatic Productions.* 14 vols. London: C. Cooke.

Genest, John. 1832. *Some Account of the English Stage, from the Restoration in 1660
to 1830.* 10 vols. Bath: Thomas Rudd.

Gilliland, Thomas. 1808. *The Dramatic Mirror: Containing the History of the
Stage . . . A Biographical and Critical Account of All the Dramatic Writers,
from 1660; and Also of the Most Distinguished Performers, from the Days of
Shakespeare to 1807.* 2 vols. London: C. Chapple.

Gray, Charles Harold. 1931. *Theatrical Critics in London to 1795.* New York:
Columbia Univ. Press.

Inchbald, Elizabeth, ed. 1808. *The British Theatre; or, A Collection of Plays, Which
Are Acted at the Theaters Royal, Drury Lane, Covent Garden, and Haymarket.*
With Biographical and Critical Remarks by Mrs. Inchbald. 25 vols. London:
Longman, Hurst, Rees, and Orme.

―――. 1980. *The Plays.* Ed. Paula R. Backscheider. 2 vols. New York: Garland.

Renwick, W. L. 1963. *English Literature 1789–1815.* New York: Oxford Univ. Press.

Critical Remarks on the Four Taking Plays of This Season By Corinna, a Country Parson's Wife

CONSTANCE CLARK

> Let it be no disadvantage to me that I am a
> Woman, since men now write like boys, it seems
> No arrogant task to censure 'em as a man.
> —Corinna

The quotation is from "Corinna's" epistle dedicatory to "The 'wits' at Button's Coffee House, Covent Garden." These wits included the likes of Richard Steele, Joseph Addison, Alexander Pope, John Dennis, and Colley Cibber, and the pseudonym comes from the Greek poetess who criticized the early work of Pindar. The tone of the dedication of *Critical Remarks on the Four Taking Plays of this Season By Corinna, a Country Parson's Wife* (1719) is bold and taunting, but Corinna is careful to present her credentials, lest she be dismissed as unqualified to pass judgment. "I have taken care to improve my understanding by making myself mistress of all the valuable criticks in French and English, and have as much Latin as is sufficient to set up a modern author." Thus she launches into a sixty-seven page critique of the most successful new plays of the London season of 1718–19, which included *Sir Walter Raleigh* by George Sewell, *The Masquerade* by Charles Johnson, *Chit-Chat* by Thomas Killigrew the younger, and *Busiris, King of Egypt* by Edward Young.[1] Young and Johnson are also known to have been regular patrons of Button's Coffee House.

Corinna complains that "These four gentlemen who have made so much noise this season, are not worthy to be continued in our society." She is "resolved to come to London, and set up a society of female wits" for the purpose of deposing the playwrights from their "usurpt authority." The mock dedication ends with the verse manifesto:

> Faith we will make an antisalick law;
> Prescribe to mankind as well as plays,
> And wear the breeches, as we wear the bays.

The title page carries a quotation from a Mr. Duke's prologue to Nathanial Lee's *Lucius Junius Brutus* (1681):

> Women for ends of government are most fit:
> Women should rule the boxes and the pit;
> Give laws to love, and influence to wit.

Dramatic criticism by a woman was rare in the period, not to mention reviews of individual plays. Lady Mary Wortley Montagu's critique of Addison's *Cato* was composed in 1713, but was not published until after her death in 1762. Although the circulation of manuscripts in literary circles was common, and Lady Montagu had returned to England from Constantinople to England in 1718, there is no evidence that Corinna would have had access to it (Montagu 1977, 62–68). Although their tenets were the same, Lady Montagu's tone was serious and respectful, whereas Corinna's is facetiously impudent. Although Corinna's identity is not established, her self-description suggests Eliza Fowler Haywood (1693–1756).

Dramatic criticism tended to generalize, often focusing on discussions of genre and debates about the conflict between the French and English versions of neoclassicism. A clear-cut and well-known example is John Dryden's *An Essay of Dramatic Poesy* (1668). It is set as a dialogue among four wits, each representing a different viewpoint. The character Crites is the proponent of the tradition of the classics, while Eugenius is a modernist. The most important argument is that between Lisideius, a champion of formal French neoclassicism, and Neander, who defends the looser English adaptations of the strictures concerning the unities of time, place, and action, the liaison of scenes, and decorum in character. He sums up: "Our variety, if well ordered, will afford a greater pleasure to the audience" (Dryden 1896, 57).

Corinna herself approvingly quotes Richard Steele's prologue to Ambrose Philips's *The Distrest Mother* (1712):

Our author does not feeble force confess,
Nor dares pretend the merit to transgress;
But strives to keep his characters entire
With French correctness and with British fire.
(Corinna 1719, 13)

Yet the critic adopts the hard line of French-style neoclassic criteria
for her own analyses, throughout bolstering her pronouncements by
prefacing them with appropriate quotations from John Sheffield,
the Duke of Buckingham's *Essay Upon Poetry* (1682). The verse
essay, though now little known, was considered a masterpiece in its
time; Alexander Pope's *Essay on Criticism* (1711) was greatly influenced by it. One of the pithier couplets, expressing the prevailing
premise of Corinna's critique is: "But to write plays is a bold pre-
tence/To judgement, breeding, wit and eloquence" (18).

The controversy over proper dramatic form was not only being
disputed in the coffee houses and taverns, it was being tested daily in
the theaters, which necessarily took a less theoretical and more
pragmatic approach. The second decade of the eighteenth century
was a time of guarded prosperity, and the competition between the
two major theater companies was ruthless; since 1714, when John
Rich had opened a new theater at Lincoln's Inn Fields, the
monopoly of the Betterton company, which was holding forth at
Drury Lane, was broken. As was to be expected, the renewed
patronage by the theater-going public of Rich's troupe cut into the
profits of Drury Lane. Both companies came to put more emphasis
on such crowd-pleasers as music, dance, and spectacle. In the season
Corinna addresses, the company at Lincoln's Inn Fields went so far
as to import a company from France to perform French and Italian
plays on an alternating schedule with the regular repertoire.

According to the *London Stage* calendar for the season of 1718–19,
the Drury Lane opened first, on 20 September, with Shakespeare's
Hamlet (2:506). The first recorded performance at Lincoln's Inn
Fields is 26 September, with Dryden's *Don Sebastian* (2:507). Drury
Lane presented *King Henry the Fourth: with The Humours of Sir
John Falstaff* on 27 September (2:507), and by the last day of the
month Lincoln's Inn Fields had mounted its own *King Henry the
Fourth, Part I*, with Drury Lane competing with *Henry the Eighth*
on the same evening (2:507). In October both companies offered

Dryden's *The Spanish Fryer* within the same week (2:508). In the same month, less than ten days separated the Rich company's and the Betterton company's productions of Addison's *Cato* (2:510, 511).

The real showdown came when the first two new plays of the season were opened by the rival troupes on the same date. Both of these are dealt with in Corinna's critique. On 16 January 1719 Drury Lane presented a comedy by popular veteran Charles Johnson, *The Masquerade*, opposite the debut of George Sewell's tragedy, *Sir Walter Raleigh* (1:524). The partisan animosity that ensued is reflected in the authors' prefaces in the published scripts. Sewell, who published first, complained that he, as a newcomer, was disadvantaged by opening on the same day that a well-established and successful author was presenting his new comedy at the more popular theater. Johnson countered with a parody of Sewell's preface, paraphrasing Sewell's charges and twisting them to his own advantage. While Sewell hotly denied that he had first offered his play to Drury Lane and had been rejected, Johnson claimed that his play had been courted by Lincoln's Inn Fields, but never offered. He went on to say that Sewell's play, had he been so fortunate, would have been better served by the other company. At this time Drury Lane was graced with such stars as actor/managers Robert Wilks, Barton Booth, and Colley Cibber, as well as the famous leading lady Anne Oldfield. Ironically, despite the supposed disadvantages, *Sir Walter Raleigh* was performed a dozen times during the season, but only seven are recorded for *The Masquerade* (*London Stage* 1960, 2:524, 526, 531, 534, 541; 2:524, 525, 534).

Chit-Chat, by Thomas Killigrew the Younger, the son of one of the two holders of the original theater patents granted after the restoration to the throne of Charles II, opened at Drury Lane on 14 February 1719 (*London Stage* 1960, 2:528). The opening was apparently considered one of great importance. The demand for seats was so intense that hundreds were turned away, and there was brief swordplay and punches were exchanged in the competition for space. The Drury Lane presented *Chit-Chat* eleven times, and in the summer it was revived by command of the king at the opening of William Penkethman's theater on Richmond Hill (2:542).

Edward Young's *Busiris, King of Egypt* debuted on 7 March at Drury Lane, and enjoyed a respectable run of nine performances, i.e.,

C R I T I C A L

REMARKS ·

Ornament from Critical Remarks on the
Four Taking Plays of This Season
by Corinna, a Country Parson's Wife.

enough for three author's benefits. It was also revived three seasons later (2:530, 534, 536, 663).

Two other "never-before-acted" plays appeared in the season, both mounted at Lincoln's Inn Fields. *The Younger Brother,* author unknown, opened 7 February and lasted for three performances (2:527). William Taverner's *'Tis Well if it Takes Well* opened 28 February and "took" for four performances, the final one augmented by a popular interlude.

This was the theater scene upon which Corinna elected to impose her standards and strictures. The piece is itself in dialogue form, and is framed as a visit from Mrs. Townley, a habitué of London's fashionable haunts, to Corinna at her country house: "The scene a pleasant mount in a country garden" (1719, 1). There ensues a debate about the virtues of the quiet country life versus the hurly-burly of London, an exchange common to the opening scenes of many comedies of manners, with the argument for the freedom of town life getting the upper hand. It seems ironic then, that Corinna, despite the tone set in her dedication, extolls the joys of being a country matron.

Before tackling the specific texts, she and Mrs. Townley exchange some remarks upon the general condition of the theater. Townley suggests that the theater is suffering from a dearth of players on the level of the former great stars: "We want your Harts, your Mohuns and Goodmans, and your Bettertons. . . ." Corinna insists, "The players of this time are much superior to those of former days; they could never carry off so much nonsense" (5).

Shortly the conversation comes around to the current theater offerings. The published scripts at hand, Corinna sets up her criteria, which are Aristotelian via Horace, as filtered through the contemporary interpreters. Her tenets consistently reflect more of the French neoclassicism than the English modifications. The format is established that Townley will read aloud portions of the texts and Corinna will comment. Occasionally Townley interjects an objection to Corinna's pronouncements that reflects popular opinion or current taste. This allows Corinna to state her case even more emphatically. On rare occasions, however, she tempers her censures with a bit of grudging praise.

Corinna gives short shrift to the comedies, but spends a good deal of time debunking the supposed merits of the tragedies. Her technique of couching her literal-minded orthodoxy in a comic vein is reminiscent of Thomas Rymer's style in *A Short View of Tragedy* (1693). Rymer, by pointing out so-called logical absurdities, reduced Shakespeare's *Othello* to farcical dimensions. Corinna's frequent allusions to *The Rehearsal* (1671) evidence her admiration for George Villiers's famous satire on Dryden's early style of heroic tragedy.

Corinna augments her credentials with the revelation of her own background in the theater. Far from always having been a country parson's wife, she herself once trod the boards. "The drama is what I have always lov'd, and made it my study as well as my diversion . . . and have, you know, perform'd something in it myself, but indeed before I was perfect mistress of that divine art" (6).

Townley opens the discussion with, "To go no farther back than this last season, what could be finer than *Sir Walter Raleigh* and *Busiris? Raleigh,* while it had the disadvantage of being produced at a house that is the contempt of the town, received general approbation" (5). Dismissing the reactions to a performance, Corinna insists that tragedy is better judged by reading the text, aside from the distraction of performance values.

> There are so many accidents and so many arts employ'd in the management of a public representation; so many prejudices or preoccupations for or against the author; such advantages from the care and action of the players, that nothing certain can be concluded from the first success; and a play to gain an established fame and reputation, must please the readers as well as the hearers. (12)

The observation certainly reinforces the author's assertion that she was well versed in the production and performance elements from her previous experience as a performer.

George Sewell, who dedicated his play to James Crags, the secretary of state, becomes the target of Corinna's criticism of the practice of dedications. "A dedicating poet has the advantage of chusing a powerful patron, who is capable of rewarding his flattery" (8).

Townley reads the opening scene of *Sir Walter Raleigh,* but only two lines into it Corinna interrupts with the stipulation that it is essential to agree upon the rules of tragedy first, in order to discuss the play. Townley dismisses the rules, citing *Chit-Chat,* in which the hero attacks the neoclassic formulas. The entire essay seems to spin off from this affront to the accepted conventions.

Corinna defines tragedy as "the imitation of one grave and important action" (14). She goes on to define fable, manners, sentiment, and diction as translated by the conservatives of the literary world. She notes that the modern authors are especially deficient in fable, mistaking cruel death, bloody execution, or the undeserved destruction of some good and virtuous man, enormous barbarity, or the history of some particular person who had suffered, for true tragedy. She is skeptical of the depiction of distress from which no general instruction can be drawn, and particularly of the true stories of people, since, "The tragick fable proposing a moral for all men, must itself be general, not particular" (15). This, she feels, is especially true in the case of *Raleigh,* which "raises not compassion, but indignation in endeavors to make us quarrel with the dispensations of Providence, that according to the story punishes the most virtuous with the ignominy and suffering which is due to the criminal alone" (15). This represents a violation of poetic justice, which requires that good be rewarded and evil punished.

Raleigh fails on other counts as well in Corinna's estimation. Act I, scene I is reprinted in the text of the essay, as if being read by Townley, and with frequent interruptions, Corinna takes it to task for infractions of the laws of unity of action, place, and especially time. Dryden is held responsible for setting a bad example on the last account. "Mr. Bays" Corinna interjects, "and some other gentlemen have a strange facility in bringing those things about in a moment, which nature and the common course of human affairs require more time to accomplish" (45).

In Corinna's dissection of the play, no fault seems more prominent than the conception of the title character who is, for one thing, too inferior in quality, i.e., in social status, to be of tragic stature, and more importantly, is passive. The tragic hero must be active, an agent in his or her own downfall.

Corinna also finds aberrations in decorum. She is shocked at the behavior of the young lady in the love story subplot:

> A word or two to the character of Olympia, which is a child of
> the poet's own brain, for which he has not so much as the excuse

of history; it is monstrous and unnatural and directly contrary
to that modesty which ought to be essential to that sex. The poet
seems unacquainted with the decorums of characters when he
makes a young virgin of great quality running up and down
after a young fellow that she has a fancy for. (40)

The entire love plot, concludes Corinna, is of no use to the action of
the play.

The character of Olympia is in fact that of an unusually independent young woman who follows her inclinations rather than the
rules of society, but Corinna, as critic, never touches on the social
content of the plays, merely their adherence to or departure from the
academic standard, in this case the "universal" stereotype of the
young virgin of quality. However much she claims equal intellectual
recognition, Corinna never disputes the traditional conceptions of
women characters in the drama.

Raleigh was popular with the public, and received the following
notice in the *Weekly Journal,* 24 January 1719:

> Sir Walter Raleigh has been acted with success, the author
> having, for his first attempt in the dramatic way, shewn
> uncommon genius: the dedication seems to be extreamly just;
> the sentiments noble; and, were it not for some irregularities in
> working up the catastrophe, it would be the best tragedy that has
> appeared these many years (*London Stage* 1960, 2:525)

Critic John Dennis was corresponding with the author at this
time. He wrote Sewell regarding Johnson's preface to *The Masquerade,* "I have lately read the preface to a certain comic rhapsody with
an odd mixture of laughter and indignation. . . . He [Johnson]
pretends to turn your own canon upon you." Dennis goes on to say
that he has it in confidence that the play would never been accepted
were not Johnson actor/manager Wilks's "favourite" (Dennis 1721,
122). While Dennis also commented on *Chit-Chat, Busiris,* and *The
Masquerade* at this time, he didn't publish his private letters until
1721, so Corinna would not have seen them. Nevertheless, they are
generally of the same school of critical thought. She may, however,
have seen his letters on poetic justice, and criticism and plagiarism in
the *Spectator* in 1712 (Dennis 1943, 2:18–22; 23–28).

Corinna disposes of *The Masquerade* in a few pages. Her main charge is plagiarism: "I don't remember any one of them [Johnson's plays], that is not stoln from other authors. . . . As for the present comedy of *Masquerade* it is almost wholly borrowed from two or three others, and those of a modern date" (49). She cites characters lifted from *The Tender Husband* (1705) by Richard Steele, and *The Artful Husband* (1716) by William Traverner. She attributes the gambling subplot in *The Masquerade* to Susannah Centlivre's *The Gamester* (1705). Centlivre's biographer, John Bowyer, corrects this attribution in *The Celebrated Mrs. Centlivre*, observing that the situation is more like that in the prolific playwright's *The Basset Table* (1968, 31–32). Both the plays had been recently performed, and Johnson contributed the epilogue to *The Gamester*. *The Tender Husband* was revived in the season of 1718–19; *The Artful Husband* was performed the previous season (*London Stage* 1960, 2:526; 497).

Of *The Masquerade*, Corinna sums up:

> There is nothing of the comic genius to be found in it, nothing of the humour which has distinguish'd Ben Johnson [*sic*], Shadwell, Wycherly [*sic*], Congreve and some others. . . . *The Masquerade* is a poor, mean performance, and awkward collection of useless characters jumbled together, with unnatural and unprepared incidents, and here and there an affected attempt at moralizing and wit. (50–51)

As did Dennis, she proposes that Johnson's plays were only performed because of the influence of Wilks. Johnson freely admitted his indebtedness in his own preface.

The Masquerade is a rather pleasant romp, albeit a pastiche of past successes. Wilks was provided with a character that was a combination of a leading man and a humorous character, Sir George Jealous, who is cured of his fears of being cuckolded by his beloved Sephronia, a charming, spirited, clever woman, which role was a perfect vehicle for Mrs. Oldfield. The second couple's plot is interestingly resolved when a cast-off mistress, a type that was usually abandoned and penalized in the drama of the time, is rewarded with an independent income and freed from the tyranny of her faithless keeper. Corinna does not comment on this pro-feminist resolution. Having taken on the task usually allotted to male wits, she seems to eschew any female bias.

Thomas Killigrew, author of *Chit-Chat*, was certainly as familiar with the approved conventions of dramatic structure as anyone, having been literally born into the theater. The thin plot of his comedy is actually a vehicle for his anarchic manifesto. Allusions to the theater are interjected throughout the simple comedy. In the opening scene the character Worthy comments on the extravagant behavior of a fellow: "This is strangely absurd, and would seem monstrous even upon the stage, where 'tis lawful to present characters larger than the life" (4). Bellamar, the hero retorts, "In my opinion the poets have no great obligation for that liberty. . . . I have seen more gigantick fools upon the theatre of the world, than were ever shewn at the Theatre-Royal" (4). When the character Alamode is asked what he is thinking about, he replies with the non sequitor: "A criticism on one of Mr. Congreve's plays, where he exposes men of quality, by making them fops and fools" (10).

The actual diatribe against the rigid rules of the neoclassic model comes in the fourth act, and is put in the mouth of leading man Bellamar. Worthy sets up the speech with an observation on a character whose nature has been seen to alter during the course of the play. "The want of unity in his character, would set all the criticks and wits at a certain coffee house [Button's] to work, if it was exposed upon the stage" (Corrinda, 1719, 49). Bellamar then proceeds to debunk formal method:

Bellamar: Hang 'em, they are like young heirs that succeed to mortgaged estates. They live upon credit of what it was;—and as soon as the one imposes beggars upon the world for rich men; so the other does fools for wits.

Worthy: Yet they read much, and know all the rules of writing.

Bellamar: Stupid pretence to judging. Method in writing is like ceremony in living , too often us'd to supply the want of better things. Wit and sincerity—and I would no more excuse a dull rogue that shou'd entertain me ill by the rule of Aristotle and Horace, than a physician who shou'd increase my disease by the rule of Hippocrates and Galen.

Alamode: Then you're no friend to those who quote Greek and Latin.

Bellamar: Dull rouge (aside)—No, 'tis an impertinent excuse for not being intelligible in their native tongue.

Worthy: But you wouldn't exclude all rule in writing.

Bellamar: No, but I wouldn't have 'em take all the wit out of a play to make it more regular, no more than the seasoning out of my meat to make it wholesome: trust me Worthy, method is the crutch of wit, a mere going cart for ricketty lame genius's, it's like cooks who make sawce from a receipt and not by taste. (Knight's Preface 49)

Corinna, of course, defends the rules and judges Killigrew's effort as living up to its own lack of standards. In her rebuttal, she makes point-by-point chop-logic of Killigrew/Bellamar's arguments. "There is no order," she concludes, "no design, no plot, nor anything that comedy requires" (55).

John Dennis was of a like mind. He mentions *Chit-Chat* a number of times in his correspondence. In particular, in a letter to William Penkethman, a leading comic actor at Drury Lane and sometimes independent entrepreneur, he urges "Pinky" to write a play—especially if he is unqualified, in view of the success of the current comic writers. "Thou hast nothing to do but write a long part for thyself, and then if thou hast no jest in thy *Chit-Chat,* thou wilt have a perpetual one in thy person" (Dennis 1721, 114). Apparently Pinky did not judge it so harshly. Even though he is not listed in the cast in the published text, he appeared in it in his own production at Richmond Hill (*London Stage* 1960, 2:542). Dennis was not in London, but in Hempstead during the season of 1718–19, so he like Corinna was judging from the text, not the performance.

From a perspective of 180 years, Joseph Knight held a more indulgent opinion of *Chit-Chat,* calling it "a pleasant, gossiping, happily named piece, with very little plot, as the author acknowledges in the prologue, but has some moderately felicitous dialogue (Downes 1886). He was, of course, evaluating it purely at face value, far removed from the heated controversy of its time.

Edward Young's *Busiris, King of Egypt* is the final play treated by Corinna. The *Critical Remarks* text indicates that Townley reads the title, epistle, prologue, and epilogue aloud, but they are not, as in the case of *Raleigh,* reprinted in the text. Corinna applauds some judicious remarks in the prologue on play structure, but she is quick to remark that they do not apply to the play that follows.

To begin with, she notes that the main story does not focus on Busiris, but on the love plot, and concludes that the whole plot of Busiris could have been left out, except that it lent a name to the play. Busiris is not a true heroic character, but "a vain, babbling, boasting coxcomb" (58). Corinna points out the similarity of one of his speeches to that of Glendower's in *Henry IV, Part 1*, with the ironic observation that the latter was intended for comic effect. Corinna sarcastically calls the king's tolerance of his wife's cheating more English than Egyptian in nature. She compares the queen to Dryden's Nourmahal in *Aurenge-Zebe* (1675), while tracing the lovers' characters and plot to French romance. On the question of decorum, she objects to the over-civilized behavior on the part of the Prince, who makes every effort to woo the heroine before restoring to rape. "The Prince, according to the manners of the climate, might have taken Mandane without all that bustle which he makes, or any crime in the opinion of anyone concerned" (62). Once again Corinna avoids any comment on the treatment of the woman per se, and regards the prince's act as in accord with the decorum of his character. She seems to go out of her way not to make any comments of subjective, nonacademic nature. John Dennis, on the other hand, deplored the action, and wrote to actor/manager Barton Booth, "A rape is a peculiar barbarity of the English stage" (1943, 2:166). *Busiris* was brought out again in the season of 1721–22, and provided one of the models for Henry Fielding's famous satire on the tragedies of the period, *Tom Thumb* (1730).

Serenely secure in the right-headedness of her judgments—every major argument being supported by the selected quotations from her infallible source, Sheffield's *Essay*—Corinna concludes her diatribe with the airy dismissal, "I have much more to say, but now I believe dinner waits for us" (67).

Who was Corinna? She was not Swift's, from his poem of that title (1711?), nor was she Pope's of *The Dunciad* (1728), women writers who have been identified as Delariviére Manley and Elizabeth Thomas, respectively (*Swift's Poems* 148–50; *Dictionary* 1985, 303). A likely candidate for this Corinna is Eliza Fowler Haywood, actress, playwright, novelist, publisher, and journalist. Haywood, as Corinna describes her circumstances, was in fact at this time a country parson's wife, living about fifty miles from London, and she had been, not long before, an actress. This comprises a fairly persuasive set of circumstantial evidence, since so few women of the time would fit that description (*Dictionary* 1985, 157).

Of her contemporary women writers, two were indeed married to clergymen, one of whom had written dramatic criticism that expressed opinions on tragedy similar to those of Corinna; two others had been dubbed "Corinna" by other writers, one of whom adopted the pseudonym; another was both a playwright and a former actress. However, none of them have the combination of attributes of the Corinna of *Critical Remarks*. The poetess Sarah Fyge Egerton, who married the Reverend Thomas Egerton, had associations with the denizens of the theater world, but isn't known to have written on the theater, and ceased to write for publication after 1703. Catherine Trotter was a playwright, and in her dedication of *The Unhappy Penitent* (1701) she evaluated the subject matter suitable for tragedy: "I have ventured to propose a doubt whether love be a proper subject for it; it seems to me not noble, not solemn enough for tragedy" (Clark 1986, 87). This certainly resembles Corinna's view. However, Trotter married the Reverend Patrick Cockburn and gave up writing for the theater after 1706 (Clark 1986, 90).

Delariviére Manley, who was Swift's Corinna, was living in London in 1719. She was not using a pseudonym at that time, and when she did, it was "Delia." Manley's play, *Lucius, The First Christian King of England,* had been a success the previous season at Drury Lane. The plot turns on two true lovers, and though serious, is resolved by a happy ending (Clark 1986, 134, 176). Elizabeth Thomas, who was coupled with Haywood in a section of Pope's *Dunciad* and referred to as Corinna, also used that pseudonym in the publication of her love letters, *Plyades and Corinna* (1731), but the poetess never married (*Dictionary* 1985, 303).

Susannah Centlivre was both a former actress and a playwright, but at the time of the publication of *Critical Remarks* she had been married to a royal cook since 1707 (Bowyer 1968, 92–93). Centlivre is referred to in the third person in the piece, and Corinna's error as to which of her plays had been plagiarized further confirms that it was not she.

The most likely candidate for the persona of the Corinna of *Critical Remarks* is Elizabeth Fowler Haywood. Born a shopkeeper's daughter in London (c. 1693), in 1710 she married the Reverend Valentine Haywood, a Norfolk clergyman who also had a parish assignment in London. In 1711 they had a son. The next record of her is when she shows up on the company roster of the Theater Royal in Smock Alley, Dublin, for the season of 1714–15 (*Dictionary* 157–60). She did play in London, but apparently didn't fare too well, and by 1717 had quit the profession due to the theater's "not answering my expectation, and the averseness of my relations to it" (Whicher 10). Recently having trod the boards, Haywood, like Corinna, would know who were the current wits and which coffee house they frequented. In 1723 Haywood made an impromptu appearance in her own play, *A Wife to be Lett*, at Drury Lane, ("By reason of the indisposition of an actress" (*London Stage* 1960, 2:731). She later performed with Henry Fielding's company at the Haymarket in the 1730s until he was silenced by the Licensing Act of 1737.

Love in Excess, the novel that launched Haywood's success as a novelist, was published either late in the same year as *Critical Remarks* or in early 1720 (Whicher 190). Shortly after, she left her husband and returned to London. In 1721 Haywood was asked to prepare a draft of an unfinished play by a Captain Hurst for a production at Lincoln's Inn Fields. If Haywood had demonstrated her knowledge of play construction as Corinna, it could explain why a sometimes actress was solicited to undertake such a task. The dedication of *The Fair Captive*, the play Haywood doctored, espouses many of the same tenets contained in Corinna's critique. She uses the same terminology in describing the process from draft to finished product:

> it was in my power to have made it much better than it is, both in the sentiment and expression. . . . I was obliged to find new employment for each character, introduce one entirely new, without which it had been impossible to guess at the design of the play; and in fine, change the diction . . .

In Haywood's *Frederick, Duke of Brunswick Lunenburgh* (1727), the printed version's preface declares:

> I have taken all imaginable care not to offend the rules they [critics] have prescrib'd for theatrical entertainment: the scenes being unbroken, the time of action not exceeding twelve hours,

and the whole business continued and executed within the walls of the Castle of Lowen-Stein.

Other points of similarity between Haywood and Corinna exist. The dedication of *Frederick* was an unabashed feminist statement similar to Corinna's dedication to *Critical Remarks:* "Nor ought a person of my sex blush in confessing herself equal to a task, in which the most improved genius of the other would be found defective." In addition, Haywood's *The Tea Table* (1725) used the same device as in *Critical Remarks,* that of two ladies having a tête à tête during a visit.

There is no hard proof, however, that Eliza Haywood was our Corinna. Corinna may simply have been a minor actress of unusual education, perspicacity and wit, who married a country parson, retired, and having made her one brief comment upon the theater of her time, was buried in the anonymity she chose, and to which the women writers have been generally consigned by historians.

Also, while one must be wary of the easy assumption that Corinna was a woman, it is possible that it was a man writing under that pseudonym. It does not seem likely, though, since the conventional use of a character of a woman who considered herself a wit or an intellectual, even in works by women writers, was generally the object of satire, i.e., a spouter of undigested learned jargon, rather than a systematic espouser of the very tenets revered by the gentlemen of letters addressed in this essay. No strong male candidate for the role of Corinna can be supported by historical evidence. Addison died in the year *Critical Remarks* was published. Steele had his own outlet for dramatic criticism in his contemporaneous *The Theatre.* Dennis, although he supports many of Corinna's opinions, was a friend and defender of the plays that were attacked. And Pope would never put intelligent words into the mouth of a woman.

Corinna's identity, whether famous or obscure, does not take away from the importance of *Critical Remarks.* Its faults, by modern standards, are its rigidity and adamant formalism, but it is easy to understand that a woman presenting herself before an impressive body of acknowledged male authorities would toe the line of conservative orthodoxy to demonstrate her own command of the accepted body of neo-classic criticism. She would be determined to outline the sources of her erudition in order to gain credibility for her pronouncements. Early on in the essay, after a dispute about strict rules, Mrs. Townley grants that "the men of best taste and sense declare for them" (13). Naturally Corinna would declare for them too. She wanted the approbation of the wits who frequented the coffee houses to which she, by virtue of her sex, was denied access.

Corinna was a feminist certainly, but not as we now understand it. She was not out to change male-established rules but to beat men at their own game. She echoes her predecessor Aphra Behn, who pleaded in her preface to *The Lucky Chance* (1686), "All I ask is the Priviledge for my Masculine Part the Poet in me."

Critical Remarks holds its own in the level of the quality of dramatic criticism of its time. It is also an exemplary demonstration of the analytic technique Corinna acquired despite the educational limitations of women in her society. Corinna's critique is an important document on the theater at a time when few women published opinions on the drama.

Works Cited

Bowyer, John. 1968. *The Celebrated Mrs. Centlivre*. New York: Greenwood.

Buckingham, John Sheffield, Duke of. 1682. *An Essay Upon Poetry*. London.

Clark, Constance. 1986. *Three Augustan Women Playwrights*. New York: Peter Lang.

"Corinna." 1719. *Critical Remarks on the Four Taking Plays of This Season, By Corinna, a Country Parson's Wife*. James Bettenham.

Dennis, John. 1943. *The Critical Works of John Dennis*. Ed. Edward Niles Hooker. 2 vols. Baltimore: The Johns Hopkins Univ. Press.

————. 1721. *Original Letters, Familiar, Moral and Critical*. London: n.p.

A Dictionary of British and American Women Writers 1660–1800. 1985. Ed. Janet Todd. Totowa, N.J.: Rowman and Allenheld.

Downes, John. 1886. *Rocsius Angelicanus*. Ed. Joseph Knight. London: J. W. Jaris and Son.

Dryden, John. 1896. *An Essay of Dramatic Poesy*. Ed. Thomas Arnold. Oxford: Clarendon.

The London Stage. 1960. Ed. Emmett L. Avery. Vol. 2. Carbondale: Southern Illinois Univ. Press.

Montagu, Lady Mary Wortley. 1977. *Essays and Poems, and Simplicity, a Comedy*. Ed. Robert Halsband and Isabel Grundy. Oxford: Clarendon.

Rymer, Thomas. 1693. *A Short View of Tragedy*. London: R. Baldwin.

Swift, Jonathan. 1958. *Swift's Correspondence*. Ed. Harold Williams. 2 vols. Oxford: Clarendon.

Three Centuries of Drama. 1960–62. Ed. Henry Willis Wells. New York: Reader Microprint.

Trotter, Catherine. 1791. *The Unhappy Penitent.* London: W. Turner & John Nutt.

Whicher, George Frisbie. 1915. *The Life and Romances of Mrs. Eliza Haywood.* New York: Columbia University Press.

6

Playbill

*"Mrs. Abington as Thalia." Courtesy of the Print Collection,
The Lewis Walpole Library, Yale University.*

"Their Empire Disjoyn'd":
Serious Plays by Women on the
London Stage, 1660–1737

WILLIAM J. BURLING

Unlike Restoration and eighteenth-century comedies of manners authored by women, serious drama has received little attention. Analysis of the serious drama reveals, however, a vibrant and vital contribution by women to the British dramatic canon and to the ongoing evolution of the London theatrical milieu. Women serious dramatists wrote with a sense of historical significance, sensing in the late seventeenth century that the time was ripe for serious plays by women to command the same respect granted to those created by their male peers. Mary Delariviére Manley sums up this new sense of pride in authorship in her remark that Catharine Trotter "snatcht a Lawrel which they [i.e., men] thought their Prize" and "their Empire have disjoyn'd" (Manley 1696, sig [A]2v).[1]

By serious drama, I mean, as Geoffrey Marshall has explained, those plays which have "in common the fact that laughter and amusement are not their primary aims" (1975, vii). Immediately we realize that the sheer number and variety of serious plays during the late seventeenth and early eighteenth centuries, by women and men alike, preclude any simple generalizations about the nature of these plays. Accordingly, scholarly discussion of serious drama is guarded and quite limited. Eric Rothstein's approach emphasizes a contrast between two basic types of plays, fabulist and affective. The fabulist play, he argues, seeks essentially to deliver a message; the affective play, on the other hand, strives to stimulate the emotions of the audience (1967, chapter 1). Philip Parsons, taking a purely performance stance, argues that the plays are simply vehicles for spectacle, the aim being impact on emotion, not appeal to intellect (1972, *passim*). Geoffrey Marshall prefers to read the plays as intellectual documents and admits that he "would not enjoy—except for historical curiosity's sake—seeing any number of these plays performed" (1975, ix). Aubrey Williams suggests that all plays, comedies and tragedies, stress the themes of providential justice and divine control (1977, 1979). I have elected, however, to emphasize the generic aspects of the plays in an attempt to classify them, basing my analysis on a scheme first suggested by Robert D. Hume, who finds eight basic types of serious plays in the period 1660–1710: heroic, horror, "high," split-plot, pattern, pathetic, "parallel," and opera/spectacle. While Hume's subgenres are unevenly defined—some by form and others by content—they have the distinct advantage of providing a niche for virtually every play, though we must remain ever mindful of his warning that "seventeenth-century playwrights did *not* work with sharp generic divisions in mind" (Hume, 1976, 252).

In particular, then, four of the types suggested by Hume emerge as most applicable: the heroic, the split-plot, the pathetic, and the horrific. The first type, the heroic, is characterized by some attention to matters of state or empire and a conflict between love and honor. Characters find themselves torn between their sense of duty and their personal feelings. As Hume rightly notes, this type of serious play has "deep roots in Fletcherian tragicomedy" (1976, 181). The second type, the pathetic play, certainly can and often does move against the backdrop of political events, but the emphasis is decidedly on the emotions of the characters. Usually great distress brought about by suffering or death is featured, and the characters often endure the worst that humans can bear, either real or imagined (psychological distress being a favorite motif in plays by women). The split-plot form, the third type, was very much favored by women serious dramatists; in fact, many of these plays are of this type. The play features at least two plots: the "high" plot was always the serious thread, while the "low" plot presented comedic elements. Such theorists as Dryden and Dennis consistently attacked this form, and dramatists sometimes complained.[2] But London audiences apparently enjoyed this variation, and women writers regularly turned them out. And finally we have the horrific play, of interest but the least favored by women playwrights. Here the emphasis is upon spectacles of suffering: tortures, deaths, poisonings, rapes, and so forth. Because each play must attempt to outdo its predecessors, diminishing returns dictate that this subgenre offers little room for consistent development, although several women did try this type at least once.

For reasons that are not as yet clear, women simply chose not to write plays in the other categories (with one exception). After discussing the plays themselves, I will return to this issue to offer some conclusions.

The years 1660–1737 can be divided into two periods regarding serious plays by women. The termini correspond to the restoration of Charles II and the passage of the so-called "Licensing Act" in 1737, an event having considerable impact on London theater (though, in fact, the final serious play we will examine was staged in 1729). The years 1660–95 are almost exclusively dominated by Aphra Behn, one of only two women to have staged an original serious play in London. The period 1696–1737, however, as Judith Stanton so vividly documents in her chapter in the present collection, saw over twenty serious plays mounted by at least six women, a truly remarkable outpouring.[3]

The history and conditions of both of these periods require separate discussion. The first woman to have staged an original, serious play was probably Mrs. Frances Boothby, whose *Marcelia* appeared in early 1669(?).[4] This love-and-honor play presents the conflict between the rights of the king (see especially the vivid defense of divine right monarchs [1670, sig. K2r]) and his obligations to his subjects. King Sigismund and Lotharicus are rivals for the love of Marcelia. Melynet, an over-zealous officer of the king, goes too far in arranging for the attempted murder of Lotharicus. At the happy conclusion, Lotharicus and Marcelia are united by the king, while Melynet is led away to execution. The play achieved no commercial success whatsoever and has variously been termed "undistinguished" (Hume 1976, 256 n.1) and "worthless" (Nicoll 1952–59, 1:130n).

Only Aphra Behn was able to achieve production of more than one serious play during the first period of our survey. In fact, she began her career as a serious playwright, and her serious plays fall into two groups, high tragedy and tragi-comedy. We find only one play, the impressive and influential *Abdelazer,* in the first category, the rest being exclusively split-plot tragicomedies.

Abdelazer appeared just as the rage for heroic drama was subsiding. Performed probably in September 1676, the play, based on

Lust's Dominion (1657), appropriately features the theme of lust as an all-pervasive motivator of actions, whether in the personal sphere or in regard to empires. A remarkable achievement hailed by Montague Summers as "apt and masterly" (Behn 1967, 2:4), the play directly influenced Edward Young's powerful and popular *The Revenge* (1721).

Behn's tragicomedies, however, constitute the more numerous component of her serious writing, four having "happy" endings and split plots. The first to appear on the stage (though not, in fact, first in composition) is *The Forc'd Marriage* (20 September 1670). The play explores the desperate circumstances resulting from an arranged marriage between Erminia and Alcippus. The latter, knowing full well that his bride actually loves Philander, strangles Erminia in a rage and leaves her for dead. The play ends with the return of Erminia, who then marries Philander. Alcippus, in a second wedding, joins with Philander's sister, Galatea, and all turns out well. The play did not enter the repertory, but it did establish Behn as a reputable dramatist and revealed her interest in feminist themes.[5]

Her second serious play followed quite soon thereafter, appearing 24 February 1671. *The Amorous Prince* begins with a famous and—to Restoration audiences—controversial scene which portrays two unmarried lovers clad in bedclothes arising from love-making. The prince seduces Chloris, a naive country lass, and then casts her aside. He later falsely learns that she has committed suicide, causing him to realize that he truly loved her. In the end, predictably, they marry. The play is thus concerned with sexual values, particularly the conflict of the joy and beauty of true and free love-making as contrasted with the hypocritical and often brutal sexual affairs Behn believed were the norm.[6]

Her third serious play, *The Dutch Lover* (6 February 1673), is especially notable for its presentation of an assertive heroine. But perhaps even more interesting is her last staged serious play, *The Young King* (c. March 1679). Behn tells us in the front matter that this was actually her first play, held back for over a decade. Stylistically the play resembles the serious plays of the 1660s in its attempt at elevated action and language, very much unlike Behn's colloquial, "natural" plays of the 1670s. The themes concern the feminine vision which juxtaposes love and war, Venus and Mars, and the nature of sexual identity for both men and women. Behn asks, what components constitute genuine male or female character? Thereafter, no more serious plays by women appeared on the London stage until 1695.

The period 1695–1737 witnessed a sudden and rapid increase in the number of serious plays by women: Mary Delariviére Manley comments in her prefatory poem to Catharine Trotter's 1695 tragedy, *Agnes de Castro,* that Trotter has filled the "Vacant Throne" left by Orinda (Katherine Philips) and Astraea (Aphra Behn) and that "Man," who had "Taught us humbly to Obey" his rule in tragedy, now must be aware that women again "their Empire have disjoyn'd" (sig. [A]2v). Manley's manifesto and the explosion of new plays initiated by Trotter's tragedy thus seemingly represent a coming of age of women playwrights or at least a recognition by theater managers that plays by women could and would be worth presenting. But while both of these factors are true to some extent, to understand properly the influx, one must recall the conditions of the theater world circa 1695–96.

The United company, London's only legitimate patent theater since 1682, had split into two companies in the spring of 1695. Thomas Betterton, Anne Bracegirdle, Elizabeth Barry, and others, displeased by the new management practices of Christopher Rich, a tight-fisted lawyer, appealed for and obtained a separate license to perform. This new company, in the old Lincoln's Inn Fields tennis court, opened in April 1695 with a smash hit, Congreve's *Love for Love,* and went on to present many new plays over the next decade.[7] Rich at Drury Lane had no choice but to respond in kind, and the ensuing competition meant new opportunities for playwrights. So why was not this need filled by existing authors? The simple reason is that few were active or available: Otway, Shadwell, Crowne, and Lee were all dead; Dryden was in disfavor; Wycherley was retired. We see then that the new theatrical war created conditions favorable to newcomers, and indeed they emerged in droves, male and female alike.

Thus conditions were ripe for the precocious sixteen-year-old Catharine Trotter. Much younger than Congreve or Fielding when they had their first plays staged, Trotter saw her tragedy *Agnes de Castro* mounted at Drury Lane, probably in December 1695, signaling a new era for women playwrights. The play, a throw-back to the heroic mode of the 1670s, features a love-honor conflict. At least three murders and an attempted suicide highlight this adaptation of Aphra Behn's novel of the same title (1688). Trotter's next play, *The Fatal Friendship* (May or June 1698), widely held to be her greatest, was admired by Farquhar and praised even by the grumpy author of *A Comparison between the Two Stages* (*Comparison* 1942, 17). As Hume notes, the "principal interest lies in the psychology of characters plunged into intolerable situations" (1976, 453). The play ends quite unhappily and exploits the pathetic mode of presentation.

Trotter returned to the theatrical scene on 4 February 1701 with *The Unhappy Penitent*. Hume has commented that we find here "sentimental mush of the most contrived sort" (1976, 453), but another explanation is that Trotter apparently attempted and failed in an experiment with irony. Her goal was to explore the process by which the *excesses* of passion overwhelmed judgment. According to Trotter's important dedicatory remarks, passion is a frailty which "becomes a Vice, when cherish'd as an exalted Vertue" (1701, sig. A3r). Far from being excessive in her depiction of extreme passion in Lorrain and Margarite, Trotter states that the play is defective because "the Distress is not great enough, the Subject of it only the misfortunes of Lovers, which I partly design'd in Compliance with the effeminate taste of the Age" (1701, sig. A2v).

Her remarks about "effeminate taste" may refer to the enormous initial and continuing popularity of Congreve's *The Mourning Bride* (1697). One of only a tiny handful of immediately and undeniably successful serious plays between the division of the companies in 1695 and Ambrose Philips's *The Distrest Mother* (1712), Congreve's tragedy concentrates on the plight of distressed lovers rather than politics or matters of state, a bold deviation from the typical concerns of tragedy. While Nicholas Rowe was later to claim in the prologue to *The Fair Penitent* (1703) that he was the first to present serious drama concerned with affairs other than those of empire and state, the so-called domestic tragedy, Congreve actually preceded him by several years.[8] Congreve's play also features a resoundingly happy ending, a structural characteristic thereafter occurring regularly, mostly in plays by women, such as Pix's *Zelmane* (1704) and *The Conquest of Spain* (1705), and Manley's *Almyna* (1706).[9]

Trotter's final serious play, *The Revolution of Sweden* (11 February 1706), also features a pathetic sensibility and a happy ending. Numerous catastrophes are averted at the last moment, and though well-crafted, the play was not a commercial success. We may conclude that after 1701 Trotter consciously moved in the direction of "soft" tragedy, which featured tests of fidelity and courage and a resolution stressing the inevitable triumph of love.

Yet another woman to emerge during these special years was Mary Delariviére Manley, who is perhaps better known as the author of such fictions as *Zara* (1705) and *The New Atalantis* (1709). She wrote three serious plays that reached the boards: *The Royal Mischief* (1696); *Almyna* (1706); and *Lucius, The First Christian King of England* (1717).

The Royal Mischief was staged at Lincoln's Inn Fields about May 1696. Another of the backward-looking love/honor plays of the period, this drama, as Hume points out (1976, 422), also featured the shock and horror techniques then enjoying a revival in such recent productions as Banks's *Cyrus the Great* (December 1695). Betterton, Barry, and Bracegirdle are featured in a steamy love triangle, and accounts tell us that their performances were compelling, particularly that of Mrs. Barry as Homais. Manley herself in the play's dedication praises Barry for her stellar performance. The play ends most unhappily and features a famous scene wherein Selima gathers up the "smoaking Relicks" of her lover Osman (who has been shot out of a cannon alive) and covers them with "burning kisses."

Her next two serious plays present happy endings and rely heavily upon pathos for effect. *Almyna* (December 1706) again featured the Betterton, Barry, Bracegirdle combination, though by this time Betterton and Barry were very much showing their ages. The company apparently went to some lengths to prepare the play in the best manner possible: records show that admission prices were raised to cover the cost of the "Extraordinary Charges for Habits" (Avery 1960, 1:135). Almyna, a royal concubine, outwits the Caliph, Almanzor, who practices the unusual and lethal habit of executing his brides after their wedding night. Fidelis Morgan asserts that this play stresses "strong feminist undertones" in its criticism of the double standard that allows men, but not women, to regain good opinion once lost (1981, 40).

Manley's final serious effort, *Lucius, The First Christian King of*

England, appeared at Drury Lane on 11 May 1717. Another love-and-honor play stressing pathos, in the happy conclusion Lucius and Rosalinda (Barton Booth and Anne Oldfield) are saved from what had appeared to be certain death or enslavement, restore the family's reputation, avenge the death of Lucius' father, and slay the evil enemies of the kingdom. This strongly moral play eschews political comment or sexual titillation, projecting, instead, a firm moral tone. The play ran only three nights, and was revived for one night only on 27 April 1720 as a benefit for Manley.[10] Of note is Matthew Prior's epilogue, explaining the status, method, and goals of women authors, especially playwrights.

The third woman playwright of the 1695–96 season was Mary Pix, who wrote more serious plays (seven) than any other authoress of this period. Her serious plays are all concerned with heroic and pathetic themes. The first play, widely admired and considered a success in its day, though it did not enter the repertory, was *Ibrahim, Thirteenth Emperor of the Turks* (May or June 1696). As Trotter and Manley did in *Agnes de Castro* (December 1695) and *The Royal Mischief* (c. May 1696), Pix chose the dated heroic mode of tragedy. Judith Milhous helpfully notes (1979, 90) that Pix's play was staged as Drury Lane's direct competitive response to *The Royal Mischief* just as *Cinthia and Endimion* (December 1696) answered Lincoln's Inn Fields' *The Loves of Mars and Venus* (14 November 1696). Love and honor are at stake, and by the play's end we have seen six deaths—four murders and two suicides. Despite the excessive gore, Hume finds the play has "considerable pathetic interest" (1976, 423).

Pix's next two plays continue her interest in serious drama. *Queen Catharine* (June 1698) takes for its subject the War of the Roses. At the play's unhappy finale, Catharine's lover, Tudor, is murdered in her presence; she enters a nunnery; and Isabella is killed accidentally. Yet another example of the love triangle favored by Betterton, Barry, and Bracegirdle, and despite their best efforts, the play found no success, but then neither did four other of the seven new serious plays staged the season of 1697–98, with only Granville's *Heroick Love* and Hopkins's *Boadicea* finding favor.[11] Pix's third serious play, *The False Friend* (May or June 1699) concludes with all four of the lovers dead and the villain, Appamia, being led off for punishment—a most unhappy conclusion. Critics have noted that the pathos is elevated to such a pitch that the play, in Milhous's terms, "was even beyond the powers of Mrs. Bracegirdle," which is saying a great deal about Pix's script (1979, 140). The play did not succeed and was never revived.

Pix next attempted a different tack in retaining the pathetic mode of development but instead supplying a happy ending. Thus *The Double Distress* (March 1701) presents a byzantine network of real and feigned love relationships that endure considerable distress to achieve their happy resolution. This play may be said to epitomize the baroque tendency toward complexity: the cast employed and taxed the talents of virtually every major actor or actress of the day, including Booth, Bracegirdle, Barry, Bowman, and Verbruggen, but, interestingly, not Betterton. Of note is the absence of a villain.

Also appearing about March 1701 was Pix's *The Czar of Muscovy* (published 15 April). Pix happily unites the two pairs of lovers in the finale: Zueski (Booth) and Alexander (Bowman) combine forces to defeat Demetrius (Hodgson), to the joy of their beloved Zarrianna (Mrs. Barry) and Marina (Mrs. Bowman). The play relies upon heroic melodrama, and as Hume notes (1976, 456), the script is written in prose rather than verse, an unusual experiment: the only other serious play of the period likewise in prose is Thomas Durfey's *The Famous History of the Rise and Fall of Massaniello* (2 parts; c. May 1699).

Zelmane, now attributed to Pix, premiered on 13 November 1704.[12] The play has often been termed an imitation of Joseph Trapp's popular and successful *Abra-Mule* (January 1704). Hume finds a "slack and slushy form" of heroics but declares Pix's play better than Trapp's, because it is "less turgid and benefits from a better villain" (1976, 475). No critic has noted, however, the strong affinities with John Banks's extremely popular and influential *The Unhappy Favourite* (1681). Both plays, for example, rotate around a queen's conflict between love and political responsibility. Banks's Elizabeth is closely paralleled by Pix's Zelmane: both queens are forced for political reasons to dismiss their principal generals with whom they are in love. And both generals, while faithful servants to their queens, are married to other women. Banks's play ends tragically, of course, but the "happy" ending of *Zelmane* is a satisfying, if less theatrically interesting, variation of the same set of problems.

The last serious play by Pix before her death in 1709 is *The Conquest of Spain* (May 1705). Based on *All's Lost by Lust* (Rowley, 1619) and yet another of the "soft" tragedies, this drama features the love/honor problems so prevalent in the serious plays by women of this period. Antonio and Margaretta survive and endure the suicides and murders that surround them; in the finale they are allowed by the Mullymumen to leave Spain together in what one must call a happy ending, though this is hardly the stuff of marital bliss.

The next major authoress of this period is Susanna Centlivre, the only woman whose reputation is equal to Behn's. Known primarily as the creator of three comedies that held the stage for more than a century, *The Busy Bodie* (1709), *The Wonder* (1714), and *Bold Stroke for a Wife* (1718), she is also responsible for three serious plays, the quality of which even her admiring biographer John Bowyer terms "hardly worth reviewing" (1952, 252).

Centlivre offered in October 1700 *The Perjur'd Husband,* which stresses the strife arising from the conflict of love and honor, again a theme more befitting the late 1660s or 1670s. Both Bowyer (1952, 34–35) and Hume (1976, 456) comment on the deplorable use of the split plot in this play (and in her next serious drama, *The Stolen Heiress,* two years later). By the bloody conclusion, all of the principals are killed or overwhelmed: Placentia stabs Aurelia; Bassino kills Placentia and then is done in by Alonzo. Her next effort, *The Stolen Heiress* (31 December 1702), is actually a tragicomedy that was advertised as a comedy. This intrigue play features some pathetic moments, but hardly qualifies as a serious play. The happy couple, Lucasia and Palante, unite in the glorious finale when the evil Count Pirro is exiled. Morgan comments that the play is of interest because of the focus on the law against marrying an heiress without the consent of her parent or guardian (1981, 52). Hume terms the play "a rather mechanical exercise" (1976, 471).

Centlivre did not attempt serious drama again for well over a decade, but then produced her best serious play, *The Cruel Gift* (17 December 1716). She relies primarily on horror and pathos: the "cruel gift," a human heart, is supposedly that of Leonora's secret husband, Lorenzo. In the happy conclusion, Antenor, the villain, dies, and the rebellion and feud are ended. Bowyer remarks that this is Centlivre's best serious play but still finds the script very weak due to shallow characterization and an unconvincing plot (1952, 52).

Four solo efforts from this period also require brief mention before we conclude with Eliza Haywood. The first, the anonymous *The*

Unnatural Mother (October 1697), follows *Agnes de Castro* and *Ibrahim* in the bloodbath fad. The anonymous "Young Lady" responsible for this play presents a variety of rapes, murders, suicides, and ghosts. Jane Wiseman's *Antiochus the Great* (November 1701), a far better play, displays the disasters that ensue when love and lust are confused. An unfortunately neglected excellent play, it ranks among the best love-triangle plots, and afforded Mrs. Barry and Mrs. Bracegirdle a vehicle for their special skills in portraying tormented women. *The Faithful General* (January 1706, by "A Young Lady"), is decidedly less successful. A wretched reworking of Fletcher's *The Loyal Subject* (1618), the play collapsed immediately in competition with Fletcher's original as staged by Drury Lane. The fourth drama, Mrs. J. Robe's *The Fatal Legacy* (23 April 1723), is an adaptation of Racine's *La Thebaide*. The plot concerns the quarrel, duel, and ultimate deaths of the two sons of Oedipus, Eteocles and Polynices, who have been left as joint rulers but must alternate on the throne. Following close on the heels of Elijah Fenton's extremely successful *Marianme* of two months earlier, Robe's play, though a workmanlike adaptation, did not please the tastes of London theatre goers and quickly disappeared, never to be revived.

We are left, then, with our final major authoress, Eliza Haywood. A woman who pursued a long career in the public eye as playwright, novelist, Grub Street hack, and actress, Haywood wrote two serious plays: *The Fair Captive* and *Frederick, Duke of Brunswick-Lunenburgh*.

Haywood explains in the advertisement to the reader of *The Fair Captive* (4 March 1721) that she is the reviser of this play, originally accepted by Lincoln's Inn Fields manager John Rich some five or six years earlier from one "Captain Hurst." She claims that "excepting the Parts of *Alphonso* and *Isabella* there remains not twenty Lines of the original" (1721, xii), so extensive were her alterations. Love-and-honor conflicts result in a happy conclusion. The moral tension in the play echoes the problem explored in *Measure for Measure:* the Mustapha demands that Isabella sacrifice her virginity and virtue to save her lover—she refuses, of course.

An attempt at capitalizing on current events is the hallmark of Haywood's only other serious drama, *Frederick, Duke of Brunswick-Lunenburgh,* which appeared, coincidentally, exactly eight years to the day after *The Fair Captive,* i.e., 4 March 1729. The play is a blatant attempt to secure royal patronage by dramatizing the life of one of George II's ancestors from about 1400. Frederick, the illustrious Brunswickian protagonist, dies in the finale (heroically, to be sure), and foretells of a descendant (guess who?) destined to be even braver and greater. Heightened heroism and elevated rhetoric characterize this drama, which did not succeed in attracting the notice of the court—not one member of the royal household attended a performance.

These twenty-six plays are considerably diverse in theme and approach, ranging from poorly conceived and executed adaptations to highly sophisticated and expertly presented original plots. But a few generalizations suggest themselves.

First, many plays are concerned with conflicts of honor or with the depiction of pathos. Indeed, the most frequent motif of all is that of lovers in distress. These plays in the main rarely explore intellectual issues, although they frequently examine social problems and are often highly moral. Above all, they were written to entertain. Given these qualifications, the best succeeded admirably, as in the case of *Agnes de Castro* and *The Fatal Friendship.* Second, many women preferred a happy ending. The reasons for this tendency can only be speculated upon, but one point can be stated with certainty: a happy ending did not guarantee the popularity of any given play. In other words, the interest in happy endings was not a concession by women serious playwrights to audience taste, at least not one that could be relied upon. And last, let us not fail to notice that while women tended generally not to write about themes radically different from what men chose, women concentrated upon affairs of the heart, love, honor, and truth.

The novel, we now know, was to become the principal literary form favored by women after 1770, notwithstanding, as Stanton also teaches us in the present volume, the increasing numbers of women who wrote for the stage during the last quarter of the century. But the history of the London literary world of the seventeenth and eighteenth centuries owes a great deal indeed to the accomplishments of women *dramatists.* And while serious plays by women never achieved the recognition that some of their comedies attained, these serious plays may now be appreciated as vibrant contributions to the London theatrical milieu.

Notes

1. All direct quotations are from the first published London editions unless otherwise noted.

2. See, for example, Thomas Southerne's epilogue to *Oroonoko* (performed 1695) which complains "Your different tasts divide our Poet's Cares: / One foot the Sock, t'other the Buskin wears" (1988, 180).

3. After 1729 a forty-year gulf exists in which only two serious plays appeared, Mrs. Hoper's *Edward the Black Prince* (1747) and *Queen Tragedy Restor'd* (1749). The production of a serious drama by Dorothea Celesia, *Almida* (1771), followed by some dozen odd plays by other women through 1800, constitutes in itself a most intriguing period unfortunately beyond the scope of this essay.

4. The precise premiére date of Boothby's play is still unknown. Katherine Philips (widely known as "Orinda") had her translation of Corneille's *Pompey* staged in the spring of 1663 in Dublin, but not, as has been long suspected, in London. For details, see Price (1979).

5. For an analysis of this play, see Goreau (1980, 122–30).

6. For a recent discussion of sexual values of the Restoration as expressed in drama, see Weber (1986). Weber does not mention *The Amorous Prince* and only briefly discusses Behn's plays.

7. The standard account of this period is Milhous (1979).

8. In fact, one could say with some justice that "domestic" tragedy had been the subject of serious plays in English at least since *Arden of Feversham* (1591), and that *Othello* (1604), a number of Fletcher's plays, Thomas Otway's *The Orphan* (1680), John Banks's plays, and Thomas Southerne's *The Fatal Marriage* (1694) and *Oroonoko* (1695) were all vehicles which prepared the public for Congreve's play in their focus on passion and pathos.

9. Hume notes that this technique was used occasionally by men, as in the case of Taverner's *The Faithful Bride of Granada* (1704) (1976, 475).

10. Morgan claims that the play ran fifteen nights the first run, made Manley 600 guineas, and was revived the next year (1981, 42). I have been unable to verify any of these assertions.

11. For discussion of the "cranky" audiences of 1697–1702, see Scouten and Hume (1983).

12. Steeves does not include or even mention the play in her edition of *The Plays of Mary Pix and Catharine Trotter*. Hume (1976, 475) cites Borgman (1935, 176–77). Surviving copies are very rare.

Works Cited

Avery, Emmett L. 1960. *The London Stage, 1660–1800*. Part 2: 1700–1729. 2 vols. Carbondale: Southern Illinois Univ. Press.

Behn, Aphra. 1915. *Works of Aphra Behn*. Ed. Montague Summers. 6 vols. Reprint New York: Benjamin Blom, 1967.

Boothby, Francis. 1670. *Marcelia*. London.

Borgman, Albert S. 1935. *The Life and Death of William Mountfort.* Cambridge, Mass.: Harvard Univ. Press.

Bowyer, John. 1952. *The Celebrated Mrs. Centlivre.* Durham, N.C.: Duke Univ. Press.

A Comparison between the Two Stages. 1942. Ed. Staring B. Wells. Princeton, N.J.: Princeton Univ. Press.

Goreau, Angeline. 1980. *Reconstructing Aphra.* New York: Dial.

Haywood, Eliza. 1721. *The Fair Captive.* London.

Hume, Robert D. 1976. *The Development of English Drama in the late Seventeenth Century.* Oxford: Oxford Univ. Press.

Manley, Mary. 1696. Prefatory poem in *Agnes de Castro.* London.

Marshall, Geoffrey. 1975. *Restoration Serious Drama.* Norman: Univ. of Oklahoma Press.

Milhous, Judith. 1979. *Thomas Betterton and the Management of Lincoln's Inn Fields 1695–1708.* Carbondale: Southern Illinois Univ. Press.

Morgan, Fidelis. 1981. *The Female Wits.* London: Virago.

Nicoll, Allardyce. 1952–59. *A History of English Drama 1660–1900.* Rev. edn. 6 vols. Cambridge: Cambridge Univ. Press.

Parsons, Philip. 1972. "Restoration Tragedy as Total Theatre." In *Restoration Literature.* Ed. Harold Love. London: Methuen.

Pix, Mary. 1982. *The Plays of Mary Pix and Catharine Trotter.* Ed. Edna Steeves. New York: Garland.

Price, Curtis A. 1979. "The Songs for Katharine Philips' *Pompey* (1663)." *Theatre Notebook* 33:61–66.

Rothstein, Eric. 1967. *Restoration Tragedy.* Madison: Univ. of Wisconsin Press.

Scouten, Arthur H. Scouten and Robert D. Hume. 1983. " 'Restoration Comedy' and its Audiences, 1660–1776." In Hume's *The Rakish Stage.* Carbondale: Southern Illinois Univ. Press. Chapter 2.

Southerne, Thomas. 1988. *The Works of Thomas Southerne.* Eds. Robert Jordan and Harold Love. Vol. II, Oxford: Oxford Univ. Press.

Trotter, Catharine. 1701. *The Unhappy Penitent.* London.

Van Lennep, William, ed. 1965. *The London Stage, 1660–1800.* Part 1: 1660–1700. With intro. by Arthur H. Scouten and Emmett L. Avery. Carbondale: Southern Illinois Univ. Press.

Weber, Harold. 1986. *The Restoration Rake Hero.* Madison: Univ. of Wisconsin Press.

Wheatley, Katherine E. 1956. *Racine and English Classicism.* Austin: Univ. of Texas Press.

Williams, Aubrey. 1977. "Of 'One Faith': Authors and Auditors in the Restoration Theatre." *Studies in the Literary Imagination* 10 (Spring): 57–76.

──────. *An Approach to Congreve.* 1979. New Haven: Yale Univ. Press.

"This New-Found Path Attempting": Women Dramatists in England, 1660–1800

JUDITH PHILLIPS STANTON

> This new-found path attempting, proud was I,
> Lurking approval on thy face to spy,
> Or hear thee say, as grew thy roused attention,
> 'What! is this story all thine own invention?'
> —Joanna Baillie

Just at the close of the eighteenth century, Joanna Baillie was embarking on one of the most productive dramatic careers in England since Susanna Centlivre's. Interestingly, she felt writing to be a "new-found path" for her, perhaps only personally, but quite probably as a woman. Women were by no means new to the stage as actresses, producers, and dramatists, and yet their achievements and successes in other genres, notably poetry and fiction, outstripped those on the stage. While we can identify 97 women who wrote plays that were either staged, published, or have survived in manuscript, at least 263 women succeeded in publishing one or more volumes of poetry and 201 in publishing novels (Stanton 1988). Religious works (170 authors) and letters and autobiographies (247 authors) also attracted more women. Playwriting did, however, appeal to women of multiple talents: only about half of the poets and novelists wrote in other genres as well; 75 percent of dramatists ventured into a variety of genres, certainly poetry and fiction, but biography, autobiography, letters, and children's books as well (Stanton). Drama is an interesting genre for a more detailed analysis of the production of women's actual works. It was the first genre to become lucrative for women. Unlike poetry, it was by its nature public when the women's sphere was private. Unlike religious writings, it had no more altruistic motive than money. And unlike the novel, which was defining its means, forms, subjects, and audience, it was an ancient and established literary genre and public activity.

Even while playwriting seemed a new path for Baillie, women playwrights had achieved a number of firsts in the world of letters. The period from 1660 to 1800 is rich with these. Margaret Cavendish, Duchess of Newcastle, published the first collection of plays in England by a woman in 1662, and she is considered the first feminist playwright (Cotton 1980, 42). Katherine Philips's *Pompey* (1663), a translation from Corneille, was performed in Dublin and then London, the first successful public staging of a play by a woman. And in 1669, Frances Boothby's *Marcelia; or, The Treacherous Friend* became the first original play by a woman to be staged. Beginning in 1670, Aphra Behn embarked on the first career as a dramatist, producing nineteen plays in as many years and becoming the first woman in England to make a living by writing in any genre. Behn's career was soon followed by the remarkable success of Susanna Centlivre, far and away the most popular woman dramatist during the eighteenth century (Cotton 1980).

Behind these notable achievements were many minor ones and many failures. Among the 314 plays that this provisional checklist offers are great successes, plays that can be acted today and have been, and abysmal failures, plays that were derided in their own time and never revived to be derided again. The checklist and analysis that follow do not attempt to revive all these works but rather to place dramatic writing by women in as large a context as possible. Whether a play is good or bad, the mere fact that it was written suggests a great deal about how accessible the stage and the dramatic form seemed to a woman who fancied herself a writer or, more likely, who needed to make her way in the world and hoped to do so by using her wits. The fact that a play was staged demonstrates the degree to which women had access to the stage and, if also published, to publication.[1] It is worth noting that no studies exist for many of these authors, and much of what does exist is old and incomplete, making a study of this nature somewhat tentative. I have included some lost works, not to send researchers on futile hunts, but to round out the analysis; a work now lost quite likely existed and adds to our picture of the climate for drama.

For any Restoration or eighteenth-century author, to be a playwright was to subject oneself to the most public and immediate of literary consequences: live audiences, payment on the third night, real applause, real derision. From 1660 to 1800, plays by women were, however, more likely to be published than staged. Of the 314 plays in the checklist, 241 were published, but only 189 staged. Table 1 and Figure 1 show the details of the stage history of plays by women. Looked at by decade, the number of plays first staged is fairly uneven: Aphra Behn is mainly responsible for the 12 plays in the 1670s; the "female wits" were very productive with 14 plays in the 1690s, 22 in the first decade of the new century, and 9 in the 1710s. During the period 1720–59, the stage did not attract women very much; only two new plays were staged in 1750. These included such forgettable productions as Elizabeth Boyd's ballad opera *Don Sancho* (1739), Charlotte Charke's comedies *The Art of Management* and *The Carnival* (1735) and her puppet show *Tit for Tat*, as well as such popular plays as Susanna Cibber's *The Oracle* (1752) and Kitty Clive's *The Rehearsal* (1750). With the 1760s, a surge of playwriting began that led to commensurately more productions. This curve is similar to, but not nearly as steep as, the increase in all writing by

Table 1. Plays presented by decade.

Decade	No. of plays first staged	% of plays first staged	All plays staged	% of all plays staged
1660	3	1.6	5	.6
1670	12	6.3	16	2.0
1680	10	5.3	6	2.0
1690	14	7.4	29	3.6
1700	22	11.6	47	5.8
1710	9	4.8	58	7.2
1720	7	3.7	57	7.1
1730	10	5.3	61	7.6
1740	6	3.2	43	5.3
1750	2	1.1	39	4.8
1760	13	7.4	50	6.2
1770	19	10.1	61	7.6
1780	33	17.4	150	18.6
1790	29	15.0	175	21.7
Total	189	100.2*	807	100.1*

*Totals do not add up to 100% because numbers are rounded.

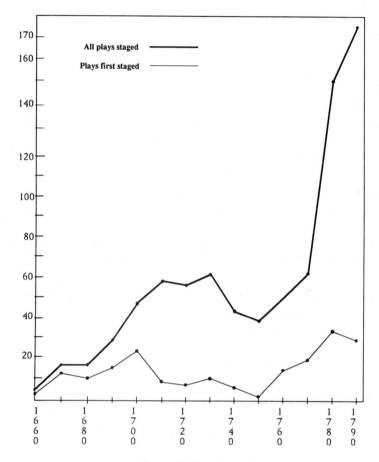

Figure 1. Plays Staged

women, especially fiction and poetry. Many of the 189 plays by
women were performed again and again, however, so that a theater-
goer would have had the impression that more and more women
were writing plays all the time. The overall falling off of new plays
staged from 1720 to 1759 contrasts sharply with the number of
women's plays actually being staged during those years. Not only
theater-goers, but also fledgling women playwrights must have come
to perceive successful plays by women as a norm. Indeed, during
those lean years for new plays, the old plays being restaged were the
very best. If 189 plays were staged over the 140 years as 807 new pro-

ductions, playwrights could hope for any given play to be staged in four different years. (But if we discount the four most popular plays discussed below, which had unusually long runs, from these figures, three years is more likely to be the average number of years in which a play would be produced.

It was easier to get a play printed than staged. As Table 2 shows, of the 314 plays written, 241 were published. A good number of these appeared in collections of plays meant only to be read, while others appeared in collections of poetry. Even though many published plays were never intended for the stage, the rate of publications of plays is very similar to the rate of staging of plays. Figure 2 illustrates these trends. More plays were published during 1690 to 1719; publications dropped by almost a third from 1720 to 1759; they rose sharply toward the end of the century. Where plays averaged new productions in three or four different years, they only averaged two editions (with the proviso, above, that plays for publication sometimes underwent multiple editions in the first year or two).

Women learned to write plays in any mode that was popular,

Table 2. Plays published by decade.

Decade	No. of first editions	% of first editions	All editions	% of all editions
1660	27	11.2	30	6.0
1670	12	5.0	15	3.0
1680	8	3.3	11	2.2
1690	13	5.4	20	4.0
1700	20	8.3	24	4.8
1710	13	5.4	24	4.8
1720	7	2.9	21	4.2
1730	8	3.3	33	6.6
1740	5	2.1	14	2.8
1750	5	2.1	21	4.2
1760	12	5.0	25	5.0
1770	22	9.1	45	9.0
1780	37	15.3	95	19.1
1790	52	21.6	119	23.9
Total	241	100.0	497	99.6*

*Total does not add up to 100% because numbers are rounded.

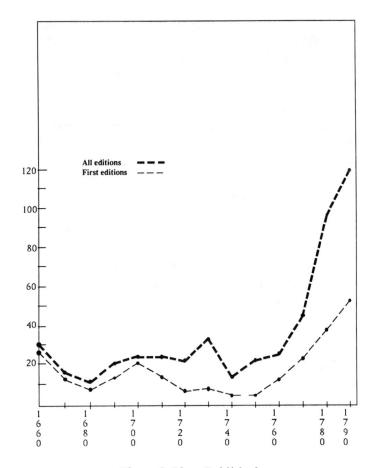

Figure 2. Plays Published

which is to say marketable, but admittedly in some much less than others. Table 3 shows their preferences: of 300 plays (14 lost plays or plays in manuscript are not included), comedies comprise 42 percent and tragedies 24.3 percent. Comedy is so predominant in this period that only in two decades (the 1690s and 1740s) does tragedy overtake it. The remaining modes—drama, farce, and opera—include a variety of types of usually shorter plays, and suggest both women's freedom to experiment and their need to write on demand for production and publication. The category of drama includes, for example, dramatic pastorals, blank verse tragedies, afterpieces, and interludes: Lady Burrell's *Comala,* a dramatic poem; Kitty Clive's afterpiece, *A Sketch of a Fine Lady's Return from a Rout;* Hannah Cowley's interlude, *The School of Eloquence;* Charlotte Lennox's *Philander, A Dramatic Pastoral;* Hannah More's pastoral drama, *The Search After*

Table 3. The popularity of modes of plays presented or published by decade.

Decade	Comedy	Tragedy	Drama*	Farce**	Opera+	Tragi-comedy	Decade Total
1660	18	7	1	0	0	2	28
1670	9	2	1	0	0	2	14
1680	6	1	1	1	0	0	9
1690	5	6	2	1	0	0	14
1700	13	8	1	0	0	0	22
1710	5	4	2	2	0	0	13
1720	4	2	0	1	0	0	7
1730	5	0	3	1	2	0	11
1740	0	4	3	3	0	0	10
1750	2	2	2	0	1	0	7
1760	7	2	6	3	0	0	18
1770	12	8	4	2	3	0	29
1780	18	4	8	7	4	1	42
1790	17	17	16	7	7	0	64
1800[1]	3	4	1	0	0	0	8
1810	2	2	0	0	0	0	4
Total in mode	126	73	51	28	17	5	300
% in mode	42.0	24.3	17.0	9.3	5.7	1.7	100.0

*Drama includes drama, verse drama, afterpiece, interlude, masque, and one puppet show.
**Farce includes burlesque and pantomime.
+Opera includes comic opera, musical piece, and musical entertainment.
[1]Many new playwrights began to present and publish plays after 1800. The totals for 1800 and 1810 include only plays by women in the checklist who began presenting or publishing plays before 1800.

Happiness and her four *Sacred Dramas* for children; Anne Penny's dramatic entertainment, *The Birthday;* and Anna Williams's drama *The Uninhabited Island.* Interestingly, farce, burlesque, and pantomime were not popular modes with women, nor was tragicomedy. A newer mode, opera, including ballad operas, comic operas, musical pieces and entertainments, appears to have become popular toward the end of the century.

Because comedy and tragedy so dominated the boards, it is useful to compare the frequency of staging and publishing of both (Table 4). On the stage, comedies were far more likely to be produced again, as many as five or six times; tragedies not quite twice. In the press, comedies and tragedies are more similar: comedies would average a little more than two editions, tragedies a little less than two.

It comes as no surprise, then, when we turn to the most popular, staged plays (Table 5) that comedies account for all but fifteen of the fifty-three most popular plays. And these fifteen plays in other modes are not near the top: Hannah More's *Percy* is seventeenth. Perhaps

Table 4. Staged and published comedies and tragedies by decade.

Decade	First year presented		All years presented		First edition		All editions	
	comedy	tragedy	comedy	tragedy	comedy	tragedy	comedy	tragedy
1660	0	2	0	4	18	7	18	10
1670	8	2	9	3	8	1	9	3
1680	6	1	9	2	5	0	6	0
1690	5	6	12	8	5	6	9	7
1700	13	8	27	10	13	7	15	8
1710	5	2	37	6	5	3	12	6
1720	3	2	42	5	3	3	14	5
1730	5	0	49	0	5	0	25	3
1740	0	0	34	0	1	3	10	3
1750	2	0	39	0	2	2	16	2
1760	7	1	43	1	5	2	16	3
1770	8	6	46	8	7	7	22	9
1780	16	2	100	8	20	3	38	10
1790	12	6	102	14	15	16	38	25
Total	90	38	549	69	112	60	248	94
% Total	70.3	29.7	88.8	11.2	65.0	35.0	72.5	27.5

Table 5. Most popular plays staged by number of years produced

Rank and author	Play title (genre)	Date first staged	No. of years produced
1. Centlivre	*The Busy Body* (c)	1709	87
2. Centlivre	*A Bold Stroke for a Wife* (c)	1718	75
3. Centlivre	*The Wonder! A Woman Keeps a Secret* (c)	1714	53
4. Behn	*The Rover* (c)	1677	51
5. Behn	*Emperor of the Moon* (f)	1687	32
6. Centlivre	*The Gamester* (c)	1705	31
7. Cowley	*Who's the Dupe?* (c)	1779	21
8. Cowley	*The Belle's Strategem* (c)	1780	20
9. Lee, Sophia	*The Chapter of Accidents* (c)	1780	20
10. Brooke, F.	*Rosina* (o)	1782	19
11. Inchbald	*The Mogul Tale* (f)	1784	16
12. Inchbald	*The Midnight Hour* (c)	1787	12
13. Inchbald	*The Child of Nature* (c)	1788	12
14. Cowley	*The Runaway* (c)	1776	11
15. Cibber	*The Oracle* (c)	1752	10
16. Inchbald	*Such Things Are* (c)	1786	10
17. More	*Percy* (t)	1777	10
18. Brooke, F.	*Marian of the Grange* (o)	1788	9
19. Cowley	*Which Is the Man?* (c)	1782	9
20. Inchbald	*I'll Tell You What* (c)	1785	9
21. Inchbald	*Everyone Has His Fault* (c)	1792	9
22. Behn	*The False Count* (c)	1681	7
23. Centlivre	*Love's Contrivance* (c)	1703	7
24. Inchbald	*Animal Magnetism* (c)	1788	7
25. Inchbald	*The Wedding Day* (c)	1794	7
26. Sheridan	*The Discovery* (c)	1763	7
27. Starke	*The Widow of Malabar* (t)	1790	7
28. Behn	*The Feigned Curtizens* (c)	1676	6
29. Centlivre	*The Man's Bewitched* (c)	1709	6
30. Centlivre	*Marplot (Busy Body II)* (c)	1710	6
31. Clive	*The Rehearsal* (c)	1750	5
32. Hook	*The Double Disguise*	1784	5
33. Pix	*The Spanish Wives* (f)	1696	5
34. Behn	*The Forc'd Marriage* (tc)	1670	4
35. Behn	*The City Heiress* (c)	1682	4
36. Behn	*The Lucky Chance* (c)	1686	4
37. Cowley	*A Bold Stroke for a Husband* (c)	1783	4

Table 5. Most popular plays staged by number of years produced (cont.)

Rank and author	Play title (genre)	Date first staged	No. of years produced
38. Pix	*Ibrahim* (t)	1696	4
39. Wiseman	*Antiochus* (t)	1701	4
40. Behn	*Abdelezar* (t)	1676	3
41. Behn	*The Young King* (tc)	1676	3
42. Centlivre	*The Beau's Duel* (c)	1701	3
43. Centlivre	*A Bickerstaff's Burying* (f)	1710	3
44. Centlivre	*A Wife Well-Managed* (f)	1724	3
45. Centlivre	*The Artifice* (c)	1720	3
46. Cowley	*More Ways Than One* (c)	1783	3
47. Cowley	*A Day in Turkey* (co)	1791	3
48. Griffith	*The School for Rakes* (c)	1769	3
49. Haywood	*A Wife to be Lett* (c)	1723	3
50. Haywood	*The Opera of Operas* (o)	1733	3
51. Inchbald	*Wives as they were* (c)	1797	3
52. Inchbald	*Lovers' Vows* (c)	1798	3
53. Philips	*Pompey* (t)	1662	3

c - comedy
t - tragedy
f - farce
tc - tragicomedy
o - opera

this table is most interesting in that it clarifies Susanna Centlivre's dominance over all other women playwrights, even over Aphra Behn and Elizabeth Inchbald, the second and third most prolific and most popular, respectively. Certainly their popularity must have encouraged all three to produce more and more plays. Of course in one sense, Centlivre and Behn cannot be compared with Inchbald because they have almost a century's head start. It is worth noting that the seventh to the thirteenth most popular plays—Hannah Cowley's *Who's the Dupe?* to Elizabeth Inchbald's *Child of Nature*—had been staged in every year to the end of the century, and went on beyond that, though that is outside the scope of this study. Still, few plays, even of Centlivre and Behn, maintained a popularity for decades. Many of the plays that enjoyed shorter runs of six, seven, eight, and nine years were enormously popular and speak to the possibility of success for women as dramatists.

Table 6 describes numerically the most successful careers. My method here is fairly experimental; I have construed the data that this table is based on in three different ways. The order given here assumes that getting a play both staged and published is the foremost mark of success: recognition on the boards and between the boards. It places all of the female wits, whose plays have traditionally been the best regarded, near the top, and there are no interlopers whose plays are bad, although Hannah More is there on the strength of *Percy*, which is no longer to our taste, and Frances Brooke on the strength of *Rosina* and *Marian*, comic operas of once enormous popularity. It seems equally sensible to construe success as an index of popularity on the stage alone (the total number of years of plays staged). Using that criterion markedly reorders the top dozen dramatists, leaving only the top three—Centlivre (289 years), Behn (128), and Inchbald (105)—in the same order. They are then followed by Cowley (80), Frances Brooke (29), Pix and Sophia Lee (21), More (13), Haywood (10), Starke and Clive (9), and Griffith (8). A third approach construes popularity by success in print—the number of years of new editions. The resulting order is again quite different, except that Centlivre remains securely on top: Centlivre (122 years of at least one new edition from all titles), More (73), Behn (37), Inchbald (34), Cowley (27), Duchess of Newcastle (25), Pix (14), Frances Brooke (12), Griffith (10), Philips, Baillie, and Plumptre (9), and Sophia Lee (8). This ordering is most suspect for providing any clue to quality because it places Hannah More second and the Duchess of Newcastle sixth. More's leaden dramas are no longer to our taste, and the duchess's dramas were never to anyone's taste. What is remarkable about her plays is that they were the first to be printed by a woman. The first *good* play by a woman was by someone else!

While we have now defined women's plays in relation to other women's plays, it would be interesting to see how women stand in relation to all playwrights and all plays. A study such as this one is possible because there are few plays and fewer women: all plays could be so analyzed, but the study would be as much as twenty times as large. If there were ninety-seven women writing 314 plays, how many men were there and how many plays did they write? Several

Table 6. Most successful dramatists by number of plays both staged and published.

Author	Plays both staged & published	Plays staged	No. years of plays staged	Plays published	No. years of plays published
Centlivre	19	20	289	20	122
Behn	19	21	128	20	37
Inchbald	16	21	105	18	34
Pix	12	13	21	12	14
Cowley	11	13	80	11	27
Griffith	5	5	8	7	10
Trotter	5	5	5	5	5
Haywood	4	6	10	4	7
More	3	3	13	8	73
Brooke, F.	3	3	29	4	12
Manley	3	5	6	3	4
Lee, S.	2	2	21	3	8
Sheridan	2	2	8	3	7
Starke	2	2	9	3	7
Philips	2	2	5	2	9
Anspach	2	4	4	3	3
Lennox	2	2	3	3	3
Ariadne	2	2	2	2	2
Clive	1	5	9	1	1
Hoper	1	4	4	1	1
Charke	1	3	3	1	1
Baillie	1	1	1	3	9
Brand	1	1	3	3	3
Lady Wallace	1	1	1	3	3
Newcastle	0	0	0	25	25
Plumptre	0	0	0	7	9
Geisweiler	0	0	0	4	6
West	0	0	0	4	5
Lady Burrell	0	0	0	3	3
Hughes	0	0	0	3	3
Ryves	0	0	0	3	3
Weddell	0	0	0	3	3

standard bibliographic works make possible some tentative estimates of the number of plays by men. Using Harbage's *Annals of English Drama: 975–1700*, we can simply count the number of plays written by men and women in each year from 1660 to 1700. Of 688 plays, only 44 are certainly by women; the 101 written anonymously can be assumed to be written by men. Almost 15 plays were written by men to every one written by a woman. Carl Stratman's *Bibliography of English Printed Tragedy, 1565–1900*, is the only source that permits a ready count of the entire 140 years. From 1660 to 1800, 585 tragedies were written by men compared to 50 by women, a ratio of about twelve to one. Finally, Dougald MacMillan's *Catalogue of the Larpent Plays in the Huntington Library* covers manuscripts submitted to Larpent from January 1737–38 through 1800. Of the 1,313 entries during this period, 93, or one in fourteen, are by women. Because the proportions from these three sources are very consistent with each other, we might well expect with a larger base of information to see for every one play written by a woman twelve to fourteen plays written by men. Based on these limited sources, too, we might expect to find this fairly constant across the 140 years: that is, the surges of playwriting by women from 1690 to 1720 and in the last three decades of the century would also be very productive for male playwrights.

Let me conclude with a few remarks on this approach. Seeing literature as data is a new and not always welcome method. The quantification of publishing facts and events lies outside conventional training in our field and outside our usual approach to literary history. Nevertheless, without making claims to determine what is good literature, we can use this approach to clarify the larger literary world in which all literature was produced. Looking at women only can help us to see how differently they entered the literary marketplace, how unevenly, how tentatively, how explosively. What I find most interesting about quantifying women's work in literature is that the very method leads me to questions I hadn't thought to ask and answers I hadn't expected to find. We knew about the dominance of comedy but might not have thought about the dominance of the stage over the printed word. And looking at the larger picture, we knew that the quality of drama was beginning to decline at the end of the century, but might not have expected to see such a marked increase in production, especially by women whose energies had become so much more absorbed in producing fiction.

Notes

1. I compiled names and plays in the checklist by searching several indispensible sources: Janet Todd's *Dictionary of British and American Women Writers 1600–1800* (1985) provided names of the most successful writers; Harbage's *Annals* (1964), Stratman's *Tragedy* (1966), Highfill's *Dictionary* (1973), and Baker's *Biographica Dramatica* (1812) were the primary initial sources for lesser-known writers. These were then checked against a number of other sources, including books and articles on individual authors, where available.

A unique part of this analysis is the data on performances of plays, made possible by Van Lennep's *The London Stage* (1960–68). The analysis of performances is done not on the number of nights performed, even though that would be possible using Van Lennep, but on the number of years in which each play was staged again. On average, a play would run three or four nights. A successful play might run ten. On being staged in subsequent years, even a successful play might run three or four nights. I believe that the number of years is as clear an indication of popularity and longevity as the actual nights run. Finally, the analysis also looks at publication as an index of popularity. Instead of listing each edition of each work—a formidable research task for this many titles—I have listed the years in which new editions or imprints were issued. In a number of cases, particularly toward the end of the century, very popular plays would go through several "editions" during the first year or two after being staged. For the analysis, such occurrences are counted as one edition in one year; in the checklist, multiple editions in a year are listed, but without naming the edition number.

Plays by Women in England, 1660–1800.

Information is presented in the following order.

The dramatist is listed by the surname under which she published. Her given name is second. The maiden name, if known, is in parentheses. Other married names are designated by the abbreviation "form" if she was formerly married or by "later" if she married after publishing under the surname given. Aristocratic titles and pseudonyms, the latter designated by "pseud.," are given last.

Each of her plays is then listed in chronological order by staging or publication, whichever occurred first. The mode of the play is given immediately after the title as a one- or two- letter abbreviation:

Comedy	c	
Tragedy	t	
Tragicomedy	tc	
Opera	o	(includes comic opera)
Musical piece	m	(includes musical farce and musical entertainment)
Farce	f	
Burlesque	b	
Pantomine	p	
Drama	d	(includes afterpieces, dramatic pastorals, interludes, melodramas, poetic dramas, and uncertain genres).

If portions of the play were written by someone else, that information follows. If the play is a translation, that is indicated by "tr" just before dates are given.

Dates of stagings, whether public or private, come next in roman type; these dates preceded by "ps" indicate a play was privately staged. Dates in boldface type are dates of publication; no distinction was made between imprints and new editions. The abbreviation "pp" indicates that the play was privately printed.

If a play survives in manuscript only, ms is indicated, and the date the play was written is given last, if known. Lost plays are so labelled; they have been retained to offer a fuller picture of the climate in which women wrote.

Other abbreviations:

attrib.	attributed to; authorship uncertain
fl.	flourished; lived; birth and death dates unknown
form.	former married name
n.d.	no date
ps	privately staged
pp	privately printed
tr	translation

ANSPACH, LADY ELIZABETH CRAVEN, MARGRAVINE OF (1750–1828)

The Somnambule; or, The Sleepwalker c tr ps 1778; **pp 1778**
The Miniature Picture c prologue by Sheridan 1780; **1780**
The Silver Tankard; or, the Point at Portsmouth m 1781
The Arcadian Pastoral mus piece ps 1782
The Statue Feast d ps 1782
The Yorkshire Ghost c ps 1794
The Georgian Princess o 1799; ps 1799
Puss in Boots p ps 1799
The Robbers t tr ps 1798; **1799**
Nourjad d ps 1803
Love in a Convent c ps 1805

"ARIADNE" (fl. 1696)

She Ventures and He Wins c 1695; **1696**
The Unnatural Mother d 1697; **1698**

AUBERT, ISABELLA (fl. 1715–20)

Harlequin Hydaspes; or, the Greshamite p 1719; **1719**

AUBIN, PENELOPE (1679–1731)

The Humours of the Masqueraders c (*The Merry Masqueraders*) 1730; **1733**

BAILLIE, JOANNA (1762–1851)

De Monfort t 1800; **1798 1799 1800** In: *Plays on the Passions* (and many subsequent eds.)
Count Basil t **1798 1799 1800** In: *Plays on the Passions.*
The Tryal c **1798 1799 1800** In: *Plays on the Passions.*

BARRELL, MARIA (fl. 1790)

The Captive d **1790**

BEHN, APHRA (1640–89)

The Forc'd Marriage; or, The Jealous Bridegroom tc 1670 1673 1687 1689; **1671 1688 1690**
The Amourous Prince; or, The Curious Husband c 1671 1785; **1671**
The Dutch Lover c 1673; **1673**
The Town Fopp; or, Sir Timothy Tawdrey c 1676 1698; **1677 1699**
Abdelazar; or, The Moor's Revenge t 1676 1692 1695; **1677 1693**
The Rover; or, The Banish'd Cavaliers Part I c 1677 1680 1685 1687 1690 1696 1703 1704 1705 1706 1707 1708 1709 1710 1711 1712 1713 1714 1715 1716 1717 1718 1720 1721 1722 1723 1724 1725 1726 1727 1728 1729 1730 1731 1732 1733 1734 1735 1736 1737 1738 1739 1740 1741 1742 1743 1748 1757 1758 1759 1760 1790; **1677 1677 1697 1709 1729 1735 1737 1741 1757**
The Debauchee; or, The Credulous Cuckold c attrib. 1677; **1677**

The Counterfeit Bridegroom; or, The Defeated Widow d attrib. **1677**
Sir Patient Fancy c 1678; **1678**
The Feign'd Curtizans; or, a Night's Intrique c 1676 1679 1680 1695 1716 1717; **1679**
The Revenge; or, a Match in Newgate c attrib. 1680; **1680**
The Second Part of the Rover c 1681; **1681**
The False Count; or, a New Way to Play an Old Game c f 1681 1696 1715 1716 1718
    1730 1762; **1682 1697**
The Round-Heads; or, The Good Old Cause c 1681; **1682 1698**
The City Heiress; or, Sir Timothy Treat-all c 1682 1697 1701 1707; **1682 1698**
Like Father, Like Son; or, The Mistaken Brothers d 1682; lost
The Young King; or, The Mistake tc 1676 1679 1698; **1683**
The Wavering Nymph; or, Mad Amyntas c 1684; lost
The Lucky Chance; or, An Alderman's Bargain c 1686 1697 1718 1786; **1687**
Emperor of the Moon f 1687 1691 1699 1702 1703 1704 1705 1706 1707 1708 1709
    1710 1714 1715 1716 1717 1718 1719 1720 1721 1722 1723 1724 1726 1728 1729
    1730 1731 1735 1739 1741 1748; **1687 1688 1757 1777**
The Widow Ranter; or, The History of Bacon in Virginia tc 1789; **1790**
The Younger Brother; or, The Amorous Jilt c 1696; **1696**

BOOTHBY, FRANCES (fl. 1670)

Marcelia; or, The Treacherous Friend tc 1669 1694; **1670**

BOWES, MARY ELLEN, COUNTESS OF STRATHMORE (1749–1800)

The Siege of Jerusalem t **1774**

BOYD, ELIZABETH pseud. LOUISA (fl. 1730–40)

Don Sancho: or, The Student's Whim with Minerva's Triumph o 1739; **1739**
Minerva's Triumph masque **1739**

BRAND, HANNA (?–1821)

Huniades; or, The Siege of Belgrade t 1791 1792 1794 (renamed *Agmunda* when
    performed second time in 1792); **1798** In: *Plays and Poems*
Adelinda c **1798** In: *Plays and Poems*
The Conflict; or Love, Honor, and Pride c **1798** In: *Plays and Poems*

BROOKE, CHARLOTTE (1740–83)

Belisarius t **1795**

BROOKE, FRANCES (MOORE) (1724–89)

Virginia, a tragedy with odes, pastorals, and translations t **1756**
The Siege of Sinope t 1781; **1781 1781** (in Dublin)
Rosina o (Music by William Shield) 1782 1783 1784 1785 1786 1787 1788 1789 1790
    1791 1792 1793 1794 1795 1796 1797 1798 1799 1800; **1783 1783 1783 1783 1783
    1783 1784 1784 1785 1786 1788 1790 1795 1796**
Marian of the Grange o (Music by William Shield) 1788 1789 1790 1792 1793 1794

1795 1798 1800; **1788 1800**; Published in 1788 as *Airs, Songs, Duetts, Trios and Choruses in Marian*

BRUNTON, ANNA (ROSS) (fl. 1788)

The Cottagers co **1788 1788 1788**

BURGESS, MRS. (fl. 1780)

The Oaks; or, The Beauties of Canterbury c 1780 (in Canterbury); **1780**

BURKE, MISS (fl. 1793)

The Ward of the Castle o 1793; Published as *Songs, Duets, Choruses &c in The Ward of the Castle*

BURNEY, FANNY aft D'ARBLAY (1752–1840)

Hubert de Vere; a Pastoral Tragedy t Berg MS.
The Seige of Pevensey d Berg MS.
Elberta t (fragments) Berg MS.
Love and Fashion c Berg MS.
The Witlings c 1779; Berg MS.
The Woman Hater c Berg MS.
A Busy Day c Berg MS.
Edwy and Elgiva t 1795; Berg MS.

BURRELL, SOPHIA (RAYMOND) aft CLAY, LADY (1750?–1802)

Comala d **1793** In: *Poems*
Maximian t 1800
Theodora; or the Spanish daughter t **1800**

BURTON, PHILLIPINA aft HILL (fl. 1768–87)

Fashion Display'd c 1770; written 1700 Larpent #308

CELESIA, DOROTHEA (MALLET) (1738–90)

Almida t 1771; **1771 1771 1771**

CENTLIVRE, SUSANNA (CARROLL) (?–1723)

The Perjured Husband; or, The Adventures of Venice t 1700; **1700 1737 1761**
The Beau's Duel; or, A Soldier for the Ladies c 1701 1782 1785; **1702 1715 1719 1727 1735 1736**
The Stolen Heiress; or, The Salamanca Doctor Outplotted c 1702 1779 (Performed in 1702 as The Heiress, LS); **1703**
Love's Contrivance; or Le Medicin malgre lui c 1703 1704 1705 1706 1723 1724 1726; **1703**
The Gamester c 1705 1706 1709 1710 1711 1714 1715 1716 1717 1718 1719 1720 1726 1727 1728 1729 1730 1731 1732 1735 1736 1737 1738 1740 1741 1742 1743 1744 1745 1756 1790; **1705 1708 1714 1725 1734 1736 1753 1756 1760 1765 1767**

The Basset-Table c 1705; **1706 1735 1735**

Love at a Venture c 1706 1782; **1706**

The Platonick Lady c 1706; **1707**

The Busie Body c (her most popular play) 1709 1710 1711 1712 1713 1714 1715 1716 1717 1718 1719 1720 1721 1722 1723 1724 1725 1726 1727 1728 1729 1730 1731 1732 1733 1734 1735 1736 1737 1738 1739 1740 1741 1742 1743 1744 1745 1746 1747 1748 1749 1750 1751 1752 1753 1754 1755 1756 1757 1758 1759 1760 1761 1762 1763 1764 1765 1766 1767 1768 1769 1770 1771 1772 1773 1774 1775 1776 1777 1778 1779 1780 1781 1782 1783 1784 1785 1791 1792 1793 1794 1795 1796 1797 1798 1799 1800; **1709 1709 1714 1725 1727 1732 1737 1737 1740 1741 1746 1746 1747 1749 1753 1754 1757 1759 1765 1766 1768 1771 1774 1776 1777 1777 1779 1782 1787 1791 1797**

The Man's Bewitched; or, the Devil to Do about Her c 1709 1730 1731 1738 1769 1784; **1709 1710 1737** (see *The Ghost*)

A Bickerstaff's Burying; or, Work for the Upholders f (later revived as *The Custom of the Country*) 1710 1711 1717; **1710 1724**

Marplot; or, the Second Part of the Busy Body c 1710 1711 1724 1755 1762 1772 (Performed in 1755, 1762, and 1772 as *Marplot in Lisbon*); **1710 1711 1737 1760** (Published in 1760 as *Marplot in Lisbon*)

The Perplex'd Lovers c 1712; **1712**

The Wonder! A Woman Keeps a Secret c 1714 1733 1734 1735 1736 1737 1741 1742 1744 1747 1748 1756 1757 1758 1759 1760 1761 1762 1763 1764 1765 1766 1767 1768 1769 1770 1771 1772 1773 1774 1775 1776 1777 1778 1780 1781 1782 1783 1784 1785 1786 1787 1788 1789 1791 1792 1793 1794 1795 1797 1798 1799 1800; **1714 1719 1725 1734 1736 1740 1756 1757 1758 1759 1766 1770 1774 1775 1776 1777 1780 1781 1782 1786 1787 1792 1794 1795 1797**

A Wife Well Manag'd; or, Cuckoldom Prevented f (adapted unacknowledged into *The Disappointment*, ballad opera, 1732) 1724 1732 1789; **1715 1737**

The Gotham Election f **1715 1737** (published in 1737 as *The Humours of Elections: The Gotham Election*)

The Cruel Gift: or, The Royal Resentment t 1716 1717; **1717 1734 1736**

A Bold Stroke for a Wife c 1718 1719 1720 1721 1722 1723 1724 1725 1726 1727 1728 1729 1730 1731 1732 1733 1734 1735 1736 1737 1738 1739 1740 1741 1744 1745 1746 1747 1748 1749 1750 1751 1752 1753 1754 1757 1758 1759 1760 1761 1762 1763 1764 1765 1766 1767 1768 1769 1770 1771 1772 1773 1774 1776 1777 1778 1779 1780 1781 1782 1783 1784 1785 1786 1787 1788 1789 1793 1794 1795 1796 1797 1798 1799 1800; **1718 1724 1727 1728 1729 1733 1735 1736 1737 1742 1749 1752 1755 1763 1766 1772 1722 1774 1776 1780 1783 1790 1791 1794**

The Artifice c 1720 1722 1781; **1723 1735 1736**

The Ghost f (from *The Man's Bewitched*) 1767 (in Dublin)

CHARKE, CHARLOTTE (CIBBER) aft SACHEVERELL (1713–60)

The Art of Management; or, Tragedy Expelled c 1735; **1735**

The Carnival; or, Harlequin Blunderer c 1735

Tit for Tat; or, the Comedy and Tragedy of War d (puppet show) 1743

CIBBER, SUSANNA MARIE (ARNE) (1714–66)

The Oracle c tr 1752 1753 1754 1755 1756 1757 1758 1759 1765 1795; **1741 1752 1752 1763 1778**

CLIVE, CATHERINE (RAFTOR) (1711–85)

The Rehearsal: or, Bays in Petticoats c 1750 1751 1753 1755 1762; **1753 1753**
Every Woman in her Humour d attrib. 1760 performed for her benefit; Larpent collection Ms #174
Island of Slaves c tr 1761 performed for her benefit
Sketch of a Fine Lady's Return from a Rout d (afterpiece) 1763; Larpent #220
The Faithful Irishwoman f 1765 performed for her benefit; Larpent #247

COOPER, ELIZABETH (fl. 1735–40)

The Rival Widows: or The Fair Libertine c 1735; **1735**
The Nobleman; or The Family Quarrel c 1736

COWLEY, HANNAH (PARKHOUSE) (1743–1809)

The Runaway c 1776 1777 1778 1779 1780 1781 1782 1783 1789 1790 1791; **1776 1776 1790**
Albina, Countess Raimond t 1779.; **1779 1779 1780 1780 1797 1812**
Who's the Dupe? f 1779 1780 1781 1782 1783 1784 1785 1786 1787 1788 1789 1790
    1791 1792 1793 1794 1795 1796 1797 1798 1800; **1779 1779 1780 1780 1787 1790**
The Belle's Strategem c 1780 1781 1782 1783 1784 1786 1787 1788 1789 1790 1791
    1792 1793 1794 1795 1796 1797 1798 1799 1800; **1782 1783 1787 1794**
The School of Eloquence interlude 1780
The World As It Goes; or, A Party at Montpelier f 1781 (also performed 1781 under
    title: *Second Thoughts are Best*)
Which is the Man? c 1782 1783 1784 1785 1786 1787 1788 1790 1791; **1783 1783 1784 1785**
A Bold Stroke for a Husband c 1783 1784 1786 1795; **1783 1784 1784 1784 1787 1793**
More Ways Than One c 1783 1784 1789; **1784 1784 1784 1784**
A School for Graybeards; or, The Mourning Bride c 1786 1787; **1786 1787 1787**
The Fate of Sparta; or, The Rival Kings t 1788; **1788 1788 1788**
A Day in Turkey; or, The Russian Slaves c o 1791 1792 1794; **1791 1792** (published in
    1791 as *Airs, Duets and Choruses in . . . A Day in Turkey*)
The Town Before You c 1794 1795; **1795**

CULLUM, MRS. (fl. 1775)

Charlotte: or One Thousand Seven Hundred and Seventy Three d 1775

CUTHBERTSON, MISS (fl. 1793)

Anna c 1793

D'AGUILAR, ROSE later LAWRENCE (fl. 1799)

Gortz of Berlingen with the Iron Hand d (historical) tr **1799**

DAVYS, MARY (1674–1732)

The Northern Heiress; or, the Humours of York c 1716; **1716 1725**
The Self-Rival c **1725**

DEVERELL, MARY (1737?–?)

Mary, Queen of Scots; An Historical Tragedy, or Dramatic Poem t pp **1792**

DU BOIS, LADY DOROTHEA (1728–74)

The Divorce m entertainment (music by James Hook) 1771; **1771**
The Haunted Grove d 1772

EDWARDS, MISS (fl. 1776–80)

Otho and Rutha: a Dramatic Tale d **1780**

EGLETON, MRS. (?–1734)

The Maggot o 1732 for her benefit

"EPHELIA" (fl. 1679)

The Royal-Pair of Coxcombs c 1678; **1679 1682** (prologue, epilogue and two songs in: *Female Poems on Several Occasions Written by Ephelia*)

GARDNER, SARAH (CHEYNEY) (fl. 1763–98)

The Advertisement; or, a Bold Stroke for a Husband c 1777 (acted under the title, *The Matrimonial Advertisement*)
Charity f n.d.
The Loyal Subject c n.d.

GEISWEILER, MARIA (fl. 1799)

Crime from Ambition d tr **1799 1800**
Joanna of Montfaucon d tr **1799 1800**
The Noble Lie d tr **1799 1799**
Poverty and Nobleness of Mind d tr **1799 1799**

GRIFFITH, ELIZABETH (1727–93)

Amana, A Dramatic Poem t **1764**
The Platonic Wife c 1765; **1765**
The Double Mistake c 1766; **1766**
The School for Rakes c 1769 1771 1776; **1769 1769 1769 1770 1795 1795 1797**
A Wife in the Right c 1772; **1772**
The Barber of Seville; or The Useless Precaution c **1776**
The Times c 1779 1780; **1780 1780**

HARLOW, ELIZABETH (fl. 1789)

The English Tavern at Berlin c **1789**

HARRISON, ELIZABETH (fl. 1756)

The Death of Socrates t **1756** In: *Miscellanies on Moral and Religious Subjects*

HAYWOOD, ELIZA (FOWLER) (1693–1756)

The Fair Captive t 1721; **1721 1724**
A Wife to be Lett c 1723 1781 1792; **1724 1724 1735 1802**
Frederick, Duke of Brunswick-Lunenburgh t 1729; **1729 1729**
The Opera of Operas; or Tom Thumb the Great o (Fielding's *Tragedy of Tragedies*
    set to music) 1733 1734 1740; **1733**
Arden of Feversham d 1736
Love in Excess d 1737 (from her novel published in 1719, 1722)

HOLFORD, MARGARET (WRENCH) (fl. 1785–1814)

Neither's the Man c 1799; **1799 1806**
The Way to Win Her c **1814**

HOOK, HARRIET HORNCASTLE (MADDEN) (fl. 1784)

The Double Disguise co 1784 1785 1786 1787 1788; **1784** (also "The Irish Lad" in
    The Double Disguise, 1784; also *Songs in the Double Disguise*, 1784)

HOPER, MRS. (HARFORD) (fl. 1747–49)

The Battle of Poinctiers; or, The English Prince d 1747
The Cyclopedia f 1748
Queen Tragedy Restor'd; A Dramatic Entertainment b 1749; **1749**

HOUSTON, LADY (?–1780)

The Coquettes; or, the Gallent in the Closet c tr n.d. (staged in Scotland)

HUGHES, ANNE (fl. 1784–90)

Cordelia t **1790** In: *Moral Dramas Intended for private representation*
Constantia t **1790** In: *Moral Dramas*
Aspacia t **1790** In: *Moral Dramas*

INCHBALD, ELIZABETH (1753–1821)

The Mogul Tale, or the Descent of the Balloon f 1784 1785 1786 1787 1788 1789 1790
    1791 1792 1793 1794 1796 1797 1798 1799 1800; **1788 1788 1796**
Appearance Is Against Them f 1785 1804 (1804 revived as *Mistake Upon Mistake; or
    Appearance Is Against Them*); **1785 1786**
I'll Tell You What c 1785 1786 1787 1788 1789 1790 1791 1792 1794; **1786 1786 1787
    1787**
The Widow's Vow f 1786 1787; **1786 1786 1787**
Such Things Are d 1786 1787 1788 1789 1790 1791 1792 1793 1796 1798; **1788 1788
    1788 1800**
The Midnight Hour; or War of Wits c tr 1787 1788 1789 1790 1791 1792 1793 1794
    1795 1796 1797 1799; **1787**

All on a Summer's Day c 1787

Animal Magnetism f 1788 1789 1790 1791 1792 1794 1797; **1789 1789 1792**

The Child of Nature c 1788 1789 1790 1791 1792 1794 1795 1796 1797 1798 1799
1800; **1788**

The Married Man c 1789 1790; **1789 1789 1796**

Next-Door Neighbours c 1791 1792; **1791 1791**

A Simple Story d 1791

Hue and Cry f 1791 1797

Young Men and Old Women f 1792

Everyone Has His Fault c 1792 1793 1794 1795 1796 1797 1798 1799 1800; **1792 1793
1793 1793 1793 1793 1793 1794 1794 1794 1795 1805**

The Wedding Day f 1794 1795 1796 1797 1798 1799 1800; **1794 1795 1806**

Wives as they were, and Maids as they are c 1797 1798 1800; **1797 1797 1797 1797 1797
1797 1797 1816**

Lovers' Vows c 1798 1799 1800; **1798 1799**

The Wise Men of the East c 1799 1800; **1799** (satirized as *The Wise Man of the East* in
1800 by T. Dutton)

To Marry, or Not to Marry c 1805; **1805**

The Massacre t **1833**

A Case of Conscience t **1833**

JORDAN, DOROTHY (BLAND) form FORD (1761–1816)

The Spoiled Child f attrib. 1790; **1799 1805** (1799: pirated Dublin ed.; 1805: pub for
her benefit)

KEMBLE, MARIE-THERESE (DE CAMP) (1775–1838)

First Faults c 1799 staged for her benefit

LATTER, MARY (1725–1777)

The Siege of Jerusalem by Titus Vespasian t 1768 (staged at Reading); **1763**

Soliloquies on Temporal Indigence d **1759 1759** In: *The Miscellaneous Works, in
Prose and Verse*

LEAPOR, MARY (1722–46)

The Unhappy Father t **1748–51** In: *Poems Upon Several Occasions*

LEE, HARRIET (1757–1851)

The New Peerage, or, Our Eyes may deceive us c 1787; **1787 1787 1787 1788**

The Mysterious Marriage; or The Heirship of Roselva t **1798 1798**

LEE, SOPHIA (1750–1824)

The Chapter of Accidents c 1780 1781 1782 1783 1784 1785 1786 1787 1788 1789 1790
1791 1793 1794 1795 1796 1797 1798 1799 1800; **1780 1780 1781 1781 1781 1782
1792 1796 1797**

Almeyda, Queen of Granada t 1796; **1796 1796 1796 1796**

The Assignation c 1807

LENNOX, CHARLOTTE (RAMSAY) (1729?–1804)

Philander, A Dramatic Pastoral d **1758 1758**
The Sister c (based on her novel *Henrietta*) 1769; **1769 1769 1769**
Old City Manners c 1775 1776; **1775**

MACCARTHY, CHARLOTTE (fl. 1745–1768)

Celia, or the Perjured Lover d (attrib.) 1749
The Author and Bookseller d **1765**

MANLEY, DELARIVIÉRE (1663–1724)

The Lost Lover; or, the Jealous Husband c 1696; **1696**
The Royal Mischief t 1696; **1696**
Almyna: or, The Arabian Vow t 1706; **1707 1717?**
Lucius, the first Christian King of Britain t 1717 1720; **1717 1720**
The Double Mistress; or, 'Tis Well 'Tis No Worse c 1720; lost
The Duke of Somerset t lost

MARISHALL, JEAN (fl. 1766–89)

Sir Harry Gaylove, or Comedy in Embryo c **1772**

METCALFE, CATHARINE (?–1790)

Julia de Roubigné t 1790 (staged at Bath)

MORE, HANNAH (1745–1833)

The Search After Happiness pastoral drama **1773 1773 1774 1774 1774 1775 1777 1778
    1785 1787 1791 1793 1794 1796 1800**
The Inflexible Captive t 1775; **1774 1774 1774 1774 1775**
Percy t 1777 1778 1779 1780 1782 1785 1786 1787 1788 1797; **1777 1778 1778 1778 1780
    1784 1785 1788 1807**
The Fatal Falsehood t 1779; **1779 1780 1789**
Moses in the Bulrushes d **1782 1782 1783 1784 1785 1789 1791 1793 1796 1798 1799 1800**
    In: *Sacred Dramas, chiefly intended for Young Persons*
David and Goliath d **1782 1782 1783 1784 1785 1789 1791 1793 1796 1798 1799 1800** In:
    Sacred Dramas
Belshazzer d **1782 1782 1783 1784 1785 1789 1791 1793 1796 1798 1799 1800** In: *Sacred
    Dramas*
Daniel d **1782 1782 1783 1784 1785 1789 1791 1793 1796 1798 1799 1800** In: *Sacred
    Dramas*

NEWCASTLE, MARGARET CAVENDISH, DUCHESS OF (1623–73)

Love's Adventures c **1662** In: *Plays*
The Second Part of Love's Adventures c **1662** In: *Plays*
The Several Wits c **1662** In: *Plays*
Youth's Glory and Death's Banquet, Part I t In: *Plays* **1662**
The Second Part of Youth's Glory and Death's Banquet t **1662** In: *Plays*

The Lady Contemplation, Part I c **1662** In: *Plays*
The Lady Contemplation, Part II c **1662** In: *Plays*
Wit's Cabal, Part I c **1662** In: *Plays*
Wit's Cabal, Part II c **1662** In: *Plays*
The Unnatural Tragedy t **1662** In: *Plays*
The Public Wooing c **1662** In: *Plays*
The Matrimonial Trouble, Part I c **1662** In: *Plays*
The Matrimonial Trouble, Part II ct **1662** In: *Plays*
Nature's Three Daughters, Beauty, Love, and Wit, Part I c **1662** In: *Plays*
The Religious d **1662** In: *Plays*
The Comical Hash c **1662** In: *Plays*
Bell in Campo, Part I t **1662** In: *Plays*
Bell in Campo, Part II t **1662** In: *Plays*
The Apocryphal Ladies c **1662** In: *Plays*
The Female Academy c **1662** In: *Plays*
The Convent of Pleasure c **1668** In: *Plays Never before Printed*
The Sociable Companions; or, The Female Wits c **1668** In: *Plays Never before Printed*
The Presence c **1668** In: *Plays Never before Printed*
The Bridals c **1668** In: *Plays Never before Printed*
The Blazing World c **1668** In: *Plays Never before Printed*

O'BRIEN, MARY (fl. 1785–90)

The Temple of Virtue o n.d.
The Fallen Patriot: A Comedy in 5 Acts c **1790**

OPIE, AMELIA (ALDERSON) (1769–1853)

Adelaide t ps 1791

PARSONS, ELIZA (PHELP) (1748?–1811)

The Intrigues of a Morning; or, An Hour in Paris f 1792; **1792**

PENNY, ANNE (HUGHES) form CHRISTIAN (1731–84)

The Birthday. An Entertainment in three acts. d **1771 1780** In: *Poems with a Dramatic Entertainment*

PHILIPS, KATHERINE (FOWLER) (1631–64)

Pompey t tr 1662 1663 1678; **1663 1663 1667 1669 1678 1710** All editions after 1663 in: *Poems. By The Most Deservedly Admired Mrs. Katherine Philips, The Matchless Orinda*
Horace t tr (Fifth act completed by Sir John Denham after her death.) 1668 1669; **1667 1669 1678 1710**. All editions in: *Poems.*

PILKINGTON, LAETITIA (VAN LEWEN) (1712–50)

The Roman Father t (first act) **1748?** In: *Memoirs of Mrs. Letitia Pilkington: 1712–1750,* Vol. II
The Turkish Court; or, The London 'Prentice b 1748 (staged at Dublin)

PIX, MARY (GRIFFITH) (1666–1709)

Ibrahim, the Thirteenth Emperour of the Turks t 1696 1702 1704 1715; **1696**
The Spanish Wives; or, The Governor of Barcelona f 1696 1699 1703 1711 1726; **1696**
The Innocent Mistress c 1697; **1697**
The Deceiver Deceived c 1697 1698; **1698**
Queen Catharine; or, the Ruines of Love t 1698; **1698**
The False Friend; or, The Fate of Disobedience t 1699; **1699 1702**
The Beau Defeated; or, The Lucky Younger Brother c 1700; **1700**
The Czar of Muscovy t 1701; **1701**
The Double Distress t 1701; **1701**
The Different Widows; or Intrique à la Mode c 1703; **1703**
The Conquest of Spain t 1705; **1705**
The Adventures in Madrid c 1706; **1706**

PLUMPTRE, ANNA (1760–1818)

The Count of Burgandy t tr **1798 1799**
The Natural Son; or, The Lovers' Vows d tr **1798 1798**
The Force of Calumny d tr **1799**
La Perouse d tr **1799**
Spaniards in Peru; or, The Death of Rolla t tr **1799 1799** (Also published as *Pizarro. The Spaniards in Peru.*)
The Virgin of the Sun d tr **1799**
The Widow and the Riding-Horse f tr **1799**

POLWHELE, ELIZABETH (?–1691?)

The Faithful Virgins t 1671; Bodleian MS.
The Frolicks, or The Lawyer cheated c ?1671; **1974**; Cornell MS.
Elysium d masque; lost

POPE, JANE (fl. 1767)

The Young Couple f (Adapted from Frances Sheridan's *The Discovery*) 1767 for her benefit

PYE, JOEL-HENRIETTA [JAEL] (MENDEZ) form CAMPBELL (1737?–82)

The Capricious Lady f 1771; Larpent #323

RICHARDSON, ELIZABETH (d. 1779)

The Double Deception; or, The Lovers Perplex'd c 1779 1780

ROBE, JANE (fl. 1723)

The Fatal Legacy t tr 1723; **1723**

ROBERTS, MISS R. (fl. 1763–88)

Malcolm t **1779**

ROBERTSON, MRS. (fl. 1800)

Ellindal or, The Abbey of St. Aubert d 1800

ROBERTSON, MRS. (patentee of Drury Land and wife/widow of Joseph Richardson)

Ethelred t n.d.

ROBERTSON, MRS. T. (fl. 1796)

The Enchanted Island 1796 (staged at Dublin)

ROBINSON, MARY (DARBY) pseud. PERDITA (1758–1800)

The Lucky Escape o 1778; **1778** Published as *The Songs, Chorusses, etc. in The Lucky Escape, a comic opera*
Nobody f 1794
The Sicilian Lover t **1796**

RYVES, ELIZABETH (1750–97)

The Triumph of Hymen masque **1777** In: *Poems on Several Occasions*
The Prude o **1777** In: *Poems on Several Occasions*
The Debt of Honour c **1777?**

SANDERS, CHARLOTTE ELIZABETH (fl. 1787–1803)

The Birds' Nest d **1797 1800** In: *The Little Family*
The Little Gamester d **1797 1800** In: *The Little Family*

SHERIDAN, ALICIA aft LE FANU (fl. 1781)
(Daughter of Frances Sheridan)

The Ambiguous Lover f 1781

SHERIDAN, FRANCES (CHAMBERLAINE) (1724–66)

The Discovery c 1763 1767 1776 1779 1780 1782 1783; **1763 1763 1763 1763 1776 1792 1797**
The Dupe c 1763; **1764 1764**
A Journey to Bath c **1890 1902** unfinished

SMITH, CHARLOTTE (TURNER) (1749–1806)

What is She? c 1799; **1799 1799 1799 1800**

STARKE, MARIANA (1762?–1838)

The Sword of Peace; or, A Voyage of Love c 1788 1789; **1788 1788 1789 1792**
The British Orphans t ps 1790 at Lady Crespigny's private theater
The Widow of Malabar t 1790 1791 1792 1794 1795 1796 1798; **1791 1791 1791 1791 1791 1791 1796 1799**
The Tournament t **1800 1803**

THOMAS, MRS. ELIZABETH (d. 1778)

Dramatick Pastoral d **1762**

TOLLET, ELIZABETH (1694–1754)

Susanna; or, Innocence Preserved In: *Poems on Several Occasions* **1724 1755 1760**

TRIMMER, SARAH (KIRBY) (1741–1810)

The Little Hermit; or, The Rural Adventure d **1788** In: *The Juvenile Magazine*

TROTTER, CATHARINE aft COCKBURN (1679–1749)

Agnes de Castro t 1695; **1696**
Fatal Friendship t 1698; **1698**
Love at a Loss, or the Most Votes carry it c 1700 (Revived years later, much revised as
    The Honourable Deceivers; or, All right at the Last); **1701**
The Unhappy Penitent t 1701; **1701**
The Revolution of Sweden t 1706; **1706**

TURNER, MARGARET (fl. 1790)

The Gentle Shepherd: A Scotch pastoral by Allan Ramsay, attempted in English d
    1790

WALLACE, EGLINTON (MAXWELL), LADY (?–1803)

Diamond Cut Diamond c tr **1787**
The Ton, or, Follies of Fashion c 1788; **1788**
The Whim c **1795**
Cortes t lost (named on the title page of *The Whim*)

WEDDELL, MRS. (fl. 1737–42)

The City Farce f **1737**
The Voyage up the Thames c (named on the title page of *Inkle and Yarico*) **1737**
Inkle and Yarico t **1742**

WEST, JANE (1758–1852)

Edmund, Surnamd Ironside t **1791 1799** In: *Miscellaneous Poetry*
Adela; or the Barons of Old t **1799** In: *Poems and Plays*
How Will It End? c **1799** In: *Poems and Plays*
The Minstrel; or, The Heir of Arundel t **1799** In: *Poems and Plays*

WHARTON, ANNE (LEE), COUNTESS OF pseud. CHLORIS (?–1685)

Love's Martyr, or Wit above Crowns t ms in British Library

WILLIAMS, ANNA (1706–83)

The Uninhabited Island d In: *Miscellanies in Prose and Verse* 1766

WINCHILSEA, ANNE (KINGSMILL) FINCH, COUNTESS OF (1661–1720)

Aristomenes: or, The Royal Shepherd t **1713 1714** In: *Miscellany Poems on several occasions*

Love and Innocence d **1713 1714** In: *Miscellany Poems on several occasions*

WISEMAN, JANE AFT HOLT (fl. 1701)

Antiochus the Great; or, the Fatal relapse t 1701 1711 1712 1721; **1702**

YEARSLEY, ANN (CROMARTIE) (1752–1806)

Earl Goodwin, an Historical Play t 1789; **1791**
The Ode Rejected c (named in *Earl Goodwin*); lost

Works Cited

Baker, David Erskine. 1812. *Biographica Dramatica; or, a Companion to the Play-house,* 3 vol. Comp. to 1764 by Baker, to 1782 by Isaac Reed, and to 1811 by Stephen Jones. London: Longman.

The British Library General Catalogue of Printed Books to 1975. 1979. London: Clive Bingley.

Cotton, Nancy. 1980. *Women Playwrights in England: c 1363–1750.* Lewisburg: Bucknell Univ. Press.

Grant, Douglas. 1957. *Margaret the First.* Toronto: Univ. of Toronto Press.

Harbage, Alfred. 1964. *Annals of English Drama 975–1700.* 2nd ed., rev. S. Schoenbaum. Philadelphia: Univ. of Pennsylvania Press.

Highfill, Philip H., Jr., Kalman A. Burnim, and Edward A. Langhans. 1973. *A Biographical Dictionary of Actors, Actresses, Musicians, Dancers, Managers & Other Stage Personnel in London, 1660–1800.* Carbondale: Southern Illinois Univ.

Jones, M. G. 1952. *Hannah More.* Cambridge: Cambridge Univ. Press.

Lock, F. B. 1979. *Susanna Centlivre.* Boston: Twayne.

Macgregor, Margaret Eliot. 1932. "Amelia Alderson Opie: Worldling and Friend." *Smith College Studies in Modern Languages* 14, no. 1 (Oct.)

MacMillan, Dougald, comp. 1939. *Catalogue of the Larpent Plays in the Huntington Library.* San Marino, Cal.: San Pasqual Press.

McMullen, Lorraine. 1983. *An Odd Attempt in A Woman: The Literary Life of Frances Brooke.* Vancouver: Univ. of British Columbia Press.

Milhous, Judith, and Robert D. Hume. 1977. "Lost English Plays, 1660–1700." Harvard Library Bulletin 25:5–33.

Morgan, Fidelis, 1981. *The Female Wits.* London: Virago.

Nash, Mary. 1977. *The Provoked Wife: The Life and Times of Susannah Cibber.* Boston: Little, Brown.

The National Union Catalogue. 1968. Chicago: American Library Assoc.

Norton, J. E. 1958. "Some Uncollected Authors: Hannah Cowley." *The Book Collector* 7:68–76.

———. 1957. "Some Uncollected Authors: Susanna Centlivre." *The Book Collector* 6:172–78, 280–85.

Polwhele, Elizabeth. 1977. *The Frolicks or The Lawyer Cheated*. Ed. Judith Milhous and Robert D. Hume. Ithaca, N.Y.: Cornell Univ. Press.

Russell, Norma H. 1964. "Some Uncollected Authors XXXVIII: Frances Sheridan, 1724–1766." *The Book Collector*, 13:196–205.

Schneider, Ben Ross, Jr., comp. 1979. *Index to The London Stage: 1660–1800*. Carbondale: Southern Illinois Univ. Press.

Schofield, Mary Anne. 1985. *Eliza Haywood*. Boston: Twayne.

Sheridan, Frances. 1984. *The Plays of Frances Sheridan*. Ed. Robert Hogan and Jerry C. Beasley. Newark: Univ. of Delaware Press.

Souers, Philip Webster. 1931. *The Matchless Orinda*. Reprint, New York: Johnson, 1968.

Small, Miriam Rossiter. 1935. *Charlotte Ramsay Lennox: An Eighteenth Century Lady of Letters*. Vol. 85 in Yale Studies in English. New Haven: Yale Univ. Press.

Stanton, Judith Phillips. 1988. "Statistical Profile of Women Writing in English from 1660 to 1800." In: *Eighteenth-Century Women and the Arts*. Ed. Frederick M. Keener and Susan E. Lorsch. Westport, Conn.: Greenwood Press.

Stratman, Carl J. 1966. *Bibliography of English Printed Tragedy, 1565–1900*. Carbondale: Southern Illinois Univ. Press.

Todd, Janet, ed. 1985. *A Dictionary of British and American Women Writers 1660–1800*. Totowa, N.J.: Rowman & Allanheld.

Van Lennep, William, Emmett L. Avery, Arthur H. Scouten, George Winchester Stone, Jr., and Charles Beecher Hogan. 1960–68. *The London Stage, 1660–1800*. 5 pts. in 11 vols. Carbondale: Southern Illinois Univ. Press.

7

Closet Drama:
From the Play to the Novel

"Mrs. Jordan as Euphrosyne." Courtesy of the Print Collection.
The Lewis Walpole Library, Yale University.

Plot and Politics in Susanna Centlivre's
A Bold Stroke for a Wife

DOUGLAS R. BUTLER

Although she is generally recognized as England's most popular woman playwright, Susanna Centlivre has inspired relatively little critical attention and even less acclaim. The standard critical observation is that she writes highly theatrical plays, full of action, that are quite innocent of thought. Perhaps Centlivre does not have a serious vision, but she does seem to share certain assumptions with the Whiggish writers of her time, with those who believed that society should guarantee (in Locke's terms) a citizen's life, liberty, and property.

Centlivre's plays, particularly one of her best, *A Bold Stroke for a Wife* (1718), manifest her Whiggish perspective. If Centlivre has political and social ideas—and I think that she does—they are not conveyed most effectively through her language, the preoccupation of the twentieth-century critic. Centlivre gives us few images and little "wit." Except when they are endowed with broad accents, her characters sound much the same. Most are so busy hatching plots that they have little time for reflection or banter. Motivation, then, is a function of the character's type and not the character's psyche.

For critics who want to hold Centlivre to standards set by the best Restoration comedies, her inability to sustain a metaphor through dialogue is obvious. Sir George Airy, the "Gentleman of Four Thousand a Year" in Centlivre's *The Busy Body* (1709), is reputed to be a man of wit. The play's audience, however, must rely on the testimony of other characters since the evidence is too thin for us to judge. Sir George is in love with two women, he thinks: one, a witty vizard who frequents the park; the other, Miranda, a wealthy heiress (of thirty thousand pounds), whose fortune and person are held hostage by her greedy guardian, Sir Francis Gripe. Sir George, of course, does not know that the two ladies are indeed the same person, and therein lies the intrigue when the lovers meet in the first act. Sir George has just given Sir Francis a hundred pounds for the chance to woo Miranda for ten minutes:

> *Sir George:* What tho' my Tongue never spoke, my Eyes said a thousand Things, and my Hopes flatter'd me hers answer'd 'em. If I'm lucky—if not, 'tis but a hundred Guineas thrown away. (Miranda *and* Patch *come forwards.*)
> *Miranda:* Upon what Sir *George:*
> *Sir George:* Ha! my *Incognito*—upon a woman, Madam.
> *Miranda:* They are the worst Things you can deal in, and damage the soonest; your very Breath destroys 'em, and I fear you'll never see your Return, Sir *George*, Ha, Ha!
> *Sir George:* Were they more brittle than *China*, and drop'd to pieces with a Touch, every Atom of her I have ventur'd at if she is but Mistress of thy Wit, ballances Ten times the Sum—Prithee let me see thy Face.
> *Miranda:* By no means, that may spoil your Opinion of my Sense—
> (10–11)

Miranda, of course, does not wish to be discovered; if she is to win Sir George, it must be as Miranda and not as a vizard. Sir George wants to know who the shadowy woman is. These conflicting desires do not let the characters really explore the metaphor of woman as commodity. Neither character really tests or explores the other; the inspirations of intrigue, the character's designs, keep the subjects and metaphors moving. Thus, Sir George soon calls his mysterious lady a "Dish of Chocolate": according to the new metaphor, women are no longer bartered but consumed. Woman as china to woman as chocolate is an intellectually acceptable progression, but most of Centlivre's shifts in metaphor are not so felicitous.

In the best Restoration comedies, metaphors are often milked dry before they are abandoned. In Wycherley's infamous "china scene," the word "china" is worked hard, serving as a metaphor for sex organs, sex acts, and sexual potency. Part of the fun is that two characters, Lady Fidget and Horner, understand the metaphor and two characters, Mrs. Squeamish and Sir Jasper Fidget, do not. Mrs. Squeamish's failure to see the innuendo does not keep her from adding life to the metaphor:

> *Mrs. Squeamish:* Oh, but it may be he may have some you could not find.
> *Lady Fidget.* What d'y think if he had had any left, I would not have had it too? for we women of quality never think we have China enough.
> (4.3–189–92)

The metaphor, here, is not merely a figure of speech, a medium for communication; it is also a dramatic device, showing us Mrs. Squeamish's inability to penetrate the surfaces. In effect, if the characters create the metaphor, the metaphor also creates the characters. This kind of dynamic relationship rarely occurs in Centlivre's drama. One often gets the feeling, for example, that in Etherege or Congreve characters meet just so the author can see what will happen, can watch the displays of wit. Centlivre's characters meet because they must—they meet to satisfy the demands of the plot. And the rapid pace of her plays does not leave much time for exhuberant displays of wit. What we have instead are language devices that move the plot or promote Centlivre's view of her society.

Most noticeable of these devices, perhaps, are the topical allusions, which Centlivre uses often. In act 4, scene 1 of *A Bold Stroke for a Wife,* Centlivre renders the stockjobbing at Jonathan's Coffee House in Exchange Alley, giving us highly realistic dialogue and an education in the business. The scene opens with stockjobbers (brokers) waving "rolls of paper and parchment" and trying to drum up buyers:

> *First Stockjobber:* South Sea at seven-eights! Who buys?
> *Second Stockjobber:* South Sea bonds due at Michaelmas, 1718! Class Lottery tickets!
> *Third Stockjobber:* East India bonds?
> *Fourth Stockjobber:* What, all sellers and no buyers? Gentlemen, I'll buy a thousand pound for Tuesday next at three-fourths.
> *Coffee Boy:* Fresh coffee, Gentlemen, fresh coffee?
> 1968, 4.1.1–7)

The litany of arcana includes references to the Sword Blade Company, the Civil List Lottery, bulls, bears, the Dutch Walk, cocoa beans, and Bohea tea.

By giving us such a close view of stock trading, Centlivre helps the credibility of her character Tradelove, whom we see trying to manipulate the market and win a fortune. Unfortunately, one of his intended victims is Jan van Timtamtirelereletta Heer van Fainwell, Dutch trader, actually Colonel Fainwell in disguise. Tradelove loses a large bet to Colonel Fainwell, but rather than lose the money, he gives up the hand of his ward, Mrs. Ann Lovely, instead. Obviously, Centlivre also uses the language of stockjobbers to poke fun at the profession.

The scene at Jonathan's shows us another feature of Centlivre's language—her fondness for accents. If Colonel Fainwell must impersonate a Dutch trader, he must sound like one, so Centlivre fits him with an accent: "Two duysend pond, mynheer; 'tis gedaen. Dis gentleman sal hold de gelt" (4.1.97–98). Accents can also create verisimilitude (the Dutch accent is part of the Colonel's disguise), but Centlivre never misses an opportunity to mock foreigners, and she likes the sheer fun of absurd speech. When the Colonel needs to trick Periwinkle, an experimental scientist and collector of curiosities (in eighteenth-century terms, a "virtuouso"), he shows off his own curiosities, among them a vial of "poluflosboio" water, which bore Cleopatra's vessel when she sailed to meet Anthony, and a belt:

> *Colonel:* But here's the wonder of the world: this, sir, is called *zona*, or *moros musphonon;* the virtues of this is inestimable.
> *Periwinkle: Moros musphonon!* What in the name of wisdom can that be? To me it seems a plain belt.
> (III.147–50)

These Greek-like neologisms are fun, of course, but they also allow Centlivre to satirize scientists, those who prize the flotsam and jetsam of ages past. Here, the corrupt language suggests the corrupt values of the world's Periwinkles.

Without denying Centlivre's linguistic ingenuity and her taste for the satirical thrust, we can see that her language serves her plot above all else. And so too with her characters. Centlivre created one original character—Marplot, the good-natured and nosey bungler of *The Busy Body*. The rest are basically stock characters, recognizable

Restoration types refurbished for the prudish and fickle audiences of the Augustan stage. In *The Busy Body*, for example, Centlivre gives us two traditional "blocking" agents, Francis Gripe and Sir Jealous Traffic. Sir Francis, a greedy curmudgeon, wants to marry his ward, Miranda, (and her money) and thus tries to thwart the suit of Sir George Airy. But Sir Francis, in comparison to stage guardians of the past, is not very oppressive. Aphra Behn's Sir Patient Fancy is splendidly lecherous, forever leering and plotting a way to get his victim into bed. Sir Francis, though, never gets near a bed, and his passion is never really very threatening:

> *Sir Francis:* And then, Adod, I believe I am Metamorphos'd; my Pulse beats high, and my blood boils, me thinks—(*Kissing and Hugging Her.*)
> *Miranda:* O fye, *Gardee*, be not so violent; Consider the market lasts all the year.
> (39)

This is mild stuff, but Centlivre never lets her characters get more passionate—at least among themselves. Absent from Centlivre's plays is Restoration comedy's exuberant portrayals of sexual encounters. We have neither bed tricks nor risque repartee. When Centlivre places her characters in situations where sex must be a motivation, she usually skirts the issue and writes only suggestively.

Centlivre does not use sex well in *A Bold Stroke for a Wife*, however, when she creates Obadiah and Mrs. Prim, hypocritical Quakers and guardians to Ann Lovely. The couple can't keep their eyes off Ann's revealing bodice, rebuking her for lewdness and demanding that she cover up temptation. Mrs. Prim tells Ann that "Thy naked bosom allureth the eye of the bystander, encourageth the frailty of human nature, and corrupteth the soul with evil longings" (1968, 2.2.26–29). Mr. Prim is less detached: "Verily, thy naked breasts troubleth my outward man; I pray thee hide 'em, Ann. Put on a handkerchief Ann Lovely" (2.2.48–50). Although Prim says that he wants Ann to cover up, he would actually like her to bare her bosom altogether. In fact, Ann is quite aware of his lechery and accuses him of molesting the maid: "Ah, you had no aversion to naked bosoms when you begged her to show you a little, little, little bit of her delicious bubby" (2.2.94–96). Mrs. Prim gives herself away when responding to Ann's scorn of Quaker dress: "Well, well make thy jests, but I'd have thee to know, Ann, that I could have catched as many fish (as thou call'st them) in my time as ever thou didst with all thy fool traps about thee" (5.9–12).

The Prims are engaging but utterly conventional. When *A Bold Stroke for a Wife* was produced, hypocritical puritans had long been a staple on the English stage. All stage puritans, like the Prims, hide their own lust or greed by pointing out the sins of others. As a rule, the stage puritans get duped, so Centlivre found a convenient character to add to her stable of eccentric guardians—all of whom will lose to Colonel Fainwell's ingenuity. Centlivre's plot dictates the nature of her characters.

I have suggested that Centlivre's language and characters serve her plots, which, ostensibly, dominate her plays. But are the intrigue elements of Centlivre's plays so dominating that we worry only about what happens next? Does Centlivre give us plot for plot's sake? On the contrary, plot serves more than itself—plot helps suggest Centlivre's view of society.

Centlivre writes about social problems—arranged marriage, gambling—exploring only occasionally personal vice and not morality. Centlivre's interest in something elemental like love, for example, is almost logistical: how do we get this couple together? She really doesn't care about what love is, what it looks like, or what it feels like. Her characters do not discover their love in the plays—there is no courtship; rather, love is a given, and the action focuses on the plots and counterplots of the lovers and guardians, who have (of course) other plans. Intrigue, not romance, is the keynote.

Centlivre's plays do not argue for specific social reforms. Unlike Aphra Behn, for example, who made it quite clear (without writing social tracts) that she felt women were getting a raw deal from society, Centlivre uses forced marriage not as a subject but as a vehicle for stage business. Nevertheless, Centlivre does display enough concern for social issues to give her plays a Whiggish tenor. Centlivre's position that human beings should be free to marry whom they choose (and have free access to their inheritance) is a subset of the Whig point of view. As H. T. Dickensen has pointed out (1981), the Whigs believed that society should guarantee individuals the rights of life, liberty, and property. Although the Whigs do not believe in democracy (that would be chaos), they believe that the individual has the right to resist tyranny, to resist any government official or function that would deprive him or her of any of these rights. Individuals must have the power to create their own destinies, to make their existence in society less than miserable.

And given the chance, the citizen is capable enough to do it. There is power within, the power of reason. We are not depraved and irrational creatures whose survival is dependent solely upon the grace of God; we are good-natured, rational creatures who, more often than not, use our reason for the good of ourselves and society. And if society is working properly, than the interests of the individual and those of society are the same. The individual is both deserving and capable of the rights that the Whigs would grant.

In one sense, Centlivre's plays are a dramatic fulfillment of Whig philosophy. Sturdy, self-reliant characters win their fortunes and future mates by virtue of their own cleverness—and some good luck. It is the middle-class ethic in operation—work hard, be smart, and success in matters of love and money cannot be too far away, an ethic clearly in operation in Centlivre's *A Bold Stroke for a Wife.*

There is nothing new in the plot of this play: four traditional butts—a scientist, a businessman, a Puritan, and a fop—are duped in succession. Centlivre's audiences were used to seeing fops and fools suffer on-stage for their excesses, usually in the subplot of a play. Centlivre, however, gives us four fools at once and makes them the main event. Naturally, the audience recognizes these refugees from plays of the past and anticipates their extravagant behavior and the just desserts they will eventually suffer. And the audience knows immediately who will dupe them (Colonel Fainwell) and why (to win Mrs. Lovely). Sackbutt, a tavern keeper, tells the Colonel in the first scene that Mrs. Lovely's father "died worth thirty thousand pounds, which he left to this daughter provided she married with the consent of her guardians. But that she might be sure never to do so, he left her in the care of four men, as opposite to each other as light and darkness" (1968, 2.1.82–86). After Sackbutt describes the humors of each guardian, no one doubts for a minute that the Colonel will claim the heiress. The only mystery left for the audience is how the dupes will be duped.

Centlivre's theater audience will certainly laugh at the fools, and to that extent, become engaged by the characters, but, primarily, the

audience is engaged by the unfolding of events. In a play, we antici-
pate the actions, but we also note the orchestration, that is, how
Centlivre has arranged it all, what patterns she has created.

As Thalia Stathas has pointed out in the introduction of *A Bold
Stroke for a Wife*, Centlivre's plot structure is unified by the character
of the Colonel—his need to gull all the guardians is the play's single
premise. Stathas believes this structure is efficient and harmonious,
suggesting that "Like tightly developed variations on a theme, the
action employs varied devices to convey a repeating motif, without
monotony or extraneous complications. It presents a cycle of repeti-
tive episodes and settings, modifying and embellishing them with
new details" (Centlivre 1968, xxiii). Indeed, the audience (with some
reflection) cannot miss the play's movement, which Stathas calls
"contrapuntal."

In act 1, the premise of the play is established when the Colonel
discovers the enormous labors facing any suitor wishing to win the
hand of Ann Lovely. The Colonel, however, is undaunted, and we
learn in the succeeding scene that Ann will not marry and leave her
fortune behind because "Loves makes but a slovenly figure in that
house where poverty keeps the door" (1.2.30–31). The Colonel has an
easy time with his first challenge, the fop; the Colonel puts on some
French finery (including snuff box, watch, and pocket glass), and
affects some French phrases (*les belles Anglaises!*), and easily wins
Sir Philip's signed consent.

Perhaps the audience, at this point, expects the Colonel to move to
the next guardian, but, instead, Centlivre gives us a preview of the
challenges that lie ahead, as Sir Philip accompanies the Colonel (still
in his fop gear) to the house of Obadiah Prim to get sanction from the
rest of the guardians. The Colonel is readily dismissed, but is able to
size up his labors and the audience sees Ann for the first time and
witnesses the abuse she suffers at the hands of the Prims, her current
overseers. Centlivre has thus slowed the pace of her action and set up
the Colonel's contest with the Prims which continues throughout
the play.

The Colonel next tries Periwinkle at the beginning of act 3, disguising himself as another scientist. The Colonel has about won
Periwinkle over with the powers of his bogus curios when his identity is revealed, which spoils the game. This forces the Colonel to find
a new expedient for trying Periwinkle again later on. In the Peri-

winkle variation, then, instead of showing us success on the first pass, or spreading out the action, Centlivre gives us two parts: the unsuccessful first try and the successful second, which comes later in the play.

Tricking Tradelove, the stockbroker, requires three parts—although the Colonel's plan, in this case, goes without a hitch. In the first part—beginning act 4—Tradelove is passed some false information, and he makes a large bet with the Colonel, who is disguised as the Dutch trader Jan van Timtamtirelereletta Heer van Fainwell. The Colonel's accomplice, Freeman, suggests in the following scene (4.2) that Tradewell relieve his debt by convincing the Colonel to accept Ann Lovely in lieu of the money, a trade which the Colonel agrees to in act 4, scene 4. Sandwiched between the second and third parts of the Tradelove affair is the second part of the Periwinkle plot, in which the Colonel uses the bait-and-switch maneuver to get Periwinkle to sign a marriage consent instead of a property lease. During this act, the Colonel also finds a means to trick the Prims. Thus, in act 4, Centlivre has interleaved three of the gulling plots.

With the signatures of the fop, the scientist, and the merchant in hand, the Colonel needs only to acquire the sanction of the Prims, which he wins in act 5. Tricking the Prims is the action that Centlivre spends the most time on, interlacing it with the other actions. Also, tricking the Prims is the only case wherein the Colonel faces the ruin of his plot and then manages to avoid it. This time he comes dressed as a "real" person, Simon Pure, a Quaker from Pennsylvania whom the Prims have never net. Predictably, the genuine Pure shows up at the Prim household, threatening to expose the imposture, but the crisis is averted, and the Colonel wins the Prims' approval.

Stathas is surely right in calling the movement of the play "contrapuntal," suggesting that each time a guardian is gulled, we see a variation on a theme. The four actions of tricking the four guardians are interwoven, and no two of the actions progress in the same way. The fop is duped in a single successful try; the first with Periwinkle is ruined, but the second succeeds; Tradelove is tricked in three parts; and gulling the Prims runs the duration of the play. Centlivre's audience (or reader) leaves the play with the impression that the play is busy, but artfully orchestrated; her plotting is a virtuoso performance, and we enjoy the order, the arrangement.

This is not to suggest, however, that the audience sees only structures. On the contrary, we delight in seeing the resourceful Colonel outwit the tyrannous guardians and steal Ann from their clutches. The delight springs first from our recognizing an old, familiar action. (The play has not developed the delight in us, but has elicited it.) Second, we delight in the Colonel's success because he is the most sympathetic character, and the play is written from his point of view. We see the guardians and Ann as he does—and we are automatically drawn to the character who, with or without our empathy, is the most attractive of the lot.

We are most tempted, of course, to compare the Colonel to the rake of the Restoration stage—but the comparison is abortive. Like a Horner or a Dorimant, for example, the Colonel tricks some foolish characters; however, the Colonel is much less the knave among fools. He enjoys the sport, but there is no evidence that he considers himself society's avenging angel, making sure that extravagant creatures suffer. There is no wasted motion, no gratuitious flagellation of fools. This is so because the Colonel's sole purpose is to marry Ann Lovely—and not merely to bed her. Even Ann's money seems to be of little concern. (Her fortune is basically a plot device to keep the lovers from eloping, which would eliminate the problem of the guardians.) Comparing the Colonel to Restoration rakes only reinforces our notions about how the tastes of theater audiences during the early 1700s differed from those of Restoration audiences.

Another way to view the Colonel is as a knight who works for both himself and society. In act 1, Ann Lovely's maid, Betty, makes us believe that the Colonel will need fantastic powers to rescue his mistress: "Well, I have read of enchanted castles, ladies delivered from the chains of magic, giants killed, and monsters overcome; so that I shall be the less surprised if the Colonel should conjure you out of the power of your guardians. If he does, I am sure he deserves your fortune" (1.2.46–50). Like the knights of Betty's romances, the Colonel, with his retainer, Freeman, defeats the trolls who keep the maiden fair confined. He is, of course, a soldier, and thus, like knights, is physically capable, but like them too, he relies primarily on his native wit and the supernatural powers of kindly magicians and demigods. In describing the Colonel to Betty, Ann suggests his knightly function: "There's something so *jantee* in a soldier, a kind of *je ne sais quois* air that make 'em more agreeable than the rest of mankind. They command regard, as who should say, 'We are your defenders; we preserve your beauties from the insults of rude unpolished foes' " (1.2.53–58). In her next speech, Ann mentions the Colonel's mind and body, invoking supernatural powers for his aid: "But the Colonel has all the beauties of the mind, as well as person.— O all ye powers that favor happy lovers, grant he may be mine! Thou god of love, if thou be'st aught but name, assist my Fainwell' (1.2.65–68).

Calling up the powers of Cupid seems to work for the lovers, and Colonel Fainwell's final speech also suggests his martial prowess and his duty to his king, his religion, and his lady:

> I must beg Sir Philip's pardon when I tell him that I have as much aversion to what he calls dress and breeding as I have to the enemies of my religion. I have had the honor to serve his Majesty and headed a regiment of the bravest fellows that ever pushed a bayonet in the throat of a Frenchman; and not withstanding the fortune this lady brings me, whenever my country wants my aid, this sword and arm are at her service. (5.546–54)

The Colonel is, then, a good knight and a good Whig.

Although Colonel Fainwell's profession has no real bearing on the action of the play—he is resourceful, but he does not need to scale any walls or fight any duels—Centlivre's use of a soldier as the hero of her play, risked the irritation of the Tories in her audience. In the first two decades of the eighteenth century, the span of Centlivre's career as playwright, the Tories had an instinctive distrust of the soldier and the standing army. Many, like Swift, believed that keeping a standing army was "the first and great Step to the Ruin of Liberty" (Swift 1941, 146). The most compelling evidence for this proposition, of course, was the New Model army, which, created by Parliament in 1645, took on a life of its own as a political and military force, a force that resisted dissolution and helped put Charles I to death in 1649.

Swift, who hated a mob in any form, never had to witness the dismantling of England's political institutions by angry brigades of political and religious radicals. On the contrary, the army helped to maintain the status quo, suppressing French imperialism in the War of Spanish Succession and defeating the Jacobite invasions of 1715 and 1745. Nevertheless, the Tories, around 1708, began to oppose the

war with France, arguing that the Whigs and the Duke of Marlborough, general of the English army, had already beaten the French
and were pursuing the war only for personal advantage.

The Tories won this debate, and Anne's Whig ministers were
replaced by Harley, Earl of Oxford and St. John, Viscount Boling-
broke. According to Geoffrey Holmes, the number of soldiers was
reduced after the war from about 100,000 to under 30,000 by 1714,
but the army by now was a fixture (1982, 265). So too was the career
officer, who, if he held a king's commission, could be discharged and
still draw half-pay—by a House of Commons resolution in 1713
(Holmes 1982, 264). Thus, it is no surprise that Swift sees soldiers
overrunning the streets of London and threatening a way of life:

> It is odd, that among a free Trading People, as we call ourselves,
> there should so many be found to close in with those Counsels,
> who have been ever averse from all Overtures towards a Peace.
> But yet there is no great Mystery in the Matter. Let any Man
> observe the Equipages in this Town; he shall find the greater
> Number of those who make a Figure, to be a Species of Men
> quite different from any that were ever known before the Revo-
> lution; consisting either of Generals and Colonels, or of such
> whose whole Fortunes lie in Funds and Stocks: So that *Power*,
> which, according to the old Maxim, was used to follow *Land*, is
> now gone over to *Money*; and the Country Gentlemen is in the
> Condition of a young Heir, out of whose Estate a Scrivener
> receives half the Rents for Interest, and hath a Mortgage on the
> Whole; and is therefore always ready to feed his Vices and
> Extravagancies while there is any Thing left. So that if the War
> continue some Years longer, a Landed Man will be little better
> than a Farmer at a rack Rent, to the Army, and to the publick
> Funds. (1941, 5)

Swift's assertion that the army officer is a new breed—in the profession for status and money—is supported by Holmes, who notes that
"Except during the Interregnum there were few, in [sic] any, periods
. . . when the self-made man flourished in the army to the extent
that he did for the quarter-century after the 1688 Revolution" (269).
And some of these "Species of Men" did use their position to become
quite wealthy. No longer did the Tory land-owner dominate the profession. Thus, Centlivre, in making the hero of her piece a soldier,

risks alienating the Tories, who believed that the army had become a Whiggish institution and a symbol of the Whigs' increasing influence in government and society at large. As a soldier for the Crown, the Colonel resists the tyranny that the Jacobites would impose on England. As a magician/artist figure, the Colonel also resists tyranny—the tyranny of those who would block the progress of romantic love. Consider Betty's verb when she says "I shall be the less surprised if the Colonel should *conjure* you out of the power of your guardians" (1.2.48–49; emphasis mine). The Colonel does not lay siege to the guardians' fortress, overwhelming them with force. He sneaks in and beats them with guile and craft. He is a protean being, artfully changing his disguise as the situation warrants. When the Colonel tries to win Periwinkle, the motif is magic. Periwinkle is impressed by the Colonel's Egyptian dress and his vial of *poluflosboio,* but he finds the *moros musphonon*—the girdle—stunning. When Periwinkle puts on the girdle, the Colonel and his accomplice, Sackbut, pretend that they can't see him. When the Colonel dons the girdle, he too disappears—through a trap door—and Periwinkle is amazed: "Ha! Mercy upon me! My flesh creeps upon my bones—this must be a conjurer, Mr. Sackbut" (3.193–94).

Like Prospero, the Colonel finds an appropriate means to trick each quarry. He appears as a scientist to the scientist and as a fop to the fop. All of the Colonel's victims are vain; all prey on society in some way. Tradelove manipulates the economy to extort money; the fop imports French customs; the scientist dwells in the past and in the fantastic; the puritans advocate, hypocritically, retirement from society. All of these creatures either corrupt or leech from society. In the context of the play, all are tyrants keeping Ann Lovely from her fortune and her lover. But through the white magic of the play's central force, the Colonel, order is restored, and love is allowed to run its course.

As the chief arranger and author of the guardians' travails, the Colonel may also remind us of Centlivre herself. The didactic function of Centlivre's plays is never too far below the surface. Although the prime business of her drama is good-natured fun, she is always aware that her audiences seemed to demand (at least from new plays) that virtuous characters find reward and vicious characters punishment. Art helps to redeem society from squalid people. And to this end, Centlivre shows tyrannies—whether the tyranny of vice as in

The Basset Table (1705) or the tyranny of parents as in *The Wonder* (1714)—thrown off through the devices of resourceful characters. Society is restored through rearrangements effected by Centlivre—and the Colonel.

Whether we see the Colonel as magician, knight, or author, he embodies the middle-class dream and sanctions Whig values. Faced with impossible odds, the Colonel uses his own wit to rescue Ann Lovely from the clutches of her guardians. The Colonel has a confederate in his merchant friend, Freeman, and gets some eleventh-hour assistance from Ann herself, but, essentially, he is alone in his labors. God and government are not around. The Colonel's self-reliance is supported, of course, by his industry and resourcefulness, both important qualities for any middle-class hero. Thus, the Colonel seizes every opportunity and finds ways to overcome obstacles. He never gives up and is thereby successful in his quest, winning a clever but graceful woman and her fortune.

If Centlivre's plays are dominated by intrigue, if wit and character are only subordinate elements, this does not make the plays second rate or rob them of meaning. In Centlivre's case, the intrigue is the point—the intrigue in *A Bold Stroke* is the method of a man who frees a woman from her oppressive guardian. Society, the play suggests, needs to accommodate the basic right of all people in freedom. Perhaps Centlivre's plays are best described as good fun, but her Whiggish assumptions resonate through the laughter.

Works Cited

Centlivre, Susanna. 1968. *A Bold Stroke for a Wife.* Ed. Thalia Stathas. Lincoln: Univ. of Nebraska Press.

———. 1981. *The Busy Body: A Comedy.* London [1709].

Dickinson, H. T. 1981. "Whiggism in the Eighteenth Century." In *The Whig Ascendancy: Colloquie on Hanoverian England.* Ed. John Cannon. London: Edward Arnold, 28–44.

Holmes, Geoffrey. 1982. *Augustan England: Professions, State and Society, 1680–1730.* London: George Allen & Unwin.

Swift, Jonathan. 1941. *The Examiner and Other Pieces Written in 1710–11.* Vol. 3 of *The Prose Writings of Jonathan Swift.* Ed. Herbert Davis. 14 vols. London: Basil Blackwell.

Wycherley, William. 1979. *The Country Wife.* Ed. Arthur Friedman. Oxford: Clarendon.

Aphra Behn: A Dramatist
in Search of the Novel

ROSE ZIMBARDO

> . . . pray tell me then
> Why Women should not write as well as Men . . .

Aphra Behn, the first *professional* female writer in our tradition (as she put it, she was "forc'd to write for Bread and not ashamed to owne it") is interesting for a number of reasons. To a historian of ideas she is important because her works, chronologically considered, reflect the drastic changes in dramatic imitation of nature that occurred during her era, which I have traced elsewhere, from imitation of nature as Idea, through imitation of the disjunction between ideal and "real," to imitation of nature as the human actual (Zimbardo 1986). To a critic who would explore the origins of the novel she is interesting as an unacknowledged pioneer in that form. Her novel *Oroonoko*, too readily dismissed by critics as a "combination of realistic action and precieuse style" to "an effect that is grotesque" (Novak 1967, xi), is to my mind the first genuine novel in English. To feminist critics Behn is interesting in two ways. First though her dramaturgic practice is indistinguishable from that of her male contemporaries, from her earliest plays the very ideas she chose to imitate (ideas of the passions) are subtly different from those they strove to capture (ideas of heroic glory). Second, with the possible exception of Ford in *'Tis Pity She's a Whore* and Webster in *The White Devil*, she is the first playwright in English to try her hand at creating *heroines* of "irregular greatness" (Waith 1962).

An outspoken feminist herself, Behn wrote,

had the Plays I have writ come forth under any Mans Name, and
never known to have been mine; I appeal to all unbyast Judges
of Sense, if they had not said that Person had made as many good
Comedies, as any Man that has writ in our Age; but a Devil on't
the Woman damns the Poet. (Preface, *The Lucky Chance*)[1]

In her own day she was assailed for impropriety by her political
enemies (Behn was most extravagantly a Tory and a skillful mocker
of Whigs); it was in the more decorous eighteenth century that she
began to be attacked on moral grounds, as in Pope's famous couplet:

> The Stage how loosely does Astrea tread
> Who fairly puts all Characters to bed.

Inevitably, that theme reached crescendo in the Victorian period.
Lady-Critics found her an embarrassment to the sex: "Even if her life
remained pure, it was amply evident that her mind was tainted to the
very core. Grossness was congenial to her. . . . Mrs. Behn's indelicacy was useless and worse than useless, the superfluous addition of a
corrupt mind and vitiated taste" (Kavanagh 1863, xxix). Gentlemen-
critics, more deeply horrified, pictured her leading her already
debased male contemporaries on a merry dance into Hell's Mouth—
"No one equalled this woman on downright nastiness save Ravenscroft and Wycherley. . . . with Dryden she vied in indecency and
was not overcome. . . . She was a mere harlot, who danced through
uncleaness and dared them [the male dramatists] to follow" (Doran
in Behn 1915, xxix). As quaintly ludicrous as we may find these
indictments to be, it is interesting, I think, that only one of Behn's
plays, *The Rover* (her worst in my judgment), was made available in
popular editions during the 1950s when revaluation of Restoration
drama was undertaken in earnest, and it is only in the very recent past
that her most interesting play, *The Lucky Chance*, has become easily
available and that critics have begun to take her seriously.

As I have suggested elsewhere, had we no other remaining evidence
than the works of Dryden and Behn upon which to judge, we could
yet trace the course in dramatic imitation that charts one of the most
important revolutions in aesthetics that has occurred in the history of
English thought. I do not mean to suggest that Behn was a great
dramatist; in my opinion she was not among the very best of her time.
Neither do I mean to suggest that she was a theorist, as Dryden was.

Quite the contrary, Behn herself, who in many respects was an accurate evaluator of her own performance, distinguishes Dryden among the male playwrights with whom she compares herself:

> Affectation hath always a greater share both in the action and discourse of men than truth and judgment have; and for our Modern [poets and playwrights] *except our most inimitable Laureate,* I dare say I know of none that write at such a formidable rate, but that a woman may reach their greatest heights. (Preface, *The Dutch Lover*)

In her method of dramatic imitation and in her understanding of what the *Nature* is that art must imitate, Behn is indistinguishable from her male contemporaries. Her earliest plays, like *The Young King* (written in the 1660s, though it was not produced until 1679; Summers 2:103), are attempts to imitate and refine upon ideas of nature exactly as those plays of Dryden or Howard that were written in the sixties (*The Conquest of Granada, Tyrannick Love, The Duke of Lerma,* or *The Vestal Virgin,* for example):

> *Orsames:* I to my self could an *Idea* frame
> Of Man in much more excellence.
> Had I been *Nature,* I had varied still,
> And made such different *Characters* of Men
> They should have bow'd and made a God of me,
> Ador'd and thank'd me for their great Creation. . . .
> (*The Young King* 2.1.4)

Here nature is a configuration of ideas and character is the delineation of essences. Characters are concepts that are placed in careful juxtaposition in the service of a rhetorical design that aims at precision of definition. As Eric Rothstein puts it, the heroic play of the 1660s "treats characters against a fixed grid of love and honor" (1967, 31). In Behn's first play she is trying her hand at the mounting dialectical progression of the heroic mode—with an important difference that I hope will be made clear later in this essay: i.e., for Behn the height of definition is usually rendered in a pastoral as opposed to a martial conception of the heroic.

Again, in an early play like *The Amorous Prince* Behn is in pursuit of the same three-tiered comic vision of ideationally conceived nature, or "reality," that we find in Etherege's *Love in a Tub* or in the

Dryden-Davenant adaptation of *The Tempest, The Enchanted Island* (1664). Here Behn's structure, like theirs, embraces a high plane wherein ideas play against one another in imitation of the stately postures of the soul:

> *Alberto:* Oh how my Soul's divided
> Between my Adoration and my Amity!
> Friendship, thou sacred bond, hold fast thy Interest
> For yonder Beauty has a subtle power.
> (1.4.4, p. 140)

On the middle plane of action, meanwhile, Idea is blunted and confused by its descent into the world of actuality:

> *Laura:* Oh where is all your Honour and your Virtue?
> *Fred:* Just where it was, there's no such real thing. I know that thou wer't made to be possess't, And he that does refuse it loves thee least.
> (3.1.162)

And on the low plane ideas are parodies in mock-heroic strain in the actions of the cowardly Lorenzo and the mercenary Isabella.

In the 1670s, in plays like *The Feign'd Courtesans* (1679), Behn is striving for the same disjunctive unity in vision and dramatic design toward which her male contemporaries aimed, wherein a heightened ideal is played against a downwardly exaggerated actual. Dryden delineated this opposition of perspectives upon reality most obviously in *Marriage à la Mode* (1673), Wycherley and Etherege more subtly in *The Country Wife* (1675) and *The Man of Mode* (1676). In this manner the high planes of the earlier comic design are absorbed into the middle plane of action where they play against one another to satiric effect, neither cancelling the validity of its opposing perspective. What is interesting is that Behn, like those masters of dramatic satire, Etherege and Wycherley, achieves her disjunctive effect dialogically:

> *Marcella:* The Evening's soft and calm, as happy Lovers thoughts;
> And here are Groves where the kind meeting Trees
> Will hide us from the Amorous gazing Croud.

Cornelia: What should we do there, sigh 'til our wandering
   Breath,
Has rais'd a gentle Gale amongst the Boughs;
To whose melancholy Musick, we
Laid on a bed of Moss, and new fall'n leaves
Will reade the dismal tale of Eccho's love!
—No! I can make better use of Famous Ovid.
(II, i)

What is perhaps as interesting is that while Etherege, Wycherley and
Shadwell choose to frame the ideal against which their satiric counters play in the heroic Homeric/Virgilian mode, Behn chooses to
frame her ideal in terms of the erotic classical model, Ovid.

In the eighties, when the actual overwhelms the ideal and satire is
no longer possible as a detached, literary design of opposing
perspectives—idealized and burlesque—upon reality, Aphra Behn
saw two alternatives and took them both. In a play like *The City
Heiress* (1682) she places the disjunctive unity that she had designed
earlier in a literary context into the actual circumstances of contemporary life. The disjunction is the same—i.e., the ideal versus the
satiric—but the dimensions of disjunctive interplay are secularized
and made present. The charming, "heroic" vices of the Tories
(drinking, gambling, and whoring) are placed in contrast to the
despicable, grotesque vices of the Whigs (hypocrisy, greed, and sedi-
tion). Character is still concept, but rendered typologically though it
is, it is realized in terms of a present contemporary situation. Like
Otway in *The Orphan* (1682) Behn translates a conflict of ideational
counters from the removed literary realm into the realm of experience.

The second alternative response to the movement in the eighties
toward imitation of nature as imitation of the human actual is that
which Behn chooses in *The Lucky Chance* (1687). The frame of this
play was borrowed from Shirley's *The Lady of Pleasure* (1635), but
what in Shirley is a stock comic situational device—i.e., Aretina, a
sexually voracious, married older woman tricks a young man into
bed with her by making him believe that he has sold himself to the
devil—is humanized and "novelized" by Behn. We are made to see
the situation from the inside and to use it to explore a real contemporary social problem, the agonies arising out of forced marriage.

Character is no longer the delineation of concept or type; it moves toward simulating people. Action is no longer in service of a rhetorical design; it is invested with *probability*. The situation of a January-May marriage, a subject for comic ridicule since Chaucer, is presented here for serious consideration and sober discussion:

> *L. Full.:* Oh how fatal are forc'd Marriages!
> How many Ruins one such Match pulls on!
> Had I but kept my Sacred Vows to *Gayman*
> How happy had I been—how prosperous he!
> Whilst now I languish in a loath'd embrace
> Pine out my Life with Age—Consumptive Coughs.
> (II, i)

The actual circumstances that cause forced marriages are explored; Lucretia is driven to marry Sir Feeble Fainwood by economic necessity. Vows are not broken, as in a play of the sixties, to present the occasion for a rhetorical "turn" that will set up a dialectical antithesis between concepts of love and honor; rather, as in life, persons are forced to break promises by social pressure and economic need. Moreover, a character's internal response to breaking a vow is considered. For example, Lucretia is saved from the loathsome necessity of consummating her marriage to Sir Feeble by a stock comic trick in which her lover, Bellmour, frightens Sir Feeble away from the marriage bed by appearing as the bloody ghost of himself. In any earlier comedy (*The Country Wife*, for example) a comic trick upon the Senex Amans is a situational device designed to draw the laughter of the audience. But here Lucretia's response is designed to give us pause: "Blest is this kind Release, and yet methinks it grieves me to consider how the old Man is frightened" (V, iii) By investing Lucretia with sympathy for the old man, Behn not only creates the illusion of interiority in Lucretia, but draws Sir Feeble and the stock comic scene in which he is engaged closer to us and make a totally improbable situation probable. Whereas by the operation of an earlier comedy our attention would rest on the surface of a situation in which stock types—Senex Amans, Juvens, and Erotia—enact a stock design, here we are forced to explore below the design and to imagine what a character might "feel" in such a situation. Lucretia's response is multi-textured, and, because it is, Lucretia becomes a "character" in our modern sense of the term. Like her male colleagues in the late eighties and early nineties (Congreve in *The Double Dealer* and Dryden in *Don Sebastian*, for example), Behn is attempting to imitate nature as the human actual and to probe beyond the surface actual to the inner "feelings" and unspoken thoughts of human beings.

But Behn goes one step further than her male counterparts. Dryden says in the preface to *Don Sebastian* that he thought his play more suitable to the study than the stage. Of necessity, drama must *show* the ideas, passions, and motives it represents in action and declaration. It cannot, as the novel does, admit us into the inner arena of human feeling and thought. When it tries to do so, it fails as drama (consider, for example, O'Neill's *Strange Interlude*). In the late 1680s and into the 1690s playwrights strained against the confining limits of their form. Their responses to the vexing problem of how to imitate the human actual in a representational idiom that required them to *show* were various. For instance, in the 1690s, soliloquy was changed from its earlier iconic function (i.e., to arrest action and provide, in emblematic declamation, a gloss upon it) to be a device by which a playwright could present a character "thinking out loud." This is Congreve's method in *The Double Dealer* and Southerne's in *The Wives Excuse*. Further, language was naturalized from declamation into dialogue, and was broken to express "unconscious" verbal tics in characters, or pauses, in which speech was suspended for "thought." Behn uses the device of the verbal tic admirably in creating the character of Sir Feeble, and Otway used it in portraying the character of Antonio in *Venice Preserved* so effectively that the portrait still manages to disgust us.

Nonetheless, the most interesting response by a dramatist under pressure to imitate a wholly new epistemological conception of nature came from Aphra Behn. If she was not a leader dancing her male colleagues to hell, she was certainly a leader in showing them the possibilities of novelization. M. M. Bakhtin says that the most salient feature involved in the novelization of classical genres is the move to "insert into these other genres an indeterminacy, a certain semantic open-endedness, a living contact with unfinished, evolving contemporary reality" (1983, 6–7). In *The Lucky Chance* Behn not only forces us to consider stock literary situations in terms of contemporary reality, and not only naturalizes discourse from declamation into dialogue, but also uses the specific, descriptive techniques of a novelist to bring ideas into contact with "evolving contemporary reality." For example, in earlier plays, including Behn's own, we are led to think of poverty in literary terms—i.e., the unknown prince or princess lives in a shepherd's cottage from which his/her majestic virtue still shines forth. Surely we are never made to imagine what the real circumstances of a young man who gives up "all for love" might be. In *The Lucky Chance* Behn forces us to envision the real circumstances behind a very old stock comic situation. The stock situation, prevalent since the Jacobean "City Comedy," is that of an aristocratic lover, down on his luck, who is forced to solicit the help of his city landlady. In Behn's play we are made by the employment of novelistic devices to envision the situation naturalistically. Lady Fullbank's servant, Bredwell, who has been her emissary in launching the trick that will bring her generous lover, Gayman, to enjoy the reward of having given his all for love of her, reports to Lady Fullbank with a description of the circumstances under which Gayman lives—a description that badly strains the limits of dramatic representation:

> *Bred:* . . . at the door [I] encountered the beastly thing he calls a Landlady; who look't as if she had been of her own Husband's making, compos'd of moulded Smith's dust. I ask'd for Mr Wasteall [Gayman's assumed name] and she began to open— and did so rail at him, that what with her Billingsgate, and her Husband's hammers, I was both deaf and dumb—at last the hammers ceased and she grew weary, and call'd down Mr Wasteall, but he not answering—I was sent up a ladder rather than a pair of Stairs. . . .
>
> 'Tis a pretty convenient Tub, Madam [Gayman's room]. He may lie a long in't, there's just room for an old join'd stool besides the Bed, which one cannot call a Cabin about the largeness of a Pantry Bin, or a Usurer's Trunk; there had been Dorex [very cheap material] Curtins to't in days of Yore; but they were now annihilated, and nothing to save his Eyes from the Light, but my Landlady's Blue Apron, ty'd by strings before the Window, in which stood a six-penny Looking Glass, that shew'd as many faces as the Scene in *Henry* the Eighth, which

cou'd just stand upright, and then a Comb case fill'd it.
(I, iii)

The scene is not the anonymous "A Room in Mrs _____'s House" of drama. Rather it sets a specific location of the kind that we find in the novel. We are made by the description to notice particular details—the sizes, shapes, and color of objects—to imagine seeing and hearing as we do in life. We *see* the ragged apron at the window; we *hear* the maddening din of the smith's hammers. Consequently, as in a novel, we are made to enter the scene that Bredwell describes. We are made to enter into, and to experience, poverty.

As I noted earlier, I do not believe that Aphra Behn was among the best playwrights of her day. On the other hand, I most heartily believe she was among the best and first early English novelists. When we begin our study of the novel with Defoe we are in grave error, for not only is Behn's most famous novel, *Oroonoko,* a worthy contender with *Robinson Crusoe* in quality, but we also find in Behn's creative history that movement in understanding that made the novel a necessary form. In Behn herself we find an innovator in the search for the novel who changed the course of literary history.

From her earliest works Behn was in search of a form that could best express the passions. It was, in fact, part of her argument for women's creative rights that women better understand the realm in which the arts exceed the sciences in providing understanding of our human condition. "Plays," she wrote, "have no great room for that which is man's great advantage over women, that is Learning." (I, p.224).

Her search for the necessary form began early, and her first response was to search for a dramatic design that would be loose enough to allow her to delineate ideas of the passions freed from the "gridwork of love and honor" (Rothstein), which demanded a dialectical progression leading to an ultimate, governing idea of glory. The original source of *The Rover,* for example, was a play, *Thomaso,* written by Killigrew during the interregnum and never meant to be presented on the stage. As Summers says, "*Thomaso* may be better described as a dramatic romance than a comedy intended for the boards" (Behn 1915, 1:4). What Behn found in Killigrew's dramatized serial form of the romance was a form that could display aspects of the passions without the necessity to put them into dialectical progression. Her intention, like that of her male contemporaries, was to imitate ideas of the passions. Her assumption was precisely that which was expressed by Thomas Stanley in his great compendium of philosophy (1669): i.e., that the amatory passion is our best conduct for transcendence from the corporeal bondage to which our human condition subjects us. Stanley writes that human beings' "only means of release from this bondage, is the amatory life; which by sensible beauties, exciting in the Soul a remembrance of the Intellectual, raiseth her from this terrene of life to the eternal; by flame of love refined into an Angel (1687, 1:34). This conception, and the conception that was wedded to it in the seventeenth century, argued that heroic virtue is a "Habit of Mind . . . inspir'd from above" that elevates us "above mankind as much as human nature could bear and renders . . . [us] like a Deity" (Anon. 1673, 18).

But how was a dramatist who had chosen to abandon the methodology whereby transcendence was figured in a dialectical progression toward metaphysical idea to delineate a conception of heroic love? Behn not only aimed at imitating heroic transcendence, but she also considered herself to *be* heroic in that attempt: "I value Fame as much as if I had been born a Hero; and if you rob me of that, I can retire from the ungrateful World and scorn its fickle favors" (Preface, *The Lucky Chance*, 3, p.186). Her early method, within the serial form she had chosen to adopt, was to create heroines of irregular greatness—Angela Bianca in *Rover I*, La Nuche in *Rover II*, and Laura Lucretia in *The Feign'd Courtesans*. All of these are figures of courtesans, outside the boundaries of any social structure. They are not characters in our modern sense; rather they are ideas of a passion so great that it breaks the boundaries, cosmic or societal, that hem the human spirit—precisely in the manner that heroes of irregular greatness, like Dryden's Almanzor and Morat are:

> *Laura Lucretia:* Honour, that hated Idol, even by those
> That set it up to worship. No,
> I have a Soul, my Boy, that is all Love;
> And I'll the Talent which Heaven lent improve.
> (*The Feign'd Courtesans*, II,I)

Two things about Behn's choice are interesting. The first is that she saw love itself as the boundary-breaking, elevating passion—not an idea of love that exists in the service of an idea of honor, as in the traditional love-and-honor formula, but rather as an idea of love that by itself *subsumes* honor and is in itself heroic. The second is that she symbolizes this idea in a figure that is *outside* the dialectical progression of love-and-honor that informs a heroic drama. We can see from this choice that at a time when other dramatists make character subordinate to rhetorical design, Behn is striving to embody an idea in a free-floating ideational figure.

Progressively, Behn attempts further and further to embody idea in character, even when character is typologically conceived. Progressively Behn is in the forefront of the movement that sought first to ground Idea in the actual, and, later, to redefine the peripheries in which "reality," or "nature" is understood.

Writing in 1696, after Behn was dead and the revolution in aesthetics in which she had participated was over, her first editor, Charles Gildon, admired in Behn her ability to approximate the actual in dialogue that was "Conversation gay and genteel" and her ability to portray love not as an idea but as a human emotion. (Behn, 1915, 4:317). Behn came into her own only when she discovered the scope for investigation of the passions that the novel afforded. What the novel form allowed her to do was to lead her readers into the millieu of her characters, and beyond that, into the inner human realm, where what in fact *is not* is often in imagination more "real" than what *is*. For example, in Behn's novel *The Fair Jilt*, an aristocratic lady, much in the mode of Laura Lucretia (*The Feign'd Courtesans*), lives in a beguinage. There she encounters a friar, who was once a prince and who is absolutely faithful to his vows. The motivation for Miranda's attempt to seduce the friar, gradually evolves within Miranda's own mind. Love is conceived here as an internal process of fantasizing:

> She imagined, if he could inspire Love in a coarse, grey, ill-made Habit, a shorn Crown, a hair-cord about his Waist, bare-legg'd in Sandals instead of Shoes; what must he do . . . with all that Youth and Beauty, set off by Advantage of Dress and Equipage? She frames an idea of him all gay and splendid, and looks at his present Habit as some Disguise proper for the stealths of Love, some feign'd put-on-Shape, with more Security to approach a Mistress and make himself happy; and that the Robe laid by, she

has the Lover in his proper Beauty, the same as he would have been, if any other Habit . . . were put off: In the Bed, in the silent Gloomy Night, and the Embraces of her Arms, he loses all the Friar, and assumes all the Prince; and that awfull Reverence due alone to his Holy Habit, he exchanges for a thousand dalliances. . . . These, and a thousand other Self-flatteries, all vain and indiscreet, took up her waking Nights and now more retired days. (*The Fair Jilt*, 5, p.224)

By way of the novel Behn had penetrated to the internal arena of human thought and imagination; she had caught the passions in their inception, before the stage in which they would be expressed in action or declaration.

Before any of her contemporaries Aphra Behn caught the direction that poetic mimesis *had* to take in order to be faithful to conceptions of Nature that were born in the Enlightenment. For that she is truly heroic and worthy of our admiration.

Notes

1. *The Works of Aphra Behn,* ed. Montague Summers, 6 vols. (London, 1915, reprint New York: Benjamin Bloom, 1967), p. xxix. All references to the works of Aphra Behn are to this edition.

Works Cited

Anonymous. 1673. *A Description of the Academy of Atheinian Virtuosi.* London.

Behn, Aphra. 1915. *The Works of Aphra Behn.* Ed. Montague Summers. 6 vols. Reprint New York: Benjamin Bloom, 1967.

Bakhtin, M. M. 1983. *The Dialogic Imagination.* Trans. C. Emerson and M. Holquist. Austin: Univ. of Texas Press.

Kavanagh, Julia. 1863. *English Women of Letters.* Quoted in Behn 1915.

Novak, Maximillian E. and David Stuart Rodes. 1967. Introduction to *Thomas Southerne, Oroonoko.* Regents Restoration Drama Series. Lincoln: Univ. of Nebraska Press.

Rothstein, Eric. 1967. *Restoration Tragedy.* Madison: Univ. of Wisconsin Press.

Stanley, Thomas. 1687. *The History of Philosophy.* 2d ed. London.

Waith, Eugene M. 1962. *The Herculean Hero.* New York: Columbia Univ. Press.

Epilogue

By the end of the eighteenth century, fewer and fewer women were writing for the stage. "To know the temper of the time with accuracy, is one of the first talents requisite to a dramatic author," Mrs. Inchbald observed in 1808, in her preface to *John Bull.* And that temper had clearly changed, both in literature and politics. As Inchbald had written in 1807, "A dramatist must not speak of national concerns, except in one dull round of panegyrick. He must not allude to the feeble minister of state, nor to the ecclesiastical coxcomb" (*The Artist,* June 1807).

Politics, though, were not the only cause for frustration. The issue of women as writers had not lost its fire. The prologue to Inchbald's *All on a Summer Day* (1787), her only theatric disaster, recalls Behn's prologue cited earlier, recalling a Golden Age when women" Once were fam'd in story, and could write, / Equal to Men; cou'd govern, nay cou'd fight." Inchbald, unlike Behn, did not write her own prologues, and the touch of a male hand is surely evident:

> When haughty man usurp'd fair learning's throne
> And made the Empire of the stage his own
> He rul'd a realm where Genius seldom smil'd
> And Nonsense hail'd him as her darling child.
> And oft when meaner subjects would avail
> Rais'd the loud laugh by Gammer Gurton's tale
> Bard follow's Bard, yet few could justly claim
> The laurell'd trophies of a lasting name
> 'Till gentle woman seiz'd the pen and writ

And shone not less in beauty than in wit.
Woman! by honest emulation fir'd
By sense directed & by wit inspir'd
Sportive, yet elegant; tho' pointed, chaste,
To mend our manners & refine our taste:
Man from her learnt the fascinating art
To please the fancy, captivate the heart
And paint the scenes of happiness and strife
The various scenes that chequer human life.

The praise of women in this passage suggests the attempt to weaken her threat, or to present it in softened language that put woman in her proper place as gentle companion. The temper of the time had clearly changed enough so that theater managers felt the need to "package" their women playwrights in conservative wrappers, to deflate the Jacobin influence of contemporary writers like William Godwin.

The temper of the times by 1793 had not improved, as a prologue to Inchbald's *Every One Has His Fault* confirms:

Our Author, who accuses great and small . . .
Sends me with dismal voice, and lengthen'd phiz,
Humbly to own one dreadful fault of his:
A fault, in modern Authors not uncommon,
It is,—now don't be angry—He's—*a woman*. . . .

The Rights of Women [*sic*] says a female pen
Are, to do every thing as well as Men.
To think, to argue, to decide, to write,
To talk, undoubtedly—perhaps, to fight.

After conceding that women may "make too free—and know too much," the prologue continues:

But since the Sex at length had been inclin'd
To cultivate that useful part—the mind;-
Since they have learned to read, to write, to spell;-
Since some of them have wit,—and use it well;—
Let us not force them back with brow severe,
Within the pale of ignorance and fear,
Confin'd entirely to domestic arts,

Producing only children, pies, and tarts,
The fav'rite fable of the tuneful Nine,
Implies that female genius *is divine.*

The author here makes many concessions, pleads rather than asserts, chooses wit and allusion rather than the aggressive demands Behn favored. But the key to the new temper of the time by 1800 is found not only in this more evasive language theater managers found necessary as prefaces to productions; tired of the constraints, the pressing censorship, the whims of audiences and actors, women turned their energy away from the stage, and wrote novels. "The Novelist," Inchbald asserted, "is a free agent. He lives in a land of liberty, whilst the Dramatic Writer exists but under a despotic government.— . . . Whilst the poor dramatist is . . . confined to a few particular provinces; the novel-writer has the whole world to range, in search of men and topics . . . Nothing is forbidden, nothing is withheld from the imitation of a novelist, except—other novels " (*The Artist*).

Women had, of course, been writing fiction for as long as they had been writing plays. Behn, like Inchbald, practiced both genres. But just as the Licensing Act of 1737 drove many off the stage and into the freer domain of the novel, so the tumultuous politics of the 1790s seems to have persuaded writers to explore the novel, bringing to it the lessons learned from the stage.

While in recent years feminist cartographers have begun to map the brave new world women pioneered in fiction, few have risked exploring the less charted domains of the stage. Yet as the twenty-two essays collected here establish, these new territories contain not the fearsome amazons or shocking anthropapagi of which critical tradition warned us, but less miraculous creatures: actresses, playwrights, entrepreneurs, editors, critics, scholars, patronesses, and prostitutes. Their critics called them whores, or praised them as blameless paradigms. For us, they are women whose journeys and discoveries merit inclusion in the literary atlas. **Curtain Calls** invites them back for one more bow.

Contributors

William J. Burling is associate professor of English at Southwest Missouri State University. A specialist in eighteenth-century drama, he has articles published or forthcoming in *Modern Philology, Philological Quarterly, Theater Survey, Theatre History Studies, Essays in Theatre, Music and Letters, Theatre Notebook, Studies in Bibliography*, and other journals. At present he is preparing *A Catalogue of New Plays and Entertainments on the London Stage, 1700–1737* and a book on summer theater in London, 1660–1800.

Douglas R. Butler is assistant professor at the College of St. Rose in New York State where he teaches courses in literature and technical writing.

Constance Clark's book, *Three Augustan Women Playwrights*, was published in 1986. She has also written introductions for the Scholars' Facsimilies reprints of Mary Pix's novel *The Inhumane Cardinal* (1696) and Sarah Fyge Egerton's *Poems on Several Occasions* (1703). Among other publications Clark has contributed articles to *A Dictionary of British and American Women Writers 1660–1800*, and *Notable Women in American Theatre*. In 1986 she was a summer fellow at the William Andrews Clark Memorial Library. She is the librarian at the Princeton Library in New York.

Nancy Cotton is professor of English and director of the Master of Arts in Liberal Studies program at Wake Forest University, where she teaches English drama to 1642 and modern drama. She is the author of *John Fletcher's Chastity Plays* (Bucknell University Press, 1973) and *Women Playwrights in England c. 1363–1750* (Bucknell University Press, 1980), as well as articles and book reviews on English drama. She is a frequent lecturer on drama and women's studies.

Ellen Donkin is an assistant professor in the theater program at Hampshire College in Amherst, Massachusetts, where she teaches theater history and playwrighting, and directs. Her current research is on the eighteenth-century playwright and anthologist, Elizabeth Inchbald. Her work focuses on the ways in which gender theory and semiotics are focusing us to rewrite the history of women in the theater. Articles include an essay called "Directing Stein," and *Theatre Three* which explores the limitations of traditional director training for the director attempting a play by Gertrude Stein and an article on Duse and Bernhardt in *Turn-of-the-Century Women*.

Frances M. Kavenik is assistant professor of English and humanities at the University of Wisconsin—Parkside, where she is director of the ACCESS Program. She is co-author (with Eric Rothstein) of *The Designs of Carolean Comedy*, Southern Illinois University Press, 1988, and associate editor of *Handbook of American Women's History*, forthcoming from Garland Press. She has taught and presented papers on Restoration drama, women in literature Jane Austen, Elizabeth Gaskell, and film.

Kendall is assistant professor of theater at Smith College. She is an actress and writer of journals, plays, fiction, and autobiography as well as academic articles, and one of her autobiographical essays is included in *Politics of the Heart*, edited by Jeanne Vaughn and Sandra Pollock, (Firebrand Press, 1987). Kendall is also the editor of *Love and Thunder*, an anthology of eighteenth-century women's plays (Methuen U.K., Ltd., 1988).

Jean B. Kern, emerita professor of English, Coe College, has been active in the eighteenth-century field for several years. The author of *Dramatic Satire in the Age of Walpole, 1720–1750*, she has written numerous articles on eighteenth-century dramatists and novelists alike for the *Philological Quarterly, Eighteenth-Century Studies, Studies in Eighteenth-Century Culture,* and *Modern Philology*. Her most recent work is on English women silversmiths, 1750–1800.

Edward A. Langhans, in addition to publishing dozens of articles and reviews, is the author of *Restoration Promptbooks* and *Eighteenth Century British and Irish Promptbooks: A Descriptive Bibliography;* co-author of *A Biographical Dictionary of Actors, Actresses, Musicians, Dancers, Managers, and Other Stage Personnel in London, 1600–1800* (12 volumes in print, 16 projected); editor of *Five Restoration Theatrical Adaptations;* and co-editor of *An International Dictionary of Theatre Language.* Langhans has presented papers at meetings of the Modern Language Association, the Educational Theatre Association, the American Society for Theatre Research, the International Shakespeare Congress, and the Society for Theatre Research, London. He served for 12 years as chairman of the department of Drama and Theatre at the University of Hawaii, where he has directed, designed, and acted in over 40 plays, many of them from the seventeenth and eighteenth centuries.

Cecilia Macheski is professor of English at LaGuardia Community College of the City University of New York. With Mary Anne Schofield she is co-editor of *Fetter'd or Free? British Women Novelists 1670–1815*. Her dissertation is a biographical and critical study of Elizabeth Inchbald. She received a Mellon grant for work on the nature of autobiography, and she was awarded a Fulbright grant to develop curriculum for the Women's Studies program at Victoria University in Wellington, New Zealand, where she also lectured on women's biography. She is at work on a study of needlework and women's writing called *Penelope's Daughters,* and has published articles on Edith Wharton and fiction about the Shakers in America.

Maureen E. Mulvihill, an independent scholar in New York City, formerly with New York's Institute for Research in History, has published essays on women writers in the journals *Restoration* and *The Scriblerian* and profiles in Todd's *Dictionary*, Todd's *British Women Writers*, and Wilson's *Encyclopedia*. She has placed editions of the writings of "Ephelia" in *Women Writers in English 1330–1830* (a new electronic database, Brown University) and with Scholars' Facsimiles & Reprints, New York. She is at work on a monograph on feminist belief and, for Garland Publishing Inc., New York, *Stuart Women of Letters 1603–1714: The Writers & Patronesses.*

Jessica Munns, associate professor of English, University of New Orleans, has taught, published and given papers in England, Poland, and the U.S. Recent publications include, " 'The Dark Disorders of a Divided State:' Otway and Shakespeare's Romeo and Juliet' " *Comparative Drama* 1986 and "Daredevil in Thomas Otway's *The Atheist*: A New Identification," (Restoration 1987). She has just completed a book on Thomas Otway, and has published "Barton and Behn's *The Rover*: or The Text Tranpos'd," *Restoration and 18th Century Theatre Research*, vol. 3, No. 2 Winter 1988.

Deborah Payne is an assistant professor at American University in Washington, D.C. She has articles published or forthcoming in *SEL, Restoration, ECTI, SECC,* and *YES.* Payne has just completed a book-length study entitled, *Patronage and the Marketplace of Restoration Theater, 1660–1685;* in addition, she is co-editor of the forthcoming collection of essays. *Restor(y)ing the Restoration and Early Eighteenth-Century Theatre* (Carbondale, 1990–91).

Linda Payne, assistant professor, the University of Southern Alabama, has published articles in the *Dictionary of Literary Biography, Studies in Eighteenth-Century Culture, Restoration, Journal of Irish Literature, Mid-Hudson Language Studies,* and *Collections,* and presented papers at ASECS conferences, regional MLA conferences and the Popular Culture Association. Her dissertation is on women writers of drama and fiction in Restoration and early eighteenth-century England.

Betty Rizzo is professor of English at The City College of New York, where she teaches eighteenth-century literature, writing, and women's studies. She is author of many articles on Christopher Smart, co-author with Robert Mahony of *Christopher Smart: An Annotated Bibliography, 1743–1983,* has written two writing texts, and will edit a forthcoming volume of Fanny Burney's journal for the McGill University edition. She has completed for publication by Southern Illinois University Press a book about the humble companions of the eighteenth century and, with Robert Mahony, a volume of the correspondence of Christopher Smart. She is also preparing literary biographies of Elizabeth Griffith and Frances Greville.

Research Professor of Literature at the American University, Katharine M. Rogers, has written extensively on eighteenth-century women authors. Her publications include *Feminism in Eighteenth-Century England* (Univ. of Illinois Press, 1982) and *The Meridian Anthology of Early Women Writers* (co-edited with William McCarthy, New American Library, 1987).

Pat Rogers, professor in the liberal arts at the University of South Florida, was educated at Cambridge and has held teaching posts at the universities of Cambridge, London, Wales, and Bristol, and has served as former president of the British Society for Eighteenth-Century Studies and of the Johnson Society. His books include *Grub Street* (1972); *The Augustan Vision* (1974); *Contexts of English Literature: The Eighteenth Century* (1979); and he has edited *The Oxford Illustrated History of English Literature* (1987). Work in progress includes the life of Joshua Reynolds and an edition of Pope for the Oxford Authors Series. He is also working on Horace Walpole, Gibbon and Boswell, and has written on Hester Thrale, Fanny Burney, and Jane Austen.

Doreen Alvarez Saar is assistant professor in the department of humanities and communication at Drexel University and co-ordinator of the Women's Studies Program. Her work in American literature of the Revolutionary period has appeared in such journals as *Early American Literature* and *MELUS*.

Mary Anne Schofield, Professor of English, St. Bonaventure University, and currently visiting Professor of English and Women's Studies, the University of Tulsa, is the co-editor of *Fetter'd or Free? British Women Novelists, 1670–1815*. She is the author of *Eliza Haywood; Quiet Rebellion: The Fictional Heroines of Eliza Haywood;* and *Masking and Unmasking the Female Mind. Disguising Romances in Feminine Fiction 1713–1799*. She has edited several novels by Eliza Haywood, Sarah Fielding, Charlotte Lennox, and Charlotte Smith and has written numerous articles on eighteenth and nineteenth-century British Fiction. Her interests also include the twentieth century. She is the editor of the recent *Cooking By the Book: Food in Literature and Culture* and is at work on a book about women writers of the second world war.

Judith Philips Stanton, assistant professor of English, Clemson University, has written a statistical profile of women's writings in the eighteenth century and a recent article on Charlotte Smith's income. Her edition of Charlotte Smith's letters is nearly completed, and she is planning a biography. She teaches women's studies courses and technical writing and editing.

Edna L. Steeves, professor of English, University of Rhode Island, has published numerous articles and reviews on eighteenth-century writers, and most recently (1982) edited two volumes on Mary Pix and Catharine Trotter in the Garland series of *Eighteenth-Century British Drama*. She is editor of *Editor's Notes*, official journal of the Conference of Editors of Learned Journals, and managing editor of *Modern Language Studies*. In 1986 she served as president of the Northeast American Society for Eighteenth-Century Studies, and was local chair of the 1988 Northeast MLA convention in Providence, R.I. Currently women's caucus representative to the MENLA Board, she also is Secretary/Treasurer of NEASECS.

Rose Zimbardo is a professor of English at S.U.N.Y. at Stony Brook. She has published in the fields of Restoration and eighteenth-century studies, in Chaucer, Shakespeare, and twentieth-century drama. Her most recent book is *A Mirror to Nature: Transformation in Drama and Aesthetics: 1660–1732* (University Press of Kentucky, 1986).

Index of Names

Note: 1. A t after a page number denotes a table; an n, a note.

2. Many variant spellings of Behn's *Feign'd Courtesans* have not been regularized, nor have Centlivre's *Busie Body* and *Busy Body* been altered. Other titles have been made consistent in the text.

A